TRIBAL NATION

TRIBAL NATION

THE MAKING OF
SOVIET TURKMENISTAN

Adrienne Lynn Edgar

PRINCETON UNIVERSITY PRESS

PRINCETON AND OXFORD

Third printing, and first paperback printing, 2006
Paperback ISBN-13: 978-0-691-12799-6
Paperback ISBN-10: 0-691-12799-9

The Library of Congress has cataloged the cloth edition of this book as follows

Edgar, Adrienne Lynn, 1960–
Tribal nation : the making of Soviet Turkmenistan / Adrienne Lynn Edgar.
p.   cm.
Includes bibliographical references and index.
ISBN 0-691-11775-6 (alk. paper)
1. Turkmenistan—History—20th century. 2. Turkmen—Ethnic identity.
3. Nationalism—Turkmenistan. 4. Turkmenistan—Social conditions. I. Title.
DK938.85.E35 2004
958.5′084—dc22   2004043423

British Library Cataloging-in-Publication Data is available

This book has been composed in Sabon

Printed on acid-free paper. ∞

pup.princeton.edu

Printed in the United States of America

10 9 8 7 6 5 4 3

For my parents

CONTENTS

viii   CONTENTS

MAPS AND ILLUSTRATIONS

ACKNOWLEDGMENTS

AFTER MANY YEARS of working on this project, it is a pleasure to acknowledge the people who have helped bring it to fruition. I am especially indebted to my adviser and mentor, Yuri Slezkine, who was unwavering in his enthusiasm for my project and had an uncanny ability to offer exactly the right advice at crucial moments in its evolution. I am also grateful to Reginald Zelnik, Daniel Brower, and Laura Nader, each of whom contributed thoughtful comments on the dissertation that was the original basis for this book.

A number of other colleagues and friends helped me greatly with their questions and comments on the manuscript. Barbara Keys, Peter Blitstein, David Brandenberger, Victoria Clement, Paul Hagenloh, Francine Hirsch, Shokhrat Kadyrov, Brian Kassof, D'Ann Penner, Barbara Walker, and the members of the U.C. Berkeley Russian history *kruzhok* commented on early versions of several of the chapters. Terry Martin generously shared research sources and advice at an early stage in the project's development. My conversations with Adeeb Khalid, a fount of knowledge about all things Central Asian, helped me to refine my ideas about elites and national identity in Soviet Turkmenistan. I enjoyed enlightening exchanges about Central Asian and Soviet history with Kathleen Collins, Douglas Northrop, Shoshana Keller, Laura Adams, Paula Michaels, Marianne Kamp, Cassandra Cavanaugh, Jeremy Smith, John Schoeberlein, and Steve Sabol.

I have benefited greatly from the willingness of other historians to discuss my work at seminars and workshops over the past few years. These have included the Workshop on Central Asian Studies at the University of Wisconsin in Madison; the Harvard Central Asian Studies Workshop; the Harvard Russian and Eastern European Historians' Workshop; the working group on Race in Europe at Harvard's Center for European Studies; the Workshop on History and Identity in Central Asia at the University of North Carolina, Charlotte; and the Department of History Colloquium at Trinity College in Hartford, Connecticut. I am grateful to the organizers and members of these groups. Since my arrival at U.C. Santa Barbara in fall 2000, my colleagues here have provided a congenial and stimulating environment in which to complete this project. I am particularly grateful to the members of the History Department's two working groups—on gender and on race and ethnicity—for their helpful comments on portions of the manuscript. The comparative dimension of my work has been enhanced by my participation in the international workshop "Race and Nation, Identity and Power" organized by Paul Spickard.

A number of institutions have provided financial support for the research and writing of this book. The early stages of research were supported by a grant from the International Research and Exchanges Board, two year-long fellowships from the Eurasia Program of the Social Science Research Council, and a MacArthur Politics of Cultural Identity Fellowship from the Institute of International Studies at U.C. Berkeley. A postdoctoral fellowship at Harvard University's Davis Center for Russian Studies in 1999–2000 was crucial in allowing me to write a large portion of the book. A Faculty Career Development Award from the U.C. Santa Barbara Academic Senate enabled me to finish the manuscript. I am extremely grateful to all of these organizations for their generous support. Naturally, none of them is responsible for the views expressed in my work.

The sixteen months I spent conducting research overseas were made productive and enjoyable by the generous assistance of friends and colleagues. In Moscow, Leonid Vaintraub and Elena Drozdova helped me with archival access and housing and showered me with hospitality. In St. Petersburg, my old friends Semion Iakerson and Tatiana Pang provided a roof over my head and the pleasure of their company on several occasions. In the Russian archives and libraries where I conducted much of my research, dedicated staff members repeatedly went out of their way to help me track down hard-to-find documents and books. In Turkmenistan, I enjoyed the sponsorship of the Institute of History at the Academy of Sciences, without which my two trips to Ashgabat would have been impossible. The employees of the rare book room at the Turkmen State Library were very kind to me, sharing tea and conversation as well as books. My first trip to Turkmenistan would have been much more arduous without the generous assistance of the deputy chief of mission at the U.S. Embassy, Doug Archard, and his wife, Claire, director of the American Educational Advising Center. Doug and Claire provided endless hospitality, helped with scholarly affiliations and visas, and tried to persuade the foreign ministry to grant me permission to work in the Turkmen State Archive. (That this permission failed to materialize was not due to any lack of effort on their part.) I owe an equally large debt of gratitude to my Turkmen friends, who explained the mysteries of Turkmen language and culture and helped me to navigate daily life in post-Soviet Turkmenistan. Although I cannot include their names here, this book literally could not have been written without them. Most important of all has been the support of my family. I am grateful to my parents, Dallas and Patricia Edgar, who always encouraged me to pursue my interests and passions; my brother, Tom Edgar, whose technical wizardry kept my computer working even when I was thousands of miles away; and my husband,

Adebisi Agboola, who has unstintingly given his love and support while enduring long periods of solitude during my overseas research trips.

An earlier and somewhat shorter version of chapter 6 was published as "Genealogy, Class, and 'Tribal Policy' in Soviet Turkmenistan, 1924–1934," in *Slavic Review* 60, no. 2 (Summer 2001): 266–88, and a portion of chapter 8 appeared as "Emancipation of the Unveiled: Turkmen Women under Soviet Rule, 1924–1929," in the *Russian Review* 62, no. 1 (January 2003): 132–49. I thank the publishers of these two journals for permission to reproduce this material here. My thanks also go to Johnnie Garcia and Susanna Baumgart, who drew the maps for this book.

Santa Barbara, California
August 2003

NOTE ON TRANSLITERATION

TRANSLITERATING the Turkmen language has posed certain technical problems. Turkmen has been written in three different scripts since the beginning of this century—four, if one counts the new Latin script to which Turkmenistan has begun to shift since gaining independence in 1991. Most of the Turkmen-language works cited in this book were published in the 1920s and 1930s, when Arabic and an earlier Latin script were used. These writing systems were highly unstable, undergoing frequent reforms to improve their phonetic correspondence to Turkmen words. Neither script was completely standardized, and word usage and orthography varied according to the spoken dialect and preferences of the writer.

The Cyrillic script adopted in 1940 did not represent the Turkmen phonetic system with great accuracy. For the two distinct sounds "h" and "kh" (one like the English "h," the other like the German "ch" in Nacht), Cyrillic used the single letter "x." For the two distinct sounds "k" and "q" (the latter similar to the Arabic letter *qaf)*, Cyrillic employed the letter "к." For the two distinct sounds "g" and "gh" (the latter similar to the *ghayin* in Arabic, pronounced similarly to the gutteral French "r"), the Cyrillic alphabet offered only the letter "г." (Both the reformed Arabic alphabet and the Latin script used in the 1920s and 1930s had two separate letters for each of these pairs of phonemes.) The Cyrillic script also failed to distinguish between long and short vowels, a distinction that Arabic script reformers and Latinizers had tried to take into account.

Despite the problems with the Turkmen Cyrillic script, I have used it as the basis for my transliteration. I made this choice mainly because the vast majority of dictionaries, published works in Turkmen, and other sources of standardized Turkmen spelling are still in Cyrillic script. Had I devised separate systems for transliterating Turkmen works written in the Cyrillic, Latin, and Arabic scripts, the result would have been multiple ways of spelling the same words. I decided against using the new Turkmen Latin script mainly because it too has undergone (and continues to undergo) frequent changes; moreover, the new script omits the same phonemes as the Cyrillic script, so it does not represent a real improvement in phonetic accuracy.

My transliteration is based on the Library of Congress system for Cyrillic, with a few modifications for greater readability and to avoid some of the eccentric spellings that result when one transliterates Central Asian languages as if they were Russian. For the Cyrillic letter "x" I use "h" rather than "kh." (While Russian lacks the "h" sound, the hard "kh" in Turkmen occurs mainly in words of foreign origin.) For "Ы" I use "ï" rather than "y," to indicate that it is a variant of the letter "i" (similar to the undotted "i" in Turkish) and not identical to the Russian "Ы." For "Я," "Ю," and "Ё," I use "ya," "yu," and "yo" (instead of ia, iu, and ë), which results in a more readable transliteration. Similarly, I render "E" as "ye" when it appears at the beginning of a word.

Turkmen proper nouns often take different forms in Russian-language and Turkmen-language sources. In general, I have tried to use the Turkmen form of Turkmen geographical and personal names. When a Turkmen appears as the author of a Russian-language book or article, however, I have transliterated his or her name as it appears on the publication in question. This seemed necessary to avoid bibliographic confusion, although it has occasionally resulted in two different spellings of the same author's name. I have also kept the forms of certain geographical terms familiar to Western readers rather than using their Turkmen forms (for example, Amu-Darya rather than Amïderya, Karakum rather than Garagum desert). Finally, certain difficulties arose because of the use of Russian-language versions of Turkmen names in Soviet archives. In most cases, I have been able to find the Turkmen version and transliterate accordingly, but in a few cases—the names of obscure villages and their residents—I have been forced to hazard a guess as to the likely Turkmen original. I hope readers will forgive any errors that may have resulted.

Unless otherwise specified, all translations from Russian and Turkmen are my own.

TRIBAL NATION

Introduction

TRIBE, CLASS, AND NATION
IN TURKMENISTAN

O N OCTOBER 27, 1991, the Turkmen Soviet Socialist Republic
declared its independence from the Soviet Union. Rejecting the
communist ideals promoted under seven decades of Soviet rule,
the new state committed itself to fostering the "all-round development of
the historical, national, and cultural traditions of the people of Turkmenistan."[1] The president of independent Turkmenistan, a former Communist Party bureaucrat named Saparmurat Niyazov, declared that he would
henceforth be known as Türkmenbashi, or "head of the Turkmen." Niyazov's regime exchanged the Soviet hammer and sickle for traditional symbols of nationhood—a flag, an anthem, and new holidays ranging from
the conventional (Flag Day and Independence Day) to the idiosyncratic
(Carpet Day and Melon Day).[2] The new patriotism found its most passionate expression in the Turkmen national oath, which was heard frequently on television and at public gatherings:

> Turkmenistan, my beloved motherland, my homeland,
> You are always with me, in my thoughts and in my heart.
> For the slightest evil against you, let my hand be paralyzed,
> For the slightest slander against you, let my tongue be lost,
> At the moment of my betrayal of the motherland, its president, or its sacred
>   banner, let my breath be stopped.[3]

Just seven decades earlier, Turkmenistan had seemed an unlikely site
for such an outpouring of nationalist fervor. A seminomadic people at
the time of the Bolshevik ascent to power in 1917, the Turkmen were
fragmented into genealogically defined groups that spoke different dia-

---

[1] Cited in John Anderson, "Authoritarian Political Development in Central Asia: The
Case of Turkmenistan," *Central Asian Survey* 14, no. 4 (1995): 510.

[2] Ibid., pp. 510–13; Annette Bohr, "Turkmenistan and the Turkmen," in *The Nationalities Question in the Post-Soviet States*, ed. Graham Smith, 2d ed., pp. 355–56 (London and
New York, Longman, 1996).

[3] On the national oath, see Shahram Akbarzadeh, "National Identity and Political Legitimacy in Turkmenistan," *Nationalities Papers* 27, no. 2 (June 1999): 275; Bohr, "Turkmenistan and the Turkmen," pp. 355–56.

lects, were often at war with each other, and were ruled by at least five different states. The Turkmen population, overwhelmingly illiterate, was scattered over a huge and largely inaccessible expanse of arid terrain. Although these Turkmen groups claimed common ancestry, they possessed no clearly bounded territory, no common political institutions, no uniform language, and no mass culture of print and education—in short, none of the trappings of modern nationhood.

What brought about this remarkable transformation from a stateless conglomeration of tribes into an independent, apparently unified nation-state? Until recently, most Western scholars viewed the Soviet regime as a "breaker of nations," a radically centralizing state that suppressed indigenous national consciousness.[4] Over the past decade, however, historians have argued persuasively that the Soviet regime itself served as midwife to the separate states that emerged on its territory in 1991. The Soviet Union, in short, was a *maker* of nations. By creating territorial republics based on ethnic criteria and promoting "national cultures" within them, the Soviet state fostered national consciousness and incipient national statehood among its numerous non-Russian minorities.[5]

Because of the remoteness of Central Asian populations from modern nationhood before 1917, some scholars have dismissed the national republics created by Soviet rule as "artificial." Like the nation-states formed out of former European colonies in the Middle East and Africa, these scholars argue, Central Asian nations were fictitious creations of their colonial masters, imposed from above with little consideration of indigenous identities and desires. A few predicted—mistakenly, as it turned out—that these nations would not survive the collapse of the Soviet Union.[6] Yet the creation of the Central Asian nations under Soviet rule is

[4] This phrase is from Robert Conquest, *Stalin: Breaker of Nations* (New York: Penguin, 1991). See also Walter Kolarz, *Russia and Her Colonies* (Hamden, Conn.: Archon Books, 1967); Olaf Caroe, *Soviet Empire: The Turks of Central Asia and Stalinism*, 2d ed. (New York: St. Martin's Press, 1967).

[5] The earliest and most influential proponent of the view of the Soviet Union as a nation-maker was Ronald Grigor Suny, in *The Revenge of the Past: Nationalism, Revolution, and the Collapse of the Soviet Union* (Stanford, CA: Stanford University Press, 1993). See also Terry Martin, *The Affirmative Action Empire: Nations and Nationalism in the Soviet Union, 1923–1939* (Ithaca: Cornell University Press, 2001); Yuri Slezkine, "The USSR as a Communal Apartment, or How a Socialist State Promoted Ethnic Particularism," *Slavic Review* 53 (Summer 1994): 414–52; Francine Hirsch, "The Soviet Union as a Work-in-Progress: Ethnographers and the Category *Nationality* in the 1926, 1937, and 1939 Censuses," *Slavic Review* 56 (Summer 1997): 251–78.

[6] For examples of works emphasizing the artificiality of the Soviet Central Asian nations, see Hélène Carrère d'Encausse, *The Great Challenge: Nationalities and the Bolshevik State, 1917–1930* (New York and London: Holmes and Meier, 1992): 177–79; Gerhard Simon, *Nationalism and Policy toward the Nationalities in the Soviet Union* (Boulder, CO: Westview Press, 1991), p. 43; Olivier Roy, *The New Central Asia: The Creation of Nations*

not in itself a reason to question their legitimacy or durability. As a vast literature on nations and nationalism has argued over the past several decades, *all* nations are "artificial" or constructed; the nation is not a primordial, organic entity, but an "imagined community" that is formed in a continual process of invention and negotiation.[7] The notion that political and ethnic boundaries should coincide is a relatively recent idea, linked to the political mobilization of the masses and, some maintain, to the needs of modern capitalism. Like the nations of Soviet Central Asia, the majority of the world's nations were formed in large measure through the actions and policies of states. As E. J. Hobsbawm has written, "Nations do not make states and nationalism but the other way around."[8]

What is striking about the Central Asian nations is not that they were constructed from above, but that their architect was a socialist state bent on bringing about a global proletarian revolution. For reasons both pragmatic and ideological, the Bolsheviks became convinced that the best way to deal with their "nationality problem"—the presence of more than one hundred different ethnic groups within Soviet borders—was to aggressively promote non-Russian nationhood. The Central Asian nations were remarkable, as well, in the rapidity with which they emerged. As a direct result of Soviet rule, aspects of nation formation that took decades or centuries elsewhere—the establishment of a national territory and government institutions, the standardization of a national language, and the emergence of a mass educational system—were accomplished in Turkmenistan and its neighbors in less than a decade. Finally, the Soviet construction of nations was uniquely ambitious and comprehensive. Modern states, whether national or imperial, typically seek to create a set of "totalizing classifications" in place of the premodern blur of diffuse and overlapping identities; in this sense, the Soviet regime's efforts to categorize its population by ethnicity were not exceptional. The Soviet state *was* unusual, however, in the lengths to which it went to elaborate these new identity categories in the non-Russian periphery.[9]

(London: I. B. Tauris, 2000), pp. vii–viii, 3; Walker Connor, *The National Question in Marxist-Leninist Theory and Strategy* (Princeton: Princeton University Press, 1984), pp. 302–3; Caroe, *Soviet Empire*, pp. xiv–xxiii.

[7] Benedict Anderson, *Imagined Communities: Reflections on the Origin and Spread of Nationalism* (London and New York: Verso, 1983).

[8] E. J. Hobsbawm, *Nations and Nationalism since 1780: Programme, Myth, Reality* (Cambridge: Cambridge University Press, 1990), p. 10, chap. 1 and 3; Ernest Gellner, *Nations and Nationalism* (Ithaca: Cornell University press, 1983), chap. 3; Thomas Hylland Eriksen, *Ethnicity and Nationalism: Anthropological Perspectives* (London and Boulder, CO: Pluto Press, 1993), p. 104.

[9] On the "totalizing" classification systems of colonial states, see Anderson, *Imagined Communities*, p. 184; on the comprehensive nature of Soviet nation-making, see Roy, *The New Central Asia*, p. vii.

The 1920s and 1930s were crucial formative years for the Soviet national republics. In this period, the Bolsheviks engaged in a mad rush of nation-building activity, conveniently if unintentionally equipping non-Russian regions with nearly everything they would need for a future existence as sovereign polities.[10] The fundamental requirement that a state possess a territory with clearly defined borders was met by Moscow through its policy of demarcating "national" republics and regions for each ethnic group. The need for administrative structures was filled by republican government and Communist Party hierarchies that duplicated in miniature those on the all-union level. Most aspiring nation-states strive for a single "national language" to replace a plethora of spoken local dialects; by supporting linguistic standardization as well as publishing and education in native tongues, the Soviet regime facilitated the consolidation of such languages. A nation-state needs an elite to rule in the name of the masses and promote "national culture"; with its policy of recruiting local nationals for service in the party and government, the Soviet regime helped to foster such elites.[11]

The nation-making efforts of modern states do not, of course, focus solely on elites; they also seek to mobilize the masses, turning them from reluctant subjects into active and concerned citizens. Here, too, the Soviet regime did a great deal to transform the regions under its tutelage. The Communist Party leadership, assisted by the native elites it so diligently cultivated, used a variety of methods to penetrate local societies and mobilize the non-Russian masses in support of the regime. Soviet authorities traveled to distant parts of the union to survey and study the indigenous inhabitants, established village schools and native-language newspapers, and created mass organizations as venues for popular participation and state control. They sought to undermine the power of traditional elites and to ban "barbaric" practices rooted in religion and custom. So far this is a familiar story, and one that is common to many aspiring nation-states.[12] Yet the Bolsheviks intended to create not just nations but *socialist* nations, and here they parted company with other modernizers. Soviet authorities campaigned to promote conflict among social classes, enlist the support of the poor and dispossessed, and eradicate existing systems of property ownership and land tenure. In the early 1930s, they sought to bring the entire countryside under state control through the forcible collectivization of agriculture. They banned "bourgeois" and "feudal"

---

[10] Suny, *Revenge of the Past*, pp. 98–126.

[11] Ibid., pp. 102–6; Simon, *Nationalism and Policy toward the Nationalities*, pp. 30–58.

[12] Historians have recently sought to analyze Russian and Soviet history within a broader framework of comparative European modernity. See the essays in David L. Hoffmann and Yanni Kotsonis, eds., *Russian Modernity: Politics, Knowledge, Practices* (New York: St. Martin's Press, 2000).

forms of literary and cultural activity and ultimately imprisoned or executed many Soviet citizens as "counterrevolutionary nationalists" and "enemies of the people."[13]

Tribal Nation focuses on the Soviet effort in the 1920s and 1930s to create a Turkmenistan that would be at once national, modern, and socialist. In many ways, Turkmenistan was a textbook case of a nation created by state fiat. It was under Soviet rule that the Turkmen first acquired a clearly defined territory, a standardized language, and other features of modern nationhood. Yet this book argues that Soviet policy was by no means the only—or even the most important—factor shaping Turkmen national consciousness. Far from being passive recipients of a national culture invented in Moscow, Turkmen themselves played a major role in shaping the institutions and discourses of nationhood in the 1920s and 1930s.

Recent works on Soviet nationality policy have emphasized the role of Moscow-based officials and ethnographers in constructing nations in the non-Russian periphery. Using newly opened archives, historians such as Terry Martin, Francine Hirsch, and Jeremy Smith have offered important insights into the evolution of Soviet nationality policy and the Soviet multinational state.[14] Moscow's role in creating nations was undeniably important, as these scholars have ably demonstrated. However, the crucial contribution of local elites in shaping Soviet nations has not received enough attention. In Central Asia, members of the cultural and political elite had their own ideas about nationhood and socialism, which they discussed with their Russian comrades at Communist Party meetings and debated among themselves in local-language newspapers. Particularly in the 1920s, when Moscow's control over cultural and intellectual life in the non-Russian periphery was relatively tenuous, indigenous intellectuals and communists often expressed views that differed substantially from those of the authorities in Moscow.

Tribal Nation draws on an array of Turkmen- and Russian-language published sources, in addition to recently declassified Soviet archives, to analyze the interaction between the transformative policies of the Soviet

---

[13] On the differences between modernity in the Soviet Union and in nonsocialist European states, see David L. Hoffmann, "European Modernity and Soviet Socialism," in Hoffmann and Kotsonis, *Russian Modernity*, pp. 256–57.

[14] Recent works examining nationality policy primarily from a central government perspective include Martin, *The Affirmative Action Empire*; Jeremy Smith, *The Bolsheviks and the National Question, 1917–1923* (New York: St. Martin's Press, 1999); Francine Hirsch, "Empire of Nations: Colonial Technologies and the Making of the Soviet Union, 1917–1939" (Ph.D. dissertation, Princeton University, 1998); and Peter Blitstein, "Stalin's Nations: Soviet Nationality Policy between Planning and Primordialism, 1936–1953," (Ph.D. dissertation, University of California, Berkeley, 1999).

state and Turkmen conceptions of identity and community.[15] Using insights gleaned from local and non-Russian sources, this study challenges certain long-standing orthodoxies about Soviet nation-making in Central Asia. Among Western scholars during the Cold War era, for example, it was taken for granted that the formation of nations in Central Asia was a process controlled entirely by Moscow, with little input from indigenous populations and little basis in pre-Soviet identities. This view continues to have wide currency among specialists in Central Asian and Soviet history. Even today, some scholars dismiss the division of Central Asia into national republics as a manipulative strategy designed to destroy the region's natural unity and enhance Moscow's control—in other words, as a policy of "divide and rule."[16] Ironically, this older belief in the top-down creation of Central Asian nations has been reinforced to some extent by the more recent recognition that the Soviet state was a "maker of nations." These two schools of thought—the "divide-and-rule" and "nation-making" perspectives—differ over the intentions of the Soviet rulers. Proponents of the former see Soviet nationality policy as Machiavellian to the core, while advocates of the latter see Soviet nation-making primarily as an effort to appease nationalist sentiment and promote historical progress. Yet both tend to underplay the significance of native involvement and local cultural and social realities in the formation of Central Asian nations.

Even in a place as remote from modern nationhood as Turkmenistan, I argue, existing conceptions of identity provided fertile ground for Soviet policies. As I show in the first chapter, a sense of "Turkmen-ness" based on genealogy long predated the Soviet era. The Turkmen population was made up of a number of tribes, subtribes, and lineages, all of which claimed descent from a single ancestor.[17] The Turkmen shared this empha-

---

[15] Unfortunately, the state archives of Turkmenistan have been closed to foreign researchers for a number of years. Instead, I was able to use the archives of the Central Asian Bureau in Moscow, which contain extensive documentation of the activities of Turkmen republican and local party organizations in the 1920s and 1930s.

[16] For a recent example of this view, see Roy, *The New Central Asia*, pp. vii–viii, 3.

[17] William Irons, *The Yomut Turkmen: A Study of Social Organization among a Central Asian Turkic-Speaking Population* (Ann Arbor: University of Michigan Press, 1975), pp. 40–44. The words "tribe" and "tribal" have gone out of fashion in certain fields, where they are considered derogatory. Anthropologists have argued that the word "tribe" is often used to distinguish "primitive" colonized groups from "modern" ethnic groups. In sub-Saharan Africa, scholars now prefer to use the term "ethnic group" instead of "tribe." Among scholars of the Islamic world, however, "tribe" is a more neutral term that refers to a society organized on the basis of patrilineal descent. Moreover, tribe and ethnicity are not equivalent in Central Asia and the Middle East, where ethnic groups—be they Arabs, Pashtuns, Kurds, Druze, or Turkmen—may be divided into many constituent tribes. Susana B. C. Devalle, *Discourses of Ethnicity: Culture and Protest in Jharkhand* (New Delhi and Newbury Park,

sis on genealogical descent with other historically pastoral nomadic groups, whose mobility and statelessness precluded forms of identity linked to territory or the state.[18] Under the right circumstances, this belief in a common ancestry had the potential to serve as a unifying factor. Although Turkmen identity had few concrete political or economic manifestations in the nineteenth and early-twentieth centuries, the idea that the tribes shared a glorious ancestry and history—and the hope that they might one day unite—had long been a staple of Turkmen discourse.[19]

Because of the existence of a genealogically defined Turkmen identity, Soviet historians maintained that the Turkmen had developed a "proto-nationalist" sensibility well before the Soviet period—a claim that served to underscore the historical correctness of Soviet nationality policy.[20] Yet this argument is misleading, since it implies that history was leading the Turkmen inexorably toward unified nationhood. In reality, the segmented genealogical structure that potentially united the Turkmen groups was equally prone to divide them. The numerous tribes and subtribes that made up the branches of the Turkmen genealogical tree had distinct identities and were often at odds with each other. While Turkmen groups were capable of uniting in the face of a common external threat, they were

---

CA: Sage Publications, 1992), pp. 29–33; Dale Eickelman, *The Middle East and Central Asia: An Anthropological Approach*, 3d ed. (Upper Saddle River, NJ: Prentice Hall, 1998), pp. 124–27; Richard Tapper, "Anthropologists, Historians, and Tribespeople on Tribe and State Formation in the Middle East," in Philip S. Khoury and Joseph Kostiner, eds., *Tribes and State Formation in the Middle East* (Berkeley and Los Angeles: University of California Press, 1990), pp. 52–53; on the relationship between ethnicity and tribe in the Middle East see also Bassam Tibi, "The Simultaneity of the Unsimultaneous: Old Tribes and Imposed Nation-States in the Middle East," in Khoury and Kostiner, *Tribes and State Formation in the Middle East*, pp. 131–41.

[18] On genealogical reckoning among the Kazakhs, see Saulesh Esenova, "Soviet Nationality, Identity, and Ethnicity in Central Asia: Historic Narratives and Kazakh Ethnic Identity," *Journal of Muslim Minority Affairs* 22, no. 1 (2002): 11–38; on genealogical identity in the Arab Middle East, see Andrew Shryock, *Nationalism and the Genealogical Imagination: Oral History and Textual Authority in Tribal Jordan* (Berkeley and Los Angeles: University of California Press, 1997).

[19] For examples of premodern calls for Turkmen unity, see Walter Feldman, "Interpreting the Poetry of Mäkhtumquli," in *Muslims in Central Asia: Expressions of Identity and Change*, ed. Jo-ann Gross (Durham, N.C.: Duke University Press, 1992), pp. 167–71, 180–83.

[20] V. V. Bartold, *Istoriia turetsko-mongol'skikh narodov* (Tashkent, 1928), p. 33; V. Karpych, "Iz istorii vozniknoveniia Turkmenskoi SSR," *Turkmenovedenie*, no. 10–11 (October–November 1928): 38–39; G. I. Karpov and D. M. Batser, *Khivinskie turkmeny i konets kungradskoi dinastii* (Ashgabat: Turkmengosizdat, 1930), pp. 89–91. The argument that the Turkmen were protonationalist has also been made by a few non-Soviet scholars; see Feldman, "Interpreting the Poetry of Mäkhtumquli," pp. 167–71, 180–83; Mehmet Saray, *The Turkmens in the Age of Imperialism* (Ankara: Turkish Historical Society, 1989), pp. 47–48.

equally likely to ally themselves with outsiders against rival Turkmen.[21] In the mid-nineteenth century, the emergence of a nation based on one of the large Turkmen tribes—Yomuts, Tekes, or Ersaris—would have seemed more plausible than the formation of a Turkmen nation. More broadly, the tribal form of social organization was in many ways antithetical to the demands of the modern nation-state. In a stateless, genealogically organized society, personalistic ties based on patrilineal kinship play a primary role in shaping behavior and allegiances. The nation-state, by contrast, is an impersonal arena that stresses the equality of all its citizens and insists on loyalty to the central government. The tendency toward divisiveness in tribal society—what anthropologist Andrew Shryock has called its "contentious multivocality"—is at odds with the unity and homogeneity sought by the nation.[22]

An existing conception of Turkmen-ness based on common ancestry was not the only local factor that favored Soviet nation-making efforts. Moscow's policies were also facilitated by the presence of a Turkmen elite willing to embrace the idea of a Turkmen national republic. In the early-twentieth century, a handful of Turkmen had been exposed to new ideas of identity then circulating in Central Asia. Some had attended schools sponsored by the Russian colonial regime, which had introduced them to European understandings of nationhood. Others had come into contact with secular forms of Turkic nationalism advocated by Muslim reformers in the Russian and Ottoman empires. In part because of their exposure to these new ideas, Turkmen elites were willing to shift their primary loyalty from particularistic genealogical affiliations to the broader idea of a Turkmen nation. In fact, their support for Turkmen nationhood frequently went beyond what Moscow expected or considered desirable. As I show in chapter 3, Turkmen elites' enthusiasm for a common Turkmen identity was reinforced in the 1920s and 1930s by the Soviet policy of nativization, which promised preferential treatment in employment and higher education to the "titular nationality" of each republic. As a direct result of this policy, a broader Turkmen identity became not merely a vague aspiration but something with real political and economic meaning.

The growing salience of a Turkmen identity was accompanied in the 1920s and 1930s by the beginning of a transformation in the understanding of Turkmen-ness. Under Soviet rule, Turkmen elites quickly learned

[21] Saray, *The Turkmens*, pp. 56–57, 97–98; Shokhrat Kadyrov, *Turkmenistan v XX veke: Probely i problemy* (Bergen, Norway: 1996), p. 100.

[22] Shryock, *Nationalism and the Genealogical Imagination*, pp. 313–14; Schirin H. Fathi, *Jordan, an Invented Nation? Tribe-State Dynamics and the Formation of National Identity* (Hamburg: Deutsches Orient-Institut, 1994), p. 30; Tapper, "Anthropologists, Historians, and Tribespeople," pp. 68, 70; see also Richard Tapper, ed., *The Conflict of Tribe and State in Iran and Afghanistan* (London: Croom Helm, 1983), pp. 10–11.

to speak the Bolshevik language of nationhood, in which a common territory and a common language—not genealogy or descent—were the main components of identity. Chapter 2 demonstrates that many Turkmen enthusiastically welcomed the creation of a Turkmen territorial republic in the 1920s, despite the lack of attachment to an ancestral homeland among the historically mobile Turkmen. Moreover, the process of drawing national borders solidified the incipient nationalist sentiments of Turkmen elites, encouraging them to view their interests as distinct from those of other Central Asians. Similarly, although language and identity were not closely linked in Central Asian history, Turkmen elites willingly adopted the Soviet emphasis on language as a critical component of national identity. As I explain in chapter 5, they rejected proposals for a pan-Turkic or pan-Turkestani language as linguistic imperialism, preferring to emphasize the distinctiveness of the Turkmen vernacular rather than its commonalities with other Turkic dialects. The evidence of strong Turkmen enthusiasm for the creation of a separate national language and territory casts doubt on the view that Central Asians were naturally inclined toward pan-Turkic unity.

Yet the shift from a genealogical to a linguistic and territorial understanding of Turkmen identity was incomplete. A person who dwelled on Turkmen lands and spoke a Turkmen dialect was not considered a Turkmen if the presumed genealogical link was absent. Moreover, genealogical considerations intruded repeatedly on efforts to create the elements of Turkmen nationhood. The ethnographers and officials responsible for drawing the boundaries of the Turkmen national republic in 1924 used genealogical criteria to determine which groups should be included within Turkmenistan. Genealogical issues also underlay a debate about where to situate the capital of the new Turkmen republic. Some Turkmen communists were concerned about the prospect of intertribal antagonism within the new republic, which brought together Turkmen populations that had never coexisted under a single government authority. They argued that the republican capital should be located in an area inhabited by smaller, weaker tribes, in order to counterbalance the influence of the powerful and demographically dominant Tekes. Similarly, genealogical concerns impinged on linguistic debates in Turkmenistan. Because each of the major Turkmen tribes spoke its own dialect, the need to create a national literary language raised the delicate question of which dialect or dialects should form its basis. Turkmen linguists interested in promoting national unity insisted that the new language should be an amalgam of all the major Turkmen dialects. In short, the discourse of Turkmen nationhood in the 1920s and 1930s was shaped in large measure by the intersection of indigenous concepts of identity with the new understandings of nationhood introduced by the Bolsheviks.

If Soviet nation-making is the primary focus of this book, a second and closely related theme is the Soviet attempt to bring socialist modernity to Turkmenistan. Although the Bolsheviks came to power with the intention of building socialism, the meaning of the term was vague and contested in the early Soviet years. The general orientation of the Bolsheviks was fairly clear; they valued the collective over the individual, advocated the dispossession of the "exploiting classes," and favored rational economic planning over reliance on markets. Yet these ideological preferences did not provide concrete guidance for the construction of a socialist system. In the 1920s, there were conflicting ideas and shifting policies on such key questions as the speed with which socialism should be built and the appropriate mix of markets and central planning.[23]

The meaning of "modernity" was less controversial. Virtually all Bolsheviks agreed on the need to eradicate "backwardness" in the form of prerevolutionary social structures, beliefs, and ways of life. The new Soviet leaders sought not just to create a new, noncapitalist economic system; they also envisioned the creation of a social order that would offer a model of justice, progress, and modernity to all humanity. For such a society to emerge, the old world of privilege, exploitation, and ignorance would have to be destroyed. This campaign against backwardness, Soviet authorities agreed, was particularly urgent among the non-Russian peoples of Central Asia. While the Bolsheviks grumbled about the "age-old backwardness of the Russian peasantry," they were even more appalled by the "oppressive" and "degrading" customs of Muslim groups in the Soviet periphery. How could socialism be built, they asked, among people who bought and sold women like livestock, murdered one another in blood feuds, based their social structures on "tribes and clans" instead of economic class, and passed their lives in a fog of illiteracy and superstition? In Turkmenistan, as in the other Central Asian republics, socialism in the 1920s meant above all an attempt to replace indigenous "backwardness" with Soviet-style "modernity."[24]

In the growing body of literature on the forging of a socialist consciousness among the Soviet population, historians have argued that Soviet citizens learned to "speak Bolshevik" during the 1920s and 1930s, internalizing the values and norms promoted by the Communist regime. Yet these works have focused almost exclusively on Russia proper, with little said

[23] Martin Malia, *The Soviet Tragedy: A History of Socialism in Russia, 1917–1991* (New York: Free Press, 1994), pp. 22, 33–34; Ronald Grigor Suny, *The Soviet Experiment: Russia, the USSR, and the Successor States* (Oxford: Oxford University Press, 1998), pp. 61–62

[24] On eradicating backwardness, see Yuri Slezkine, "Imperialism as the Highest State of Socialism," *Russian Review* 59 (April 2000): 228–29.

about what socialism might have meant to other Soviet peoples.[25] Did the Turkmen, too, learn to "speak Bolshevik"? *Tribal Nation* shows that they did, but that they spoke it with their own accents and lent it their own meanings. As a result, there were continual conflicts in the 1920s and 1930s over whose values and norms would dominate the newly established Soviet institutions in Turkmenistan.

A case in point is the Soviet attempt to promote class conflict among the Turkmen rural population. For the Soviets, class struggle was the driving force of history. In order to progress toward socialism, the Turkmen would have to replace their archaic "tribal-clan structures" with a modern class system. As I show in chapter 6, many Turkmen did learn to speak the Bolshevik language of class in the 1920s and 1930s, but they interpreted Soviet class categories in ways that made sense within the Turkmen cultural context. Infusing Bolshevik class rhetoric with Turkmen genealogical content, Turkmen villagers used Soviet terminology to promote the interests of their own kin groups and carry on older rivalries. Similarly, as I show in chapter 7, some Turkmen made adroit use of the Soviet preoccupation with class to undermine the campaign to emancipate Muslim women. The Soviet ban on traditional marriage customs was extremely unpopular among Turkmen men, who perceived it as an assault on the foundations of Turkmen culture. Seeking to frame their opposition in a language Russian Bolsheviks would understand, Turkmen communists argued that the policies of female emancipation would alienate poor and landless male peasants—the very social groups on whom the Soviet regime hoped to rely. A correct class policy, they insisted, must take precedence over solving the "woman question."

At the end of the 1920s, Soviet socialism acquired a more concrete and radical meaning as the government launched a new revolution from above. Abandoning the gradualism of the New Economic Policy, the Stalinist regime sought to transform Soviet society through an accelerated assault on all forms of backwardness and a massive program of centrally directed industrialization. The government squeezed the resources for this transformation out of the rural population through the compulsory collectivization of agriculture, which brought the peasantry and its grain under the control of the state. At the same time, the Soviet regime stepped up its attack on "class enemies," persecuting "kulaks" in the countryside

[25] On "speaking Bolshevik" and the making of Soviet citizens, see Stephen Kotkin, *Magnetic Mountain: Stalinism as a Civilization* (Berkeley and Los Angeles: University of California Press, 1995); see also Jochen Hellbeck, "Laboratories of the Soviet Self: Diaries from the Stalin Era" (Ph.D. dissertation, Columbia University, 1998); Anna Krylova, "Soviet Modernity in Life and Fiction: The Generation of the 'New Soviet Person' in the 1930s" (Ph.D. dissertation, Johns Hopkins University, 2001).

and rooting out "bourgeois intellectuals" in cultural institutions. Among the Turkmen elite, many prominent figures were driven from their posts in the early 1930s by accusations of "counterrevolutionary nationalism." In rural areas of Turkmenistan, where collectivization was accompanied by a drive to force peasants to plant cotton, Soviet policies provoked one of the most massive and violent popular uprisings anywhere in the Soviet Union.

In recent years, some historians have argued that the Soviet multinational state was a form of European imperialism, and that Bolshevik policies aimed at "modernizing" the Muslim peoples under their tutelage were comparable to the efforts of British and French rulers in the Middle East, India, and Africa. Even the Soviet Union's nation-making efforts were a means of imperial control, in this view, since European powers typically codified and reified ethnic and "tribal" differences within colonized populations.[26] Yet historians have also pointed to important differences between the Soviet Union and the empires maintained by other European states. The Soviet regime did not subscribe to the notions of biologically based racial inferiority that underpinned most European colonial projects.[27] Moreover, while the word "empire" implies the existence of a privileged, metropolitan group exercising hegemony over subordinate groups in the periphery, the Soviets did not institutionalize Russian superiority. On the contrary, the Soviet state aimed at equality for all its citizens—and all its nations—under an ideology of socialist internationalism. Many of the "imperial" strategies carried out in the non-Russian periphery were used with similar effect—and with similar violence—in the Russian countryside. Among Russian peasants, as among the Turkmen, the Soviet regime tried to break down old social structures, emancipate women, and transform the rural economy.[28]

---

[26] On the "imperial" features of Soviet rule in Central Asia, see Douglas Northrop, "Uzbek Women and the Veil: Gender and Power in Stalinist Central Asia" (Ph.D. dissertation, Stanford University, 1999); Douglas Northrop, "Nationalizing Backwardness: Gender, Empire, and Uzbek Identity," in *A State of Nations: Empire and Nation-Making in the Age of Lenin and Stalin*, ed. Ronald Grigor Suny and Terry Martin (Oxford and New York: Oxford University Press, 2001), pp. 193–96; Paula A. Michaels, "Medical Propaganda and Cultural Revolution in Soviet Kazakhstan, 1928–1941," *Russian Review* 59 (April 2000): 159–78; Roy, *The New Central Asia*, p. 11. For an interesting view of the USSR as a self-consciously antiimperialist empire, see Hirsch, "Empire of Nations." On the consolidation of tribal identities in the Middle East under colonial rule, see Eickelman, *The Middle East and Central Asia*, pp. 139–40.

[27] Francine Hirsch, "Race without the Practice of Racial Politics," *Slavic Review* 61, no. 1 (Spring 2002): 30–43.

[28] Slezkine, "Imperialism as the Highest Stage of Socialism," pp. 227–34. For a thoughtful analysis of the concepts of nation and empire in the Russian context, see Ronald Grigor Suny, "The Empire Strikes Out: Imperial Russia, 'National Identity,' and Theories of Empire," in Suny and Martin, *A State of Nations*, pp. 23–66.

Because of these distinctive features of the Soviet multinational state, it would be a mistake to consider it an empire like any other. It would be equally wrong, however, to view the Soviet Union as a rapidly homogenizing unitary state in which the gap between Russian and non-Russian regions was negligible. This study shows that there were significant differences in the ways in which Russians and Central Asians experienced Soviet rule. The equality that the Soviet Union pledged to its non-Russian citizens was impressive on paper, but not always scrupulously followed in practice. Despite the policy of indigenization, which mandated preferential treatment for the indigenous nationality and language within each republic, the behavior of local Russian communists often left Turkmen feeling that they belonged to an inferior group. Many Russians objected to ethnic preferences and undermined them at every opportunity. Moreover, indigenous communists did not enjoy the same career opportunities as their European counterparts. As I show in chapters 3 and 4, the assumption of non-Russian "backwardness"—read inferiority and incompetence—often prevailed among even the most committed communists and internationalists. The ethnic tensions that plagued non-Russian republics as a result of indigenization had no direct equivalent within Russian regions.

Soviet nationality policy created another important difference between metropole and periphery in the Soviet Union. In the 1920s and 1930s, the Bolshevik regime *encouraged* national culture and consciousness among the non-Russians, whom it considered former victims of tsarist colonial oppression, while *discouraging* overt national self-expression among the former colonizers—the Russians.[29] As a result, the dynamics of Soviet rule in the periphery were different from those in the Russian heartland. In non-Russian areas, there was a fundamental contradiction between nationality policy, which pledged to support the autonomy and unique identity of each Soviet people, and the construction of socialism, which sought the homogenization of the Soviet population under a centralized government. While other historians have pointed to this contradiction in general terms, *Tribal Nation* seeks to analyze its manifestations and impact within a particular "national" context.[30]

In Turkmenistan, the projects of nation-making and socialist transformation were visibly at odds with each other. The Soviet assault on "back-

---

[29] On the status of Russians within the Soviet multinational state, see Yuri Slezkine, "The USSR as a Communal Apartment."

[30] Ron Suny has argued that Soviet policies of socioeconomic transformation were antithetical to nativization. *Revenge of the Past*, pp. 106–10; see also Simon, *Nationalism and Policy toward the Nationalities*, chap. 5. More recently, Peter Blitstein has described a conflict between "ethnic" and "statist" discourses of nationhood under Stalin. "Stalin's Nations," p. 253.

wardness" targeted the practices that most clearly defined Turkmen identity, including their distinctive genealogical structures and practices relating to marriage and the family. The Soviet attempt to emancipate Turkmen women, which I discuss in the book's final chapter, was particularly contentious. For the communist leadership in Moscow, Turkmen gender practices were archaic customs that could only hinder the development of Turkmen nationhood. National identity, in the communist view, was based on language, territory, and certain acceptable folkloric practices. Yet Turkmen themselves considered the customs surrounding kinship, marriage, and family life to be essential expressions of Turkmen identity. The attempt to eradicate these practices was therefore resisted as an attempt by outsiders to "Europeanize" Turkmen life.

Other aspects of socialist modernity were similarly incompatible with the fostering of Turkmen national identity. The attempt to eradicate Turkmen "tribalism" conflicted with the historical basis of Turkmen identity in genealogy. The promotion of class conflict, an essential part of constructing Soviet-style socialism, perpetuated the very social fragmentation Turkmen elites hoped to overcome as they built a unified Turkmen nation. The purges of leading cultural figures as "nationalists" and "class aliens" in the early 1930s eliminated most of the literate Turkmen capable of creating and promoting a "national culture." Finally, collectivization and the compulsory planting of cotton violated the regime's promises of autonomy and equal development for all national republics. Throughout the more than seven decades of Soviet Turkmenistan's existence, these tensions between nationality policy and the construction of socialism remained both unacknowledged and unresolved. Only at the end of the Soviet era—when the new rulers of independent Turkmenistan abandoned Marxism-Leninism with few apparent regrets, while hastening to wrap themselves in the cloak of nationalist legitimacy—did it become clear which of the two policies had the more profound impact on Turkmen society.

PART I

MAKING A NATION

Chapter One

SOURCES OF IDENTITY AMONG THE TURKMEN

WHEN NINETEENTH-CENTURY EUROPEAN adventurers wrote of their travels in Central Asia, some of the most vivid passages described the formidable desert nomads known as the Turkmen. Clad in high wool hats and mounted on Ahal-Teke horses noted for their speed and stamina, the Turkmen were infamous for their slave raids on settled villages. Stateless themselves, they were continually at war with neighboring states. As tenaciously as they fought against outsiders, the Turkmen were said to oppose one another with equal fervor. The Turkmen population was divided into a number of tribes, each of which possessed an intense pride in its own ancestry and considered its own members to be the only "true Turkmen."[1] In the words of a nineteenth-century Russian officer, "The hatred of the various Turkmen clans toward each other is scarcely less than their hatred toward other peoples."[2]

Even if one allows for some exaggeration of the "warlike" qualities of the Turkmen by European observers, it is hard to see the Turkmen as a "people," let alone a "nation," prior to the twentieth century. The question that Russian colonizers, Soviet officials, and the Turkmen themselves would have to resolve in the early decades of the century was this: Were the Turkmen tribes distinct ethnic groups, or were they merely subdivisions of a larger Turkmen nation? Did the word "Turkmen," in other words, encompass one people or many? By the 1920s, this question had been officially answered by the architects of Soviet nationality policy. The Turkmen were one people—a "backward" people with many internal di-

---

[1] K. Bode, "O turkmenskikh pokoleniiakh yamudakh i goklanakh," *Zapiski russkogo geograficheskogo obshchestva*, kn 2 (1847), p. 224.

[2] A. Kuropatkin, *Turkmeniia i Turkmeny* (Saint Petersburg, 1879), p. 33. For nineteenth-century accounts of the Turkmen by other European travelers, see *The Country of the Turcomans: An Anthology of Exploration from the Royal Geographic Society* (London: Oguz Press and the Royal Geographical Society, 1977); Edmund O'Donovan, *The Merv Oasis: Travels and Adventures East of the Caspian during the Years 1879–1880–1881* (London: Smith, Elder, and Co., 1882); Arminius Vambery, *Sketches of Central Asia* (Philadelphia: J. B. Lippincott and Co., 1868; reprint, New York: Arno Press and the New York Times, 1970).

visions, to be sure, but a people destined eventually to become a unified and homogeneous Soviet nation. The anointing of the Turkmen as a nation was just one aspect of a broader consolidation of Central Asian identities that occurred under Russian and Soviet rule.

Central Asia is an area of extraordinary ethnic complexity. Historically a frontier between nomadic and sedentary civilizations in the heart of the Eurasian continent, the region has long been buffeted by massive population movements and a wide range of cultural influences. The demographic structure of Central Asia took shape over a period of many centuries, as successive waves of nomadic Turkic migrants from the East conquered and mingled with settled agricultural populations speaking Indo-European languages. The result was a rich patchwork of peoples, tribes, languages, and cultures, all living intermingled within a diverse landscape of deserts, mountains, and oases. This diversity existed within the framework of a broad cultural unity, an Islamic Central Asian civilization that was a synthesis of Turkic and Persian elements.[3]

It is difficult to identify distinct, let alone cohesive, ethnic groups in Central Asia prior to the twentieth century. The labels that formed the basis for Soviet "national republics"—Uzbek, Tajik, Turkmen, Kyrgyz, and Kazakh—were not unknown, but the identities they referred to were neither exclusive nor the most compelling for Central Asians. Subethnic and supraethnic loyalties were generally more important to people than these ethnic categories. Asked to identify themselves, most nineteenth-century Central Asians would have named their kin group, neighborhood, or village; others might have referred to their religion or the state in which they lived. Moreover, there was no historical relationship between ethnicity and statehood in the region. Prior to the Russian conquest in the late-nineteenth century, the prevailing form of statehood in Central Asia was the Muslim dynastic state ruling over a multiethnic population. State legitimacy depended on dynastic claims and a pledge to uphold the Islamic faith. The notion that a state should exist for the benefit of a single ethnic group was unfamiliar. On the contrary, multiethnicity was part of the structure of Central Asian states. Rulers descended from Turkic nomads used Persian as their language of culture and government, maintaining their power by promoting rivalry among the different population groups.[4]

---

[3] John Samuel Schoeberlein-Engel, "Identity in Central Asia: Construction and Contention in the Conceptions of 'Özbek,' 'Tajik,' 'Muslim,' 'Samarquandi,' and Other Groups" (Ph.D. dissertation, Harvard University, 1994), pp. 19–26; Beatrice Manz, "Historical Background," in Beatrice Manz, ed., *Central Asia in Historical Perspective* (Boulder, CO: Westview Press, 1994), p. 4; Roy, *The New Central Asia*, pp. 1–10.

[4] Manz, "Historical Background," p. 12; see also Roy, *The New Central Asia*, pp. 2–3, 10, 72.

It is hard to imagine a less congenial setting for the late-nineteenth-century European doctrine of nationalism. Nationalists insist that human-ity is divided into discrete, homogeneous nations, each of which has the right to self-determination within its own territorial state. Wherever this ideology takes hold, it requires the superimposition of an idealized unifor-mity onto the real complexity of prenational identities. It also requires a rewriting of the past, since the newly formed nation prefers to represent itself as a unified community whose "national history" can be traced far back into the mists of time. Alternative identities and stories that conflict with the national narrative are obscured or erased.[5]

One of the most important themes in the modern history of Central Asia has been the consolidation of the many identity narratives of the premodern era into a handful of national narratives. During the twentieth century, large numbers of Central Asians became convinced that they be-longed to cohesive, mutually exclusive, homogeneous groups—"ethnic groups" that would ultimately become "nations" through the possession of national territories and the development of national languages. This required that previously porous boundaries within the larger Central Asian cultural sphere become hardened into absolute dividing lines be-tween groups. People who shared a great many beliefs and cultural prac-tices came to view their differences—in dialect, in the rituals of daily life, in historical memory—as more important than their similarities.[6] At the same time, differences *within* each ethnic group had to be minimized, so that the nation would appear as a homogeneous, undivided whole. These changes began under tsarist colonial rulers, who categorized the region by ethnicity and introduced new ideas about the relationship between language and identity. But it was the Soviet state, with its radical and unprecedented "nationality policy," that was primarily responsible for the transformation of Central Asia. In the 1920s, the Soviets launched a process of ethnic categorization and consolidation that created a handful of discrete "nationalities" and national territories where there had pre-viously been hundreds of overlapping and nested identities.

Among the sedentary population of Central Asia, the blurred and po-rous boundaries between groups posed the chief obstacle to Soviet de-signs. During the creation of national-territorial republics in the 1920s, the majority of settled residents of the core areas of Soviet Central Asia were designated as either Uzbeks or Tajiks. This seemingly straightfor-

---

[5] Gellner, *Nations and Nationalism*, pp. 139–40; Prasenjit Duara, *Rescuing History from the Nation: Questioning Narratives of Modern China* (Chicago and London: University of Chicago Press, 1995), pp. 3–4.

[6] On the hardening of previously "soft" boundaries between identity groups, see Duara, *Rescuing History from the Nation*, pp. 65–66; Eriksen, *Ethnicity and Nationalism*, pp. 94–95.

ward process actually required the disentangling of populations and dialects that had previously shaded into each other without any clear boundaries. In the official Soviet view, the Uzbeks were a Turkic group speaking
Uzbek, a Turkic language, while the Tajiks were an Indo-European population speaking a language related to Persian. In reality, the distinction
between Uzbeks and Tajiks was not so clear. Before the Russian revolution, many people in the region were bilingual in both Turkic and Persian,
regardless of ancestry. Intermarriage between Turkic-speakers and Tajik-
speakers was common. "Uzbek" dialects had many "Tajik" elements, and
vice versa. Language and descent did not necessarily coincide; some people declared themselves to be Uzbeks although they spoke Tajik as their
first language. When queried in population surveys in the late-imperial
and early-Soviet periods, many Central Asians were unable to say whether
they were Tajiks or Uzbeks.[7]

Among the nomadic and seminomadic populations of Central Asia,
the most serious problem was not the porous boundaries *between* ethnic
groups but the divisions *within* them. In contrast to the intermingled populations living in settled areas, the Turkmen were relatively easy to identify. Like many historically pastoral nomadic peoples, the Turkmen were
organized along lines of patrilineal descent, and their elaborate genealogies defined with a fair amount of precision who belonged to their group
and who did not. All those who called themselves Turkmen traced their
ancestry back to a single individual, the mythical Turkic warrior Oguz-
khan. Individuals and groups who did not claim descent from Oguz were
not considered Turkmen, even if they lived among the Turkmen and spoke
their language. Groups claiming to be Turkmen could be found throughout Central Asia and the Middle East, from the North Caucasus to Iraq,
Iran, and Anatolian Turkey.[8] Despite this belief in a common ancestry,
one cannot speak in the singular of "Turkmen history" or the "Turkmen
people" before 1917. The various Turkmen tribes had fought against,
allied with, or submitted to the domination of at least five different states;
they had also fought against, allied with, and been dominated by each
other. They had never acted in concert as a political force. The people
who identified themselves as Turkmen had not one story to tell about
themselves, but many—stories that often conflicted and competed with
each other.

[7] Roy, *The New Central Asia*, p. 16–17; Schoeberlein-Engel, "Identity in Central Asia,"
pp. 53–54, 118, 128–29, 137–39; Maria Eva Subtelny, "The Symbiosis of Turk and Tajik,"
in Manz, *Central Asia in Historical Perspective*, pp. 49–52.

[8] Irons, *The Yomut Turkmen*, p. 40; on the origins and early history of groups calling
themselves Turkmen, see Peter Golden, *An Introduction to the History of the Turkic Peoples: Ethnogenesis and State-Formation in Medieval and Early Modern Eurasia and the
Middle East* (Wiesbaden: Otto Harrassowitz, 1992), pp. 207–19, 221–25, 307.

The genealogical notion of Turkmen-ness was almost entirely abstract and certainly not the most compelling affiliation for those who claimed it. Indeed, a broader Turkmen identity had little political or economic significance before the advent of Soviet rule. The descent groups that were subdivisions of the larger category "Turkmen" were the primary sources of solidarity and mutual assistance. The Turkmen population was divided into a number of tribes, each of which was thought to descend from one of Oguz's sons or grandsons. Each tribe was named after the putative ancestor who founded that branch of the family tree. Thus, the Yomut tribe was named for Yomut, said to have been the great-grandson of Oguz's grandson Ogurjïk. These tribes were divided into a series of ever smaller sections and subsections, each of which was also presumed to descend from a common ancestor.[9]

The largest subgroups of the Turkmen population—groups such as the Tekes, Salïrs, Sarïks, Yomuts, Choudïrs, Göklengs, and Ersarïs—were known as *halq* or *il* in the Turkmen language (both terms literally mean "people" but are usually translated as "tribe"). Each of these Turkmen tribes had its own genealogy, history, legends, and myths. Each was associated with a specific Turkmen dialect and had its own distinctive forms of dress and carpet ornaments.[10] In the mid-nineteenth century, shortly before the Russian conquest, the most numerous and politically powerful tribe was the Teke, which primarily inhabited the Ahal and Marï regions in the southeastern part of Turkmenia. The second largest tribe was the Yomut, located mainly in two geographic areas: the Gurgan and Balkhan regions of southwestern Turkmenistan near the Caspian Sea and along the Persian border, and the northeastern regions near Khiva. The Göklengs lived near the Gurgan Yomut regions in northern Khorasan, on both sides of the Persian border. The Ersarïs lived along the Amu Darya near Bukhara in the east. The Salïrs and Sarïks lived to the south of the Marï oasis, near Afghanistan. The Choudïrs occupied the desert region between Khiva and Mangïshlak, to the west of the northern Yomuts.[11]

Like the "Turkmen people" as a whole, tribes such as the Tekes and the Yomuts were too large and impersonal to inspire unqualified loyalty. They were further divided into sections and subsections, which also possessed their own genealogies and distinct identities. Smaller, local descent

[9] Irons, *The Yomut Turkmen*, pp. 40–44.

[10] Wolfgang König, *Die Achal-Teke: Zur Wirtschaft und Gesellschaft einer Turkmenengruppe im XIX Jahrhundert* (Berlin: Akademieverlag, 1962), p. 81; Irons, *The Yomut Turkmen*, p. 40.

[11] Irons, *The Yomut Turkmen*, p. 9. See also Saray, *The Turkmens*, pp. 8–12; G. Karpov, "Turkmeniia i Turkmeny," *Turkmenovedenie*, no. 10–11 (October–November 1929), pp. 39–40.

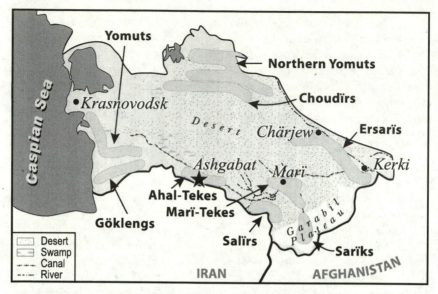

Figure 1. Location of major tribes in Soviet Turkmenistan

groups were the institutions with the greatest political and economic importance in people's daily lives. The smallest kin unit, called the *bir ata* among the Tekes, was a group of families claiming a single ancestor three to five generations in the past. Members of the bir ata had many mutual political and economic obligations. They pooled their resources to pay for wedding and circumcision celebrations, to ransom members captured by enemies, and to replace stolen livestock. In addition, they were collectively responsible for the protection of guests to whom the group had extended its hospitality.[12]

Most studies of Central Asia relate genealogical forms of social organization to pastoral nomadism. Among nomadic groups, whose mobility precludes strong identification with a particular territory, genealogy commonly forms the basis for identity.[13] At one time, all Turkmen were nomadic pastoralists in the arid steppe and desert regions of Central Asia. They raised sheep, goats, camels, and horses, consuming animal products such as milk, cheese, and wool and trading these products to settled peoples for grain, tea, sugar, and manufactured products such as guns and

[12] König, *Die Achal-Teke*, pp. 72–73, 80–81.

[13] A. M. Khazanov, *Nomads and the Outside World* (Cambridge: Cambridge University Press, 1984), pp. 138–39.

cloth.[14] Several hundred years before the Russian conquest, Turkmen began to move into the fertile oases along the edges of the Karakum desert and take up agriculture, growing wheat and barley, vegetables, fruit and nut trees, grapes, rice, cotton, and melons.[15] By the late-nineteenth century, nomadic and sedentary life formed a continuum among the Turkmen, with more arid regions relying to a greater extent on livestock herding and more fertile regions featuring greater dependence on agriculture. Predominantly settled Turkmen were known as *chomur*, while mainly nomadic Turkmen were known as *charwa*. The line between the two groups was not always sharply defined. In the early-twentieth century, a significant minority still led a completely nomadic existence, but most Turkmen practiced some combination of agriculture and livestock herding.[16]

Despite the shift toward settled life in recent centuries, there was a strong cultural preference among Turkmen for nomadic pastoralism. It was considered "more Turkmen" to migrate with one's flocks than to plow one's fields. Thus, Turkmen nomads generally turned to settled agriculture only if forced to do so by impoverishment or inadequate pasture, while agriculturalists who improved their financial standing would gladly abandon their settled existence and take their flocks on the road.[17] Because of this preference, even those Turkmen who worked the land maintained some features of nomadic life, making short migrations with their livestock and continuing to live in the traditional movable Turkmen dwelling, the yurt. As one nineteenth-century observer wrote, "strictly speaking, even the settled ones don't live all the time in the same place." Turkmen, like other pastoral nomads, tended to see mobility as their guarantee of independence and autonomy and looked down on neighboring peasant peoples as weak and easily victimized.[18]

[14] Saray, *The Turkmens*, pp. 26–27, 30–31; Irons, *The Yomut Turkmen*, pp. 7, 25–26.

[15] Some Soviet and post-Soviet scholars have claimed that the Turkmen were "semisedentary" as early as the sixteenth century. Marat Durdyev, for example, has argued that the Turkmen have long combined agriculture and pastoralism. Yuri Bregel believes the shift toward agriculture took place somewhat later, and that it was only in the mid-nineteenth century that the majority of Turkmen became sedentary. See Marat Durdyev, *Turkmeny* (Ashgabat: Kharp, 1991); Yuri Bregel, "Nomadic and Sedentary Elements among the Turkmens," *Central Asiatic Journal* 25, no. 1–2 (1981): 5–37. See also König, *Die Achal-Teke*, pp. 41–43.

[16] "Turkmeny iomudskogo plemeni," *Voennyi sbornik* no. 1 (January 1872): 65–66; Bode, "O turkmenskikh pokoleniiakh," pp. 218–20; Saray, *The Turkmens*, pp. 23–24, 26; Irons, *The Yomut Turkmen*, pp. 21–27.

[17] Irons, *The Yomut Turkmen*, pp. 26–27, 69–71; Bregel, "Nomadic and Sedentary Elements," pp. 36–37.

[18] "Turkmeny iomudskogo plemeni," p. 65; See also Kuropatkin, *Turkmeniia i Turkmeny*, p. 34; O. Tumanovich, *Turkmenistan i Turkmeny* (Ashgabat: Turkmengosizdat, 1926), p. 65; Irons, *The Yomut Turkmen*, pp. 22, 36, 70–71.

Even as Turkmen became more sedentary, genealogy retained its historical importance in their political, economic, and social life. The local descent group was a vital economic unit among both pastoral and agricultural Turkmen. The ownership of natural resources was based on the system of patrilineal descent. Rights to land and water belonged to the kin group; individual ownership and the buying and selling of land were unknown.[19] Kin groups were not just a source of political solidarity and economic support but the primary structuring principle of social conflict as well. On the local level, severe outbreaks of conflict were relatively rare; people with many shared interests generally sought to stay on good terms and turned to mediators—elders or genealogically neutral parties— to solve intractable conflicts. Among larger-level groups, shared interests were fewer and the potential for conflict was greater. The major Turkmen tribes were often at war with each other in the centuries prior to the Russian conquest. Much of this conflict was over territory. In the eighteenth and early-nineteenth centuries, large numbers of Tekes had migrated southward from the Mangïshlak peninsula to the Ahal and Marï oases. In addition to conquering lands formerly occupied by Persians, they pushed the Yomuts out of their lands in the Balkhan region of the Ahal oasis into the Etrek valley, previously settled by Göklengs. This caused persistent hostility among Tekes, Yomuts, and Göklengs. In the Marï oasis, Teke expansion had pushed out Salïrs and Sarïks, again causing sustained hostility.[20]

The role of kinship in political conflict was perhaps most graphically illustrated in the custom of the blood feud. In a stateless society, an individual who was offended or injured had little recourse but to seek help from relatives. In the absence of state enforcement mechanisms, crimes were not viewed as offenses against society as a whole; only victims and their kin had the right and obligation to respond. The closer the relationship, the greater the obligation to provide support. Thus, in the rare event of a murder, customary law required the victim's close patrilineal relatives—those who traced their common descent back no more than seven generations—to avenge the crime. If the victim was a stranger or for some other reason lacked relatives to avenge his or her death, the crime would go unpunished.[21]

[19] M. A. Nemchenko, *Dinamika turkmenskogo krest'ianskogo khoziaistva* (Ashgabat: Turkmengosizdat, 1926), p. 5; Irons, *The Yomut Turkmen*, pp. 47–48.

[20] Irons, *The Yomut Turkmen*, pp. 61–65, 115; Saray, *The Turkmens*, pp. 55–57; Bode, "O turkmenskikh pokoleniiakh," p. 224; Kuropatkin, *Turkmeniia i Turkmeny*, p. 38; König, *Die Achal-Teke*, p. 84.

[21] A. Lomakin, *Obychnoe pravo turkmen* (Ashgabat, 1897), p. 52; Irons, *The Yomut Turkmen*, pp. 61, 114.

Genealogy, then, was the structuring principle of Turkmen society—an important basis for political solidarity, economic activity, and social conflict. Nevertheless, we should be wary of taking genealogical claims at face value. Genealogy itself is highly malleable and not always a reliable guide to a group's origins. A genealogical tree, like a "national history," is to some extent a backward projection of present concerns and relationships onto the past. Thus, tribal genealogies often reflect current political and social relationships as much as they do biological kinship. When groups establish close and enduring political relationships, they may eventually "discover" common ancestors and rewrite their genealogies accordingly.[22]

There were many examples of biologically unrelated individuals and groups who had been grafted onto the Turkmen genealogical tree. In Turkmen communities, nonkin often lived in close symbiosis with Turkmen—they might be slaves, prisoners, members of small client tribes, or individuals who had fled their homes to escape blood vengeance. While such people were initially considered "outsiders" (gongshï), over an extended period of time they might be incorporated into the local genealogy.[23] For example, a number of small lineages of non-Oguz Turkic origin had "become Turkmen" with the passage of time. Freed slaves, usually of Persian origin, formed their own lineages and were eventually incorporated into the genealogical tree of their former masters; every major tribe had its "slave" (gul) subsections.[24] In the Ahal region, there were culturally "Turkmenized" groups who claimed Turkmen genealogy but were believed to be descended from the original Persian inhabitants of the regions conquered by the Tekes.[25] The absorption of non-Turkmen groups provided the basis for hierarchies of prestige within Turkmen society, since those with the "purest" Turkmen pedigrees held themselves to be superior to those of "mixed" or "slave" ancestry.[26] The important point is not that all Turkmen were in fact descended from a single ancestor, but that the Turkmen living under Russian and Soviet rule believed this to be the case. Even in the absence of biological kinship, in other words, genealogy was the most important idiom on the basis of which solidarities and conflict were understood and justified. The belief in a shared ancestry

---

[22] On the malleability of genealogy, see Khazanov, *Nomads and the Outside World*, pp. 142–43; on the links between historical and genealogical thought, see Shryock, *Nationalism and the Genealogical Imagination*.

[23] König, *Die Achal-Teke*, pp. 72–73, 78–79; Irons, *The Yomut Turkmen*, pp. 51–56.

[24] Yu. E. Bregel, *Khorezmskie turkmeny v XIX veke* (Moscow: Izdatel'stvo vostochnoi literatury, 1961), pp. 28, 161–64; on slavery among the Turkmen, see F. A. Mikhailov, *Tuzemtsy Zakaspiiskoi oblasti i ikh zhizn': Etnograficheskii ocherk* (Ashgabat, 1900), p. 35.

[25] Karpov, "Turkmeniia i Turkmeny," p. 39; König, *Die Achal-Teke*, p. 84.

[26] Bregel, *Khorezmskie turkmeny*, pp. 161–64.

formed the "ethnic core" of myth and memory that some scholars argue is essential to the formation of a nation.[27]

Genealogy was the most important factor in one's identification as a Turkmen, but it was not the only factor. In order to be a "real Turkmen," one also had to lead a Turkmen way of life—in other words, a life in conformance with Turkmen customary law. Customary law, or *adat*, was an elaborate unwritten code that regulated all aspects of life, from marriage and family relationships to land distribution and the conduct of war.[28] Turkmen customary law was interpreted and enforced by the elders of each community, known as *yashulïs* (old men) or *aksakgals* (white beards), who were chosen by consensus from among the group's oldest, most experienced, and most influential men. Unlike the neighboring Uzbeks and Kazakhs, the Turkmen lacked a hereditary aristocratic stratum or tribe that monopolized positions of leadership. Leadership within each community was based to a large extent on seniority; personal qualities, wealth, and membership in a well-respected lineage were also important.[29]

Being Muslim was also a part of Turkmen identity. Like a number of rural and tribal peoples throughout the Islamic world, the Turkmen practiced a variety of popular or "folk" Islam focused on the veneration of saints' shrines and saintly lineages. Although many Turkmen observed the Islamic practices of prayer, fasting at Ramadan, and almsgiving, they had little familiarity with the great textual traditions of Islam and little institutionalized religion in the form of mosques or professional clergy. Any man who could read and recite prayers was respectfully called a *mullah*, or cleric. Although the Turkmen held themselves to be devoted followers of Muhammad, they gave precedence to tribal customary law over Islamic law, or *shariat*. A Turkmen proverb made the relative standing of the two legal systems clear: "You can leave religion if you like, but you can't leave your people." Because Russian orientalists believed that "true Islam" resided in the texts and doctrines of urban Muslims, they considered the spiritual life of the Turkmen to be primitive and impoverished.[30]

---

[27] The term "ethnic core" is from Anthony Smith, *The Ethnic Origins of Nations* (Oxford: Basil Blackwell, 1986).

[28] Lomakin, *Obychnoe pravo turkmen;* see also Karash-Khan Ogly Yomutskii, "Bytovye osobennosti turkmen Turkmenskoi SSR," *Izvestiia sredne-aziatskogo komiteta po delam muzeev, okhrany pamiatnikov stariny, iskusstva i prirody,* Vypusk 3-ii (1928), pp. 191–203.

[29] Yomutskii, "Bytovye osobennosti," p. 200. The council of elders was called the *maslahat.* On leadership among the Turkmen, see also RGASPI, f. 62, op. 2, d. 286, l. 165; König, *Die Achal-Teke,* p. 74; Irons, *The Yomut Turkmen,* pp. 47–48; Saray, *The Turkmens,* p. 41; Bregel, *Khorezmskie turkmeny,* pp. 123–25, 132–33, 139–42.

[30] On religion among the Turkmen, see P. S. Vasiliev, *Akhal-tekinskii oazis: Ego proshloe i nastoiashchee* (Saint Petersburg, 1888), pp. 49–50; F. A. Mikhailov, "Religioznye vozzreniia turkmen Zakaspiiskoi oblasti," in *Sbornik materialov po musul'manstvu,* vol. 2, ed. V. P. Nalivkin (Tashkent, 1900), pp. 95–96; Mikhailov, *Tuzemtsy Zakaspiiskoi oblasti,* pp.

Until the nineteenth century, most Turkmen groups had not come under the effective control of any state. Although they were stateless themselves, their contact with sedentary peoples and states was extensive. For centuries, Turkmen tribes had traded with and preyed upon neighboring settled peoples, acknowledged khans and emperors as their nominal sovereigns, and provided military services to the rulers of neighboring states.[31] During the eighteenth and nineteenth centuries, the Turkmen tribes fought continual battles against the Persian empire and the Khivan khanate, which were determined to subjugate them. Gradually, states succeeded in bringing Turkmen areas under control, and the nominal Turkmen recognition of neighboring sovereigns became more real. By the late-nineteenth century, the Ersarï Turkmen and a few smaller tribes were subordinate to the Bukharan emir; the Yomut nomads in Khiva were subjects of the Khivan khans; the Tekes and Western Yomuts had been incorporated into the Russian empire; and some Yomuts and Göklengs were under Persian rule.[32] In each of the states to which they declared their allegiance, the Turkmen tended to be regarded as unruly and potentially disloyal. Although valued as military allies, they were feared for their tendency to make raids for slaves and livestock on the border regions even of states to which they were nominally subject. As one nineteenth-century tsarist officer wrote, the states of Bukhara, Khiva, Persia, and Afghanistan "always paid dearly whenever they let down their guard" against supposedly submissive Turkmen tribes.[33]

The khanate of Khiva, also known as Khorezm, illustrated the complicated Turkmen relationship with state power. Some of the mostly Yomut Turkmen who lived in the region began to acknowledge themselves as subjects of the Khivan khan in the second half of the eighteenth century, paying tribute and participating in the khanate's military expeditions. However, the subordination of the Yomuts to Khiva was always conditional, since their nomadic way of life allowed them simply to flee whenever the government tried to impose unwanted obligations on them. They were also prone to turn on the khan when provoked, deposing the govern-

---

49–50; Sev, "Zametki o turkmenskom dukhovenstve," *Turkmenovedenie*, no. 2 (February 1928): 8–9. On saintly lineages, see V. N. Basilov, "Honour Groups in Traditional Turkmenian Society," in *Islam in Tribal Societies: From the Atlas to the Indus*, ed. Akbar S. Ahmed and David M. Hart (London: Routledge, 1984), pp. 220–43. The proverb was cited by a Turkmen informant in an interview, May 2000.

[31] G. Karpov, *Ocherki po istorii turkmenii i turkmenskogo naroda* (Ashgabat: Turkmengosizdat, 1940), pp. 14–15; Irons, *The Yomut Turkmen*, pp. 5–7.

[32] See Saray, *The Turkmens*, esp. chap. 4; Irons, *The Yomut Turkmen*, p. 7.

[33] Kuropatkin, *Turkmeniia i Turkmeny*, p. 32; see also V. V. Bartold, *Istoriia turetsko-mongol'skikh narodov* (Tashkent, 1928), pp. 32–33.

ment and pillaging the city of Khiva on several occasions.[34] In 1869, the
Khivan khan concluded an agreement with the Yomuts that essentially
made them into a privileged military caste, granting them land and water
and privileges not held by other groups, such as freedom from taxes and
the right to own slaves. This agreement between the khan and the Yomuts
did not last long, however. In 1873, Russian troops subjugated the khanate and massacred the Yomut Turkmen who made up most of the Khivan
military force. After the Russian conquest, the khan was able to call on
Russian regiments for aid in suppressing the frequent rebellions of the
Yomuts.[35] A Russian officer described the khan's attitude toward the
Turkmen in a 1909 report to the Turkestan governor-general:

> The relationship of Khiva to the Turkmen tribes is most original. The khan does
> not regard them as his subjects, but sees in them solely a restless independent
> people, against whom, due to their close proximity, he is forced to conduct a
> merciless war with the aid of all means known to eastern despots. His most
> sincere desire would be to see a single head belonging to all the Turkmen, which
> he would immediately command to be chopped off.[36]

The Tekes of the Marï and Ahal oases of Transcaspia remained independent and stateless longer than other Turkmen groups. In the mid-nineteenth century, the Tekes repeatedly fought against Persian attempts to
subdue them, occasionally allying themselves with other Turkmen tribes
against the common foe.[37] In the second half of the nineteenth century,
the Tekes were forced to turn their attention from their frequent wars
with Persia to the new threat posed by the Russians. The Russian empire
had been steadily adding to its conquests in Central Asia for some time.
Kazakhstan, Central Asia's northern steppe, had been gradually conquered in the early nineteenth century. In the early 1860s, the Russians
moved south into the fertile oases of Central Asia, subjugating the Kokand khanate (which was subsequently dissolved) and taking the city of
Tashkent. In the late 1860s and early 1870s, Russia turned Khiva and
Bukhara, both of which had significant Turkmen minorities, into vassal
states. In 1869, a Russian division was stationed on the eastern shore of

[34] Saray, *The Turkmens*, p. 18; Karpov and Batser, *Khivinskie turkmeny*, pp. 20–21; Kuropatkin, *Turkmeniia i Turkmeny*; p. 32.

[35] Richard Pierce, *Russian Central Asia, 1867–1917: A Study in Colonial Rule* (Berkeley
and Los Angeles: University of California Press, 1960), p. 33; Karpov and Batser, *Khivinskie
turkmeny*, pp. 6, 23, 31, 48, 51–52; on the Khivan Turkmen, see also Bregel, *Khorezmskie
turkmeny*; and Seymour Becker, *Russia's Protectorates in Central Asia: Bukhara and Khiva,
1865–1924* (Cambridge: Harvard University Press, 1968), pp. 229–36.

[36] Karpov and Batser, *Khivinskie turkmeny*, pp. 45–46.

[37] Saray, *The Turkmens*, pp. 56–59; V. Karpych, "Iz istorii vozniknoveniia Turkmenskoi
SSR," *Turkmenovedenie*, no. 10–11 (October-November 1928), pp. 38–39.

Figure 2. Teke family near their yurt, Gökdepe region, late nineteenth or early twentieth century. (From the collection of the Russian State Archive of Film and Photographic Documents at Krasnogorsk.)

the Caspian Sea, laying the foundations of the city of Krasnovodsk, which would later become part of the Turkmen republic.[38] Russian encroachment on Turkmen territory culminated in two major military assaults on the Ahal Tekes. The Tekes offered stiff resistance to the Russian attackers, who eventually sealed their victory with the massacre of thousands of Turkmen men, women, and children at the fortress of Gökdepe in January 1881. The Teke regions of Ahal and Marï were subsequently incorporated into the Russian empire as the Transcaspian province, which became part of Turkestan governor-generalship in 1892.[39]

After the Russian conquest, the experience of Turkmen in Transcaspia diverged in significant ways from that of the Bukharan and Khivan Turk-

[38] Saray, *The Turkmens*, chap. 4; Pierce, *Russian Central Asia*, pp. 22–34; Becker, *Russia's Protectorates*, pp. 26–78; Karpov, *Ocherki po istorii Turkmenii*, pp. 17–18.

[39] Karpov, *Ocherki po istorii Turkmenii*, p. 22–23; Pierce, *Russian Central Asia*, pp. 40–42; Saray, *The Turkmens*, pp. 210–12.

men. Unlike Turkestan, Bukhara and Khiva were never subjected to direct colonial rule. Subordination to Russia did result in a greater opening to outside economic and cultural influences within the two principalities, because of the construction of the Central Asian Railroad in the second half of the 1880s and the arrival of Russian troops, merchants, and political agents. Russian influence also played a role in stimulating the emergence of native movements for political and cultural reform in Bukhara and Khiva in the early-twentieth century. As a general rule, however, the Russians avoided interfering in the internal affairs of the two protectorates. When they did become involved, they sought to prop up the indigenous structures of power in Bukhara and Khiva and to discourage challenges to the prevailing political and social order.[40]

In Transcaspia, which became an integral part of the Russian empire, the social and economic changes resulting from the Russian presence were more far-reaching. Ironically, the tsarist regime did not deliberately try to transform Transcaspia or its other Central Asian possessions; rather, it sought to promote stability and forestall violent opposition to colonial rule. The administration refrained from attacking Islam in the Turkestan governor-generalship, concerned that this would provoke native resistance. Russian officials, while vehemently anti-Muslim, were convinced that Islam was a weak religion that would crumble on its own if it were ignored by colonial authorities. Thus, the proselytizing of Orthodox Christianity among Central Asian Muslims was prohibited. Russia ruled indirectly, using local elites to collect taxes and administer justice on the village and *volost'* (district) levels. Instead of imposing the Russian legal system on the region, colonial authorities dispensed justice to natives based on local codes of Islamic and tribal customary law.[41]

Nevertheless, colonial rule brought profound change to Transcaspia. Russian authorities created a new stratum of hereditary aristocrats among the relatively egalitarian Turkmen. The tsarist regime formalized the council of elders into the popular court, or *narodnyi sud*, and made the aksakgal—now called by the Russian term *starshina*—responsible for collecting taxes and other administrative duties. Preferring to deal with a formal aristocracy that would resemble the Russian nobility, tsarist au-

[40] Becker, *Russia's Protectorates*, pp. xii–xiii, chap. 8–13. Reformers in Bukhara and Khiva were also influenced by liberal reforms taking place in Turkey and Persia in the early-twentieth century. See Becker, *Russia's Protectorates*, p. 205.

[41] Adeeb Khalid, *The Politics of Muslim Cultural Reform: Jadidism in Central Asia.* (Berkeley and Los Angeles: University of California Press, 1999), pp. 52–55, 58–61; Daniel Brower, "Islam and Ethnicity: Russian Colonial Policy in Turkestan," in *Russia's Orient: Imperial Borderlands and Peoples, 1700–1917*, ed. Daniel R. Brower and Edward J. Lazzerini (Bloomington: Indiana University Press, 1997), p. 130; Karash Khan Ogly Yomut Khan, *Mestnyi sud v Zakaspiiskoi oblasti. Istoriko-kriticheskii ocherk* (Tashkent: 1922).

thorities appointed representatives of leading families from each tribe or descent group as hereditary "khans." For their cooperation, these prominent Turkmen were rewarded with large land grants, administrative positions, high salaries, and officers' ranks in the tsarist military. The new khans were invited to visit Moscow as honored guests, while their sons were admitted to study in Russian military academies. Under colonial rule, familiarity with Russians and the Russian language became a new source of power and prestige. The tsarist regime made no attempt to train a large local administrative elite or to promote mass education in Turkmenistan. However, it did establish a small number of so-called Russian-native schools for Turkmen boys. The goal of these schools was to "educate the natives in the spirit of respect for the throne and state, Russian law and power" and to prepare future Russian-speaking translators, clerks, military officers, and teachers.[42] A small Russian-speaking intelligentsia, for the most part educated in the Russian-native schools, began to emerge in the cities. Russian rule also resulted in the opening of Transcaspia to the outside world through the railroad and the linking of the Transcaspian economy to the world market. (The first railroad in Turkestan was in Transcaspia.) One-time subsistence farmers began to grow cash crops, especially cotton. These policies resulted in the rise of new social strata, including large landowners and merchants.[43]

Russian colonial rule also played a role in introducing new conceptions of identity to Central Asia, particularly the notion that humanity is divided into ethnic groups speaking distinct languages. Traditionally, the Russian empire had categorized its subjects according to religion. Russian identity was not primarily linked to descent or language but was a matter of practicing Russian Orthodoxy. Muslims within the Russian empire were classified as *inorodtsy*, a term that arose in the seventeenth century to describe the non-Christian subjects of the tsar.[44] In the late-nineteenth century, influenced by ideas of ethnolinguistic nationalism then gaining currency in Europe, Russian authorities began to see language and race as

[42] Karpych, "Revoliutsionnyi put' Turkmenistana," p. 9; Khalid, *Politics of Muslim Cultural Reform*, pp. 67–68; RGASPI, f. 62, op. 2, d. 286, ll. 165–66; B. A. Khodjakulieva, "Russko-tuzemnye shkoly v Zakaspiiskoi oblasti (konets XIX–nachalo XX v.) *Izvestiia Akademii Nauk TSSR*, seriia obshchestvennykh nauk, no. 4 (1995): 13, 18. See also B. A. Khodjakulieva, *Turkmenskaia natsional'naia intelligentsiia v kontse XIX–nachale XX v.* (Ashgabat: Ylym, 1995).

[43] Karpych, "Revoliutsionnyi put' Turkmenistana," p. 10; Khalid, *Politics of Muslim Cultural Reform*, pp. 61–65.

[44] Michael Khodarkovsky, "'Ignoble Savages and Unfaithful Subjects': Constructing Non-Christian Identities in Early Modern Russia," in Brower and Lazzerini, *Russia's Orient*, pp. 9, 15; John Willard Slocum, "The Boundaries of National Identity: Religion, Language, and Nationality Politics in Late Imperial Russia" (Ph.D. dissertation, University of Chicago, 1993), p. 54.

the main criteria for distinguishing among population groups.[45] Colonial administrators supported the work of ethnographers seeking to classify the Central Asian natives by ethnicity. These Russian scholars used physical type, language, ancestry, and other criteria to divide the population into distinct "peoples" who were presumed to have innate and identifiable characteristics.[46]

Tsarist colonizers also began to separate the peoples of Central Asia from each other administratively and territorially—a process that had a major impact on the Turkmen. The Transcaspian province, where most of Central Asia's Turkmen lived, was physically cut off from the rest of Turkestan by the intervening vassal states of Bukhara and Khiva. The Russians created a separate administration for Transcaspia with a judicial system based on tribal customary law, rather than the Islamic law used elsewhere in Turkestan. The special treatment of the Turkmen arose out of a conviction among the colonial rulers of Turkestan that nomads needed to be protected from the religious "fanaticism" of settled and urban Muslims.[47] One result of these measures was to institutionalize the distinction between the Turkmen and the sedentary population of Turkestan's core provinces.

The notion of a Turkmen identity linked to language and territory was not only a product of Russian rule, but was also fostered by the advent of new indigenous intellectual and cultural trends in Central Asia in the early-twentieth century. The most important of these was the rise of the jadid movement. In the early part of the twentieth century, the Muslim reformers known as jadids began to question traditional religious and communal understandings of identity. The Central Asian jadids, like reformers elsewhere in the Muslim world, were urgently concerned with the need for reform of their own society in order to face the challenges of modernity and European colonialism. They called for a modern educational system that would teach children in the vernacular language, rather than requiring rote memorization of sacred texts in Arabic and Persian, and would include

[45] Slocum, "Boundaries of National Identity," pp. 3–6; Brower, "Islam and Ethnicity," pp. 115–16, 122–30.

[46] Brower, "Islam and Ethnicity," pp. 122, 124–28; see also Peter Holquist, "To Count, to Extract, to Exterminate: Population Statistics and Population Politics in Late Imperial and Soviet Russia," in *A State of Nations: Empire and Nation-Making in the Age of Lenin and Stalin*, ed. Ronald G. Suny and Terry Martin (Oxford: Oxford University Press, 2001), pp. 115–16. On the use of the language category in census questions, see Henning Bauer, Andreas Kappeler, and Brigitte Roth, eds., *Die Nationalitäten des Russischen Reiches in der Volkszahlung von 1897. Band A: Quellenkritische Dokumentation und Datenhandbuch* (Stuttgart: Franz Steiner Verlag, 1991) pp. 137–51.

[47] Khalid, *Politics of Muslim Cultural Reform*, pp. 54–55. In Transcaspia, in contrast to the rest of Turkestan, local native officials were not elected by the village population but were appointed by the district commander. Pierce, *Russian Central Asia*, pp. 85–86, 304.

secular subjects such as history and science. Influenced by the ideas of the Young Turk nationalists in the Ottoman Empire, the Central Asian jadids also began to promote more secular notions of linguistic and territorial nationality.[48] But while the Young Turks insisted on the use of Ottoman Turkish as a lingua franca by all Turks, the Central Asian jadids sought instead to create a common Central Asian Turkic language. Instead of a pan-Turkic nation, they envisioned a territorial and linguistic Turkestani nation based on a common Central Asian Turkic culture.[49]

A few Turkmen accepted the jadid idea that identity was linked to language, but they rejected the prospect of a pan-Turkestani literary language and an inclusive Turkestani nation-state. As Adeeb Khalid has noted, the jadids were city dwellers, and the majority lived in the three central provinces of Turkestan and Bukhara—Syr Darya, Fergana, and Samarkand. The common Turkestani language they envisioned was essentially the Chaghatai literary language, which was close to what later became literary Uzbek. The Turkestani identity they claimed was based largely on the culture of sedentary Central Asians. Most Turkmen were geographically and culturally isolated from the goals of the jadid movement. They lived far from the urban cultural centers of Central Asia, spoke Western Turkic dialects that differed from those of the sedentary population, and led a collective life that retained many nomadic and "tribal" elements. Moreover, they believed themselves to be genealogically distinct from other Central Asians. As a result, they felt excluded from the jadid view of a Turkestani nation.[50] Just as the Central Asian jadids rejected the notion of pan-Turkic unity imposed by Istanbul, Turkmen resented being asked to submerge their identity in a larger Turkestani whole. The Turkmen linguist Muhammet Geldiev, for example, was educated in Bukharan religious schools and later at a jadid *medrese* in Ufa, where he received a modern, secular education and studied along with Tatar, Kazakh, and other non-Turkmen students. Rather than converting him to the cause of Turkic unity, however, his expe-

<hr>

[48] Khalid, *Politics of Muslim Cultural Reform*, pp. 1–11; Hisao Komatsu, "The Evolution of Group Identity among Bukharan Intellectuals in 1911–1928: An Overview," *Memoirs of the Research Department of the Toyo Bunko* no. 47 (1989): 122–23.

[49] Khalid, *Politics of Muslim Cultural Reform*, pp. 209–15. Khalid provides an extremely interesting account of changing conceptions of identity in Central Asia in the late-tsarist period. See also Seymour Becker, "National Consciousness and the Politics of the Bukhara People's Conciliar Republic," in *The Nationality Question in Soviet Central Asia*, ed. Edward Allworth (New York: Praeger, 1973), p. 161.

[50] The Kazakhs and Kirgiz were similarly excluded from the *jadid* vision of Central Asia. Adeeb Khalid, "The Politics of Muslim Cultural Reform: Jadidism in Tsarist Central Asia," (Ph.D. dissertation, University of Wisconsin at Madison, 1993), pp. 252–53; Adeeb Khalid, "Nationalizing the Revolution in Central Asia: The Transformation of Jadidism," in Suny and Martin, *State of Nations*, pp. 156–59. On the Bukharan jadids, see also Becker, *Russia's Protectorates*, pp. 205–9.

riences seem to have consolidated a feeling of Turkmen distinctiveness. Geldiev became a leading promoter of a separate Turkmen language in the Soviet period.[51]

The era of war and revolution that began with the outbreak of World War I was cataclysmic for Turkmen and other Central Asians. They faced several years of political upheaval, violence, and famine, all driven by distant political events that were incomprehensible to most of the indigenous inhabitants. Along with the worsening economic situation, two events in 1916 contributed to an atmosphere of crisis in Turkmen regions. Early in the year, the Khivan Turkmen under the leadership of Muhammad Qurban Junaïd Khan launched one of their frequent uprisings against the Khivan government. Russian troops helped the khan to suppress the rebellion, massacring many Yomuts in the process.[52] In the summer of 1916, some Turkmen took part in a massive Central Asian uprising in response to the imperial regime's attempt to mobilize native workers into labor battalions for service in the war. (Natives had previously been exempt from any form of compulsory military service.) Workers were recruited peacefully in the Teke regions of Ahal and Marï, but other Turkmen, most notably the Yomut nomads in western Transcaspia, resisted violently. The harsh reprisals of tsarist authorities included massacres, looting, and burning of nomadic encampments; many Turkmen nomads fled to Persia to escape the Russian state's coersion.[53]

The brutality of the tsarist regime during the war angered many Turkmen. Alienated from the Russian imperial state, they welcomed the revolutionary overthrow of the tsarist regime that took place in Petrograd in March 1917 (February 1917 according to the old Russian calendar). Politically aware Turkmen believed that the installation of the liberal Provisional Government would usher in a government more respectful of the rights of natives. In this they were similar to other Central Asians, who hoped that the establishment of a liberal and constitutionalist regime would bring democracy and greater autonomy to the region.[54] Like other Central Asians, however, the Turkmen soon discovered that local Russians intended to do whatever was necessary to retain their privileged position relative to the

[51] T. Tächmïradov, *Muhammet Geldieving ömri we döredijiligi* (Ashgabat, 1989), pp. 14–15.

[52] Edward Allworth, ed., *Central Asia: 130 Years of Russian Dominance, A Historical Overview*, 3d. ed. (Durham, NC: Duke University Press, 1994), p. 210.

[53] Karpych, "Revoliutsionnyi put' Turkmenistana," pp. 11–12; Pierce, *Russian Central Asia*, pp. 286–89; Karash-khan Ogly Yomutskii, "Turkmeny i revolutsiia: Desiat' let tomu nazad v Turkmenii," pt. 1, *Turkmenovedenie*, no. 1 (September 1927): pp. 12–15.

[54] Yomutskii, "Turkmeny i Revoliutsiia," pt. 1, p. 15; Adeeb Khalid, "Tashkent 1917: Muslim Politics in Revolutionary Turkestan," *Slavic Review* 55, no. 2 (Summer 1996): 276–78.

native population. In Central Asia as in Russia, the period between the overthrow of the old regime and the Bolshevik takeover of November 1917 featured a system of "dual power," under which the liberal organs of the Provisional Government shared power with the more radical soviets (councils) of workers' and peasants' deputies. In Turkestan, political authority was divided between the the liberal Turkestan Committee and the socialist Tashkent Soviet. Both halves of the dual power structure in Turkestan were dominated by Russians and determined to deny natives real political power. Despite calls by the Provisional Government in Petrograd for full and equal citizenship for native Turkestanis, local institutions seemed to be interested in serving only the European population in the cities. Even after the Bolsheviks took power in Turkestan in November 1917, the government continued to be dominated by non-Muslims; in fact, the third Congress of Soviets held in Tashkent in mid-November voted to deny Muslims the possibility of holding government positions. The new Soviet rulers justified their exclusion of natives on class grounds, noting that there were no proletarians among the native population.[55]

Central Asians made several attempts to organize in the face of their political disenfranchisement. At congresses of Turkestani Muslims held in Tashkent in April, September, and November 1917, delegates demanded autonomy and self-government for Muslims within the Russian state. In early December 1917, delegates to the Fourth Extraordinary Muslim Congress met in the town of Kokand to proclaim the autonomy of Turkestan and form a Muslim government.[56] Transcaspian Turkmen made a similar effort to organize after the Bolshevik takeover, convening an all-Turkmen congress and dispatching a representative to the Kokand government. Turkmen leaders proposed the creation of an autonomous Turkmen government that would rule the villages where most Turkmen lived, while Russians would govern the Russian-dominated cities. But these attempts by Turkmen and other Central Asians to establish autonomous native governments were suppressed. The Kokand government was destroyed in a Red Army assault on February 14, 1918, in which thousands of Muslims perished and the town of Kokand was destroyed. The Turkmen movement

[55] Becker, *Russia's Protectorates*, pp. 239–40; Yomutskii, "Turkmeny i Revolutsiia," pt. 1, pp. 15–17; Khalid, *Politics of Muslim Cultural Reform*, pp. 246–51, Khalid, "Tashkent 1917," pp. 276–80, 292; Alexander Park, *Bolshevism in Turkestan, 1917–1927* (New York: Columbia University Press, 1957), pp. 12–23; Sh. Tashliev, *Grazhdanskaia voina i angliiskaia voennaia interventsiia v Turkmenistane* (Ashgabat: Turkmenistan, 1974), pp. 30–31; Allworth, *Central Asia*, p. 225.

[56] Park, *Bolshevism in Turkestan*, pp. 14–21; Allworth, *Central Asia*, pp. 217–21. Adeeb Khalid has argued that the formation of the Kokand government reflected tensions between liberal and conservative Muslims as much as it did conflict between Muslims and Russians. Khalid, "Tashkent 1917," pp. 292–94.

for autonomy was similarly put down by force. In February 1918, when the Turkmen congress tried to create a national army based on the tsarist-era Turkmen Cavalry Squadron, Red Army troops arrived from Tashkent to crush the movement.[57]

Tensions between natives and European settlers were further aggravated by a severe famine that gripped Turkestan in 1917. The grain shortage resulted from a variety of factors: poor harvests; a shift to growing cotton by native farmers; a decline in grain shipments from Russia; and the upheavals caused by the 1916 revolts. The food supply problem was exacerbated during the Civil War, when Turkestan's rail links with Russia were cut. Once again, the burden was borne disproportionately by the native population, as the struggle for survival pitted Europeans against Turkestanis. Russian-dominated government organs reserved scarce grain for the city populations, leaving the natives to fend for themselves.[58]

The Civil War period from 1918 to 1920, when the infant Soviet regime fought for survival against a host of political enemies, was a time of tremendous political upheaval in Central Asia. Physically cut off from Russia by White forces, the Soviet government in Tashkent faced severe local challenges to its power. The most serious of these occurred in Transcaspia. In July 1918, a group of rebels led by Socialist Revolutionaries (a rival socialist party resentful of the Bolshevik monopoly on power) overthrew the Bolshevik government in Ashgabat, executed most of the Bolshevik commissars, and established a moderate socialist government. Facing Red Army determination to reestablish Bolshevik power in Transcaspia, the rebels solicited military support from the British command in neighboring Iran. After more than a year of fighting, Bolshevik forces finally retook Transcaspia in early 1920.[59] These upheavals were led by Europeans fighting political battles that had their origins in Russia; nevertheless, Turkmen became involved on both sides of the conflict. Some rejoiced at the overthrow of the Bolsheviks in 1918 and offered their military services to the rebel government. The supporters of the White rebels included an unlikely group of anti-Bolshevik bedfellows: Socialist Revolutionaries, Armenian nationalists, Russian monarchists, Teke war-

[57] Karpych, "Revoliutsionnyi put' Turkmenistana," pp. 13–14; Park, *Bolshevism in Turkestan*, pp. 13–24; Yomutskii, "Turkmeny i revoliutsiia," pt. 1, pp. 16–17.

[58] Marco Buttino, "Politics and Social Conflict during a Famine: Turkestan Immediately after the Revolution," in *In a Collapsing Empire: Underdevelopment, Ethnic Conflicts, and Nationalisms in the Soviet Union*, ed. Marco Buttino (Milan: Fondazione Giangiacomo Feltrinelli, 1993), pp. 257–58; Yomutskii, "Turkmeny i revoliutsiia," pt. 1, p. 18; Becker, *Russia's Protectorates*, p. 273.

[59] I. G. Ivanchenko. "Pravda i domysli ob odnoi neordinarnoi lichnosti (shtrikhi k politicheskomu portretu Khadjimurada Khodjamuradova)" *Izvestiia Akademii Nauk TSSR, seriia gumanitarnykh nauk*, no. 1 (1991): 38–41; Park, *Bolshevism in Turkestan*, pp. 26–29.

riors, and supporters of the Khivan Yomut leader Junaïd Khan.[60] Other Turkmen supported the Bolsheviks, serving in the Red Army or joining the Bolshevik Party. While their numbers were small, these Red Turkmen would play a disproportionately large role in the early political and cultural evolution of Soviet Turkmenistan.

Most Turkmen, however, had little understanding of the conflict and what the various parties represented. According to the Russian-educated Turkmen scholar Karashkan Yomutskii, ordinary Turkmen had only a vague and largely inaccurate sense that the Civil War pitted "Bolshevoi" (Bolsheviks) against "Menshevoi" (Mensheviks). Moreover, they generally had no idea what these terms meant: "Some thought that 'Bolshevoi' was a separate nation, which had conquered Russia and was fighting with the Russians, while others thought that both 'Bolshevoi' and 'Menshevoi' were non-Russian groups fighting for power."[61] Recruits for both Red and White forces in Transcaspia came primarily from the ranks of the homeless and hungry, who served not for ideological but for economic reasons. As one Turkmen soldier said, "I went to the White Guards because they were giving out boots, and the Red Army wasn't giving any."[62] For the majority of Turkmen, the Civil War was a time of unmitigated suffering. All parties to the conflict stole from and abused the rural population. Famine and war produced a demographic catastrophe of immense proportions, as the indigenous population of Turkestan declined by more than 25 percent between 1915 and 1920. Many Turkmen came to believe that they were in the last days before the apocalypse. They fled from the cities and railway lines where Europeans concentrated, retreated into the desert, and hid their families and possessions from the rapacious warring parties.[63]

Khiva and Bukhara were also caught up in the events of the revolution, despite the nominal independence and relative isolation they had enjoyed in the imperial era. Each of the former tsarist protectorates had a small modernizing intelligentsia that was eager to implement political and social reforms. Some of these reformers were willing to ally themselves with the Soviet regime in their struggle against conservative opponents and the traditional political system. Along with tensions between conservatives and reformers, the Khivan khanate was also plagued by the long-sim-

[60] Ivanchenko, "Pravda i domysli," pp. 38–39; Karpych, "Revoliutsionnyi put' Turkmenistana," p. 14; Park, *Bolshevism in Turkestan*, pp. 26–30.

[61] Yomutskii, "Turkmeny i revolutsiia: Desiat' let tomu nazad v Turkmenii," pt. 2, *Turkmenovedenie*, no. 2–3 (October–November) 1927, p. 17.

[62] Ibid., pp. 15–16.

[63] Buttino, "Politics and Social Conflict," pp. 257–58, 264–65; Marco Buttino, "Study of the Economic Crisis and Depopulation in Turkestan, 1917–1920," *Central Asian Survey* 9, no. 4 (1990); 59–62; Yomutskii, "Turkmeny i revolutsiia," pt. 2, p. 18.

mering conflict between sedentary Uzbeks and nomadic Turkmen tribes. This conflict burst forth once again in 1918, when the Turkmen under Junaïd Khan captured Khiva and executed the khan, setting up their own government. A group of jadid-oriented Uzbek intellectuals organized into a party known as the Young Khivans sought help from the Red Army, which in January 1920 drove out the Turkmen and declared Khiva to be a Soviet people's republic. In Bukhara, jadids who had been persecuted by the emir organized a political party called the Young Bukharans. The pro-Bolshevik wing of this party enlisted Red Army aid against their conservative Muslim opponents. After a first failed attempt in March 1918, the Young Bukharans and their Bolshevik allies managed to overthrow the emir in late 1920. Bukhara was declared a people's republic in October 1920.[64] Both republics were nominally independent but in reality subordinate to Moscow; in each, the Turkmen remained a marginalized and restive minority.

In the chaos of war and revolution, the Bolsheviks faced yet another challenge that greatly complicated their attempts to consolidate power in Central Asia—a Muslim guerrilla movement determined to resist Soviet rule. The Muslim rebels, known to the Soviets as "Basmachi" (a Turkic word for "bandit"), were motivated by a variety of causes, including famine and economic crisis, the disenfranchisement of indigenous Muslims, and the Soviet government's disrespectful and often brutal treatment of the native population.[65] Gaigïsïz Atabaev, a Turkmen communist who investigated the reasons for the Basmachi rebellion, argued that it was primarily caused by the Bolsheviks' harsh and culturally insensitive policies toward the rural population.[66] Far from representing a unified movement with a clear political program, the rebels were fragmented and incapable of coordinated activity. Some were defeated supporters of the Kokand government; others were religious conservatives who declared their goal to be the defense of Islam against infidels. Many of the Turkmen Basmachi had no real political program but were simply adventurers or men who were "expressing some sort of protest in one form or another," as the

[64] Park, *Bolshevism in Turkestan*, pp. 43–44, 47–48; Becker, *Russia's Protectorates*, pp. 294–95. On tensions between Muslim reformers and conservatives in 1917, see Khalid, "Tashkent 1917."

[65] Park, *Bolshevism in Turkestan*, pp. 34–42. On the Basmachi, see Baymirza Hayit, *Basmatschi: Nationaler Kampf Turkestans in den Jahren 1917 bis 1934* (Cologne: Dreisam Verlag, 1992); Richard Lorenz, "Economic Bases of the Basmachi Movement in the Farghana Valley," in Andreas Kappeler, Gerhard Simon, Georg Brunner, and Edward Allworth, eds. *Muslim Communities Reemerge: Historical Perspectives on Nationality, Politics, and Opposition in the Former Soviet Union and Yugoslavia* (Durham, NC, and London: Duke University Press, 1994), pp. 277–303.

[66] Rossiiskii Gosudarstvennyi Arkhiv Sotsial'no-politicheskoi Istorii (henceforth RGASPI), f. 670, op. 1, d. 11, ll. 3–4.

Turkmen scholar Yomutskii put it. While some guerrilla bands were overtly anti-Russian, attacking only Soviet garrisons and Russian settlements, others attacked and robbed their fellow Muslims, seeking to settle personal scores or to satisfy a lust for power. In Transcaspia, the rebels were not brought under control until 1924; in other regions, the uprising simmered at a low intensity for years longer. The Soviet regime ultimately defeated the Basmachi rebellion with military force. At the same time, it reduced popular support for the rebels by making concessions to native opinion. During the Civil War, Bolshevik leaders in Moscow had become aware that they needed to rein in the discriminatory tendencies of local communists and do more to win the support of the native population. After Moscow regained control of Central Asia in late 1919, central authorities stepped up their efforts to force local officials to involve natives in Soviet government institutions and to avoid actions that would inflame Muslim religious sentiments.[67]

The Bolsheviks also sought to win the support of Central Asians by satisfying—at least superficially—native demands for autonomy and self-determination. Even as the Bolsheviks struggled to control Central Asia in the early 1920s, they took the first steps toward implementing their nationality policies in the region. In regions inhabited primarily by Turkmen, a number of measures adopted between 1920 and 1923 promoted the Turkmen language and culture and reinforced the tsarist-era administrative separation of Turkmen from other Central Asians. The Transcaspian *oblast'* (province) of the Turkestani republic was renamed the Turkmen province in deference to its majority Turkmen population. Moscow urged local authorities to recruit Turkmen into local party and government institutions. Moreover, these measures were extended for the first time to the Khivan and Bukharan Turkmen. In Bukhara, an autonomous Turkmen province with its own Central Executive Committee (TsIK) was formed out of the Chärjew and Kerki provinces in October 1923. In addition, a Turkmen section was created within the Bukharan Central Executive Committee in September 1921. In Khiva, the Soviet government created a section for ethnic Turkmen within its executive committee. In Tashkent, a new Turkmen cultural commission was charged with standardizing the Turkmen language and publishing Turkmen textbooks.[68]

---

[67] Yomutskii, "Turkmeny i revolutsiia," pt. 2, p. 18; Park, *Bolshevism in Turkestan*, pp. 49–58; Allworth, *Central Asia*, pp. 250–53; R. Vaidanyath, *The Formation of the Central Asian Republics: A Study in Soviet Nationalities Policy, 1917–1936* (New Dehli: People's Publishing House, 1967), pp. 100–103.

[68] Komatsu, "Group Identity among Bukharan Intellectuals," p. 130; Becker, "National Consciousness," pp. 164–66; B. F. Sultanbekov, ed. *Tainy natsional'noi politiki TsK RKP, chetvertoe soveshchanie TsK RKP s otvetsvennymi rabotnikami natsional'nykh respublik i oblasteii v g. moskve 9–12 junia 1923 g., stenograficheskii otchet* (Moscow: Insan, 1992);

On the eve of the "national delimitation" of Central Asia in 1924, the people about to become the Soviet Turkmen nation were heirs to an ambiguous and complex legacy. The Turkmen population remained divided genealogically as well as politically. Subethnic identities remained more important than an overarching Turkmen identity, and the experiences of Turkmen living under Russian colonial rule had diverged substantially from those of their Khivan and Bukharan counterparts. In short, there were still many Turkmen stories rather than a single "national narrative." Nevertheless, both tsarist and early Soviet policies had paved the way for the creation of a Turkmen national republic. The introduction of ethnolinguistic notions of identity to the region under Russian and later Bolshevik rule reinforced existing Turkmen conceptions of identity based on genealogy. The administrative separation of the Transcaspian Turkmen from the rest of Turkestan—begun under tsarist rule and continued in the early 1920s—encouraged a sense of separate identity linked to territory. Moreover, the promotion of vernacular-language education within tsarist Russian-native schools institutionalized the link between identity and language. Russian colonial officials had introduced these new ideas and institutions without any intention of bringing about major changes in Turkmen society. The Soviets, by contrast, would promote nationhood and social transformation in Turkmenistan in a far more deliberate and systematic fashion.

Ia. Khudaiberdyev, *Obrazovanie Kommunisticheskoi Partii Turkmenistana* (Ashgabat: Turkmengosizdat, 1964), p. 18; "Turkmenizatsiia sovetskogo apparata," *Turkestanskaia pravda*, April 25, 1924, p. 2; A. A. Rosliakov, *Sredazburo TsK VKP: Voprosy strategii i taktiki* (Ashgabat, Turkmenistan, 1975), pp. 78–79.

Chapter Two

ASSEMBLING THE NATION

THE CREATION OF A TURKMEN NATIONAL REPUBLIC

FOR THE COMMUNIST OFFICIALS charged with delineating the boundaries of national republics in Central Asia in 1924, the tribe known as the Khïdïr-Alï posed a vexing problem. Soviet policy required that administrative borders correspond as closely as possible to the boundaries between ethnic groups. Yet it was difficult, if not impossible, to ascertain the ethnicity of the Khïdïr-Alï. The members of the tribe, who inhabited a region between the prospective Uzbek and Turkmen republics, claimed to be Turkmen. Soviet ethnographers refused to accept this claim, noting that the Khïdïr-Alï did not resemble Turkmen in dress, dialect, or way of life. A commission studying the ethnic composition of the region declared the group to be Uzbek, arguing that "even though some members of this tribe call themselves Turkmen . . . their statements are not reflective of reality."[1] The ethnographers speculated that the Khïdïr-Alï's claim to be Turkmen did not reflect their "true" identity, but their desire to retain their links to the neighboring markets of Chärjew, which were due to become part of Turkmenistan. Meanwhile, indigenous communists of both ethnic groups entered the fray, seeking to aggrandize the territory of their own future republics by claiming the Khïdïr-Alï as their own. Uzbek party members insisted that the tribe was Uzbek, while Turkmen declared that the entire region in which the Khïdïr-Alï lived was "exclusively Turkmen."[2]

The tug of war over the Khïdïr-Alï illustrates important features of the political climate of Soviet Central Asia in the early and mid-1920s. First, it shows the earnestness with which Soviet authorities sought to follow ethnographic criteria as they created "national-territorial republics"; the idea of including the Khïdïr-Alï in the Uzbek republic if they were "really" Turkmen (or vice versa) was simply unacceptable. Second, it underscores the fluidity of Central Asian identities, which complicated Soviet efforts to divide the region along ethnic lines. In fact, the Khïdïr-Alï were one of many Central Asian groups whose ethnicity could not be easily deter-

[1] RGASPI, f. 62, op. 2, d. 102, l. 62.
[2] Ibid., d. 100, ll. 15, 27.

mined during the national delimitation. Finally, the competition over the Khïdïr-Alï among Uzbek and Turkmen communists reveals the alacrity with which native elites adopted the Soviet rhetoric of territorial nation-hood when it was in their interest to do so. Eager to increase the territory of their own republics, the prospective leaders of Uzbekistan and Turk-menistan were more than willing to overlook the ambiguous ethnicity of some of their future citizens.

In Soviet Central Asia, the decision to redraw borders along ethnic lines brought about major changes in the region's political geography. Before 1924, the region contained three multiethnic territories: Turkestan, a for-mer Russian colony that became a Soviet republic in 1918, and the Mus-lim dynastic states of Bukhara and Khiva, which were transformed from tsarist protectorates into nominally independent "people's Soviet repub-lics" in 1920. The 1924 "national delimitation" dissolved these three enti-ties, establishing in their place a handful of territories based on ethnic criteria. Uzbeks, Kazakhs, Turkmen, Kyrgyz, and Tajiks now would have their own "national homelands."

In Turkmenistan, the resulting changes in mental and cultural geography were every bit as profound as the transformation of the physical landscape. The making of a modern nation-state requires a shift from a local concep-tion of territorial belonging—the view that one's village is one's homeland, in essence—to a broader understanding of the "national space."[3] But the leap required of the Turkmen was larger still. Like many other historically nomadic groups, the Turkmen conceptualized community boundaries in terms of genealogy rather than territory.[4] Instead of a spatial landscape of interconnected villages and towns, they conceived of a network of inter-connected kin groups and ancestors, a genealogical tree whose branches had no necessary relationship to specific geographical locations. This did not mean that the Turkmen were indifferent to territory; on the contrary, even nomadic tribes claimed tracts of land as their own and defended them fiercely against interlopers. Yet the boundaries of tribal territory were fluid and shifted frequently with changing historical circumstances and power relationships.[5] As a result, the Turkmen sense of identity was not bound

[3] Robert Kaiser, *The Geography of Nationalism in Russia and the USSR* (Princeton: Princeton University Press, 1994), pp. 16–17. On "national" borders in non-European areas and their consequences, see Basil Davidson, *The Black Man's Burden: Africa and the Curse of the Nation-State* (New York: Times Books, 1992); William F. S. Miles, *Hausaland Di-vided: Colonialism and Independence in Nigeria and Niger* (Ithaca: Cornell University Press, 1994). On boundaries and national consciousness in Europe, see Peter Sahlins, *Boundaries: The Making of France and Spain in the Pyrenees* (Berkeley and Los Angeles: University of California Press, 1989).

[4] Khazanov, *Nomads and the Outside World*, pp. 138–39.

[5] Anita Sengupta, *Frontiers into Borders: The Transformation of Identities in Central Asia* (London: Greenwich Millennium Press, 2002), p. 23.

up with the knowledge that generations of ancestors had occupied a specific piece of land. In theory, Turkmen individuals and groups could move about in the physical world to their heart's content without altering their positions on the genealogical map. The making of a Soviet Turkmen nation, then, meant the fixing of Turkmen identity in space.

The creation of the Turkmen republic in 1924 would provide the impetus for this transformation. The first decade of Soviet rule saw the beginning of a shift from a genealogical to a territorial conception of Turkmen identity, as a small coterie of Turkmen Communist Party members adopted the Soviet emphasis on territory as a crucial element of Turkmenness. For this Turkmen elite, the process of drawing national borders in 1924 served to solidify incipient nationalist sentiments. Turkmen communists were expected to negotiate with other Central Asian nationalities over the division of the region's land, population, and economic assets. This process required them to pit the needs of their own future republic against those of neighboring peoples, reinforcing a sense of common Turkmen identity and destiny. Yet even as Turkmen communists sought to defend their "national interests," they struggled to define those interests—and the Turkmen nation itself—in a region where the concept of a clearly bounded, homogeneous nation was unfamiliar. Not only was the Turkmen population fragmented along genealogical lines, but the boundaries of the prospective republic contained numerous non-Turkmen and groups whose nationality could not be ascertained. Although Soviet officials described Turkmenistan as the most ethnically homogeneous part of Central Asia, the republic faced challenges from the very beginning to the integrity of its borders and the cohesiveness of its population.

WHY CREATE NATIONAL TERRITORIES?

The demarcation of national territories in Central Asia was part of a broader "nationality policy" that emerged in the early 1920s, under which the Soviet state pledged to support national autonomy and cultural development for its non-Russian minorities.[6] With this policy, the Bolsheviks hoped to win the allegiance of the minorities of the former Russian Empire and forestall any secessionist inclinations. They were determined to show that the newly reconstituted Russian state would be a union of equal nationalities, not a perpetuation of the tsarist colonial empire. At a time when empires were collapsing and minorities were demanding independence throughout Eastern Europe and the Near East, this strategy made a great

---

[6] For a general discussion of Soviet nationality policy, see Suny, *The Revenge of the Past*; Martin, *The Affirmative Action Empire*.

deal of sense; in fact, it proved critical to the Soviet regime's survival during the Civil War.[7] There were other practical reasons for the policy as well. Soviet authorities believed that the non-Russian masses would embrace the message of socialism more willingly if it were transmitted by native elites, and that Soviet citizens would gain a greater understanding of Marxist-Leninist concepts if they were explained in Georgian, Yakut, or Uzbek.[8]

Moroever, the Soviet leaders believed that promoting nationhood was the best way to foster progress and modernity in the Soviet periphery. For Lenin and Stalin, nations and nationalism were real phenomena that could not be wished away even by fervent proletarian internationalists. Nations were a natural and essential stage of historical development, closely linked to capitalism, modernization, and the emergence of a modern class structure. Put simply, a people had to become a nation before it could move on to the more advanced socialist and internationalist stages of human existence. By promoting national distinctiveness, the Soviets would ensure a speedier passage through this stage; eventually, in true dialectical fashion, the promotion of nationhood would lead to the disappearance of nations and the emergence of a united humanity. Lenin argued that it would be counterproductive to attempt to force the non-Russians to abandon their national cultures and languages, since this would only intensify their nationalist sentiments.[9] The Bolsheviks were particularly sympathetic toward the nationalism of oppressed and colonized peoples, viewing national sentiments among non-Russians as an understandable response to the oppression they had suffered at the hands of tsarist colonizers. Russian nationalism, on the other hand, was to be suppressed as "great power chauvinism."[10] By promoting the national development of oppressed nations, the Soviets would both win their trust and encourage their more rapid progress toward socialism.

The foundation for Soviet nationality policy was the creation of "national territories," which would provide the spatial and institutional framework for the development of socialist nationhood. Within each national-territorial republic, the "titular nationality" would enjoy special privileges: preferential hiring for Soviet jobs, preferential admission to higher education, and the development of its native language for use in schools, books, and newspapers. At the same time, ethnic minorities living on another nation's territory would have the right to cultural autonomy

---

[7] Kaiser, *Geography of Nationalism*, p. 102.

[8] Yuri Slezkine, "The USSR as a Communal Apartment," p. 418; Martin, *The Affirmative Action Empire*, p. 12.

[9] Slezkine, "The USSR as a Communal Apartment," p. 420; Smith, *The Bolsheviks and the National Question*, pp. 16–17; Martin, *The Affirmative Action Empire*, p. 5.

[10] Martin, *The Affirmative Action Empire*, pp. 6–8; Slezkine, "The USSR as a Communal Apartment," pp. 418–21.

as well; in many cases, they would receive their own, smaller national territories within the boundaries of larger republics.[11]

The decision to base the Soviet state on national territories was by no means a foregone conclusion at the time of the Russian revolution; rather, it emerged from debates within the Communist Party about how to address the "nationality question" while modernizing and rationalizing the administrative structure of the Russian Empire. Lenin and Stalin rejected the idea of extraterritorial autonomy, in which individuals would be able to exercise their national rights anywhere within the territory of a multinational state. The Bolshevik leaders argued that this policy, proposed by the Austrian Marxists to deal with the complexities of minority nationalism within the Habsburg Empire, was not appropriate for a socialist state; it would make national identity more important than class affiliation, hinder identification with the Soviet Union as a whole, and exacerbate ethnic conflict. The creation of self-contained national territories, they believed, would satisfy nationalist aspirations and thereby diminish ethnic conflict.[12] Writing in 1913, Lenin had argued that national territories within a multinational state should be as ethnically homogeneous as possible, in order to "eliminate all national oppression" and to ensure the progress of these peoples toward modernity. While socioeconomic factors should also be taken into account, ethnographic data and the will of the affected population should be the primary factors determining the boundaries.[13]

In addition to those favoring extraterritorial autonomy, there were communists who disagreed entirely with the primacy accorded to ethnicity in structuring the Soviet state. Officials of Gosplan, the state planning organization, argued that administrative units should be based primarily on economic rationality and efficiency, even if this meant cutting across ethnic boundaries. The economic and ethnographic principles were

[11] Kaiser, *Geography of Nationalism*, p. 112, chap. 3; Martin, *The Affirmative Action Empire*, pp. 10, 47–48; Slezkine, "The USSR as a Communal Apartment," p. 430; Rogers Brubaker, *Nationalism Reframed: Nationhood and the National Question in the New Europe* (Cambridge: Cambridge University Press, 1996), p. 30; Smith, *The Bolsheviks and the National Question*, pp. 43–46, chap. 3.

[12] Kaiser, *Geography of Nationalism*, pp. 101–5; Martin, *The Affirmative Action Empire*, pp. 10, 32; Smith, *The Bolsheviks and the National Question*, pp. 18–19. Within the Soviet Union, the Jewish Bund and some Tatars favored extraterritorial autonomy, a reflection of the territorial dispersion of these two peoples. See Martin, *The Affirmative Action Empire*, p. 32; Serge Zenkovsky, *Pan-Turkism and Islam in Russia* (Cambridge: Harvard University Press, 1967), pp. 146–50.

[13] V. I. Lenin, "Critical Remarks on the National Question," in *National Liberation, Socialism, and Imperialism: Selected Writings by V. I. Lenin* (New York: International, 1968), pp. 42–43. Stalin also argued for a territorial approach to national autonomy in his 1913 article "Marxism and the National Question." See Joseph Stalin, *Marxism and the National and Colonial Question* (London: Lawrence and Wishart, 1936), pp. 3–61.

in active competition with each other during the early 1920s. Despite the twelfth Communist Party congress's declaration of the importance of national-territorial autonomy in 1923, Gosplan forged ahead with proposals for the division of the Soviet Union along economic lines. However, the support of Lenin and Stalin ensured that the ethnoterritorial principle ultimately carried the day. The Commissariat of Nationalities argued for the ethnoterritorial principle as the basis for the Soviet federation, maintaining that the inclusion of "backward" peoples in more "advanced" administrative units would hinder the economic development of the former and violate Leninist promises of national autonomy.[14]

Central Asia was the last major region of the Soviet Union to be divided along national lines. Communist officials viewed the national delimitation of Central Asia as a way of speeding up a natural process of nation formation in the Soviet periphery. This, in turn, was an essential precondition for the "modernization" that would allow Central Asians to enter the mainstream of Soviet life. Moscow also hoped that the creation of national republics would ameliorate the ethnic conflicts that plagued Central Asia and facilitate the emergence of class struggle. Instead of ethnic groups vying with each other for political influence and economic resources within each republic, the indigenous exploiting classes of each new national republic would struggle with their own impoverished classes. As an added bonus, the delimitation was expected to have positive foreign policy benefits, leading Turkmen, Uzbeks, and others outside Soviet borders to look with admiration to the new republics enjoyed by their ethnic brethren.[15]

A number of Western scholars have argued that the creation of national republics in Central Asia was an attempt to "divide and rule" Turkestan in order to combat pan-Turkic and pan-Islamic sentiments.[16] But this view neglects the larger context of Soviet nationality policy. Central Asia was

---

[14] D. Krasnovskii, "Administrativnoe-khoziaistvennoe raionirovanie Turkestana," *Turkestanskaia pravda*, no. 246 (November 20, 1923): 2; Hirsch, "Empire of Nations," pp. 44–54; Martin, *The Affirmative Action Empire*, pp. 33–34; Slezkine, "The USSR as a Communal Apartment," p. 422; Jeremy Smith, "Delimiting National Space: The Ethnographical Principle in the Administrative Division of the RSFSR and USSR, 1918–1925," paper presented at the conference "The Concept of Space in Russian History and Culture," Helsinki, Finland, June 1998.

[15] Terry Martin refers to the foreign policy effects of Soviet nationality policy as the "Piedmont Principle." *The Affirmative Action Empire*, pp. 8–9.

[16] For examples of the "divide and rule" argument, see Carrère d'Encausse, *The Great Challenge*, pp. 177–78; Connor, *The National Question in Marxist-Leninist Theory and Strategy*, chap. 9; Simon, *Nationalism*, p. 43; Roy, *The New Central Asia*, pp. vii–viii, 3. A few scholars have sought to challenge this view of Soviet nation-making in Central Asia, but it has proved remarkably durable. See, for example, R. Vaidanyath, *The Formation of the Central Asian Republics: A Study in Soviet Nationalities Policy, 1917–1936* (New Delhi: People's Publishing House, 1967).

not singled out for division; on the contrary, national territories were springing up everywhere in the Soviet Union in the 1920s. With republics being created for Ukrainians, Tatars, and Buriats, the exclusion of Central Asians from this process would have been tantamount to admitting that they were too "backward" to travel the path of other Soviet peoples and become modern Soviet nationalities. Far from imposing the delimitation on an unwilling population, Soviet authorities believed that the measure would be welcomed by many Central Asians. Interest in a unified Turkestan was limited to a small group of urban intellectuals, many of whom subsequently became leading figures in the Uzbek republic. The elites of other groups were less enthusiastic, fearing that pan-Turkestani unity would mean Uzbek domination. Turkmen and Kazakhs, in particular, complained that they were underrepresented and ill-treated in republics where they were in the minority.[17]

In creating national republics in Central Asia, then, Moscow did not divide a unified region, but merely institutionalized and deepened divisions that already existed. National delimitation could be presented as a response to ethnic conflict and the grievances of oppressed minorities. The notion that larger nations were oppressing smaller nations in Central Asia fit neatly into the Soviet dichotomy of great-power and oppressed-nation nationalism, in which the latter was always a justified response to the chauvinism of the former. Stalin argued that great power chauvinism was not limited to Russians; non-Russian nations were equally capable of national chauvinism and oppression of their own minorities. Thus, in 1923 Stalin condemned "Uzbek chauvinism directed against the Turkmen and the Kirgiz . . . [Kazakhs] in Bukhara and Khorezm."[18] Just as it supported the rights of non-Russians against "great Russian chauvinism," the Soviet regime would protect Turkmen and Kazakhs in Central Asia from their Uzbek oppressors.

Soviet rhetoric created the impression that there were a finite number of clearly bounded, easily identifiable ethnic groups in Central Asia, each eagerly awaiting the day when it would be granted its own territorial republic. In Soviet discourse, Kazakhs were in conflict with Turkmen, Uzbeks oppressed Turkmen and Kyrgyz, and so forth—all facts that necessitated the creation of a national republic for each group. In reality, ethnic groups in Central Asia were neither cohesive nor clearly marked. The

---

[17] Sultanbekov, *Tainy natsional'noi politiki*, pp. 164–65; RGASPI, f. 62, op. 2, d. 101, l. 10; A. A. Rosliakov, *Sredazburo TsK VKP: Voprosy strategii i taktiki* (Ashgabat: Turkmenistan, 1975), p. 81.

[18] Cited in Seymour Becker, "National Consciousness and the Politics of the Bukhara People's Conciliar Republic," in Allworth, *The Nationality Question*, p. 165; see also Kaiser, *Geography of Nationalism*, p. 106. The term "Kirgiz" at that time referred to the people we now call Kazakhs. "Kara-kirgiz" was used to refer to the present-day Kyrgyz.

people labeled by the Soviets as Uzbeks and Tajiks lived intermingled, often spoke more than one language, and did not necessarily regard each other as belonging to a different "nationality." The nomads competing over pastureland along the Caspian Sea were more likely to identify themselves as members of smaller tribes and lineages than as Turkmen and Kazakhs. Some groups in Central Asia did not belong to any of the now-familiar ethnic categories at all.[19] How, then, did the architects of nationality policy determine which groups were "nationalities" in need of their own territories? In particular, what led Moscow to decide that the Turkmen, a small, fragmented group of largely illiterate nomads and peasants, deserved their own republic?

In Stalin's famous definition, a nation was a "historically evolved, stable community" sharing a "common language, territory, economic life, and psychological makeup manifested in a community of culture."[20] Language was the criterion most commonly used to determine ethnicity in the European parts of the Soviet Union. In the tsarist empire, the late-nineteenth and early-twentieth centuries had seen the rise of the concept of linguistically defined "nationality," replacing religion as the main determinant of group identity.[21] The Bolsheviks generally adhered to this linguistic understanding of nationhood; Stalin once argued that Belorussia was a separate nation because it "has its own language, different from Russian."[22] In Central Asia, however, language was often of little use in determining identity. Because the region featured numerous Turkic dialects that had not yet been standardized into uniform written languages, it was not easy to determine the boundaries between the "national languages" of Turkmen, Uzbeks, and Kazakhs. Many settled Central Asians spoke both Uzbek and Tajik, and sometimes Persian and Arabic as well. Some individuals who spoke Tajik as their first language claimed to be Uzbeks, while others who spoke Uzbek or Turkmen dialects considered themselves to be Arabs.[23]

Soviet ethnographers familiar with Central Asia were well aware of the problems with linguistic identity. Accordingly, they were flexible in the criteria they used to determine the nationality of Central Asians. They introduced additional "objective" factors, such as customs, religion, and

---

[19] For an excellent discussion of the complexities of identity in Central Asia, see Schoeberlein-Engel, "Identity in Central Asia."

[20] Stalin, "Marxism and the National Question," p. 8.

[21] Slocum, "The Boundaries of National Identity," pp. 3–6.

[22] *Desiatyi s"ezd RKP (b), mart 1921 goda—stenograficheskii otchet* (Moscow: Gosudarstvennoe Izdatel'stvo Politicheskoi Literatury, 1963), p. 252.

[23] Vl. Kun, "Izuchenie etnicheskogo sostava Turkestana," *Novyi vostok*, no. 6, 1924, p. 351; Schoeberlein-Engel, "Identity in Central Asia," pp. 19–21, 56–60.

byt (way of life), to aid in classifying ethnic groups in Central Asia.[24] They also took into account the genealogical loyalties of the peoples concerned. For the Turkmen, as we have seen, genealogical consciousness was the main basis for their identification as a potential nation. Certainly, they had little else to recommend their candidacy from the Soviet perspective. They lacked a clearly bounded territory, a single national language, or a single national history. Nor was there any uniformity in their economic life; some Turkmen were nomads, some were settled cultivators, and some were a combination of the two. They did not possess a "common psychology," given their exposure to a wide range of historical and political influences. In short, the Turkmen could hardly be called a community, let alone a stable one.

Yet the Turkmen claimed a shared ancestry that provided a potential basis for unity. This genealogical structure, and the tribal customary law that went along with it, provided the basis for a Turkmen national identity. Interestingly, Soviet ethnographers and administrators in the 1920s accepted the existence of genealogically defined nations even though Bolshevik ideology officially rejected a biological or racial definition of nationality. (Stalin had seemingly excluded groups such as the Turkmen from nationhood when he wrote in 1913 that the nation is "not racial, nor is it tribal.")[25] In Central Asia, ethnographers and census takers queried the population about "tribes" and "clans" as well as nationality and language. They drew up detailed genealogical charts showing how different tribes were related to each other and to larger ethnic categories.[26] Yet genealogical consciousness did not in itself make a nation, in the Soviet view; it merely provided a foundation for future nationhood. Groups such as the stateless and fragmented Turkmen were potential nations, "backward" peoples who would require the help of the Soviet state in order to evolve. As I. Vareikis, secretary of the Turkestani Communist Party Central Committee, wrote in 1924:

> National delimitation will have especially great significance for peoples such as the Turkmen, who have not yet attained the formation of a unified nation in their historical development. . . . By creating a Turkmen national state, we will

[24] Slezkine, "The USSR as a Communal Apartment," p. 428. For an excellent account of Soviet ethnographers' debates about how to define nationality, see Hirsch, "Empire of Nations," pp. 16–42, 74–84.

[25] Stalin, "Marxism and the National Question," p. 5. See also Hirsch, "Empire of Nations," pp. 84, 98.

[26] Rossiiskii Gosudarstvennyi Arkhiv Ekonomiki (henceforth RGAE), f. 1562, op. 336, d. 26, l. 157; SSSR komissiia po raionirovaniiu Srednei Azii, *Materialy po raionirovaniiu Srednei Azii. Kniga 1, territoriia i naselenie Bukhary i Khorezma* (Tashkent, 1926), pp. 13–14.

speed up the process of forming a single nation at the expense of the tribal, clan, and village structure.[27]

If the reasons for identifying the Turkmen as a potential nation were relatively clear, it is more difficult to explain why the Turkmen were deemed worthy of the status of a Soviet Socialist Republic (SSR) or "union republic." Union republics stood at the apex of the Soviet hierarchy of national territories and formed the primary building block of the Soviet multinational state. In theory, at least, the union republics were sovereign entities that had the right to conduct their own foreign policy and to deal directly with Moscow. Within Central Asia, only Uzbekistan and Turkmenistan were granted union republic status in 1924. Tajiks, Kazakhs, and Kyrgyz initially received lower-level Autonomous Soviet Socialist Republics (ASSRs) located within the boundaries of larger union republics. (The Tajik ASSR was a constituent part of Uzbekistan, while the Kazakh and Kyrgyz ASSRs were within the Russian federation.) Tajikistan became a union republic in 1929; the Kyrgyz and Kazakh ASSRs seceded from the Russian Federation and acquired union republic status only in 1936.

Why did the Turkmen, with their small and scattered population and weak sense of common identity, receive a union republic in 1924 while the Tajiks and Kazakhs did not? One can only speculate, since the evidence does not provide a definitive answer. Turkmenistan's location may have worked in its favor, since like all other union republics it was located on an international border. Yet this is not in itself a satisfactory explanation, since the regions that became the Tajik autonomous republic similarly bordered on Afghanistan and China. Like other union republics, the Turkmen inhabited a relatively large territory; they were allotted nearly 40 percent of the land mass of Central Asia, even though they made up only 10.5 percent of the region's population. Yet size is also inadequate as an explanation, since the Kazakhs' territory was even larger.[28] The decades-long administrative separation of the Turkmen under tsarist rule may have played a role in the decision to give Turkmenistan union republic status, since it resulted in a sense among Russians that the Turkmen were a breed apart—a belief the Turkmen themselves constantly sought to reinforce. The Turkmen scholar Shokhrat Kadyrov has noted an additional pragmatic reason for creating a Turkmen SSR. Unlike the Kazakhs, the Turkmen did not share a border with Russia and thus could not easily

[27] I. Vareikis and I. Zelensky, *Natsional'no-gosudarstvennoe razmezhevanie Srednei Azii* (Tashkent: Sredazgosizdat, 1924), pp. 59–60.
[28] Connor, *The National Question in Marxist-Leninist Theory and Strategy*, p. 221; Vaidyanath, *Formation of the Soviet Central Asian Republics*, pp. 218, 196; Kadyrov, *Turkmenistan v XX veke*, pp. 107–8.

be attached to the Russian Federation as an autonomous republic. At the same time, Turkmen territories could not comfortably be incorporated into neighboring Uzbekistan because of the long-standing enmity between Uzbeks and Turkmen in Khiva and Bukhara.[29]

CENTRAL ASIAN COMMUNISTS AND THE "NATIONAL DELIMITATION"

In early 1924, the Soviet leadership in Moscow decided to proceed with the division of Central Asia along "national" lines. Most of the Soviet Union had already been subjected to national-territorial division by this time, and autonomous national regions and republics were ubiquitous features of the Soviet landscape. Between March 1919 and January 1921, the Soviet regime had granted national territories to a number of other groups within the Russian Federation, including the Tatars, the Bashkirs, the Chuvash, and the Kalmyks. In April 1918, the former tsarist colony of Turkestan was declared an autonomous republic within the Russian Federation; like Bukhara and Khiva, however, the Turkestani republic was multiethnic in composition.[30]

The trend in the early 1920s was to divide larger territories into ever smaller, more narrowly "national" autonomous units. Thus, the multiethnic North Caucasus was initially established as the Republic of Mountaineers in November 1920, but was later dissolved and subdivided into autonomous regions and republics for the Ingush, Ossetians, Chechens, Kabardins, and others.[31] In Central Asia, similarly, Soviet officials recognized early on that a further division of the multiethnic Turkestani, Bukharan, and Khivan republics was desirable. However, because of Soviet officials' unfamiliarity with the region and its instability in the early 1920s due to the "Basmachi" uprising, the further subdivision of Central Asia was postponed.[32]

By early 1924, the rebels had been subdued and the nominally independent Khivan and Bukharan republics had been brought under Soviet control. On February 25, 1924, an expanded plenum of the all-union Communist Party Central Committee adopted a decree calling for the reorganization of Central Asia into national-territorial republics. The pro-

---

[29] Kadyrov, *Turkmenistan v XX veke*, p. 108.

[30] Jeremy Smith, "The Origins of Soviet National Autonomy," *Revolutionary Russia* 10, no. 2 (December 1997): 65–66, 74; Smith, *Bolsheviks and the National Question*, pp. 43–65.

[31] Smith, "Origins of Soviet National Autonomy," pp. 71–73.

[32] Vareikis and Zelensky, *Natsional'no-gosudarstvennoe razmezhevanie*, p. 44.

Figure 3. Soviet Central Asia before the "national delimitation" of 1924–25.

posal mandated the creation of Uzbek and Turkmen union republics and a Tajik autonomous province, and the unification of part of the Kazakh (then called Kirgiz) population of Central Asia with the existing Kazakh autonomous republic. The Turkmen republic was to be created by merging the Turkmen-populated regions of Bukhara, Khiva, and Turkestan. In the words of the Central Committee resolution, delimitation would "completely solve the national problem, opening real, stable opportunities for economic, political, and cultural construction among all peoples," and would "strengthen the USSR as a Soviet Union of peoples of Europe and Asia."[33] From the moment of this declaration, the creation of the Central Asian republics proceeded with remarkable rapidity. In March and April, Central Asian communists discussed the broad outlines of the delimitation; over the summer, national subcommittees negotiated over

[33] RGASPI, f. 62, op. 2, d. 101, ll. 3–4.

borders and territory; by September, the new republics had acquired their final form. The delimitation became official in February 1925, with the inaugural meeting of a new Congress of Soviets in each republic.

The division of Central Asia was not simply imposed unilaterally by the Bolshevik leadership in Moscow. Rather, it involved a great deal of give and take between central Soviet authorities in Moscow and indigenous communists in Central Asia. At each stage of the delimitation, Moscow laid down general principles and asked local party organizations and specially designated committees in Central Asia to work out the details. Party leaders in Moscow, knowing relatively little about the national composition and popular mood of Turkestan, and even less about Bukhara and Khiva, sought the opinions of Central Asian communists before deciding on the details of the delimitation. The precise location of borders was generally negotiated by indigenous communists, with Moscow stepping in only in the case of intractable disputes. Lenin had argued that ethnographic criteria and the will of the population should determine the boundaries of national territories. In Central Asia, where popular sentiment on the "national question" could be difficult to determine, ethnographic data and the desires of local communists were the deciding factors.

Turkmen communists were highly receptive to the Soviet argument that the Turkmen deserved their own "nation," and they quickly learned to use the Soviet terminology of nationhood to promote this goal. Between 1920 and 1923, Turkmen communists had been exposed to the rhetoric and practices of Leninist nationality policy, with its promises of national autonomy and cultural development. Ethnic Turkmen had received their own "national territories" within the Turkestani, Bukharan, and Khivan republics, as well as specially designated cultural institutions and sections within the Communist Party.[34] These measures paved the way for the creation of a Turkmen republic and encouraged Turkmen to view identity as linked to territory.

Turkmen communists shared the official Soviet view that the Turkmen population formed a single nation artificially fragmented by internal divisions and by its dispersion among several different states. They hoped that the creation of a republic would help to overcome those divisions and consolidate a feeling of nationhood. Moreover, Turkmen communists shared a strong sense of grievance against other Central Asian groups. The Turkmen elite maintained that Turkmen minority populations were politically and economically oppressed in Turkestan, Bukhara, and Khiva. They willingly followed Moscow's lead and redefined these long-standing

---

[34] Khudaiberdyev, *Obrazovanie Kommunisticheskoi Partii Turkmenistana*, p. 18; "Turkmenizatsiia sovetskogo apparata," *Turkestanskaia pravda*, April 25, 1924, p. 2; Rosliakov, *Sredazburo TsK VKP*, pp. 78–79.

communal disputes as "national" conflicts, arguing that the solution was
the creation of a Turkmen republic in which Turkmen would be the dominant nationality. Turkmen officials believed that the Turkmen would get
a larger share of resources—jobs, power, spending on education and economic development—as masters of their own republic than as a minority
in other republics. These officials also knew that the planned creation of
a Turkmen republic would transform them from relatively minor officials
in the larger Central Asian context into the leading political figures within
their own republic. As a direct consequence of the national delimitation,
they would become the founding fathers of the first Turkmen national
state. The Turkmen communists' ready acceptance of Moscow's views on
national delimitation may also have been due to their educational background. A significant number of them had attended Russian schools prior
to the revolution, making them generally more "russified" and more willing to follow Moscow's lead than their Uzbek and Tajik counterparts.
(Many of the latter were educated in Muslim schools and came out of the
jadid tradition, which tended to favor a unified Turkestan.)

In the aftermath of the February decree, the Politburo asked the Central
Committees of all the Central Asian communist parties to prepare draft
delimitation proposals for presentation at the thirteenth party congress
to be held in Moscow at the end of May 1924.[35] In March and April,
officials of the communist party organizations of Turkestan, Bukhara, and
Khiva worked out the broad issues related to the delimitation: the number
of national republics to be created, their constitutional status within the
Soviet federation, and the nature of their links to each other and to Moscow.[36] They were supervised in this work by the Central Asian Bureau of
the Russian Communist Party Central Committee. The Bureau, formed
in April 1922, was a regional party organization based in Tashkent that
was assigned the task of coordinating and overseeing the work of all the
Central Asian communist parties.[37]

In Communist Party debates during the spring of 1924, Turkmen officials consistently emerged as the most avid and forceful supporters of the
plan for delimitation. They favored a self-sufficient republic that would
incorporate all the Turkmen of Soviet Central Asia, including Bukhara
and Khiva, with as few political or economic links as possible to other
republics. At a March 10 party meeting in Tashkent, Gaigïsïz Atabaev, the
Turkmen vice chairman of the Bukharan republic's Council of People's

[35] RGASPI, f. 62, op. 1, d. 25, ll. 27–28.
[36] Ibid., ll. 26–27.
[37] The Central Asian Bureau succeeded the Turkestan Bureau, which had a similar function; the main difference between the two was that the Central Asian Bureau supervised the
communist parties of Bukhara and Khiva in addition to the Turkestani party organization.
Rosliakov, *Sredazburo TsK VKP*, pp. 11–13.

Commissars, presented a lengthy document calling for the creation of a Turkmen republic.[38] Not long after this meeting, a group of sixteen Turkmen party officials from Turkestan, Bukhara, and Khiva passed a resolution approving Atabaev's proposal:

> Taking into account the political, economic, and cultural unity of the Turkmen settled in Central Asia, artificially disunited by the course of historical events and by despotic states— [we] acknowledge the current necessity of separating the Turkmen from the Turkestani, Bukharan and Khivan states in order to form an independent, autonomous republic.[39]

Nadïrbai Aitakov, chair of the Turkestani Central Executive Committee, added that Turkmen communist officials were unanimously in favor of a national republic that would unite the Turkmen population of all three republics.[40]

The Turkmen officials made the reasons for their position clear at subsequent meetings. At the Central Asian Bureau's April 28 meeting, Atabaev argued that the governments of Buhkara, Khiva, and Turkestan were failing to meet the special economic needs of Turkmen minority populations. The Turkmen, he said, were reduced to begging for government services and assistance from other nationalities—a fact that bred resentment and conflict between Turkmen and their neighbors:

> The Turkmen are a minority surrounded by other nations. Everywhere they are cast in the role of supplicant among other dominating nations. The Turkmen and their way of life require . . . specific economic conditions, and since this circumstance is not being considered by Turkestan, Bukhara, or Khorezm, it deepens the hostile attitude of the Turkmen tribes toward these nationalities.[41]

For this reason, Atabaev said, "it is my deep conviction that the unification and separation of the Turkmen into an independent republic is a necessary historic step in the life of the Turkmen people."[42]

Turkmen communists were particularly concerned about the situation in Khiva, where relations between Turkmen groups and the predominantly non-Turkmen government and population had long been tense. While Turkmen and Uzbek peasants competed over access to scarce water resources, the Khivan Communist Party and government were almost totally dominated by Uzbeks, Kazakhs, and Tatars. Only two or three of the six hundred Communist Party members in Khiva were Turkmen, al-

---

[38] RGASPI, op. 2, d. 101, l. 56; Karpych, "Iz istorii vozniknoveniia Turkmenskoi SSR," p. 37.

[39] RGASPI, f. 62, op. 2, d. 101, l. 56.

[40] Ibid., ll. 28–29.

[41] Ibid., op. 1, d. 25, ll. 33–34.

[42] Ibid.

though Turkmen made up around 25 percent of the republic's population. Khiva was the site of an uprising against Soviet power in January 1924, and secret Central Asian Bureau reports portrayed its government as incompetent and totally lacking in support. Viewing the Khivan government as an alien force incapable of defending their interests, Turkmen residents bypassed the Khivan government and turned to Moscow's local representatives whenever they had a problem or complaint.[43]

The future status of Khiva became one of the thorniest problems raised by the delimitation. The Khivan and Bukharan states, multiethnic in composition, possessed considerable legitimacy in the eyes of many of their residents. The Soviet leadership apparently toyed with the idea of defining Khiva and Bukhara as entities deserving territorial autonomy. At the tenth party congress in March 1921, for example, Stalin listed Bukharans, Khivans, Kazakhs, Uzbeks, Turkmen, and Tajiks as Central Asian "nationalities" deserving the help of the Soviet state.[44] As national autonomy came to be defined in more narrowly ethnic terms, however, Khiva and Bukhara came to be seen as anachronisms. The uprising in Khiva in January 1924 and the complaints of the Turkmen and Kazakh minority populations of Khiva and Bukhara convinced Soviet leaders that the two republics should be disassembled into separate ethnic components.

The Bukharan Communist Party rapidly passed a resolution approving the breakup of its own republic. However, Khivan officials refused to cooperate, and the status of Khiva remained unresolved for several months largely because of their resistance.[45] Khivan officials argued that their republic was a unified economic entity that should not be broken up. They denied that the Turkmen minority population was in any way oppressed or neglected, and they insisted that "their Turkmen" had no desire to join a Turkmen republic. They declared, moreover, that the merging of all Turkmen in a single republic was impractical because Khivan Turkmen were culturally and linguistically distinct from other Turkmen.[46] Turkmen communists disputed all these points. Atabaev noted that the handful of ethnic Turkmen who held positions of authority in Khiva supported the idea of a Turkmen republic but were "under the thumb of Uzbek officials" and therefore "afraid to express their opinion."[47] Aitakov argued that a republic that did not include the Bukharan and Khivan Turkmen would be a sham.[48]

[43] Ibid., op. 2, d. 97, ll. 28–30; op. 1, d. 20, ll. 45–46.
[44] Becker, "National Consciousness," pp. 162–63.
[45] RGASPI, f. 62, op. 1, d. 25, ll. 31–32.
[46] Ibid., ll. 30, 46–48.
[47] Ibid., l. 46.
[48] Ibid., op. 2, d. 101, ll. 83–84.

Another controversial question in the discussions of national delimitation was whether the new national republics would join the Soviet Union
as independent entities or as part of a Central Asian federation. Even
among those communists who supported delimitation, many believed
that national republics were only a short-term step toward the creation
of a single Central Asian republic. As Vareikis remarked in 1924, "Sooner
or later, we will see the formation of a Central Asian federation. This
is historically inevitable—the shared interests and ideas that the Soviet
republics have fought for are too numerous."[49] This point of view was
widespread among European communists, many of whom regarded the
promotion of national-territorial autonomy as a betrayal of internationalism. As one party member asked, "When are we finally going to drop
all this self-determination business? Can't we all live under a single International?"[50] Some Central Asians also favored a federation, mainly Uzbeks and Kazakhs who hoped that their own ethnic group would dominate a unified Central Asia.[51] The creation in 1923 of the Central Asian
Economic Soviet (SredazEKOSO), a regional economic coordinating
body, was a source of satisfaction for those communists who favored
greater regional integration.[52]

For Turkmen party members, however, the idea of a Central Asian federation was anathema. Turkmen feared falling under the domination of more
powerful and demographically numerous ethnic groups in such a federation; for this reason, they preferred to see the new Turkmen republic establish direct political and economic links to Moscow. The majority of Turkmen communists also argued against an economic union of the republics,
a course favored by the leaders of the future Uzbekistan. Atabaev indicated
that he himself favored some sort of Central Asian economic regulatory
organ, but was overruled by some of his Turkmen colleagues. In good
Marxist fashion, they reminded him that since the economic base determined the political superstructure, political autonomy would be meaning-
less if the new republic lacked full economic autonomy.[53]

On April 28, the Central Asian Bureau approved the plan for delimitation of all three republics over the vehement objections of the Khivan
officials.[54] A resolution adopted at the May 10 meeting of the Bureau
decreed that Turkestan, Bukhara, and Khiva would be divided into Uzbek
and Turkmen national republics and Tajik and Kara-Kyrgyz (soon to be

[49] Vareikis and Zelensky, *Natsional'no-gosudarstvennoe razmezhevanie*, p. 53.

[50] Ibid., p. 57.

[51] RGASPI, f. 62, op. 2, d. 97, ll. 68–69; d. 101, ll. 15, 20–23, 53.

[52] Rosliakov, *Sredazburo TsK VKP*, pp. 10–13; *Turkestanskaia Pravda*, no. 95 (372)
(April 30, 1924), p. 5.

[53] RGASPI, f. 62, op. 2, d. 101, l. 56; see also d. 100, ll. 10, 15–16.

[54] Ibid., op. 1, d. 25, l. 62.

known simply as Kyrgyz), autonomous provinces. (The Tajik entity was to be part of the Uzbek republic, while the Kara-Kyrgyz would join the Russian federation.) In contrast to the initial Politburo decree, the Bureau called for the Kazakhs in Turkestan to form their own autonomous unit, rather than uniting with the existing Kazakh republic. The resolution also rejected the establishment of a Central Asian federation, while calling for the retention of the Central Asian Bureau and the Central Asian Economic Soviet as suprarepublican coordinating bodies.[55]

The Politburo decree adopted on June 12 followed most of the committee's recommendations, with two important exceptions: first, it emphasized that the Turkestani Kazakhs were to be united with the Kazakh republic, not left to form their own separate autonomous region within Turkestan. Second, the Khivan republic was not to be dissolved, although its Turkmen population would be permitted to join the Turkmen republic.[56] It is not entirely clear why the Politburo overrode the Central Asian Bureau committee on these questions. One possible explanation is that the Politburo was responding to lobbying by Khivan officials and Kazakh communists, who felt strongly about these issues. However, this was not the end of the story for Khiva. On July 26, the Khivan Communist Party passed a resolution saying that it had rethought its position and now "welcomed" the dissolution of the republic. Heavy pressure from the Central Asian Bureau, including a visit by Bureau vice chair Karklin, appears to have produced the change in Khivan sentiments. Clearly anticipating opposition to this decision among the party rank and file, the Khivan Central Committee ordered party members not to "agitate" among the village population, send telegrams or petitions, organize delegations, or in any way voice their opinions on delimitation without explicit instructions from the party.[57]

If the enthusiasm of Turkmen communists at the prospect of a national republic showed that they had already absorbed new ideas about territorial nationhood, the process of delimitation only served to further stimulate a sense of common Turkmen identity. The broad outlines of national delimitation were determined for the most part between late April and mid-June. On April 28, the Central Asian Bureau created a committee to work out the practical implementation of a preliminary plan for national delimitation. The committee was divided into subcommittees by nationality, with each subcommittee assigned to come up with a draft plan for its

[55] Ibid., op. 2, d. 100, ll. 3–4.
[56] Ibid., f. 17, op. 3, d. 443, l. 17. The Politburo decree was drafted on May 28 by members of the Central Asian Bureau Committee on National-Territorial Delimitation who were in Moscow for the thirteenth party congress. Ibid., f. 62, op. 2, d. 100, ll. 7–8.
[57] RGASPI, f. 62, op. 1, d. 21, l. 125.

own national republic and present it to the Central Asian Bureau for review on May 10.[58] These draft proposals were presented to the Moscow
leadership at the end of May. During the summer, after the Politburo had
made final decisions on the contentious issues of Khiva's status and a
Central Asian federation, the difficult process of drawing borders and
distributing economic assets began. New committees designated by the
Central Asian Bureau hammered out the specific details of borders, territory, capitals, and the division of economic resources. (These details were
subject, of course, to Moscow's approval.) A Politburo decree of June 12
called for the delimitation to be completed by September 1924 and created a territorial commission, consisting of representatives of five Central
Asian nationalities, to determine the precise borders of the republics and
handle the mechanics of delimitation.[59]

In July, the Central Asian Bureau divided the territorial commission into
subcommittees by nationality, known as temporary national bureaus. Each
of these was asked to submit a precise plan for its own republic to the
Bureau by August 12, including territory, borders, internal administrative
divisions, and information on the projected number of inhabitants and the
composition of the new Communist Party organizations.[60] The national
bureaus, whose members were in many cases the future leaders of their
republics, naturally had an interest in maximizing their republics' territory.
The drafts inevitably contradicted each other, and bitter conflicts erupted
over borders, territory, and the distribution of cities and economic assets.

The Turkmen Republic: Disputed Borders and Contested Identities

The prospective Turkmen republic was generally considered one of the
easiest to demarcate. Soviet officials noted that the Turkmen oblast' was
the least ethnically mixed part of Turkestan.[61] A study conducted by the
Central Statistical Administration in the spring of 1924 concluded that
"building a Turkmen republic purely on the ethnographic principle is entirely possible" and predicted that the national composition of the republic would be "very homogeneous."[62] Nevertheless, border disputes did
arise between the prospective Turkmen republic and its neighbors.

[58] Ibid., op. 2, d. 100, l. 1.
[59] Ibid., f. 17, op. 3, d. 443, ll. 17–18; see also f. 62, op. 2, d. 100, ll. 7–8.
[60] Ibid., op. 1, d. 21, ll. 74–75.
[61] Ibid., op. 2, d. 101, l. 19.
[62] Ibid., ll. 125–26.

In a conflict that predated the Soviet era, nomadic Kazakhs and Turkmen each claimed the pasture land along the projected border between the Turkmen and Kazakh republics in Mangïshlak.[63] It was impossible to sort out who had the historical right to the disputed territory, since it fell along the migratory routes of both Turkmen and Kazakh nomads. Repeated efforts by tsarist and Soviet authorities had failed to end the conflict, and the two sides continued to raid each other's villages and steal each other's livestock.[64] Elsewhere, the most vexing problems had to do with distinguishing Turkmen from non-Turkmen. Compared with the monumental task of disentangling Uzbeks from Tajiks, it was relatively easy to identify core Turkmen populations in Transcaspia and parts of Bukhara and Khiva. Yet despite the precision with which most Turkmen calculated their genealogies, there were ambiguities of identity that complicated the process of drawing borders. In frontier areas between the future republics of Turkmenistan and Uzbekistan, there were groups whose identity could not easily be determined; in many cases, they spoke dialects that fell somewhere between Turkmen and Uzbek, claimed ambiguous genealogies, and could not name the ethnic group to which they belonged.

Soviet ethnographers were responsible for sorting out the identities of Central Asian populations, and they provided much of the information on which the national delimitation commissions based their decisions. In the years prior to the delimitation, ethnographers collected extensive data on the ethnographic composition and socioeconomic characteristics of Central Asia.[65] Continuing work that had begun under the tsarist regime, they labored to produce ethnographic maps that included not just "nationalities" but also tribes and lineages.[66] Yet many regions, including the more remote parts of Bukhara and Khiva and the steppes inhabited by Turkmen nomads, remained poorly studied well into the 1920s. Because of Civil War violence and Basmachi raiding, ethnographers could move through these regions only with a Red Army Cavalry escort. When they succeeded in penetrating the steppe, their attempts to query individuals about their ethnicity often produced unsatisfactory results. Some of those questioned would refuse to answer; others would name their tribe or clan but could not name their nationality. When village elders, or aksakgals, were asked about the number of people in their communities, their re-

[63] Gosudarstvennyi Arkhiv Rossiiskoi Federatsii (henceforth GARF), f. 3316, op. 19, d. 309, ll. 11, 15; see also op. 64, d. 46, l. 43.

[64] Ibid., op. 19, d. 309, ll. 15–17.

[65] Ibid., f. 6892, op. 1, d. 32, ll. 90, 120–24.

[66] Ibid., l. 90; *Materialy po raionirovaniiu Srednei Azii*, pp. 13–14; Sanktpeterburgskii Filial Arkhiva Rossiiskoi Akademii Nauk (henceforth SPF ARAN), f. 135, op. 1, d. 18, ll. 1, 4–5, 36–37. See also Hirsch, "Empire of Nations," pp. 26–27, 34–37, 66–67.

sponses were maddeningly imprecise: "God knows," they would sigh. "We have never counted, and no one has."[67]

In border regions with Uzbekistan, ethnographers were frequently hard-pressed to determine whether a given population was Turkmen or Uzbek. In 1923, members of a commission attempting to determine the boundaries of a Turkmen autonomous area within the Bukharan republic were perplexed by the Salur and Bayad tribes, who sometimes called themselves Uzbeks, sometimes Turkmen, and sometimes refused entirely to name their nationality.[68] The Amu Darya region in the former Bukharan republic posed special problems because of centuries of intermingling among its diverse population groups. On the right bank of the Amu Darya, a tribe known as the Kurama was sometimes recorded as belonging to the Uzbek ethnic group and sometimes described as Turkmen; during the delimitation, the Uzbek and Turkmen national bureaus each sought to claim the group as their own.[69] In the Farap region along the right bank of the Amu Darya, the Khïdïr-Alï became the object of close scrutiny by ethnographers and national bureau members. While the Uzbeks maintained that the Khïdïr-Alï were Uzbek, the group's elders unanimously declared themselves to be Turkmen; they were suspected of misidentifying themselves because of their economic connections to Turkmen regions.[70] In the end, these residents of Farap were—with a wink and a nod—classified as Turkmen, a triumph for the principle of self-identification as well as a tacit recognition of the importance of economic factors in drawing borders.[71]

Other groups in border regions also created headaches for ethnographers. There were tribes in Bukhara that claimed to be Ersarï Turkmen, but were not accepted as kin by other Ersarïs.[72] An Uzbek tribe called "Turkman" claimed genealogical ties to the Turkmen even though its dialect and way of life were considered "typically Uzbek" by Soviet ethnographers. (Ultimately, the "Turkman" were counted as Uzbek.) In the Garagul, Bukharan, and Garshï oases along the Amu Darya, certain groups claiming to be Uzbek carried tribal and clan names more typically found among Turkmen; ethnographers suspected that they were former Turkmen who had been absorbed by the Uzbek population.[73]

Groups of ambiguous ethnicity were not located exclusively along republican borders; they also lived within core Turkmen areas, where they

[67] *Materialy po raionirovaniiu Srednei Azii*, pp. 5–9, 11.

[68] RGASPI, f. 62, op. 2, d. 102, l. 62.

[69] Ibid., d. 100, ll. 15, 27. Leningrad ethnographers in 1930 were still debating whether the Kurama were Uzbek or Turkmen. See SPF ARAN, f. 135, op. 1, d. 332, l. 1. Kurama means "mixed-blood" in several Central Asian Turkic languages.

[70] RGASPI, f. 62, op. 2, d. 102, l. 62.

[71] *Materialy po raionirovaniiu Srednei Azii*, pp. 7–9.

[72] Ibid., pp. 241–42.

[73] Ibid., pp. 205, 223–24.

posed a challenge to the very idea of an ethnically homogeneous republic. The Ahal region contained people who called themselves Turkmen and spoke Turkmen dialects, but were not considered full-fledged Turkmen; they were believed to be descended from Persians who had lived in the region before the Teke conquest.[74] Another problematic group was the collection of "saintly" tribes known as the Ewlad, who claimed descent from the early Arab caliphs. Despite their linguistic and cultural resemblance to Turkmen, they were not counted genealogically as Turkmen.[75] It was not clear how the identity of such groups would be defined by a Soviet state perpetually in search of ethnographic clarity. Should a group be considered Turkmen based on self-ascription, even if other Turkmen rejected their claim? Should the Ewlad be considered Turkmen despite their own view—and that of other Turkmen—that they were not? Could they be considered Arabs, in accordance with their putative ancestry, even though they did not speak Arabic?

These ambiguities made life difficult for the ethnographers who earnestly sought to draw clear lines between ethnic groups. For members of the temporary national bureaus, however, they offered a prime opportunity to exploit ethnographic uncertainty in the interest of gaining additional territory. In cases where the identity of border populations was disputed, Turkmen communists generally took an expansive view of Turkmen nationality, lobbying intensively to maximize the territory of their republic. They claimed the entire right bank of the Amu Darya for Turkmenistan, saying that the population there was "exclusively Turkmen." When the members of the Uzbek subcommittee countered that the population in question was Uzbek, Atabaev called for the formation of an ethnographic commission to decide the matter.[76]

Conflicts between the national bureaus were negotiated in sessions that were competitive and frequently acrimonious. Committee members occasionally referred contentious matters to ethnographers and demographers for further investigation, but they were willing to abandon the ethnographic principle when it proved inconvenient. In such cases, they cited economic factors or simply engaged in outright horse trading over disputed regions. Turkmen negotiators, for example, tried to compensate for the fact that there were no Turkmen-populated cities by claiming Uzbek urban areas for their republic. Atabaev calmly observed that since Turkmenistan had no cities of its own, the republic had the right to annex

---

[74] Karpov, "Turkmeniia i Turkmeny," p. 39; König, *Die Achal-Teke*, p. 84; *Materialy po raionirovaniiu Srednei Azii*, pp. 241–42.

[75] Basilov, "Honour Groups in Traditional Turkmenian Society," pp. 220–43; Mikhailov, *Tuzemtsy Zakaspiiskoi oblasti*, pp. 38–39; Irons, *The Yomut Turkmen*, pp. 65–66.

[76] RGASPI, f. 62, op. 2, d. 100, ll. 15, 27.

those cities that served as Turkmen "national markets." Thus, he and the other Turkmen officials lobbied successfully for the inclusion of the city of Dashhowuz in Turkmenistan, although it was widely known that the population of that city was overwhelmingly Uzbek.[77] In ethnically mixed border regions, the subcommittees struggled to find mutually agreeable compromises. The Uzbek and Turkmen national bureaus tried to strike a deal that would give the Farap region to Uzbekistan in exchange for leaving Dashhowuz and Chärjew in Turkmenistan—even though there were many self-proclaimed Turkmen in Farap and large Uzbek populations in the latter two regions.[78] At one meeting devoted to difficult border questions, the chairman grew exasperated at hearing the local communists haggle like merchants at a Central Asian bazaar. The question of Farap would be decided by ethnographic investigation, he said, not in bargains struck in back rooms. "We are not a conciliation committee trading in mutual concessions. We will decide the question according to what is fair."[79] Exactly what was "fair," however, was open to question in such a context of ethnographic uncertainty.

In some cases, Moscow decided contentious questions unilaterally. Tashkent, Central Asia's largest city, was noisily claimed by both Kazakhs and Uzbeks until a preemptive Politburo decree assigned it to Uzbekistan.[80] In general, Moscow's attitude toward the future Uzbekistan was the cause of considerable resentment among communists of other ethnicities. Kyrgyz, Turkmen, and Kazakh officials maintained that the Soviet leadership regarded Uzbekistan as the "main" Central Asian republic, viewing the other republics as secondary.[81] In a joint letter to the Central Asian Bureau, they accused the Uzbeks of bullying the "weaker nationalities" and blamed Moscow for favoring the future Uzbekistan in these disputes. They also expressed dismay about the composition of the territorial commission, which, they claimed, was stacked so as to guarantee Uzbekistan a majority of votes. Instead of "protecting the interests of weaker nationalities against the dominance of economically powerful nationalities," as the principles of Leninist nationality policy required, Moscow was caving in to Uzbek demands.[82]

Tensions grew so sharp that the Central Asian Bureau issued a reprimand to local party members on August 16, 1924, warning them to avoid "nationalist deviations" and the public airing of national disagreements in their discussions of national delimitation. The members of the national

---

[77] Ibid.; see also d. 104, l. 89.
[78] Ibid., d. 100, ll. 9–20; d. 104, l. 91.
[79] Ibid., d. 104, l. 90.
[80] Ibid., d. 100, ll. 7–8, 13–14.
[81] Ibid., d. 101, ll. 3–4.
[82] Ibid., d. 110, l. 14–16.

delimitation commission, said I. A. Zelenskii, the new head of the Bureau, were particularly guilty of fomenting national discord.[83] At a secret meeting of the Central Asian Bureau on August 20, a decree condemned the "personal, uncomradely attacks" made by some members of the commission on their colleagues.[84] Another Central Asian Bureau decree of August 31 noted that the propaganda campaign for national delimitation was in some quarters assuming an "incorrect character." Instead of educating the masses by explaining communist views on the national question, communists were publicly discussing the merits of specific territorial questions, which could lead to "conflict between nationalities." The Bureau admonished party members to refrain from publicly airing national disagreements, discussing undecided questions with nonparty members, or making personal attacks on fellow communists.[85]

Nationalist bickering was an unavoidable result of the process of dividing Central Asia according to ethnicity. Despite the Soviet leadership's hope that national-territorial autonomy would prove less ethnically divisive than extraterritorial autonomy, the territorial division of Central Asia produced an inordinate amount of conflict. It served to heighten and consolidate a sense of national distinctiveness among communists of various ethnicities who had previously worked together in a multiethnic context. Conflicts between the Central Asian republics over borders and territory persisted for several years after the delimitation and ultimately had to be resolved by special commissions appointed in Moscow.[86] Communists who disagreed with the results of delimitation wrote "dissenting opinions," while individual citizens and occasionally entire villages sent petitions to Moscow or Tashkent complaining about their assignment to the "wrong" republic.[87] Republican officials learned to rally the support of border populations in disputes with neighboring republics—a practice that not only served to solidify the sometimes ambiguous identity of border groups, but also mobilized the rural population in support of questions of national interest once limited to communist elites.

In addition to the difficult task of defining the external boundaries of the Turkmen community, the Turkmen republic faced serious threats to its internal cohesion. Despite the optimistic projections of Soviet statisticians, the new republic was far from ethnically homogeneous. Turkmen made up only about 77 percent of the republic's total population of around one million. The remainder were Uzbeks, Russians, Kazakhs,

[83] Ibid., d. 104, l. 2.
[84] Ibid., op. 1, d. 21, l. 194.
[85] Ibid., d. 22, ll. 39–40.
[86] GARF, f. 3316, op. 64, d. 410; also op. 19, d. 309.
[87] A number of these petitions can be found in RGASPI, f. 62, op. 2, d. 109.

Tajiks, Persians, Armenians, Karakalpaks, Jews, Baluchis, Kurds, and members of other minority groups.[88] The dearth of Turkmen in urban areas posed a particular problem for Soviet modernizers. Although Soviet cities were supposed to spread national culture and Soviet ideology to rural peasants and nomads in their own languages, the cities of the future Turkmen republic were overwhelmingly populated by non-Turkmen— Tatars, Russians, Uzbeks, Armenians, and Persians. According to 1923 data, fewer than 1,000 of the 943,701 residents of the cities of Turkestan and Khiva were Turkmen. (No figures were available for Bukhara's cities.)[89] As Isaak Zelenskii wrote, "Can capitals which have a different national composition from the basic majority of the population fulfill the task of planting national culture and national progress? Of course not." The solution, he added, was "to change the national composition of capital cities."[90]

While Soviet policy privileged the titular nationality within each republic, it also guaranteed "national development" and cultural autonomy to minorities. Thus, Kurds, Uzbeks, and Armenians in the Turkmen republic had the right to their own national soviets and native-language schools.[91] Despite the pledge that minorities would be treated as full and equal citizens, however, non-Turkmen were concerned about their status in the new republic. Rank-and-file party officials of Turkmen extraction were reportedly "ecstatic" when the news of national delimitation was made public in the summer of 1924, but European workers and party members were noticeably less enthusiastic. At a party meeting in Ashgabat on August 11, Russian workers expressed "confusion as to how they will live and work in Turkmenistan if everyone is speaking the native language."[92] Muslim minorities were also worried about their fate in a Turkmen republic. Sultan Kary, the chairman of the Khivan TsIK, was one of a number of Uzbeks upset about the ceding of Dashhowuz to Turkmenistan. In a letter to Zelenskii, he cited an incident in which Turkmen "bandits" had attacked Uzbek settlements, driving away 410 sheep and taking seven people captive. The Turkmen authorities, Kary maintained, had done nothing to help the victims—an indication of the neglect Uzbeks could expect in a Turkmen republic.[93]

If the officials of the new Turkmen republic were relatively sanguine about the fate of ethnic minorities, they were more concerned at the pros-

---

[88] GARF, f. 3316, op. 20, d. 156, l. 48.

[89] Vareikis and Zelensky, *Natsional'no-gosudarstvennoe razmezhevanie*, p. 72.

[90] Ibid., p. 80.

[91] On national minority soviets, see Martin, *The Affirmative Action Empire*, pp. 31–74.

[92] RGASPI, f. 62, op. 2, d. 101, ll. 148–49; Vareikis and Zelensky, *Natsional'no-gosudarstvennoe razmezhevanie*, pp. 54, 83.

[93] RGASPI, f. 62, op. 2, d. 109, l. 75.

pect of intra-Turkmen conflict. The members of the Turkmen national bureau recognized that it would not be easy to promote a sense of unity and cohesion among the various Turkmen groups making up the new republic. The delimitation would unite the Turkmen minority populations of Turkestan, Khiva, and Bukhara into a single political entity. Of the Turkmen in Soviet Central Asia before the national delimitation, about 43 percent lived in the Turkmen oblast' of the Turkestani republic, while 27 percent were in Bukhara and 30 percent in Khiva.[94] In Turkestan, Turkmen were a tiny minority—266,672 out of a total population of 5,664,481. In Bukhara, too, Turkmen made up less than 10 percent of the population—246,646 out of a population of 2,682,130. In Khiva, Turkmen made up closer to 25 percent of the population—184,200 out of a total of 640,040.[95]

These three Turkmen populations differed not only in their tribal composition but also in their historical experiences. The Marï and Ahal oases in the former Turkmen oblast' were home predominantly to Teke Turkmen and were considered by the Russians—and by the Tekes—to be the most economically and culturally developed part of the republic. This central region of the republic, having been the longest under Russian domination, had the largest number of Turkmen who spoke Russian and was the main source of native officials for the Soviet regime. To the east of the former Turkmen oblast', the Yomut regions of Khiva and the predominantly Ersarï regions of Bukhara were considered to be more "backward." Unlike the Teke lands, these areas had little exposure to Soviet institutions and the Russian language prior to 1924. Similarly, the Western portion of Transcaspia, home to numerous Yomut nomads, was considered economically and culturally underdeveloped.[96]

The concern of some Turkmen officials about the potential for friction among these diverse Turkmen populations was reflected in the debate over where to locate the republican capital. Four members of the Turkmen national bureau—Aitakov, Atabaev, B. Nazarov, and V. Naubatov—favored moving the capital immediately to Chärjew, near Bukhara. The other two members, Halmïrad Sähetmïradov and Nikolai Paskutskii, insisted that the capital should remain in Ashgabat (known briefly in the 1920s as Poltoratsk), the center of the former Transcaspian province of tsarist Turkestan.[97] The proponents of Chärjew were primarily concerned

[94] Khudaiberdyev, *Obrazovanie Kommunisticheskoi Partii Turkmenistana*, p. 15.

[95] Vareikis and Zelensky, *Natsional'no-gosudarstvennoe razmezhevanie*, p. 72; RGASPI, f. 62, op. 2, d. 108, l. 68.

[96] Turkmenskoe Natsional'noe Buro, "Gde byt' stolitse Turkmenii?" *Turkestanskaia Pravda*, September 9, 1924, p. 2.

[97] RGASPI, f. 62, op. 1, d. 22, l. 205, ll. 209–12. See also Karpych, "K istorii vozniknoveniia Turkmenskoi SSR," pp. 46–52.

about the political unity of the republic. They argued that moving the capital would show the government's commitment to developing the less advanced parts of the republic, proving to the newly incorporated Yomut and Ersarï Turkmen that national unification did not simply mean they were being "colonized" by Tekes. In an editorial published in September 1924, the proponents of Chärjew argued that a successful "tribal" policy was essential to the future cohesion of the new republic. In parts of former Bukhara and Khiva, they wrote, the population is "armed to the teeth" and individual tribes are afflicted with a "downright pathological self-love." If the concerns of these tribes were not respected, they might try to secede from the Turkmen republic.[98] The majority of bureau members considered Chärjew to be an ideal compromise capital because of its location in a "neutral" area between the three main regions of the new republic: "Making Poltoratsk into the capital, given the ignorance and backwardness of the Khorezmian and Bukharan Turkmen, will create the impression of their subordination to the Tekes and will threaten us with a real rupture." The choice of Chärjew would also be instrumental in attracting back the many Bukharan Turkmen who had fled to Afghanistan during the Civil War. Many of these emigrants "looked with hope on the newly born republic, but only in the context of their own tribes." For those Turkmen, the authors added, "Tekes are just as hostile an element as Uzbeks, and subordination to Poltoratsk will be a deadly insult.[99]

The proponents of Chärjew prevailed at a meeting of the national bureau on August 24, 1924, but Sähetmïradov and Paskutskii continued to campaign for Poltoratsk/Ashgabat.[100] They scoffed at the concerns of those who favored Chärjew, arguing that the most important thing for the new republic was to set to work immediately establishing schools, hospitals, and newspapers. Such a "running start" could be made only if Ashgabat were used as the capital, at least for the time being. All the "cultured" people in the republic, both European and native, lived in and around Ashgabat, they noted, while Chärjew lacked the facilities to accommodate the new government and its employees. Thus, a "correct policy" would locate the capital in the center of the republic, "employing all of its dynamic cultural strengths and technical potential, [and] using the center's resources to *raise the east and the west to the necessary level*" (emphasis in original).[101]

The two factions do not appear to have been motivated by regional or tribal patriotism. The four members of the pro-Chärjew camp had diverse

[98] Turkmenskoe Natsional'noe Buro, "Gde byt' stolitse Turkmenii?" p. 2.
[99] Ibid.
[100] RGASPI, f. 62, op. 1, d. 22, ll. 205–6.
[101] Ibid., ll. 211–15.

backgrounds. Atabaev was a Teke from Transcaspia and Aitakov a Yomut from Western Transcaspia, while Nazarov and Naubatov were from Khiva and Bukhara, respectively. It may be significant that at least three of these individuals had worked in Bukhara or Khiva before the delimitation. This experience may have made them more aware than the two promoters of Ashgabat—Paskutskii, a Russian, and Sähetmïradov, a Teke who was perhaps the most russified and Moscow-oriented of the Turkmen communists—of the potential resentments and centrifugal tendencies within the republic.

The Central Asian Bureau approved the choice of Chärjew on September 1, 1924, after hearing the arguments of each side.[102] A committee was formed to begin preparing Chärjew for its role as republican capital.[103] However, the move to Chärjew never took place, apparently because of the practical difficulties involved in moving government institutions and their staffs to a new town.[104] Ashgabat, the former tsarist administrative center, became the capital of the new Turkmen republic, and many of the "tribal" problems anticipated by the proponents of Chärjew did in fact arise.

The Turkmen National Bureau's final proposal for a Turkmen Soviet Socialist Republic was adopted by the Central Asian Bureau on September 7, 1924.[105] The republic would include the five districts of the Turkmen (formerly Transcaspian) province of Turkestan, the Chärjew and Kerki provinces and a portion of the Shirabad (Kelif) province of the Bukharan republic, and the Turkmen or Dashhowuz province of the Khivan republic. It would be bounded by Persia and Afghanistan in the south, by the Caspian Sea in the west, by Uzbekistan in the east and northeast, and by Kazakhstan in the northwest. The new republic would be divided into five provinces, or *okrugi:* Poltoratsk, Marï, Chärjew (now renamed Leninsk), Kerki, and Dashhowuz. Each of these provinces, in turn, would be broken down into four or five districts, or *raiony*.[106] In the months leading up to the first meeting of the Turkmen republic's new Congress of Soviets on February 14, 1925, Soviet officials worked to organize and staff the central party and state institutions of the republic.[107] A revolutionary committee under the leadership of Aitakov took over the day-to-day administration of the republic until permanent institutions could be formed.[108]

[102] Ibid., l. 194.
[103] Ibid., l. 57.
[104] *Materialy po raionirovaniiu Srednei Azii,* pp. 75–76.
[105] RGASPI, f. 62, op. 1, d. 22, ll. 84–85.
[106] Ibid., ll. 55, 84–85; GARF, f. 3316, op. 18, d. 250, l. 285; Khudaiberdyev, *Obrazovanie Kommunisticheskoi Partii Turkmenistana,* p. 29.
[107] GARF, f. 3316, op. 18, d. 250, l. 286.
[108] Ibid., f. 6892, op. 1, d. 32, l. 218.

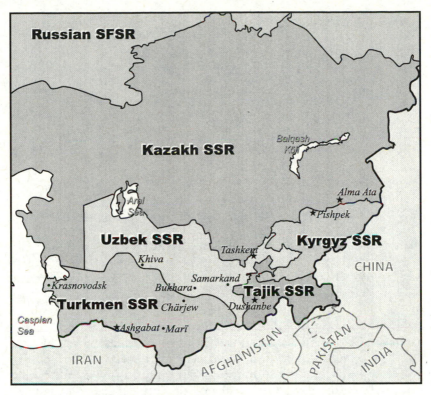

Figure 4. Soviet Central Asia after the "national delimitation." This map reflects the later upgrading of the Tajik (1929), Kazakh (1936), and Kyrgyz (1936) autonomous republics to union republic status.

The Turkmen republic officially became a member of the Union of Soviet Socialist Republics at the third all-union Congress of Soviets in May, 1925.[109] The infant republic embarked on the process of *natsional'noe stroitel'stvo*, or nation-building, with a distinct set of assets and liabilities. On the one hand, it possessed a small but enthusiastic coterie of native officials who were deeply committed to the idea of Turkmen political and cultural autonomy—a commitment that had been reinforced by their participation in the process of delimitation. On the other hand, the new republic faced significant threats to its cohesion: a divided Turkmen population, restive ethnic minorities, and a tenuous connection between an urban-based regime and an overwhelmingly rural population.

[109] Khudaiberdyev, *Obrazovanie Kommunisticheskoi Partii Turkmenistana*, p. 34.

Chapter Three

ETHNIC PREFERENCES AND
ETHNIC CONFLICT

THE RISE OF A TURKMEN NATIONAL ELITE

I N MAY 1925, the women's department of the Turkmen Communist Party received an urgent assignment: find seven young women of indigenous nationalities to enroll in the new Central Asian Communist University in Tashkent. For the 1925–26 academic year, the university had reserved 20 percent of its admissions slots for native Central Asian women. The Turkmen republic was allotted seven places—five for women of the titular nationality and one each for members of the republic's Uzbek and Kazakh minorities. The deputy director of the women's department, Comrade Ross, asked her subordinates in local offices throughout Turkmenistan for help in finding seven prospective scholars. The problem, she wrote, was that the university accepted only literate people, "that is, those able to read and write in their native language and familiar with the four operations of arithmetic," yet few Turkmen women possessed these abilities. In seeking out "suitable candidates," therefore, local officials should simply look for women between sixteen and twenty-five years of age, "healthy people, not suffering from trachoma or venereal diseases," who were willing to study in Tashkent and whose departure would not cause "family difficulties." An inability to read and write was no obstacle, since the chosen seven would "liquidate their illiteracy" over the summer before beginning their university studies.[1]

Comrade Ross's task illustrates both the uniquely ambitious and the uniquely problematic nature of Soviet nationality policy. In the brave new world of Soviet Central Asia in the 1920s, there was nothing at all implausible about plucking a young woman from her parental home in a remote Turkmen village, teaching her to read and write, and sending her off to the big city to study Marxist-Leninist political economy. Nor was there anything unusual about the party's attempt to manipulate the ethnic and gender composition of the Tashkent university's student body. If the 1924–25 Soviet partition of Central Asia into national-territorial repub-

[1] RGASPI, f. 62, op. 2, d. 440, l. 84.

lics based on ethnic criteria had been unprecedented, so, too, was the ambitious Soviet effort to promote local elites, languages, and cultures within each republic. With good reason, the Soviet Union of the 1920s and 1930s been called an "affirmative action empire."[2]

According to the tenets of Soviet nationality policy, the promotion of national cultures and elites in non-Russian republics would help to atone for the past oppression of these regions by tsarist colonizers. Moreover, local elites fluent in the native language and familiar with the native way of life would be better able than outsiders to introduce socialist ideas to the non-Russian masses. The Soviet efforts to recruit native cadres and foster the use of local languages in education and government adminstration came to be known as *korenizatsiia*, a term derived from the Russian words *koren'* (root) and *korennoi* (indigenous) and usually translated as "indigenization." Indigenization was intended to make Soviet power seem homegrown and approachable. In strictly pragmatic terms, it meant that non-Russians would be able to communicate with the Soviet government in their native language, whether they were applying for a job, consulting a doctor, registering a marriage, or complaining about a high-handed official. In political and psychological terms, indigenization sought to distance the Soviet government from tsarist colonialism and convince non-Russian nationalities that it supported their aspirations for self-determination and cultural autonomy.[3]

In the 1920s and the first part of the 1930s, Soviet authorities passed decree after decree on indigenization, adopting ever higher quotas for the recruitment of local nationals and ever more stringent deadlines for the use of indigenous languages in government work and education. In Turkmenistan, however, this campaign faced an uphill struggle. The Soviet administration needed individuals who could execute bureaucratic commands and document government work in protocols and reports. But the overwhelming majority of Turkmen were illiterate and lived in rural areas, far from the cities where the new Soviet administration was based. Traditional Muslim confessional education, which emphasized oral transmission of knowledge and the memorization and recitation of sacred texts, was not well suited to the production of Soviet bureaucrats. Moreover, there was no history of modern state administration using the native language in Turkmen-inhabited areas. Individuals had to be attracted to the

---

[2] This phrase was coined by Terry Martin.

[3] See Martin, *The Affirmative Action Empire*, chap. 1 for a comprehensive analysis of the goals and strategies of indigenization. See also Slezkine, "The USSR as a Communal Apartment," 414–52; George Liber, "Korenizatsiia: Restructuring Soviet Nationality Policy in the 1920s," *Ethnic and Racial Studies* 14, no. 1 (January 1991), pp. 15–22; Simon, *Nationalism*, pp. 20–70.

city, acclimatized to urban life, and taught basic literacy before they could even begin training for government work.[4]

In the decades before the Second World War, the pace of indigenization was slow in Turkmenistan. Despite the strong support for the policy at the highest levels of the Soviet state, Turkmen remained a minority within the Soviet government and Russian continued to serve as the administrative lingua franca. The most obvious reason for the slow progress was that the goals of Soviet-style affirmative action were unrealistic, given the tiny number of Turkmen who were culturally equipped to work in a modern state bureaucracy. Another reason was the deep hostility of many Europeans toward preferential policies for the titular nationality. Viewing indigenization as a form of reverse discrimination against the competent and the qualified, they resisted the policy strenuously. Finally, there was a high level of dissatisfaction among the beneficiaries of ethnic preferences. Turkmen who worked and studied in Soviet institutions were often poorly prepared for their new roles, shabbily treated by colleagues and classmates, and ambivalent about adapting to a Russian-dominated cultural environment. The result, all too often, was a high rate of attrition among Turkmen officials and students.

Although designed to appease national sentiments among non-Russians, the policy of indigenization led to sharp interethnic tensions within the Turkmen republic and the emergence of an aggrieved and resentful Turkmen nationalism. The incessant drumbeat of pro-indigenization propaganda raised expectations among Turkmen that they would soon be masters of their own republic; when Russians and the Russian language remained dominant, Turkmen frustration was palpable. Moreover, dissatisfaction was greatest among those who were the main beneficiaries of the policy—Turkmen who had been recruited into the Communist Party, state bureaucracy, and higher education. Just as colonized elites in Asia and Africa used the democratic rhetoric of their European rulers to justify their demands for independence, Turkmen elites learned to turn the Soviet rhetoric of national equality against its Russian originators. Citing the principles of Leninist nationality policy, these Turkmen demanded that the regime make good on its promises that natives and the native language would predominate in the republic.[5]

[4] In Russian-ruled Turkestan, administrative business had been conducted in the Russian language. After the revolution, the republic's new Soviet administration was dominated by Russians and urban Central Asians, while Russian continued to be the dominant language. In the Bukharan and Khivan republics, state administration prior to 1924 was conducted mainly in the Turkic dialects eventually codified as Uzbek. RGASPI, f. 62, op. 2, d. 490, ll. 149–50; GARF, f. 3316, op. 20, d. 156, l. 47. On Muslim schools in Central Asia, see Khalid, *Politics of Muslim Cultural Reform*, pp. 20–34.

[5] On the tendency of colonized elites to appropriate the ideology of the "mother country," see Dagmar Engels and Shula Marks, eds., *Contesting Colonial Hegemony: State and*

THE ORIGINS OF SOVIET ETHNIC PREFERENCES

Within the Soviet Union as a whole, the policy of indigenization received its authoritative form in 1923. Resolutions adopted by the twelfth Communist Party congress in April of that year declared that the administration of national republics should be "made up predominantly of local people, knowing the language, way of life, morals and customs of the corresponding peoples" and called for "special laws, guaranteeing the use of the native language in all government agencies and all institutions serving the local non-Russian population and national minorities."[6]

The policy laid out by the party was quite clear; the government should be made up *predominantly* of local people and the native language should be used in *all* government agencies and *all* institutions serving the local non-Russian population. How to accomplish this, however, was open to debate. Most officials recognized that there was a close link between the recruitment of native personnel and the use of the native language. Soviet authorities could hope to recruit and retain large numbers of Turkmen only if their native language were widely used in the bureaucracy, since few Turkmen knew Russian. But the use of the Turkmen language could not be ensured without the presence of a critical mass of Turkmen employees, since even fewer Russians spoke Turkmen.

In the first years of the republic's existence, Soviet authorities made a concerted effort to forge ahead in both spheres of indigenization. The campaign to create a Turkmen elite began before the division of Central Asia into national republics in 1924–25. Within the Turkestani, Bukharan, and Khivan republics that were subsequently dismantled by the "national delimitation," Soviet authorities attempted to recruit Turkmen into village soviets, district executive committees, and the Communist Party. Local authorities also made the first steps toward promoting the use of the Turkmen language in education and publishing in the first half of the 1920s. In May 1920, the Turkmen-language newspaper *Türkmenistan* began to appear in Ashgabat. In Tashkent, a Turkmen cultural commission was established in 1922 and charged with standardizing the Turkmen language and publishing Turkmen textbooks.[7] Training courses for Turkmen-speaking teachers were offered in the cities of Tashkent, Ashgabat,

---

Society in Africa and India (London: British Academic Press, 1994), pp. 1–15; J. C. Scott, *Weapons of the Weak: Everyday Forms of Peasant Resistance* (New Haven and London: Yale University Press, 1985), p. 338.

[6] *Dvenadzatyi s"ezd RKP (b): stenograficheskii otchet* (Moscow: Izdatel'stvo Politicheskoi Literatury, 1968), p. 696.

[7] V. G. Mel'kumov, *Ocherki istorii partorganizatsii Turkmenskoi oblasti Turkestanskoi ASSR* (Ashgabat: Turkmengosizdat, 1959), pp. 38, 140.

and Marï, and a new Turkmen pedagogical school opened its doors in April 1922.[8]

The creation of a Turkmen national republic in 1924–25 meant that indigenization would need to be practiced on a much more ambitious scale. The republic would have an extensive hierarchy of party organizations, ranging from the Central Committee at the top to village party cells at the bottom; a complete hierarchy of soviet organizations, from the Central Executive Committee of Soviets (TsIK) to the village soviets that dotted the countryside; and a republican Council of People's Commissars (Sovnarkom) overseeing commissariats devoted to agriculture, education, criminal justice, health, finance, labor, and other spheres of government activity. The republic would also have its own economic organs duplicating those on the all-union level, including its own branches of the state economic planning agency (Gosplan) and the Central Statistical Administration (TsSU). Finally, every national republic had to have a full complement of cultural institutions—book publishers, newspapers, museums, libraries, and institutes of higher education. Finding the huge number of employees required to staff all of these new institutions became an urgent problem.

The campaign to recruit local people was stymied from the start by the shortage of literate Turkmen; Soviet sources estimated that between 97 and 99 percent of Turkmen were unable to read and write.[9] In order to meet the critical need for native government officials, the Soviet regime initially employed all those who were even remotely qualified, whatever their class background and political orientation. This meant that many of those hired were members of the "exploiting classes"—wealthy landowners, merchants, Muslim clergymen, former tsarist army officers and administrators—since such individuals were the ones most likely to have the necessary qualifications for civil service. In the early and mid-1920s, some compromise of the regime's class principles was thought to be unavoidable in the non-Russian periphery; as Stalin said in 1923, "In the eastern republics and provinces, intellectuals, thinking people, even literate people are so few in number that you can count them on your fingers—how, in view of this, can we not treasure them?"[10] Over the long term,

---

[8] Ibid., p. 139; D. Chersheev, *Kul'turnaia revoliutsiia v Turkmenistane* (Ashgabat: Izdatel'stvo Turkmenistan, 1970), p. 46.

[9] RGASPI, f. 62, op. 3, d. 42, l. 2; op. 2, d. 545, l. 23; GARF, f. 3316, op. 19, d. 105, l. 11. Soviet illiteracy figures may have been exaggerated. Just a few years earlier, tsarist administrators had estimated that around 88 percent of the native population of Transcaspia was illiterate. *Obzor Zakaspiiskoi oblasti za 1912–1913–1914 g.* (Ashgabat, 1916), p. 237.

[10] Sultanbekov, *Tainy natsional'noi politiki*, p. 81.

the plan was to replace this "old intelligentsia" with a new Soviet elite forged in socialist educational institutions.[11]

In Turkmenistan, the small number of natives who had received more than a rudimentary education in the prerevolutionary period fell into two main categories: those who were Russian educated and those who had attended Muslim confessional schools. The former had attended the so-called Russian-native schools established by the tsarist regime in Transcaspia, which sought to train local boys as Russian-speaking translators, clerks, and assistants.[12] The second group of Turkmen had received a traditional Muslim education and had had relatively little contact with Russian colonial authorities; many of them lived in Bukhara and Khiva, which were nominally sovereign states under tsarist protection.

Cutting across this line between Russian-educated and Muslim-educated Turkmen was a division between Communist Party members and "nonparty intellectuals." Most of the leading political jobs within the new republic were occupied by Turkmen Communist Party officials who had joined the party between 1917 and 1924. Party members tended to be russified Turkmen; many of them had attended tsarist Russian-native schools prior to the revolution and spoke Russian well, and most were from the Russian-colonized Transcaspian province of the Turkestani republic. A typical example was the influential communist Gaigïsïz Atabaev, who had attended a Russian-native school in Tejen and worked as a teacher in Russian-native schools in Marï and Bäherden before the revolution.[13]

While the Communist Party members were mainly Russian-educated, the "nonparty intellectuals" included both russified and nonrussified Turkmen. Some of the non–party members recruited to work for the Soviet regime had attended Russian schools or served in the tsarist army. These individuals were most often recruited into the new republic's cultural and educational institutions, rather than into positions of political leadership.

[11] T. Durdyev, *Formirovanie i razvitie Turkmenskoi sovetskoi intelligentsii* (Ashgabat, 1972), pp. 35–43.

[12] Pierce, *Russian Central Asia*, pp. 214–17; B. A. Khodjakulieva, "Russko-tuzemnye shkoly v Zakaspiiskoi oblasti (konets XIX–nachalo XX v.)," *Izvestiia Akademii Nauk TSSR, seriia obshchestvennykh nauk*, no. 4 (1995): 18. These schools were similar to the Il'minsky schools founded earlier in the nineteenth century by tsarist authorities in Kazan, in that they stressed bilingual education in Russian and the native tongue. Unlike the Il'minsky schools, however, the Russian-native schools in Turkestan did not proselytize for the Russian Orthodox faith, since the Turkestani governor-general had prohibited attempts to convert the Muslims of Central Asia. On Il'minsky schools, see Robert P. Geraci, *Window on the East: National and Imperial Identities in Late Tsarist Russia* (Ithaca and London: Cornell University Press, 2001).

[13] Khudaiberdyev, *Obrazovanie Kommunisticheskoi Partii Turkmenistana*, pp. 190–91; Berdi Kerbabaev, *Chudom rozhdennyi (Kaigysyz Atabaev): Roman-khronika* (Moscow: Sovetskii Pisatel', 1967), pp. 7–14.

The prominent Teke leader Seidmïrad Övezbaev, for example, was an officer in the tsarist army and commanded the Ahal cavalry regiment for the Whites during the Civil War. After defecting to the Bolsheviks, he first worked as an education official and later became a member of the presidium of Gosplan.[14] Hajïmïrad Hojamïradov, a graduate of the Aleksandrov military academy and a highly decorated veteran of the tsarist army in World War I, served as director of the state museum of the Soviet Turkmen republic.[15] Karash-Khan Ogly Yomut Khan (known as Yomutskii in Russian-language sources) received a Russian military education and served as an officer in the tsarist army. After retiring from military service, Yomutskii became a scholar, ethnographer, and critic of Russian colonial rule in Turkmenistan, writing extensively on Turkmen culture and traditions. He held various cultural posts within the Turkmen republic after 1925.[16]

A second group of noncommunist intellectuals had a traditional Muslim education. They were educated in local *mekdeps* (confessional elementary schools) and in some cases had attended *medreses* (Muslim secondary schools) in Bukhara and elsewhere. They were literate in Turkic languages and in many cases Arabic and Persian, though not necessarily in Russian. The most prominent among them were Muhammet Geldiev, a Mangïshlak Yomut educated in medreses in Bukhara and Ufa who played a leading role in creating a standardized Turkmen language; Berdi Kerbabaev, born in Tejen and educated in a Bukharan medrese, who became editor of the satirical journal *Tokmak* and perhaps the best-known of all Soviet Turkmen writers; and the Bukharan Turkmen leader Abdïlhekim Gulmuhammedov, a poet and literary scholar who became deputy editor of the Turkmen-language newspaper *Türkmenistan* and wrote extensively on Turkmen culture in the 1920s.[17]

Even after the recruitment of virtually every qualified Turkmen—communists and noncommunists, graduates of Russian and Muslim schools alike—the Soviet government's voracious hunger for manpower was not slaked. Nor were republican institutions even close to being staffed predominantly by indigenous Turkmen, although the number of Turkmen had increased slightly. Between January 1925 and January 1926, the proportion of Turkmen employees in the republic's central bureaucracy had risen from 8.6 percent to 13 percent. In absolute terms, 109 of the 804 employees in central republican institutions in early 1926 were Turkmen. The remainder were overwhelmingly Russians and other Europeans, along with representatives of other "Eastern nationalities" such as Uzbeks and

[14] Kerbabaev, *Chudom rozhdennyi*, pp. 168–70; RGASPI, f. 62, op. 2, d. 3086, l. 12.

[15] Ivanchenko. "Pravda i domysli ob odnoi neordinarnoi lichnosti," pp. 37, 41–42.

[16] *Turkmenskaia iskra*, April 21, 1929, p. 3.

[17] On Geldiev, see T. Tächmïradov, *Muhammet Geldieving ömri we döredijiligi* (Ashgabat, 1989), pp. 14–15; on Kerbabaev, see A. Aborskii, *Vremia oglianut'sia: sapiski literatora* (Moscow: Sovetskii Pisatel', 1988), pp. 27–29.

Kazakhs.[18] Even though Turkmen officials were disproportionately placed in highly visible leadership positions, their presence was not enough to ensure that the Turkmen language would be the lingua franca of the bureaucracy or that the Soviet regime would seem "indigenous."

To address this problem, the republican Central Executive Committee (TsIK) established the Central Commission on the Indigenization of the State Apparatus on October 13, 1926. Nadïrbai Aitakov, chair of the TsIK, was the commission's formal head. His deputy—and the man who actually did most of the day-to-day work—was TsIK deputy chairman Begjan Nazarov.[19] The indigenization commission was responsible for increasing the recruitment of Turkmen into industrial and governmental jobs. Nazarov attempted to fulfill this mandate by wheedling, cajoling, and twisting the arms of employers throughout Turkmenistan. The commission had little enforcement power, however, and most non-Turkmen regarded its efforts with a jaundiced eye.

In the mid-1920s, the indigenization commission tried a variety of strategies to encourage the employment of Turkmen. One was the *praktikant-stvo*, or internship program, under which Turkmen recruits received a salary while participating in on-the-job training with a government agency. The ineffectiveness of this approach quickly became evident. Because nearly every minimally qualified person in the republic was already employed by the state, the people recruited as interns had absolutely no qualifications for government service. They were often illiterate and completely unfamiliar with the conventions of office work. As a result, they were simply a burden on the institutions that employed them. For the most part, they failed to receive the training they had been promised, but instead were assigned to run errands or simply given nothing at all to do.[20] A slightly more successful approach involved the training of Turkmen recruits in special courses before placing them in jobs. Republican-level institutions such as the commissariats of justice, finance, education, and internal affairs offered specialized training for potential employees.[21] Once again, however, the high level of illiteracy among the population and the small number of Turkmen living in the cities made it difficult to find people eligible for such training. Preparatory courses in basic literacy had to be offered in order to create a contingent of qualified students.[22]

---

[18] GARF, f. 3316, op. 20, d. 156, ll. 42–3; RGASPI, f. 62, op. 2, d. 545, l. 14.

[19] RGASPI, f. 62, op. 2, d. 490, l. 119, l. 128; GARF, f. 3316, op. 20, d. 156, l. 43.

[20] GARF, f. 3316, op. 20, d. 156, ll. 40–41, 119. Terry Martin has pointed out that host institutions disliked the *praktikantstvo* system since they had to pay the interns' salaries out of their own budgets. By 1926–27, this system was being phased out throughout the USSR. Martin, *The Affirmative Action Empire*, p. 135.

[21] GARF, f. 3316, op. 20, d. 156, l. 40.

[22] RGASPI, f. 62, op. 2, d. 490, l. 120.

The effort to create a Turkmen "technical intelligentsia" by recruiting students into higher education faced similar problems. Soviet authorities believed that the formation of cadres of Turkmen "specialists"—doctors, accountants, agronomists, and so forth—would have beneficial effects for indigenization more generally. First, it would create a new pool of Soviet-educated people from which to recruit for government jobs. The emergence of Turkmen technical specialists would also ensure the presence of Turkmen-speaking individuals in professions that required considerable contact with the rural population. Yet the quotas for recruitment of Turkmen students were rarely met. So few Turkmen were qualified for entry into technical institutes that prospective students generally had to attend special preparatory courses before they could begin the actual program of study.[23]

On a basic level, these problems were caused by the Turkmen population's lack of exposure to modern, secular education. Comrade Ross's casual approach to the liquidation of illiteracy notwithstanding, it was extremely difficult to go directly from the mekdep to the medical institute or budget office without at least a brief sojourn in European-style elementary and secondary schools. Only the spread of Soviet schools throughout the republic could create a larger pool of potential recruits for the Soviet regime. Yet Soviet authorities did not expect to introduce universal primary education in the Turkmen republic until the 1939–40 academic year. Moreover, the "universal education" envisioned by republican authorities would guarantee every child just one year of schooling; only children in urban and "more advanced" rural areas would be entitled to attend for a longer period. It would be decades before a contingent of Turkmen youngsters would graduate from Soviet secondary schools.[24]

"IF I WERE SOME AHMET-BAI, THEY WOULD HAVE TAKEN ME."

Given all the difficulties involved in transforming members of a largely rural and partly nomadic population into cogs of a modern bureaucratic state, a sizable and competent Turkmen Soviet elite simply could not be

[23] On preparatory divisions, see T. Durdyev, "Rol' rabfakov v podgotovke kadrov intelligentsii v Turkmenistane," *Izvestiia Akademii Nauk TSSR, seriia obshchestvennykh nauk*, no. 1 (1981): 50–51; RGASPI, f. 62, op. 2, d. 1611, l. 25; f. 17, op. 30, d. 123, l. 57.

[24] M. Vereshchagin, "Balans kadrov narodnogo khoziaistva i kul'turnogo stroitel'stva Turk. SSR," *Revoliutsiia i natsional'nosti*, no. 10–11 (October–November 1931): 101; M. Mikhailov, "VNO i likbez v Turkmenii," *Revoliutsiia i natsional'nosti*, no. 9 (September 1931): 95–98. On weaknesses in secondary education in the national republics more generally, see Martin, *The Affirmative Action Empire*, pp. 374–75; Blitstein, "Stalin's Nations," p. 192.

conjured up overnight. Nevertheless, many Turkmen expected rapid results from indigenization and blamed the obstructionist tactics of Russian officials for the slow progress. They were not entirely wrong to do so. Throughout the 1920s and 1930s, there was considerable resistance to the policy among Russians and other non-Turkmen, especially at the lower echelons of the Soviet bureaucracy and the Communist Party. Opponents of indigenization complained that important jobs would be filled by unqualified and illiterate natives. Typically, a European employer would object, "How can I take a Turkmen into my organization? I won't fulfill the plan and I'll mess up the work."[25] A Russian agronomist at the Bairamalï state farm declared in 1931 that a job opening "should be filled by a literate and intelligent Russian. Placing an illiterate and undeveloped national minority person in this position is not desirable—they won't be able to handle the work. I categorically protest against this."[26]

Russian industrial workers and students vigorously opposed preferential hiring and admissions policies for the titular nationality, believing that such preferences came at their expense. As a Russian applicant said after being rejected by the Higher Communist Agricultural School: "If I were some Akhmet-Bai, they would have taken me, but they won't take a Russian."[27] Factories were often reluctant to hire Turkmen. According to an October 1926 estimate, only about 11 percent of all workers in industry and transport were Turkmen.[28] Many employers refused to cooperate with the efforts of the indigenization commission to raise these numbers. When Nazarov called the director of a meat processing plant to complain about the plant's failure to hire Turkmen workers, the director retorted, "Comrade Nazarov, you're not responsible for my job, so don't interfere."[29] The railroad, one of the leading employers in Turkmenistan, was notorious for its resistance to indigenization. In early 1925, fewer than 4 percent of its workers were Turkmen.[30] Railway workers in Krasnovodsk expressed their opposition to the preferential hiring of Turkmen, claiming that "Turkmen are poorly trained, but they make lots of material demands," and "they're throwing out Russians and putting in Turkmen."[31]

While some Russians believed that they were victimized by preferences for the titular nationality, Turkmen maintained that they were unfairly

[25] Ia. A. Popok, *O likvidatsii Sredne-Aziatskikh organov i zadachakh kompartii Turk-menii: Doklad sekretaria TsK KPT na sobranii partaktiva Ashkhabada, 16. okt. 1934* (Ashgabat, Turkmenpartizdat, 1934), p 30.

[26] RGASPI, f. 62, op. 2, d. 2587, l. 36.

[27] Popok, *O likvidatsii*, pp. 28–29.

[28] RGASPI, f. 17, op. 60, d. 814, l. 81.

[29] Ibid., f. 62, op. 3, d. 397, l. 108.

[30] GARF, f. 3316, op. 20, d. 156, ll. 40–41.

[31] RGASPI, f. 62, op. 2, d. 545, l. 35.

passed over in favor of "foreigners" within their own republic.[32] A Turkmen newspaper correspondent lamented in 1927 that Persians and Europeans were invariably able to land jobs in the Turkmen republic, while "our own people" were unable to find a position.[33] Mirroring the Russian complaints about incompetent Turkmen, Turkmen officials maintained that Russians came to work in Turkmenistan because they were unqualified for jobs elsewhere. An official in the Sayat region told villagers that most of the Russians working in the Turkmen republic were dishonest and only came to Turkmenistan because they couldn't find jobs "in the USSR."[34] Turkmen proponents of indigenization believed that an understanding of local conditions was more important than the formal qualifications emphasized by Russians; it was unfair, in their view, that Russians who lacked a basic knowledge of the local language were taking jobs away from native Turkmen.[35] Turkmen also accused Russians of having little commitment to the republic; those who worked in Turkmenistan were merely building up "political capital" in the periphery in order to land a more prestigious job in Moscow.[36] This dual sense of victimization, in which Turkmen and Europeans each felt deprived of their rightful due by ethnic rivals, proved to be a potent source of conflict in the 1920s and 1930s.

In addition to disputes over sheer numbers of Turkmen hired, controversy erupted in the mid-1920s over the responsibilities and behavior of Turkmen officials on the job. In 1925 and 1926, a number of Turkmen had been appointed to highly visible positions in the state and party apparatus. They were people's commissars, first secretaries of party committees, and leaders of a host of other government organizations. However, it was widely acknowledged that Turkmen officials often did not wield the authority that should go with their positions. Frequently, a European deputy working behind the scenes had the real decision-making power. Everyone agreed that this was a problem, but there was little consensus on who was to blame.

In August 1926, Atabaev, chairman of the Turkmen republic's Council of People's Commissars, and Shali Ibragimov, the Tatar first secretary of the Turkmen Communist Party, addressed a harshly critical letter to high-

[32] *Tokmak*, no. 69 (1927). Cited in RGASPI, f. 62, op. 2, d. 1185, l. 100.

[33] *Tokmak*, no. 20–21 (1927) and no. 31 (1927). Cited in RGASPI, f. 62, op. 2, d. 1185, ll. 70, 82. Within the Central Asian republics, the term "European" was used to refer to all nonindigenous, non-Muslim residents, including Russians, Ukrainians, Armenians, and Jews. Occasionally, even Muslim Tatars were included in the "European" category.

[34] RGASPI, f. 62, op. 2, d. 882, l. 22.

[35] Ibid., d. 1185, l. 70.

[36] Ibid., d. 838, l. 11. For other examples of ethnic conflict surrounding indigenization, see Matthew J. Payne, *Stalin's Railroad: Turksib and the Building of Socialism* (Pittsburgh: University of Pittsburgh Press, 2001), pp. 138–39.

ranking Turkmen officials. The two claimed that Turkmen officials placed in high positions "have not yet devoted enough attention to learning their jobs and are more figureheads than genuine leaders."[37] As a result, Atabaev and Ibragimov wrote, "all questions that arise in the process of an institution's work are dealt with by European comrades, and a question often will not receive the essential corrective from the point of view of local specificities." For this situation, "the main share of blame falls on the native employees."[38] Atabaev and Ibragimov urged Turkmen officials to make a greater effort to become the "genuine leaders" of their organizations.

Begjan Nazarov responded indignantly to the charge that Turkmen officials were themselves to blame for their lack of authority. In a letter to the Turkmen Central Committee, he argued that Turkmen officials found themselves in an impossible position due to the "Europeanization" of the government—in other words, the dominance of Europeans and the Russian language. This, he argued, prevented Turkmen-speaking officials from understanding what was going on around them, let alone exercising real leadership. Moreover, it was unfair to blame Turkmen officials for failing to provide a local perspective when policies were formulated, since European officials almost never turned to natives for advice and information.[39]

This dispute underscored the tensions that had arisen not just between Turkmen and Europeans, but also between russified and nonrussified Turkmen. Nazarov noted that Bukharan and Khivan Turkmen were at a disadvantage relative to those who lived in the tsarist-colonized Transcaspian province, since government business in the first two republics had been conducted in Persian or Turkic and officials there had not been exposed to Russian. The result of the "Europeanization" of republican institutions, therefore, was to divide Turkmen officials into two groups: "those who know Russian, and are therefore able to cope with their work, and those who don't know that language, whom we are now calling 'figureheads.' "[40] To Nazarov, a Bukharan Turkmen who did not speak Russian, the Russian-educated Atabaev appeared to be criticizing his fellow Turkmen from a position of unfair advantage.

Accusations of differential treatment were not limited to the highest echelons of the Soviet bureaucracy. In factories, state farms, schools, and libraries, Turkmen complained that they were treated as second-class citi-

[37] GARF, f. 3316, op. 64, d. 265, ll. 1–2.

[38] Ibid., l. 2. An editorial in *Turkmenskaia iskra* made a similar point. K. Sakhatov, "O turkmenskikh rabotnikakh," *Turkmenskaia iskra*, March 4, 1926, p. 1.

[39] RGASPI, f. 62, op. 2, d. 490, ll. 147–49, 152.

[40] Ibid., ll. 149–50. Nazarov himself did not speak Russian and used an interpreter at party meetings. On language use in Bukhara before 1924, see Timur Kocaoglu, "The Existence of a Bukharan Nationality in the Recent Past," in Allworth, *The Nationality Question in Soviet Central Asia*, p. 155.

zens within their own republic. At a January 1927 meeting of the Central Asian Bureau, the chair of the Turkmen Central Executive Committee, Aitakov, said that unequal treatment of Turkmen industrial workers was hindering the development of a Turkmen proletariat. Because "certain European comrades . . . think that Turkmen are used to living in their yurts and therefore don't need to live in a building," Turkmen workers were not permitted to live in factory housing along with their Russian comrades. Instead, "at the end of the work day, Turkmen are forced to walk three or four versts home to their yurts, only to return to work the following morning." Denied the opportunity to socialize with Russian workers after hours, Turkmen were unable to become acquainted with true proletarian culture.[41] The Turkmen Communist Party secretary Halmïrad Sähetmïradov agreed, noting that under such conditions Turkmen production workers would never shed their backward peasant mentality.[42]

Along with segregated housing conditions, Turkmen workers claimed that they were given last priority in the allocation of consumer goods. A party cell secretary at the Bairamalï state farm in 1931 told Central Asian Bureau investigators, "Russian workers throw Turkmen and national minorities out of line at the cooperative stores—the most and best groceries are always given out to the Russians, while the leftovers are for Turkmen and national minorities."[43] Turkmen also reported separate and unequal treatment in educational and cultural institutions. In the republic's institutes of higher education, they complained about being assigned to inferior dormitories and special "preparatory divisions" for those without knowledge of Russian. In one particularly egregious case, Turkmen students at the Bairamalï polytechnical institute in May 1928 claimed that the school's director, a former professor at Tomsk University, had prohibited them from entering the Russian dorm or socializing with Russian students.[44] Even in the public reading rooms where citizens could peruse the latest newspapers and magazines, Russians reportedly received better treatment. A Turkmen-language satirical magazine claimed that the Russian reading room in Ashgabat boasted two large lamps that "shone like the moon," while Turkmen readers were forced to decipher their newspapers by the light of a single dim bulb. Seeking to explain this difference, the editors slyly suggested that the authorities were simply trying to protect Turkmen eyesight: "In the old days, our eyes weren't used to so much bright light, so they might be damaged if suddenly exposed to too much of it."[45]

[41] RGASPI, f. 62, op. 1, d. 220, l. 59.
[42] Ibid., l. 93.
[43] Ibid., op. 2, d. 2587, l. 36.
[44] Ibid., d. 1611, ll. 38–39.
[45] *Tokmak*, no. 28–29 (1927), p. 8.

Figure 5. Turkmen worker at lunch in a Soviet cafeteria, 1930. (From the collection of the Russian State Archive of Film and Photographic Documents at Krasnogorsk.)

Like the campaign to recruit Turkmen personnel, the attempt to mandate the use of the Turkmen language was fraught with problems. In August 1924, the Turkmen National Bureau adopted a decree calling for the linguistic "Turkmenization" of the state apparatus. It declared that village and district-level organs should conduct their work exclusively in Turkmen, while higher-level organs should conduct correspondence simultaneously in Turkmen and in Russian.[46] The first Turkmen Congress of Soviets passed a similar resolution in 1925, adding that the Kerki, Chärjew, and Dashhowuz provinces—those that had been part of Bukhara and Khiva—should conduct all correspondence in the local language.[47] These were the first of many such decrees within the republic. Throughout the 1920s and 1930s, however, attempts to require the use of Turkmen enjoyed little success, largely because most government institutions were still dominated by Russian speakers.

Around 1927, the Central Asian Bureau signaled a new, more language-oriented approach to indigenization throughout Central Asia. There would be less emphasis on recruiting members of the titular nationality; the focus now would be on hiring individuals able to speak the local language, regardless of their ethnicity. This shift resulted from a growing awareness of the difficulties involved in recruiting indigenous nationals. The hostility of Russians to ethnic preferences may have also played a role; the new approach to indigenization was less overtly discriminatory, allowing Russians a chance to compete for the best jobs as long as they were willing to learn the local language.[48] Under the new policy, the main focus of linguistic indigenization would be on those organizations that "served the masses" most directly, such as the commissariats of agriculture, justice, education, and health. While most state institutions would be expected to produce paperwork in both Russian and Turkmen, these commissariats would be required to use Turkmen exclusively in their work.[49]

Central Asian Bureau chairman Isaak Zelenskii presented the rationale for the new, language-focused approach to indigenization at a Bureau plenum in January 1927. Indigenization did not mean simply increasing the number of natives in Soviet jobs, he argued. The most important thing was that Soviet officials should be able to speak the local language, whatever their ethnic background.[50] The result of this new policy was not just a narrowing of the scope of indigenization efforts, but also a shift to a more strictly practical view of the policy and a discounting of its political

[46] RGASPI, f. 62, op. 2, d. 114, l. 12.
[47] Ibid., d. 490, l. 147.
[48] Terry Martin has described this as a shift from "mechanical" to "functional" indigenization. See *The Affirmative Action Empire*, pp. 144–45.
[49] RGASPI, f. 62, op. 2, d. 490, l. 97.
[50] Ibid., op. 1, d. 220, ll. 17, 22.

and psychological aspects. The goal now was not so much to make the Soviet government seem truly indigenous as to render it comprehensible in practical terms. A government unable to communicate with its population simply could not function effectively. To illustrate his point, Zelenskii discussed the potentially dangerous consequences of a doctor's inability to speak the local language:

> People come to him with the most intimate diseases . . . and it's very unpleasant to explain such things through an interpreter, especially since the interpreter doesn't always convey the explanation of the ill person accurately or correctly. What guarantee do we have that when a patient tells the translator that he has tuberculosis, he won't be treated for syphilis?[51]

Many Turkmen officials were critical of this more narrowly focused approach to indigenization. In a lead editorial in the Turkmen-language newspaper *Türkmenistan* in April 1927, Begjan Nazarov accused "some comrades" of showing a "lack of understanding of the essence of indigenization," believing that it meant simply "the translation of outgoing and incoming documents into the Turkmen language."[52] Not only did the new approach violate the premise that Soviet cadres in the national republics were supposed to be made up predominantly of local people: it also made little sense in practical terms. Since few Europeans knew Turkmen or were willing to learn it, it was unrealistic to imagine that government agencies would communicate with the population in the native language if they were staffed mainly by Russians. For many Turkmen, moreover, the Turkmen language was not just a tool for the practical purposes of medical treatment or mail delivery, but a symbol of national identity and the basis of national culture. Its psychological and political value was even more important than its practical function as a means of communication. If the Turkmen language were not used regularly in schools, government, and the press, Turkmen intellectuals feared, their national culture would stagnate.[53]

Because the Turkmen language had such immense symbolic value for many Turkmen, its use—or rather, its nonuse—became a focal point of contention in the republic. There were frequent complaints in the press and at party meetings about bureaucrats who refused to accept peasants' petitions written in Turkmen, demanding instead that they submit the paperwork in Russian.[54] A 1928 article in the republican newspaper *Türkmenistan* complained that shop employees in the city of Chärjew had no knowledge of Turkmen: "Peasants who don't know Russian can't buy

[51] Ibid., ll. 26–27.
[52] *Türkmenistan*, no. 61 (April 1, 1927), p. 1.
[53] RGASPI, f. 62, op. 2, d. 397, l. 100.
[54] Ibid., l. 109.

what they need, and are even afraid to go into the store, because they fear they'll be scolded."[55]

Russian officials sometimes balked at providing translators at meetings, leaving their Turkmen colleagues to languish in frustrated incomprehension. An official in the town of Pöwrize reported that Russian colleagues had cursed him when he requested that the proceedings of a meeting be translated into Turkmen.[56] Turkmen officials also complained that it was hard to find published materials in their native language, while Russian publications were widely available. Except for the newspaper *Türkmenistan*, the satirical magazine *Tokmak*, and a handful of propaganda pamphlets, few publications existed to help Turkmen-speaking officials keep up with current events and broaden their political and cultural horizons.[57] A 1927 article in *Tokmak* decried this situation: "Turkmen literature, like the Turkmen woman, is ashamed to show itself—or perhaps our officials are ashamed of their own literature," the editors commented.[58] Some Turkmen maintained that their language was even being neglected in native-language schools, since parents and teachers alike believed that a child's future success depended on knowledge of Russian.[59] As a Turkmen official lamented, "Once again, we're putting the Turkmen language into such a position so that no one will be interested in it, not just Europeans but even the Turkmen themselves."[60]

European officials often dismissed Turkmen demands as impractical, downplaying or ignoring the symbolic significance of Turkmen language use. The first secretary of the Turkmen Communist Party, G. N. Aronshtam, suggested in 1929 that non-Russian speaking Turkmen officials should be given "one or two months off" to learn the language. Having revealed a certain lack of appreciation for the intricacies of Russian grammar (not to mention the basic principles of Leninist nationality policy), Aronshtam went on to explain that this strategy would ultimately save time and money: "It's much easier for us to completely eliminate illiteracy in Russian than to guarantee a full translation of all materials into the Turkmen language." Aronshtam's response to the complaints about the unavailability of published materials in Turkmen was similarly inventive. European subscribers to the Russian periodicals *Pravda* or *Bolshevik* should summarize the contents for their Turkmen colleagues, he sug-

[55] *Türkmenistan*, no. 211 (September 16, 1928). Cited in RGASPI, f. 62, op. 2, d. 1641, l. 58.

[56] *Tokmak*, no. 32–33 (1927), p. 10.

[57] RGASPI, f. 62, op. 2, d. 490, ll. 148–49.

[58] *Tokmak*, no. 31 (1927), p. 3.

[59] *Türkmenistan*, no. 173 (August 3, 1927). Cited in RGASPI, f. 62, op. 2, d. 1185, l. 116.

[60] RGASPI, f. 62, op. 3, d. 397, l. 109.

Peasants: "Comrade! Do you have any Turkmen books left?"
Sales clerk: "The old ones are all gone, and the new ones haven't come in yet."

Figure 6. "In the bookstore of the Turkmen State Publishing House." (*Tokmak*, no. 31 [1927]: 8.)

gested, thus helping to keep them up to date.[61] This would be both cheaper and easier than increasing the number of Turkmen-language publications. With such suggestions coming from the republic's top Moscow-appointed official, it is little wonder that many Turkmen questioned the regime's commitment to linguistic indigenization.

In the absence of a sufficient number of Turkmen officials, the only way to ensure the use of Turkmen in government work was to require non-Turkmen to speak it. "Learn the Turkmen language!" urged the leading Russian-language republican newspaper, *Turkmenskaia iskra*, in 1928. If Europeans were required to study Turkmen for an hour every morning before work, the newspaper's editors noted, within six months they would have a basic vocabulary of three hundred words. This would allow them to communicate with the Turkmen masses in their own language.[62] For most Europeans, however, this was three hundred words too many. They regarded Turkmen as an inferior tongue whose acquisition would be a monumental waste of time; wouldn't it make more sense, they asked,

[61] Ibid., l. 131.
[62] K., "Voprosy natsionalizatsii: Izuchaite turkmenskii iazyk," *Turkmenskaia iskra*, May 15, 1928, p. 2.

for the natives to learn the language of Pushkin and Lenin? Faced with demands that they learn the local language, Europeans would offer feeble excuses, citing overwork, business travel, or a shortage of Turkmen-language textbooks. To counter such attitudes, Turkmen Commissar of Education K. A. Böriev proposed that officials who demonstrated a "malicious unwillingness" to learn Turkmen should be fired from their jobs. "We can fire ten or fifteen people and publish their names in the press. This will have a strong moral impact and will force others to learn Turkmen language," he suggested at a 1929 party plenum.[63]

For the most part, the more limited, language-focused approach to indigenization was a failure. A 1929 investigation of twenty-one government institutions in Ashgabat found that none of them were meeting the requirement that they use the Turkmen language in their work. In central republican institutions such as the Central Executive Committee, the Council of People's Commissars, and the commissariats, the proportion of employees who knew the Turkmen language actually dropped between January 1, 1927, and January 1, 1928, from 7.7 percent to 7.1 percent. Only in provincial and district Soviet organs did the situation improve somewhat in the same period, with the proportion of Turkmen-speaking employees rising from 15.4 percent to 24.7 percent.[64]

"TURNING INTO RUSSIANS": AMBIVALENCE AMONG THE TURKMEN ELITE

The cultural revolution and launching of the first Five-Year Plan in 1928 brought an accelerated push for indigenization. Opponents of the policy hoped that the cultural revolution's radical campaign against all forms of "backwardness" would bring about a declining emphasis on national and ethnic distinctions. Instead, Stalin declared that the Soviet Union would accelerate its efforts to promote non-Russian nationhood. In the Central Asian republics, there were new campaigns for the recruitment of natives into government work and higher education, along with new decrees on the use of native languages.[65] At the same time, the increased tempo of "socialist transformation" emboldened the opponents of indigenization, who argued that the employment of illiterate and poorly qualified natives would slow down the tempo of economic development.

[63] RGASPI, f. 62, op. 3, d. 397, ll. 100, 109.
[64] Ibid., ll. 82, 151–52.
[65] Slezkine, "The USSR as a Communal Apartment," pp. 437–38; Blitstein, "Stalin's Nations," p. 9; Martin, *The Affirmative Action Empire*, pp. 154–56.

A special plenum of the Turkmen Central Committee in July 1929 deplored the unsatisfactory results of indigenization and called for the accelerated promotion of Turkmen into the bureaucracy and greater attention to teaching Europeans the local language. The Central Committee also called for the translation of all bureaucratic paperwork into the Turkmen language, with the greatest emphasis to be placed, once again, on those branches of government that directly served the "peasant masses."[66] In August 1931, a joint plenum of the republican party's Central Committee and Central Control Commission adopted "final" deadlines for the translation of all government work into the Turkmen language: for the central bureaucracy, the deadline was January 1, 1933; for the regional government, June 1, 1932. By January 1933, all officials within the republic were also expected to learn the Turkmen language.[67]

There were also ambitious new quotas for the recruitment of Central Asians into higher education and a major new campaign for *vydvizhenie*, the promotion of natives into positions of responsibility. In the Turkmen republic, the 1932 plan called for 303 Turkmen nationals to be promoted into republican-level government agencies and 212 into district agencies. In a departure from the earlier willingness to hire prominent members of the "old intelligentsia," Soviet officials were now expected to hire only members of "exploited classes." Since the number of Turkmen industrial workers was small, the usual Soviet policies favoring proletarians were insufficient; promotion efforts focused instead on poor and landless peasants. A certain number of slots were also set aside for women and members of national minorities.[68]

This intensified push heightened the tensions surrounding indigenization. At a special July 1929 party plenum devoted to indigenization, Nazarov called the slow progress in this area "intolerable." Another Turkmen official argued that government organizations should be prosecuted for their failure to hire more Turkmen.[69] The Russian official Mikhailov, a leading opponent of indigenization, responded by accusing Turkmen party members of "placing national questions above class ones, when the reverse should hold true." Indigenization should be pursued only when it did not conflict with the needs of central economic planning, he argued. Promoting large numbers of Turkmen would undermine economic efficiency because of their "natural sluggishness, inertia, and excessive ambition."[70]

[66] RGASPI, f. 62, op. 3, d. 397, ll. 153–54.
[67] Ibid., op. 2, d. 3163, l. 169.
[68] Ibid., d. 3133, l. 19; d. 2589, l. 59.
[69] Ibid., op. 3, d. 397, l. 110.
[70] Ibid., ll. 113–14.

While Mikhailov may have been gratuitously offensive in his description of the Turkmen national character, it was true that Turkmen recruits were often fresh from the countryside and totally unprepared for the jobs into which they were thrust. The fact that Russian was the dominant language in the bureaucracy only compounded their difficulties. Some European officials simply refused to take Turkmen promotees. At the state bank, the party member Beksler refused to hire the Turkmen promotee Durdï because he was "semiliterate in the Russian language." He told the prospective recruit, "We write our reports only in Russian, it will be hard for you." When Turkmen promotees did get jobs in the bureaucracy, they often had no idea what they were supposed to be doing, and Russians resented having to take time away from their own duties to teach them. At the cotton procurement agency, the head accountant and his assistant refused to train the promotee assigned to them, a Turkmen named Övez-merad. "We're compiling an annual report and we don't have time to occupy ourselves with you. Anyway, there's no work for you to do," the two Europeans explained. At the Commissariat of Agriculture, a Turkmen party member hired in 1931 as inspector of animal husbandry complained that his Russian colleagues refused to give him any assistance, even though he was "barely literate" and unable to understand the Russian documents that came his way. The new inspector's colleagues scarcely concealed their eagerness to be rid of him, neglecting to assign him a desk or chair and continually sending him off to the countryside on assignments that had nothing to do with his job.[71]

Turkmen promotees had other concerns as well. Many feared that their lack of experience and poor understanding of Russian would lead them to make mistakes in their work, which could cause them to be fired or stripped of their party membership. Some left their jobs rather than risk such consequences.[72] Other problems were created by the fact that most Turkmen officials starting new jobs were former peasants who were living in the city for the first time. They needed help not only with work, but also with finding housing and adjusting to city life. The republican party secretary Charï Vellekov described the psychological state of a Turkmen recruit in such circumstances:

> Imagine the situation of this comrade. This guy arrives from the village, from the collective farm, barely literate and seeing the city for the first time. He sits in an office or in an institution where business is conducted in the Russian language, but no one translates for him, no one gives him any work to do, and even if they do, they don't explain how to complete the assignment. Therefore

[71] Ibid., ll. 17, 24.
[72] Ibid., l. 24.

it's totally understandable that this person is miserable and offended and demands: either help me or send me back home.[73]

The attempt to accelerate indigenization during the first Five-Year Plan was for the most part unsuccessful. Although there was an initial surge of recruitment into industry, the bureaucracy, and higher education, by 1933 many of these gains had been lost. In June 1933, investigators found a decline in the proportion of Turkmen employees of people's commissariats between March 1932 and June 1933, from a peak of around 19 percent to under 14 percent. In absolute terms, out of 1,125 employees of commissariats in June 1933, only 154 were Turkmen. In the republic's economic and financial organizations, the percentage of Turkmen decreased from 15 percent to 11.7 percent. The Commissariat of Education, one of the few with a high proportion of Turkmen, saw a decrease in Turkmen employees from 69.7 percent to 28.2 percent, largely because of a major purge of cultural and educational officials in 1933. Only the republican Central Executive Committee saw an increase in the proportion of Turkmen officials, from 64 percent to 71 percent.[74]

The effort to recruit Turkmen into higher education had similarly disappointing results during the first Five-Year Plan. The republic's institutions of higher education were ordered to increase the proportion of Turkmen students to 70 or 75 percent—figures that corresponded roughly to the proportion of Turkmen within the population of the republic. Not enough prospective students could be found, however, and many who were admitted lasted only a few months before dropping out. At the pedagogical institute, the most heavily Turkmen of all educational institutions in the republic, only 36 percent of the students were Turkmen. At the medical institute, a mere 4 percent of the aspiring doctors were Turkmen.[75] Finally, the resolutions mandating the use of the Turkmen language were not implemented. Not a single institution had complied with the requirement that it translate all its paperwork into Turkmen by January 1933, and most European officials remained ignorant of even the barest rudiments of the Turkmen language.[76] Industry was one of the few spheres that showed gains in indigenization during the first Five-Year Plan; the proportion of Turkmen industrial workers rose from 24 to 27 percent between 1929 and 1933. Even so, there were extremely high rates of dissatisfaction and turnover among Turkmen production workers, in part because of inadequate access to food, housing, and transportation.[77]

[73] Ibid., op. 1, d. 1039, l. 143.
[74] Ibid., op. 2, d. 3133, ll. 8–9; d. 3163, l. 169.
[75] Ibid., d. 3133, ll. 12, 13–14.
[76] Ibid., l. 6.
[77] Ibid., op. 1, d. 1039, ll. 138–39.

As we have seen, the dearth of qualified Turkmen and the resistance of non-Turkmen were primary reasons for the failure to achieve rapid indigenization. Another problem—less tangible but nonetheless important—was the pervasive sense of ambivalence and anxiety that gripped many Turkmen who were recruited by the Soviet regime. Much of this discontent was due to the frustrations of working in an alien and unwelcoming environment. Because the bureaucracy remained dominated by Europeans and the Russian language, working for the Soviet regime required adapting to a foreign environment and an alien worldview. Many Turkmen, even as they welcomed the political influence and economic advantages brought by government service, were ambivalent about becoming russified. They feared that assimilation into the urban, Russian-speaking Soviet elite would bring estrangement from their roots in the rural Turkmen community.

Certainly, there was evidence that some ordinary villagers resented fellow Turkmen who imitated foreign ways. Turkmen who attended Soviet schools, learned Russian, or worked for the Soviet regime were sometimes accused of betraying Turkmen values or "turning into Russians."[78] Turkmen boys who returned to their home villages from Soviet boarding schools complained of fathers who refused to acknowledge them or older brothers who chased them away, saying, "Get out of here, Russian kid."[79] Yet it was the members of the Turkmen elite themselves, particularly those who worked for Soviet-sponsored cultural institutions and publications, who monitored their compatriots most closely for signs of russification. Articles in the Turkmen-language press ridiculed those Turkmen who enthusiastically adopted Western or urban ways, such as carrying a briefcase, wearing a necktie, or drinking vodka. One correspondent reported in mock seriousness the "good news" that "city culture" was at last beginning to spread into the Turkmen village; young Turkmen were approaching Russian levels in their consumption of the "water that increases bravery."[80] Turkmen who abandoned their own language and culture for Russian became special targets of scorn. A Turkmen official in Gïzïlarbat drew criticism in the press when he refused to speak Turkmen with the local population and shouted at Turkmen peasants, "Quit bugging me, speak Russian!"[81] A commentator in *Tokmak* wrote scathingly about Turkmen who were attracted by the greater "prestige" of the Russian language:

---

[78] Ibid., op. 2, d. 287, l. 107; d. 757, l. 17.

[79] Ibid., d. 287, l. 107; see also *Tokmak*, no 20–21 (1927), p. 5.

[80] *Tokmak*, no. 6–7 (1927), p. 10.

[81] *Türkmenistan*, no. 212 (September 17, 1928). Cited in RGASPI, f. 62, op. 2, d. 1641, l. 59.

Newspaper vendor: "Comrade! Would you like to buy a copy of
  Türkmenistan?"
Official: "No, get out of here with your *Türkmenistan*! Hey, boy! Do you have
  [*Turkmenskaia*] *iskra*? Give me a copy!"

Figure 7. A Turkmen government official reveals his preference for Russian-language newspapers. (*Tokmak*, no. 31 [1927]: 8.)

Some Turkmen officials are indifferent to literature in their own language. As soon as they arrive from the desert, these thirsty camels throw themselves upon *Russian* literature, even though they themselves are unable to put together two words in Russian. They are only interested in having other people say, "This guy learned Russian and became a human being."[82]

A 1926 discussion in the newspaper *Türkmenistan* revealed the social and professional dilemmas faced by Turkmen who sought to join the Soviet elite. The topic was interethnic marriage; specifically, whether it was acceptable for young Turkmen men to marry Russian women. Some of the participants in the debate insisted that such marriages were a good thing. A Russian wife could be highly advantageous, they noted, since fluency in the Russian language was essential for a successful career in Turkmenistan. Moreover, since Turkmen girls scorned Russian-educated Turkmen as "infidels," such men had little choice but to marry foreigners.

[82] *Tokmak*, no. 31 (1927), p. 4.

Other contributors were strongly opposed to the idea of intermarriage, arguing that it would result in the russification of the Turkmen elite and the destruction of the Turkmen language and culture.[83]

There were good reasons for the preoccupation of Turkmen elites with the threat of russification. The notion of a Turkmen national identity was still new and insecurely rooted in this period. Rural villagers, who had not yet been exposed to modern mass education and its powerful nation-making capabilities, tended to identify with their local community and kinship group; a "national" identity was of little interest to them. Urbanized Soviet elites, on the other hand, were much more likely to identify with an overarching sense of Turkmen-ness. These new elites were drawn to Ashgabat from all tribes and all regions of Turkmenistan. In their positions as Soviet officials, they encountered members of other Turkmen subgroups along with Russians and other Europeans. In this environment, the subdivisions within the Turkmen population came to seem less important than the huge cultural and linguistic gap between Turkmen and Europeans. The policy of indigenization, too, had the effect of making a broader Turkmen identity politically and professionally relevant to a growing number of Turkmen. It was now less important to be a Yomut or a Teke than to be a member of the titular nationality, with all the preferences and privileges this implied. Finally, the new identification with "Turkmen-ness" among the elite was intensified by the conviction that Turkmen were not accorded the preeminence they deserved within their own republic. The educated elite was well aware that Russians looked down on them and their language, notwithstanding the official Soviet rhetoric of national equality. They also knew that some Turkmen had internalized this hierarchy of values, imagining that they had to learn Russian to "become a human being." This knowledge stimulated resentment not just against Russians, but against those Turkmen who tried to act like Russians.

The comments in the Turkmen-language press of the 1920s suggest that Turkmen intellectuals were coming to define their identity by contrasting it with Russian-ness. A true Turkmen was a person who did *not* do the things Russians typically do: carry a briefcase, drink vodka, or speak Russian in everyday life. Ironically, the Turkmen putting forward this definition of national identity were those who were most likely to adopt "Russian" attributes—living in the city, holding an office job, perhaps even speaking Russian and drinking vodka. These Turkmen had been recruited

---

[83] A series of articles and letters on this topic appeared between October 15 and November 7, 1926 in *Türkmenistan*. Cited in RGASPI, f. 62, op. 2, d. 757, ll. 16–18. A number of the leading Turkmen officials in the republic, including Atabaev and Sähetmïradov, were married to European women.

to work for the Soviet regime because of their Turkmen-ness, yet their new way of life threatened to make them less Turkmen.

The slow progress on indigenization had potentially ominous political consequences within the republic. For one thing, it ensured that the Soviet regime and its goals continued to be popularly viewed as "Russian" rather than as home grown—precisely the perception Soviet nationality policy had originally sought to combat.[84] For many members of the Turkmen elite, indigenization had the effect of fostering an aggrieved sense of Turkmen identity and a resentment of the Russian "other." Tensions over indigenization also laid the foundation for future persecution of Turkmen officials and intellectuals in the terror and purges of the 1930s. In the late 1920s, despite the official position that Russian chauvinism was the most dangerous threat to Soviet internationalism, the secret police devoted considerable attention to the search for signs of Turkmen nationalism. Turkmen who insisted on proper implementation of the stated goals of Soviet nationality policy, such as the use of the Turkmen language or the hiring of Turkmen cadres, risked being identified as "nationalists." So, too, did those who vociferously condemned "Great Russian chauvinism." The OGPU, an organization overwhelmingly dominated by Europeans in the 1920s, closely monitored the Turkmen-language press and the public and private utterances of Turkmen officials for evidence of such "anti-Russianism" or "anti-Europeanism." They could be labeled "nationalists" if they showed a preference for hiring Turkmen over Russians, reading the Turkmen poet Mägtïmgulï rather than Pushkin, or speaking Turkmen instead of Russian in government offices—all attitudes ostensibly sanctioned by Leninist nationality policy.

OGPU analysts ferreted out any hint that Turkmen considered themselves "masters of their own republic" and able to dispense with the support and guidance of their Russian elder brothers. Thus, Artïk Rahmanov, chief prosecutor of the Turkmen republic and former first secretary of the Chärjew provincial party committee, was identified as a "nationalist" in 1927 because he gave preference in hiring to Turkmen officials over Europeans.[85] Articles criticizing the dominance of the Russian language in the republic or lamenting the unavailability of Turkmen-language publications similarly drew sharp criticism. In response to the claim that non-Russian-speaking Turkmen peasants were treated rudely by store clerks, one OGPU analyst wrote: "The author clearly is exaggerating the situation when he says that Turkmen who don't know Russian can't buy anything. This is

[84] RGASPI, f. 62, op. 2, d. 396, l. 119.
[85] Ibid., d. 874, l. 22.

factually untrue. Sariev [the author] deliberately chooses negative facts, leaving out a number of positive aspects of indigenization."[86]

The frequent articles lamenting the shortage of Turkmen language publications, meanwhile, were said to be "exclusively intended to fuel Turkmen antagonism toward the European population." "The significant quantity of published literature in the Turkmen language can serve as a fact to disprove these attacks," an OGPU analyst wrote. "The claim of a dearth of Turkmen literature is just an excuse for attacks against the study of the Russian language, especially since every correspondent knows perfectly well that a significant number of Turkmen publications have come out since the national delimitation." Turkmen journalists who wrote critically of the dominance of the Russian language in government offices were accused of "adhering to the view that a Turkmen should know exclusively his own language."[87] These OGPU comments were at odds with the official Soviet policy of the time, which sought to end the dominance of the Russian language and to require the use of Turkmen within the republic.

Turkmen were treading on dangerous ground even if they criticized tsarist colonial rule, although Moscow's official stance in the 1920s was to draw a sharp distinction between oppressive tsarist colonialism and progressive Soviet rule.[88] A November 1927 article by the commissar of education, Bäshim Perengliev, drew fire because the author claimed that the tsarist regime had suppressed Turkmen education, denigrated the Turkmen language and culture, and practiced russification in the schools of Transcaspia. Perengliev, in the view of the OGPU analyst, was slandering the Russians by suggesting that they were solely to blame for Turkmen backwardness. Instead, he should have pointed out that "the backwardness of the Turkmen people was not only the fault of the Russian capitalists, pursuing a policy of oppression, but also the fault of the population itself."[89]

The comments of these OGPU analysts convey the hostility some Europeans felt toward the indigenous population of Turkmenistan, and they foreshadow the persecutions of "local nationalists" that would come in the 1930s. Despite the official discourse of national equality and condemnation of "great Russian chauvinism" in the 1920s, an alternative discourse held sway among many Russians within Central Asia. In this parallel universe of ideas, Russian dominance and non-Russian inferiority were taken for granted, and natives who insisted on equality and respect were viewed as troublemakers. In the 1920s, those Turkmen accused of being

[86] Ibid., d. 1641, ll. 58–59.
[87] Ibid., l. 59.
[88] See Lowell Tillett, *The Great Friendship: Soviet Historians on the Non-Russian Nationalities* (Chapel Hill: University of North Carolina Press, 1969).
[89] RGASPI, f. 62, op. 2, d. 1185, ll. 88–89.

too zealous in their approach to indigenization did not face any serious consequences. As we will see in the next chapter, however, the most vocal proponents of indigenization were among the first to be accused of "counterrevolutionary nationalism" when the OGPU began arresting Turkmen officials in the 1930s.

Retreat from Indigenization?

By 1934, the ambitious push for indigenization within the Turkmen republic had sputtered to a halt. For several years, little was said about the policy in public or at party meetings. The apparent abandonment of indigenization was not limited to Turkmenistan; a similar shift took place throughout the Soviet Union. Until recently, in fact, most Western historians believed that the Soviet regime ended its campaign to promote native elites and languages in the 1930s and adopted a more russocentric policy in its place.[90]

There were indeed indications in the mid- and late 1930s that the Soviet regime was shifting away from its enthusiastic promotion of non-Russian nationhood. There was an increasing emphasis on the Russian language, as exemplified by a 1938 law mandating the study of Russian by all non-Russian schoolchildren.[91] Moreover, the threat posed by non-Russian nationalism was being reconsidered. In 1923, the twelfth party congress had unambiguously declared Great Russian chauvinism to be more dangerous than local forms of nationalism, especially since such "great power nationalism" was responsible for inflaming local national sentiments.[92] Stalin had repeated this formulation in 1930 at the sixteenth congress, noting that Great Russian chauvinism was the main threat to the party's nationality policy. Yet in 1934 Stalin changed his position, declaring that "local nationalism" could be just as harmful as "great power chauvinism," depending on the circumstances.[93]

None of this meant the wholesale abandonment of indigenization, however. Well into the 1940s and beyond, Soviet authorities continued to promote native elites into Soviet jobs, set quotas for natives in higher education, and support native-language education. However, these efforts were transformed in several important ways in the mid- to late 1930s. First, there was a retreat from the noisy, public indigenization campaigns of the

[90] See, for example, Simon, *Nationalism*, chap. 2.
[91] Blitstein, "Stalin's Nations," pp. 10–11, 104.
[92] *Dvenadzatyi s"ezd RKP (b)*, p. 697.
[93] Blitstein, "Stalin's Nations," p. 189; Martin, *The Affirmative Action Empire*, pp. 156, 361; Simon, *Nationalism*, p. 73.

1920s and early 1930s, possibly because of an awareness that the rhetoric of ethnic preference was exacerbating ethnic conflict. Second, preferential policies came to focus primarily on the national or union republics, while smaller autonomous republics and regions saw their national cultures and languages neglected. Third, indigenization came to refer almost exclusively to the recruitment of native elites, as attempts to require the use of native languages in government administration were gradually abandoned.[94]

In Turkmenistan, concern about the promotion of local elites remained evident in the late 1930s, but the results continued to be disappointing. In June 1937, a lead editorial in *Turkmenskaia iskra* called the slow pace of indigenization within the republic "intolerable." In higher education, the proportion of Turkmen students within the republic averaged only 14 percent in institutes and 28 percent in technical schools. Meanwhile, in government institutions the all-too-meager gains of indigenization were evaporating. The proportion of Turkmen employees in the Commissariat of Agriculture, for example, had dropped from 8.9 percent in 1935 to 3.8 percent in January 1937. Not surprisingly, government business was still being conducted in Russian.[95] Even in the mid-1940s, studies continued to find that Turkmen constituted a small minority within republican institutions of higher learning and that they remained underrepresented in central and regional government institutions.[96]

More than two decades after the twelfth party congress, then, the resolutions requiring that local institutions be staffed predominantly by the local nationality and that all administrative organs use the local language remained unfulfilled. The Soviet bureaucracy and higher educational institutions within the Turkmen republic were still dominated by Europeans and the Russian language. Yet it would be wrong to conclude from this that indigenization was a failure. Because of the inflated expectations surrounding the policy, Soviet authorities viewed even modest successes in recruiting an indigenous elite with disappointment. In fact, the gains brought by indigenization were far from trivial. The number of Turkmen students in technical institutes in the late 1930s seems more impressive when one recalls the complete absence of such institutions in the region before 1917. Similarly, the fact that nearly 30 percent of white-collar workers in 1939 were Turkmen should be seen as a remarkable achieve-

[94] Martin, *The Affirmative Action Empire*, pp. 372–73, 376–79; Blitstein, "Stalin's Nations," pp. 140–41, 163, 190–91; Slezkine, "The USSR as a Communal Apartment," pp. 442–46.

[95] "Korenizatsiia i natsionalizatsiia apparata—ser"ezneishaia zadacha partorganizatsii," *Turkmenskaia iskra*, June 23, 1937, p. 1; RGASPI, f. 17, op. 30, d. 123, l. 57; *Turkmenskaia iskra*, July 15, 1937, pp. 2–3.

[96] Blitstein, "Stalin's Nations," pp. 202–3, 223–24.

ment in light of the nearly universal illiteracy of the native population just two decades earlier.[97]

Nevertheless, the policy of ethnic preferences failed to achieve the goals set by its originators. It had not produced a Soviet apparatus that had a "Turkmen face" and was accessible to the masses, nor had it undercut potential anti-Russian feeling within the republic. If anything, the policy had exacerbated conflict between Turkmen and non-Turkmen. Turkmen officials took for granted that the republic belonged to them, as the titular nationality, and that most if not all important posts should be filled by Turkmen. Europeans generally believed that the Turkmen were not capable of running things themselves and should therefore be suitably grateful for any positions they were offered. In the end, the grandiose promises of indigenization served to antagonize Turkmen and Europeans alike.

[97] The figure on white-collar workers is based on 1939 census data. Cited in Martin, *The Affirmative Action Empire*, p. 381.

Chapter Four

HELPERS, NOT NANNIES

MOSCOW AND THE TURKMEN COMMUNIST PARTY

A T A SECRET MEETING of the Turkmen Communist Party (KPT) leadership in June 1929, Turkmen communists complained bitterly about ethnic discrimination within the party. Although they were technically the equals of their Russian comrades, the Turkmen claimed that they were bypassed whenever important decisions were made. Russian party leaders, instead of consulting with native communists about conditions in the republic, listened solely to the opinions of "Petrov" and "Smirnov." Charï Vellekov, first secretary of the KPT Central Committee and the highest-ranking Turkmen communist in the republic, spoke for many when he described his own feelings of powerlessness: "I have the impression that no one takes me into account at all, that I was just placed in my job nominally as a representative of the titular nationality."[1]

Ethnicity was not supposed to matter within the Communist Party. The party was, in theory, a multinational vanguard of politically conscious individuals who would lead the masses to socialism. In a Soviet state structured along ethnic lines, however, no institution was immune to the pervasive importance of ethnicity. Ethnic affirmative action extended to the ranks of the KPT, which recruited aggressively and successfully among the Turkmen rural population in the 1920s and 1930s. At the same time, Moscow placed Turkmen communists at the highest levels of party leadership within the republic. Like the indigenization policies discussed in the previous chapter, which focused primarily on government agencies dealing directly with the "native masses," the recruitment of Turkmen into the Communist Party was a way of ensuring that the republic would present a "Turkmen face" to its own people and the rest of the world. In the party, too, the preferential recruitment of Turkmen served to foster a sense of Turkmen identity and to heighten tensions between Turkmen and non-Turkmen.

Of course, not all divisions within the party were ethnic in nature. Cobbled together out of fragments of the predelimitation communist parties of Turkestan, Khiva, and Bukhara, the KPT was far from cohesive. The

[1] RGASPI, f. 62, op. 2, d. 396, ll. 207, 210–13.

"local Europeans" who had dominated the region's party organizations before 1924 resented the European career communists sent from Tashkent and Moscow after the delimitation.[2] Turkmen communists themselves were divided by tribe, region, ideology, and personal loyalties. As the party expanded rapidly beyond its original core and recruited large numbers of Turkmen, new fracture lines appeared. In particular, the Russian-speaking Turkmen communist elite found that it had little in common with the rural members of village party cells, who soon made up the overwhelming majority of Turkmen communists.

Most disturbing in its implications for nationality policy, however, was the rift between Turkmen and European communists that emerged within the upper reaches of the party in the late 1920s and early 1930s. Before the creation of the Turkmen republic, Turkmen party officials had seen European communists as potential allies in their disputes with other Central Asians and as supporters in their quest for Turkmen autonomy. After 1924, other Central Asian ethnic groups no longer posed a threat to Turkmen national aspirations; the main competition for jobs and political power now came from Europeans. As more Turkmen were promoted into positions of responsibility within the party, there was fertile new ground for friction between Turkmen and European communists.

Soviet hiring and promotion policies contributed to this rift. Despite the rhetoric of a single internationalist Communist Party, Turkmen and European communists were treated differently by Moscow and could expect different career trajectories. Turkmen officials tended to spend their careers within their own republic, while Europeans (who might be Russians, Jews, Armenians, Latvians, or even Muslim Tatars) alternated between jobs in national republics and positions with the central party apparatus in Moscow.[3] Moreover, the Soviet leadership relied on European communists to carry out central policies and to report on the views and activities of their "national" comrades. Within the Turkmen republic, this two-tiered system was epitomized by the appointment of dual secretaries—one Turkmen and one European—at every level of the party bureaucracy. Despite the rhetoric of equality, the European secretary was always the real decision maker and the one entrusted with the implementation of central directives.

[2] Ibid., f. 17, op. 67, d. 205, l. 46.

[3] Turkmen were often sent to Moscow or Leningrad to study, and occasionally they worked in the capital (usually in nationalities-related positions). They might also hold positions with the Central Asian Bureau apparatus in Tashkent. But they were less likely to be transferred to Latvia or Armenia or promoted to a regular position in Moscow, as European communists routinely were. Benedict Anderson describes a similar lack of vertical and horizontal mobility among creole elites in Latin America. See *Imagined Communities*, pp. 47–65.

In the second half of the 1920s, Turkmen communists began to chafe at their second-class status within the party, arguing that it violated the spirit of communist internationalism. Like the complaints about the slow pace of indigenization, however, this criticism ultimately served to fuel the suspicions of an increasingly paranoid regime. In the early 1930s, Moscow launched a major campaign to purge Soviet government and party institutions in non-Russian republics of "counterrevolutionary nationalists," and Turkmen cultural officials who had complained about the dominance of Russians and the Russian language were among its first victims. In the Great Terror of 1937–38, these accusations of nationalism expanded to encompass the republican communist elite. Even Turkmen communists previously considered beyond reproach by Moscow fell victim to allegations that they were "counterrevolutionaries" seeking independence from Soviet rule.

The Formation of the Turkmen Communist Party

The Soviet system of rule was formally divided into party and state branches. In broad terms, the Communist Party served as the behind-the-scenes force determining the overall direction of policy, while state institutions were charged with executing the party's directives. Within the Turkmen republic, the Communist Party of Turkmenistan formed a pyramid headed by the Central Committee. At the apex of the Central Committee was the executive bureau (Ispolburo), the republican equivalent of the all-union Politburo and the real ruling body within the republic. The leading institutions on the state side were the Central Executive Committee (TsIK) and the Council of People's Commissars (Sovnarkom). The TsIK supervised the network of elected soviets, or councils, throughout the republic, ranging from the Congress of Soviets (in theory the main legislative body in the Soviet system) to the village soviets that were the primary point of contact between the regime and the rural population. The Sovnarkom oversaw the commissariats that were the Soviet equivalent of ministries, each of which was responsible for a specific sphere of government activity. In a small republic such as Turkmenistan, the party-state distinction was not nearly as rigid as the formal structure implied, and there was a great deal of overlap in personnel between party and state institutions. At the highest levels, many of the individuals who served on the republican Central Committee and its executive bureau were simultaneously leading officials of the Sovnarkom or the TsIK; in the countryside, the same group of people often dominated both the village soviet and the village party cell.[4]

---

[4] See, for example, RGASPI, f. 62, op. 2, d. 2589, l. 7; d. 618, l. 171. The overlapping of party and state has been noted in other areas as well. See Merle Fainsod, *Smolensk under Soviet Rule* (1958; reprint, Boston: Unwyn Hyman, 1989), p. 93.

Figure 8. Building housing the offices of the Turkmen republic's Council of People's Commissars, Central Executive Committee, and KPT Central Committee, Ashgabat, 1930. Note misspelling of the Russian word "commissars." (From the collection of the Russian State Archive of Film and Photographic Documents at Krasnogorsk.)

The Turkmen Communist Party was formed at the same time as the Turkmen republic. The Politburo decree of June 12, 1924, mandating the creation of national-territorial republics called for the creation of national communist parties in each of them.[5] Through a series of institutional reorganizations, the Turkmen National Bureau, the six-member committee responsible for delineating the new Turkmen republic, became the nucleus of the new Turkmen Communist Party. The National Bureau was reconstituted in the autumn of 1924 as the Turkmen National Party Bureau and then as the organizational bureau of the Communist Party of Turkmenistan. On October 30, 1924, the Politburo appointed a twelve-member Turkmen Temporary Party Bureau, which included most of the membership of the earlier committees and ultimately became the executive bureau of the KPT Central Committee.[6]

[5] RGASPI, f. 62, op. 2, d. 100, l. 7; f. 17, op. 3, d. 443, ll. 17–18.
[6] Khudaiberdyev, *Obrazovanie Kommunisticheskoi Partii Turkmenistana* (Ashgabat: Turkmengosizdat, 1964), pp. 29–30.

The membership of the new KPT was an amalgamation of three different components: the Turkmen (formerly Transcaspian) provincial party organization of the Turkestani republic, the Dashhowuz (also known as Turkmen) provincial party organization of the Khivan Communist Party, and the Turkmen section of the Bukharan Communist Party.[7] The core of the Turkmen communist elite within the republic was made up of officials who had joined the party between 1917 and 1924 and worked in the state and party organs of Bukhara, Khiva, and Turkestan prior to the national delimitation. This group consisted of only a few dozen individuals, yet it played an extremely important role in the first decade and a half of the republic's existence. Not only were these early Turkmen communists instrumental in negotiating the borders of the Turkmen republic, but they also held most of the leading positions within its party and state structures.

As a group, these prominent Turkmen communists shared a number of characteristics. Many of them had attended tsarist Russian-native schools prior to the revolution. Unlike most Turkmen, therefore, they were Russian speaking and familiar with Russians and Russian culture. The majority were from the former Transcaspian province of the Turkestani republic; that is, they lived in the Turkmen areas that had been longest under Russian rule and influence. The main Turkmen groups represented in the Communist Party were Tekes from the Ashgabat and Marï regions of Transcaspia and western Yomuts from Mangïshlak, near the Caspian shore.

The three most important Turkmen officials in the new republic—Gaigïsïz Atabaev, Nadïrbai Aitakov, and Halmïrad Sähetmïradov—all fit this dominant profile. Atabaev, the most influential of the Turkmen communists, was a Teke Turkmen from the Tejen district of Transcaspia. He was born in 1887 to a prominent family, but was orphaned in infancy. Atabaev attended a Russian-native school in Tejen and the Tashkent Teacher's Seminary, then worked as a teacher in Russian-native schools in Marï and Bäherden before the revolution. He joined the Bolshevik Party in February 1919 after a brief period of membership in the left Socialist Revolutionaries and served as deputy chair of the Bukharan Council of People's Nazirs (the local equivalent of the Sovnarkom). After the national delimitation, Atabaev became the first head of the Turkmen republic's Sovnarkom, a position he held until 1937.[8]

Nadïrbai Aitakov, another leading Turkmen communist who participated in the creation of the Turkmen republic, was born in 1894 to a fisherman's family in a Yomut region along the Caspian Sea. Like Ata-

[7] *Ocherki istorii Kommunisticheskoi Partii Turkmenistana*, 2d ed. (Ashgabat: Izdatel'-stvo "Turkmenistan," 1965), p. 288.

[8] Khudaiberdyev, *Obrazovanie Kommunisticheskoi Partii Turkmenistana*, pp. 190–91; Kerbabaev, *Chudom rozhdennyi*, pp. 7–14.

baev, he was orphaned at an early age.[9] He attended a Russian-native school in Fort Aleksandrovsk and later worked at a variety of menial jobs. Aitakov began his career with the Soviet regime as chairman of a village soviet, later rising to become a member of a district executive committee. He joined the Communist Party in January 1922. After the national delimitation, Aitakov became chair of the Turkmen Central Executive Committee, where he remained until 1937.[10]

Halmïrad Sähetmïradov was a Teke, born in 1898 in the Ashgabat region. He too received a Russian-language education, attending a Russian agricultural school and the Tashkent Teacher's Seminary. Sähetmïradov joined the Bolshevik Party in November 1919, and in the same year became secretary of the Transcaspian branch of the Muslim Bureau of the Communist Party. Prior to the national delimitation, he served as a member of the Turkmen provincial party committee and the Poltoratsk (later Ashgabat) district-city party committee. Sähetmïradov also spent time in Moscow in 1921 as a deputy representative of the Turkestani republic. In 1925, Sähetmïradov became first secretary of the Central Committee of the Turkmen republican Communist Party.[11]

A smaller number of Turkmen communists were from the less-russified Turkmen regions of Khiva and Bukhara. One prominent Bukharan official was Artïk Rahmanov, who joined the Communist Party in 1918. He served as chairman of the Chärjew and Kerki executive committees before the national delimitation. In 1925 he became first secretary of the Chärjew province party committee, and was subsequently appointed chief prosecutor of the Turkmen republic.[12] Begjan Nazarov, from the Dashhowuz province of the Khivan republic, was educated in a traditional Muslim confessional school and did not speak Russian. Nazarov joined the party in 1921 and worked for the Khivan Central Executive Committee prior to the national delimitation. Nazarov was a member of the organizational bureau of the Turkmen Communist Party when the republic was formed, and in 1924 was appointed deputy chair of the Turkmen republic's Central Executive Committee.[13]

---

[9] It was often orphaned or poor children who attended Russian-native schools, since many Turkmen parents were reluctant to deliver their offspring into the hands of Russian educators. Khodjakulieva, "Russko-tuzemnye shkoly v Zakaspiiskoi Oblasti," p. 18. One can speculate that the lack of close family ties made it easier for these individuals to distance themselves from Turkmen society and adopt Russian or communist values.

[10] *Turkmenskaia iskra*, no. 50 (March 4, 1925), p. 2; Khudaiberdyev, *Obrazovanie Kommunisticheskoi Partii Turkmenistana*, p. 190; RGASPI, f. 17, op. 9, d. 3256, l. 206.

[11] RGASPI, f. 17, op. 9, d. 3280, l. 195; B. P. Palvanova, *Tragicheskie 30-e* (Ashgabat: Turkmenistan, 1991), pp. 56–57.

[12] RGASPI, f. 62, op. 2, d. 874, l. 22.

[13] Palvanova, *Tragicheskie 30-e*, p. 63.

The KPT, like the other Central Asian communist parties, dealt with Moscow through the Central Asian Bureau of the Russian Communist Party Central Committee. The Bureau, formed in April 1922 to coordinate and supervise the work of local party organizations, was one of several regional party organs in the Soviet Union that served as intermediaries between Moscow and local communist parties.[14] Moscow considered the Bureau necessary in order to keep a close watch on local communists, whom it viewed as less than politically reliable and prone to succumb to nationalist tendencies.[15] The Bureau, based in Tashkent, was in frequent contact with local communists and thus was better able than far-off Moscow to spot brewing problems. Its officials reported to Moscow on the political situation in Central Asia and recommended personnel and policy changes when necessary. Leaders of republican party organizations received instructions from the Bureau and reported to its leadership on their successes and failures.[16]

VILLAGE COMMUNISTS: "POLITICALLY AND ALPHABETICALLY ILLITERATE"

The KPT went through a tremendous expansion in the first years of the Turkmen republic's existence, recruiting with particular success among the Turkmen population. In 1920, when the Transcaspian province was reconquered from the Whites in the Civil War, the provincial party organization had had 1,818 members and 788 candidates, only a few hundred of whom were Turkmen and other Muslims. The overwhelming majority were Russians and other Europeans. By the time of the first congress of the Turkmen Communist Party in February 1925, there were 5,240 members and 2,484 candidates within the republic, 24.5 percent of whom were Turkmen.[17] On January 1, 1930, out of a total of 10,448 communists in the republic, 40.5 percent were Turkmen. Fifty percent were Russians and other Europeans, and 9 percent belonged to other "Eastern nationali-

---

[14] Rosliakov, *Sredazburo TsK VKP*, pp. 11–13. For a useful discussion of the Central Asian Bureau, see Shoshana Keller, "The Struggle against Islam in Uzbekistan, 1921–1941: Policy, Bureaucracy, and Reality" (Ph.D. dissertation, Indiana University, 1995), pp. 29–38.

[15] The Politburo decree of June 12, 1924 outlining the basic principles of national delimitation explicitly called for the retention of the Central Asian Bureau. RGASPI, f. 62, op. 2, d. 100, l. 7. also f. 17, op. 3, d. 443, ll. 17–18.

[16] Rosliakov, *Sredazbiuro TsK VKP*, pp. 10–12.

[17] Mel'kumov, *Ocherki istorii partorganizatsii Turkmenskoi oblasti*, p. 37; V. Vorshev, "Osnovnye etapy razvitiia partorganizatsii Turkmenistana," *Revoliutsiia i natsional'nosti*, no. 12 (December 1934), p. 69.

ties." By January 1, 1933, Turkmen made up more than half the Communist Party members in the republic (8,586 out of 17,005 total), while the
proportion of Russians and other Europeans had dropped to about 35
percent.[18] In strictly quantitative terms, the Communist Party was one of
the most successful arenas of indigenization in the Turkmen republic.

The quality of the new members was another matter entirely. The vast
majority of Turkmen communists belonged to village party cells. These
representatives of the socialist vanguard were mostly peasants described
by party leaders in Ashgabat as "politically and alphabetically illiterate."
Even among secretaries of party cells—those who were supposed to be
producing minutes of meetings and keeping track of written instructions
sent from the regional center—some 30 percent were functionally illiterate.[19] In 1933, some party organizations were still reporting that half of
their members could not read. Those who claimed to be literate often
were only marginally so.[20]

Party members were frequently drawn from the wrong social classes.
Since the party was the main source of power and influence under the
Soviet system, those who joined tended to be wealthy and influential members of dominant lineages, rather than the poor and landless peasants
from whom the Soviet regime hoped to gain support. While these nominal
communists continued to dominate their villages in their traditional roles
as aksakgals, or elders, the party cell often existed only on paper. "Despite
the great personal influence of its individual members," one investigator
wrote, "the cell as such has no connection with the population and does
not take any part in the public life of the village."[21] Frequently new recruits to the party had little comprehension of the Soviet enterprise, let
alone commitment to its goals. In what investigators described as a "typical village party cell" in the village of Shorgala in 1926, the communists
were mainly interested in the economic and political benefits of party
membership:

> They all have no understanding of the party whatsoever. They have totally
> wrong ideas about their role as members of the party and about their responsi-
> bilities. For them, the party is a path to power, to the extraction of material
> benefits from the Soviet regime, to the improvement of their personal situa-
> tion. . . . When asked why they joined the party, they even respond with naive
> candor that otherwise (without belonging to the party) it's impossible to find a
> job anywhere.[22]

[18] RGASPI, f. 62, op. 2, d. 3145, l. 15.
[19] Ibid., d. 2589, ll. 2–3.
[20] Ibid., d. 3200, l. 96; op. 3, d. 293, ll. 16–17.
[21] Ibid., op. 2, d. 618, l. 174.
[22] Ibid., l. 171.

Established in 1922, the Shorgala cell consisted of four party members and seven candidate members. The membership was drawn from seven settlements in the area. Three of the members were employees of the local Soviet apparatus, while three of the candidates were secretaries of village soviets. Three of the four members were illiterate. Two candidates had recently been expelled: one for smoking opium, the other for theft and "selling" his own sister into marriage.[23] In this group, even those who made a genuine effort to learn about the party were thwarted by the utterly alien nature of its tenets:

> Only one of the candidates, the most cultured and literate, has read political brochures and said a few words about defending the proletariat. However, this is so far over his head and so foreign to his disposition that beyond the most general and formulaic phrases he could not say anything and was unable to draw any conclusions.[24]

The cell rarely called meetings on its own initiative, doing so only when regional officials or the arrival of an investigator demanded it. Its activity was limited to passing formal resolutions on topics dictated by higher-ups. A party instructor doubted whether some of the meetings documented in the cell's protocols had ever taken place.[25]

In order to produce better-informed and more active communists, the party had to educate Turkmen villagers about party doctrine and goals. This was difficult in view of the illiteracy of many communists and the shortage of written materials in the Turkmen language. The alternative was to educate communists at meetings and in face-to-face interactions, but this posed problems as well. Politically sophisticated European communists could not speak Turkmen, and those Turkmen-speaking individuals recruited to work as propagandists were often vague on the details of the Marxist-Leninist class theory they were supposed to be expounding. In a conversation with a party investigator in 1925, an agitprop worker in the Sayat region revealed a rather idiosyncratic understanding of the term "proletarian":

> *Investigator*: What is a worker?
> *Agitprop worker*: A poor person.
> *Investigator*: What is a proletarian?
> *Agitprop worker*: A poor person.
> *Investigator*: A peasant, even a middle peasant is poorer than a factory or railway worker, does that mean he's a proletarian?
> *Agitprop worker*: Of course.

[23] Ibid.
[24] Ibid., ll. 171–72.
[25] Ibid., l. 175.

Investigator: Then a beggar, a starving person, or a petty thief is also a proletarian.
Agitprop worker: Of course.
Investigator: But some workers have their own gardens and small houses, they receive a salary.
Agitprop worker: Then they're bourgeois.
Investigator: Nowadays, generals and merchants often go hungry.
Agitprop worker: They're proletarians, they've become completely impoverished.[26]

Rural communists were not only self-serving, illiterate, and politically uninformed; they were also incapable of setting a good example for other Turkmen villagers. In the view of communists from Ashgabat and Moscow, joining the party implied that one was ready to abandon the "backward" customs of one's ancestors and embrace a modern, European lifestyle. Instead of serving as shining models of Soviet humanity, however, many Turkmen communists behaved no differently from the noncommunist villagers around them. The Soviet officials from Ashgabat who paid visits to their comrades in outlying areas reported that the villagers' conversion to communism had not brought about a corresponding conversion to European domestic habits. Investigators who visited rural party cells throughout the Turkmen republic in 1926 found organizations that were permeated by "tribal-clan conflict" and communists who continued to observe tribal customary law and Muslim religious traditions.[27] In the village of Yarïgala, party members visited a traditional healer rather than a European doctor when they fell ill, went to the mosque to pray, and refused to allow their wives to attend school.[28] In Irigalï, the wives of communists sat in the presence of their husbands with their mouths covered as a sign of modesty. "No matter which village I visited, I saw absolutely no sign of change in the sense of communist influence on family life," wrote the Communist Party women's department official Anna Aksentovich in 1927.[29] In Shorgala, "religious superstitions" continued to hold sway among communists, according to a party investigator: "In response to my question 'does Satan exist?' they all answered evasively that they don't know—perhaps he does exist, and perhaps not—but it was completely obvious that they sincerely believe in his existence."[30] It was clear that Moscow could not expect much assistance in carrying out its rural policies from communists like these.

[26] Ibid., d. 287, ll. 17–18.
[27] Ibid., f. 121, op. 1, d. 42, ll. 7–9, 19, 36, 107.
[28] Ibid., f. 62, op. 3, d. 293, ll. 20–22.
[29] Ibid., op. 2, d. 1218, ll. 50–51.
[30] Ibid., d. 618, l. 172.

THE PARTY ELITE: COMMUNISTS OF THE "SECOND RANK"

In the upper echelons of the KPT, the difficulties plaguing the party were quite different. Here the problem was how to cobble together a cohesive party organization out of a number of seemingly incompatible components. At the time of the national delimitation, the need to defend Turkmen interests against those of other Central Asians produced a solidarity that obscured the divisions within the future KPT. Communists from Khiva, Bukhara, and Turkestan, including individuals of European as well as Turkmen descent, had all worked together to draw the borders of the republic and create its new institutions. At the founding congress of the KPT in Ashgabat on February 14–19, 1925, this solidarity was still very much in evidence. Isaak Zelenskii, head of the Central Asian Bureau, reported to Moscow that the congress went smoothly, "with no noticeable internal tensions."[31] The post-delimitation honeymoon did not last long, however. Within two years, the KPT was virtually immobilized by factionalism arising out of personality conflicts, ideological differences, and ethnic tensions.

At the first republican party congress, Ivan Ivanovich Mezhlauk and Halmïrad Sähetmïradov were named co–first secretaries of the KPT Central Committee. Mezhlauk, a Latvian, was a former Menshevik who had joined the Bolshevik Party in 1918. He chaired the Central Asian Economic Council prior to the national delimitation and served as secretary of the organizational bureau of the KPT.[32] But Mezhlauk proved to be tremendously unpopular with his fellow communists. In particular, he was disliked by Turkmen party officials for his condescending attitude toward local nationals.[33] After a little more than a year, the Moscow leadership replaced Mezhlauk with Shali Ibragimov, a Tatar who had joined the party in 1915 and had previously been an instructor of the Central Committee of the all-union Communist Party.[34] Ibragimov and Sähetmïradov were now to serve as co–first secretaries of the republican party Central Committee.

---

[31] *Ocherki istorii Kommunisticheskoi Partii Turkmenistana*, p. 292; Vorshev, "Osnovnye etapy," p. 69; RGASPI, f. 17, op. 67, d. 206, l. 7.

[32] *Turkestanskaia pravda*, no 95 (April 30, 1924), p. 5; Khudaiberdyev, *Obrazovanie Kommunisticheskoi Partii Turkmenistana*, p. 193; RGASPI, f. 17, op. 67, d. 206, l. 11.

[33] RGASPI, f. 62, op. 2, d. 838, l. 10; f. 17, op. 30, d. 10, l. 26. Mezhlauk had previously alienated Uzbek national communists in Bukhara and Khiva, who sent a petition to the Politburo in October 1924 demanding his removal from party work in Central Asia. They alleged that he had taken sides in factional struggles between Turkestani communists, on the one hand, and Bukharan and Khivan communists, on the other. See RGASPI, f. 670, op. 1, d. 11, ll. 136–38.

[34] Sultanbekov, *Tainy natsional'noi politiki*, p. 289.

Ibragimov's tenure ran into problems almost immediately. He was a weak leader, incapable of maintaining party discipline and ensuring the implementation of Moscow's directives. Sähetmïradov challenged Ibragimov's authority, refusing to accept that the Tatar official was his superior. Officially, the two first secretaries were equals, with each responsible for overseeing half of the government agencies within the republic.[35] In reality, however, Ibragimov was Moscow's man and the true first secretary, while Sähetmïradov was the local communist expected to play a secondary role. Sähetmïradov, an experienced party official, considered himself every bit as qualified to run the republic as Ibragimov, a Muslim Tatar who was not even a "real European." Concerned by these tensions, Zelenskii proposed a restructuring of the Central Committee Secretariat to make it clear that Ibragimov outranked Sähetmïradov.[36]

At the same time, Ibragimov was unable to manage the escalating conflict within the party organization between party secretary Sähetmïradov and Sovnarkom chair Atabaev. This conflict was both ideological and personal, with the two Turkmen communists battling for influence and popularity within the party and the republic as a whole. Atabaev was in some ways a typical "national communist," willing to take local cultural constraints into account and to work with prerevolutionary elites to bring socialism to the masses. Atabaev quietly opposed the coercive transformation of Turkmen society, arguing that such change should take place gradually. He also argued that class distinctions and class struggle were relatively unimportant among the Turkmen. Sähetmïradov was a more doctrinaire Bolshevik, presenting himself as the defender of the working class and the village poor. Thus, he criticized Atabaev for his blindness to class distinctions and his conciliatory attitude toward the "bourgeois intelligentsia."[37]

The infighting within the party weakened its ability to deal with corruption and other "unhealthy manifestations," since parties to the conflict unhesitatingly supported members of their own faction even when the latter were accused of crimes. Bairam Sähedov, an official of the Central Control Commission who was a supporter of Sähetmïradov, was allowed to remain in his position despite having embezzled official funds.[38] Atabaev and Aitakov were able to arrange the release of several supporters imprisoned for crimes committed while working as Soviet officials.[39] The conflict between Atabaev and Sähetmïradov was a form of the left-right

[35] RGASPI, f. 17, op. 30, d. 16, l. 26.
[36] Ibid., f. 62, op. 2, d. 832, ll. 3–4.
[37] Ibid; f. 17, op. 30, d. 10, ll. 9–22. For Stalin's view of the "nationalist" intelligentsia in this period, see Sultanbekov, *Tainy natsional'noi politiki*, p. 81.
[38] RGASPI, f. 62, op. 2, d. 832, l. 4.
[39] Ibid., f. 17, op. 67, d. 382, l. 99.

factionalism that divided the party organizations of many Muslim repub-lics. The "rightists" tried to make communism compatible with national-ism and demanded a more rapid implementation of indigenization. The "leftists" were internationalists, who criticized the right's efforts to ele-vate national concerns above class issues. Stalin had declared in 1923 that the left faction was the more dangerous, perhaps because he feared alienating the more popular and numerous rightists.[40] In Turkmenistan, where the rightist viewpoint had more support within the party, Sähetmï-radov soon found himself isolated.

By February 1928, Zelenskii reported to the all-union Central Commit-tee that the condition of the party organization in Turkmenistan had "sig-nificantly deteriorated" and that the "relationship to comrade Ibragimov of a significant portion of the active Turkmen and European party mem-bers" had worsened. European communists had become completely de-moralized as a result of the factional fighting.[41] Many committed commu-nists were unwilling to remain in Turkmenistan because of the "constant wavering and vacillation on all important questions facing the Turkmen organization." Even worse, Zelenskii reported that Ibragimov had en-tered the factional conflict on Atabaev's side, instead of staying above the fray in a manner befitting Moscow's representative. "Ibragimov, evi-dently, is so closely connected to Atabaev that he cannot carry out a policy that would ensure the TsK's actual leadership of the Soviet apparatus."[42] The polarization of the party between the Sähetmïradov and Atabaev fac-tions, which was not limited to the central republican leadership but ex-tended to the provincial and local level, was paralyzing the party. Even the all-important business of promoting and transferring personnel had come to a virtual standstill, Zelenskii wrote:

> As a general rule, all sorts of appointments, shifts, and transfers are inevitably looked at from the point of view of maintaining or securing the influence of either Atabaev or Sähetmïradov. This has meant that in an organization with a very small core of active party members, it has become completely impossible to promote officials who do not belong to either faction. In fact, promotions have hardly taken place at all over the past year.[43]

In early 1928, the Central Asian Bureau moved to address the problem. At Zelenskii's suggestion, Moscow removed both Ibragimov and Sähetmï-radov from their posts. Sähetmïradov was transferred to the Central

[40] Martin, *The Affirmative Action Empire*, pp. 228–38; See also Alexandre A. Bennigsen and S. Enders Wimbush, *Muslim National Communism in the Soviet Union* (Chicago: University of Chicago Press, 1979).
[41] RGASPI, f. 17, op. 67, d. 382, ll. 99–100.
[42] Ibid, ll. 98–100.
[43] Ibid., l. 98.

Asian Bureau, where he became head of the party department for village work. His nemesis, Atabaev, was allowed to remain in his position as Sovnarkom chair. Zelenskii noted that Atabaev "has significant ties to the masses and is popular among them. With firm guidance he may be retained as an official of the Soviet apparatus."[44]

To replace the two departing Central Committee secretaries, Zelenskii recommended appointing Nikolai Antonovich Paskutskii and Charï Vellekov as co–first secretaries of the Turkmen TsK. Paskutskii was a Russian with considerable political and military experience in Central Asia. A party member since 1919, he was the former chair of the revolutionary military soviet of the Transcaspian front, a major player in the Civil War in Central Asia, and a close associate of the veteran Bolsheviks Kuibyshev and Frunze.[45] After the national delimitation, he became deputy chair of the Turkmen Sovnarkom under Atabaev. Paskutskii was unusual in that he maintained good relations with all the diverse factions of the KPT. The European party members from predelimitation Transcaspia considered him to be "one of their own," yet he was also respected by the newer arrivals from Tashkent and Moscow and by the leading Turkmen communists, most notably Atabaev.[46] Zelenskii wrote of Paskutskii, "He is quite a strong organizer and has a great deal of experience in Soviet work. The relationship of the European *aktiv* and the vast majority of Turkmen toward him is positive; he may well be the most authoritative and popular figure in all of Turkmenia."[47]

Vellekov, a twenty-six-year-old Teke from the Tejen area, had received his education in Russian-native schools, served as an enlisted man in the Red Army from 1920 to 1922, and joined the Communist Party in 1922. After the national delimitation, he served as first secretary of the Turkmen republic's Young Communist League (Komsomol) and subsequently as first secretary of the Chärjew province's party committee.[48] Zelenskii described Vellekov as "an individual who stands outside all factions, and who belongs to that group of Turkmen young people who are seriously striving to become Bolsheviks."[49] Along with his freedom from factional links, Vellekov's youth and relative lack of experience may have been an attraction. He was less likely than the more experienced Bolshevik Sähetmïradov to demand equality with the first secretary sent from Moscow.

[44] Ibid., ll. 99–100; Palvanova, *Tragicheskie 30-e*, p. 57.

[45] Palvanova, *Tragicheskie 30-e*, p. 53.

[46] RGASPI, f. 17, op. 67, d. 205, l. 45.

[47] Ibid., d. 382, l. 100.

[48] Khudaiberdyev, *Obrazovanie Kommunisticheskoi Partii Turkmenistana*, p. 192; Palvanova, *Tragicheskie 30-e*, p. 58.

[49] RGASPI, f. 17, op. 67, d. 382, l. 100.

Despite Paskutskii's qualifications and popularity, he was passed over for the post of first secretary. Paskutskii had spent much of his career in Central Asia and was viewed as a "local Russian"; this was a disadvantage in the eyes of Moscow. The all-union Central Committee preferred to appoint experienced communists without local entanglements to fill top republican posts, in the belief that they would be more likely to carry out central policies in a firm and dispassionate manner.[50] Instead of Paskutskii, the Central Committee chose G. N. Aronshtam, an old Bolshevik who had joined the party in 1913, to serve with Vellekov as co–first secretary of the KPT. Aronshtam was a dedicated communist who could be relied on to carry out Moscow's policies, but he was less successful in winning the support of Turkmen communists. Unfamiliar with the local culture and often insensitive to Turkmen concerns, his tenure contributed to a sharpening of ethnic tensions in the republic.

By 1927, a serious rift between Turkmen and European communists had begun to emerge. This conflict was exacerbated by Moscow's way of staffing republican party organizations. One of the main features of the republican party structure was a dual secretary system in which a local national and a European were jointly appointed as first secretaries of the Central Committee. The European was usually a reliable long-time Bolshevik sent from Moscow. Generally he (and it was always a "he") knew little about the culture and language of the place; his job was to ensure that Moscow's orders were carried out and report back to the Central Asian Bureau or, with increasing frequency, directly to Moscow. These officials moved frequently from one republic to another, alternating such posts with jobs in the central party apparatus in Moscow. The local national—in this case a Turkmen—was usually a party official who had spent and would spend most of his or her career within the borders of the republic in question.[51] This system was duplicated at lower levels of the party hierarchy, where the secretary of the regional or provincial party committee was most often a Turkmen while the head of the local organization department—the person responsible for personnel appointments and effectively the real decision maker—was a European. Although this two-tiered system of appointments was not publicly acknowledged, most Europeans accepted it as natural, given the political "backwardness" of the Turkmen.

[50] Ibid.
[51] According to Terry Martin, Stalin always appointed a nontitular national as first secretary in the non-Russian republics because he believed that local nationals would not be able to resist the temptation of nationalism. A European first secretary was presumed to be more capable of balancing the demands of titular nationals for more rapid *korenizatsiia* against the grievances of Russians who were opposed to nationality-based preferences. *The Affir-*

Among Turkmen party members, however, the two-tiered party soon became a source of resentment. Shali Ibragimov, who visited Turkmenistan as a party instructor before becoming secretary of the Turkmen Central Committee in 1926, noted that the condescending attitude of European officials was "agitating a broad circle of party activists." "Europeans are not doing a good job of instructing the Turkmen with whom they work," he wrote. "In most cases, Europeans order the Turkmen around and decide a large number of important questions without the Turkmen."[52] These resentments burst into the open with the 1927 Tumailov affair. Mahmut Tumailov, a young Turkmen party official and self-proclaimed Trotskyist, caused a scandal when he publicly criticized the way nationality policy was carried out in Turkmenistan. Tumailov, a twenty-five-year-old member of the tiny community of Stavropol Turkmen in the North Caucasus, was deputy commissar for worker-peasant inspection and a member of the presidium of the Central Control Commission.[53] Like many other Turkmen party members, he had been educated before the revolution in a Russian-native school. He frequently noted with pride that when he joined the Communist Party at the age of seventeen, he was the first Turkmen from the North Caucasus to do so.[54]

Tumailov maintained that the party was not living up to the promises of self-determination it had made to the non-Russians. In a speech to the plenum of the Central Committee and Central Control Commission in the summer of 1927, he argued that European communists assigned to Turkmenistan were failing to abide by the Leninist requirement that they be "not pedagogues and nannies, but helpers" to the local communists in non-Russian regions.[55] Turkmen were treated as communists of the "second rank" and not fully trusted within their own republic, while officials sent from Moscow had all the real decision-making power. The dual secretary system, in which a "real" European secretary shared power with a Turkmen "figurehead," was a prime example:

> As for Turkmenia, it's no secret that many of our [Turkmen] nationals sit [in their positions] as formal representatives and don't adequately control their own staffs, thanks to their backwardness, on the one hand, and the minimal attention of European officials to [the Turkmen's] mastery of their jobs, on the other.[56]

---

mative Action Empire, pp. 232–33. Martin also notes that in many republics the European first secretary allied himself with the local leftist faction. This did not occur in Turkmenistan.

[52] RGASPI, f. 17, op. 67, d. 382, ll. 15–16.

[53] Ibid., f. 62, op. 2, d. 836, l. 15.

[54] Ibid., d. 838, l. 46; d. 1740, ll. 103–4.

[55] Ibid., d. 838, ll. 7, 9.

[56] Ibid., l. 15.

Tumailov also claimed that pan-regional institutions such as the Central Asian Economic Council were "unconstitutional" because they impinged on the economic autonomy of the national republics.[57] Tumailov was offended by the fact that European national republics had more rights than Central Asian republics; Ukraine and Belorussia were allowed to send trade representatives directly to Moscow, he noted, while Uzbekistan and Turkmenistan had to go through the Central Asian Economic Council. Tumailov was also critical of the Soviet of Nationalities attached to the all-union TsIK, which, unlike its predecessor, the Commissariat of Nationalities, "does nothing at all." He argued that the Soviet should be turned into a functioning agency, a true defender of the economic and cultural interests of union republics and autonomous provinces.[58]

Many of Tumailov's views were shared by other Turkmen communists; he was not the first to criticize the marginalization of Turkmen officials or to question the need for common Central Asian economic institutions. Tumailov's major mistake was to tie his own fate to that of the Left Opposition. Prior to 1927, Trotsky and his allies had shown little interest in the nationality question. In fact, given their aggressively internationalist orientation, there was little reason to expect them to endorse the regime's promotion of ethnicity. In 1927, however, the Left Opposition suddenly came out with demands for a more rapid and comprehensive implementation of Leninist nationality policy. The Opposition platform demanded more rapid indigenization, additional attention to developing industry in non-Russian regions, stronger resistance to "great Russian chauvinism," and the transformation of the Soviet of Nationalities into an institution capable of representing the interests of non-Russians. The Opposition evidently hoped to win the support of the national right with this program, but it found little response in the Muslim republics; the Tatar rightists who might have supported such a platform were suspicious of the Opposition's sincerity based on its past record.[59] Tumailov, however, was young and inexperienced enough to take the platform at face value, thus becoming quite possibly the only Turkmen Trotskyist in history. He was one of only a handful of signers within the Turkmen republic of the Opposition document known as the Platform of the 83 in May 1927.[60]

Tumailov was far from discreet about his pro-Opposition views. In addition to speaking out at the 1927 plenum, he sent copies of an article outlining his positions to the main republican party newspaper, *Turkmenskaia iskra*, the Opposition leaders Trotsky and Zinoviev, every party cell

[57] Ibid., ll. 9–10, 15–16.
[58] Ibid., ll. 14–16
[59] Martin, *The Affirmative Action Empire*, pp. 235–37.
[60] RGASPI, f. 62, op. 2, d. 838, ll. 5, 31.

in the republic, and a number of individual party members.[61] He tried to persuade Bäshim Kulbesherov, the Turkmen head of the Soviet of Nationalities, to sign the Platform of the 83.[62] Tumailov even wrote to Trotsky and Zinoviev on August 25, 1928, with advice on how to win the support of local communists. He assured the two Opposition leaders that they would enjoy great success among Central Asian communists if they advocated greater trust in local non-Russian communists, an end to the system of dual party secretaries, and the elimination of regional institutions such as the Central Asian Economic Council. Tumailov claimed that many Turkmen party members agreed with his views privately, but feared for their families if they spoke out.[63]

By joining forces with the Left Opposition, Tumailov had made it impossible for other communists to support him even if they agreed with his criticisms of nationality policy. Moreover, by pointing to the unspoken yet obvious reason for the "figurehead" status of Turkmen officials, Tumailov had gone too far in his criticism. Instead of demanding better implementation of a basically sound policy, he drew attention to the real power dynamic in operation—the progressive centralization of the party that made republican autonomy little more than a fiction. Tumailov violated a strict taboo by saying publicly that the Turkmen, notwithstanding the Soviet rhetoric of self-determination, were not the masters of their own republic.

Tumailov's party colleagues, both Russian and Turkmen, closed ranks to deny his allegations and denounce him at a party plenum in the summer of 1927.[64] He was vilified in the press as a nationalist and a Trotskyist.[65] Tumailov was accused of stirring up trouble between Turkmen and Europeans, putting national interests before class interests, and treating the Russian proletariat as a colonizing force. He was said to be taking orders from the Opposition leaders in Moscow.[66] His criticism of the Central Asian Economic Council was alleged to be an attempt to gain Turkmenistan's independence from the Soviet Union. Similarly, his criticism of the dual secretaries system amounted to a rejection of Moscow's guidance of national communist parties.[67]

At the sixth unified plenum of the Turkmen Central Committee and Central Control Commission in July–August 1927, party members lined

[61] Ibid., ll. 21–22, 46–47.

[62] Ibid., f. 17, op. 30, d. 13, l. 152.

[63] Ibid., f. 62, op. 2, d. 838, l. 5.

[64] Ibid., f. 17, op. 30, d. 13, ll. 67–68, 92–93, 112.

[65] *Pravda vostoka*, October 7, 1927; V. Nodel', "Menshevistskie spletni v Srednei Azii," *Za partiiu*, no. 4 (December 1927), pp. 53–65.

[66] RGASPI, f. 17, op. 30, d. 13, l. 106.

[67] Ibid., f. 62, op. 2, d. 836, l. 13.

up to attack Tumailov. They vehemently denied Tumailov's assertion that
there were "first-class" and "second-class" secretaries of the TsK. In the
words of the Central Committee member O. Nïyazov, "Such a situation
does not exist, never will exist, and never did exist."[68] Sähetmïradov and
Ibragimov, the feuding first secretaries of the Central Committee, united
to deny the existence of a "two-tiered" party. Ibragimov said that it was
"demagoguery" to claim that he was really in charge of the Central Committee.[69] Sähetmïradov argued that Tumailov had insulted the party with
his allegations: "to say that communists are figureheads is an anti-party
statement."[70] Other communists took issue with Tumailov's claim that
the Central Asian Economic Soviet was an impediment to republican autonomy. Common Central Asian organizations were essential, they argued, because of the many regional problems that transcended the boundaries of individual republics.[71] Tumailov's punishment was swift and
severe. A closed meeting of the Secretariat of the Turkmen Central Committee on August 22, 1927, condemned Tumailov's article as "sheer slan-
der of the party." Tumailov lost his job with the Central Control Commission and was expelled from the party.[72]

Despite the protestations of his fellow party members, Tumailov's account of the situation within the party was fundamentally accurate.[73] This
became clear in 1929, when rising ethnic tensions led the KPT Central
Committee to call a secret meeting to discuss the problem. At a joint
plenum of the Ispolburo and the Presidium of the Central Control Commission in June, leading party officials were willing to say things that they
had been reluctant to express in the context of an open party debate about
the Left Opposition.[74] At this meeting, Turkmen officials led by Charï
Vellekov complained bitterly about their lack of real authority and the
failure of Russian colleagues to take them seriously. Vellekov said that he

[68] Ibid., f. 17, op. 30, d. 13, l. 67.

[69] Ibid., l. 112.

[70] Ibid., l. 93.

[71] Ibid., ll. 38, 42, 98, 117–18.

[72] Ibid., f. 62, op. 2, d. 838, ll. 23, 30. Tumailov was eventually readmitted after writing
a letter to the Central Asian Bureau and TsK KPT on December 11, 1927 promising to
submit himself to party discipline.

[73] Private communications between Zelenskii and Aronshtam and officials of the all-
union Central Committee showed clearly that they did view the republican party organization as divided into "two ranks," with the Turkmen first secretary subordinate to the European first secretary, and the head of the organizational department in each province in reality
the superior of the Turkmen party secretary. RGASPI, f. 17, op. 67, d. 382, ll. 149–51; f.
62, op. 2, d. 832, ll. 3–4.

[74] Ibid., f. 62, op. 3, d. 396, l. 207. The stenogram of this meeting is reproduced in Shokhrat Kadyrov, *Rossiisko-turkmenskii istoricheskii slovar'*, vol. 1 (Bergen, Norway: Biblioteka Almanakha "Turkmeny," 2001), pp. 380–423.

saw "a kind of negation and ignoring of local national cadres" in party organizations, so that "local workers occupy their positions only in a formal sense and are kept away from leadership of practical work, while all decision-making is concentrated in the hands of European officials." To make the isolation of Turkmen communists even worse, European communists often failed to provide translators for their non-Russian-speaking colleagues during meetings.[75]

According to Vellekov, disregard for Turkmen communists permeated even the highest levels of the republican Communist Party. As an example, he cited his relationship with his co–first secretary Aronshtam. Officially the two first secretaries were equals, dividing responsibilities for the various spheres of party and government activity among themselves. But in reality, Aronshtam decided everything:

> It turned out that the division of labor that was agreed upon between comrade Aronshtam and myself was never implemented. I get almost no mail at all, officials don't come to see me, and even when there is a line outside Aronshtam's office no one comes to see me. They only stop by my office if somehow they don't manage to get an audience with Aronshtam.[76]

Vellekov complained about being excluded from discussions between the KPT and party leaders in Tashkent and Moscow; Aronshtam, for example, went to Tashkent to meet with Zelenskii without telling Vellekov, and Central Asian Bureau officials visiting Ashgabat often did not bother to meet with the Turkmen party secretary. Vellekov also complained, tellingly, that he never received the secret police reports on conditions in the republic that were supposed to be delivered to him regularly. While acknowledging that Turkmen officials needed guidance because they were not as well trained in Marxist-Leninist theory as their European comrades, Vellekov accused those comrades of "not acting in a way so as to really help us grow."[77]

A number of other high-ranking Turkmen communists present at the meeting echoed Vellekov's complaints. Atabaev agreed that "this neglect is going on everywhere, and we must correct it." Always the conciliator, Atabaev emphasized that European party members' disregard of their Turkmen comrades was not deliberate. Nevertheless, he suggested that the most egregious offenders should be punished in order to set an example. Aitakov said, rather mournfully, that this was the first time in the existence of the Turkmen republic that he could remember such a rift; while there had been conflict in the past based on differences of opinion

---

[75] RGASPI, f. 62, op. 3, d. 396, ll. 207, 210–12.
[76] Ibid., ll. 210–11.
[77] Ibid., ll. 211–13.

or factional infighting, "we have never before had a situation in which the European and Turkmen party leadership fought with each other."[78]

The European communists in attendance claimed to be mystified by their colleagues' distress and eager to clear up the problem. They offered complicated and implausible excuses to explain why they had been forced to consult with the Russian party secretary rather than his Turkmen counterpart. Some Europeans blamed the situation on the Turkmen communists, accusing them of being overly sensitive to slights.[79] In addition to suffering from "excessive touchiness," Turkmen communists had an exaggerated sense of their own capabilities, believing that they "can direct all the work independently, when in fact this is not true."[80] In what was perhaps the most implausible claim of all, given the tight controls over who was allowed to see secret police reports, the head of the OGPU in Turkmenistan blamed the "technical apparatus" for failing to deliver these reports to Vellekov: "Comrades, we sent them," he insisted. "It's not our fault."[81] Left unmentioned by all the party members at the meeting were the structural dimensions of the problem; the lines of power ran from Moscow through its hand-picked emissaries in the republic, for the most part bypassing local officials. This was even truer of the party hierarchy than of state institutions such as the Sovnarkom. Officials lined up outside Aronshtam's office and ignored Vellekov because they knew who was really in charge.

The two-tiered party was Moscow's way of ensuring its control in non-Russian republics despite doubts about whether local communists could always be trusted to carry out Moscow's bidding. High-ranking Turkmen party officials suffered potentially from divided loyalties. They walked a fine line between their desire to please higher-ups in Moscow and their commitment to the autonomy and development of their own republic. While many of the Turkmen communists were russified and distant from the concerns of the Turkmen rural masses, they were far more attuned to Turkmen realities than the communists sent from Moscow, who did not speak the local language and knew little about the society they were charged with transforming. As a result, Turkmen officials, especially those of the "nationalist right," were more likely than Europeans to criticize Soviet policies as inappropriate for Turkmenistan. In theory, such attention to local conditions was welcomed. In practice, any hesitation in implementing Soviet policies could cast doubt on Turkmen officials' loyalty and steadfastness as communists.

[78] Ibid., ll. 214–15.
[79] Ibid., ll. 216–24.
[80] Ibid., ll. 224–26.
[81] Ibid., ll. 218–19

Figure 9. Meeting of the Sovnarkom of the Turkmen republic, 1930. Sovnarkom chair Gaigïsïz Atabaev is presiding at the head of the table, beneath the "no-smoking" sign. (From the collection of the Russian State Archive of Film and Photographic Documents at Krasnogorsk.)

The Turkmen official who most successfully straddled this line was Gaigïsïz Atabaev. Although he frequently questioned the wisdom of Bolshevik measures in Central Asia, Atabaev's loyalty to Moscow was never seriously called into question prior to 1937. Atabaev's outspokenness began in the early 1920s, when he served as chair of the Turkestani republic's Sovnarkom and of a special commission on the Basmachi rebellion. At that time, Atabaev argued that misguided Soviet policies had fanned the Basmachi rebellion then raging throughout much of Central Asia. In a report to the Orgburo's Commission on Military-Political and Party-Organizational Questions in Turkestan on August 11, 1922, Atabaev called the Basmachi movement "the strongest reproach to all of our work in Turkestan, and perhaps even in the entire East." The rebels, he said, were provoked by Bolshevik insensitivity to their way of life: "All of our work in the years of the revolution stood in complete contradiction to the way of life, customs, and traditions that had evolved here among the native population over centuries."[82]

The counterproductive methods used by the Bolsheviks in the fight against the Basmachi rebels, Atabaev argued, reflected Soviet ignorance of the local society and culture. In Khiva, Soviet officials had caused a disaster by allowing themselves to be drawn into local political intrigue and ethnic conflict. Believing the allegations of Uzbeks that Turkmen leaders were planning an anti-Soviet coup, Moscow's representatives in Khiva had arrested and summarily executed a number of Turkmen. This had resulted in a mass panic and the flight of many Khivan Turkmen.[83] In Bukhara, Atabaev argued, crude antireligious propaganda and the harsh tactics of the secret police—which included the practice of shooting entire groups of hostages in response to Basmachi attacks—had caused virtually the entire population to rise up in rebellion against the Soviet regime. In the Turkmen province of the Turkestani republic, too, the secret police had terrorized the population. Atabaev advocated the creation of native militias, led by influential local citizens, to fight the Basmachi. He called on the party to rein in the secret police and ensure that leadership of the anti-Basmachi movement remained in the party's hands.[84]

Atabaev's strong stance on the Basmachi rebellion set the tone for his later interventions in policy debates. After the creation of the Turkmen republic, Atabaev raised eyebrows with his unorthodox positions on eradicating "backwardness" among the population. One example was his stance on *galïng*, the bridewealth traditionally paid by a Turkmen groom to his bride's family at the time of marriage. Abolishing bridewealth was a centerpiece of Bolshevik policy in Central Asia, since it was regarded as the literal buying and selling of a woman. Atabaev dutifully repeated the Soviet formula that bridewealth was "the crudest sort of assault on the personality and freedom of a woman." However, he argued that it would not be feasible to criminalize overnight a practice that was universally observed among the population.[85] Atabaev took a similarly conciliatory position on Muslim confessional schools, arguing in 1925 that the Soviet regime should not ban these schools, but should encourage them to teach scientific subjects and employ Soviet-trained teachers.[86]

Despite his willingness to make concessions to local traditions and mores, Atabaev was generally viewed as a "loyal Turkmen" by Moscow.

[82] Ibid., f. 670, op. 1, d. 11, l. 3.

[83] Ibid., ll. 3–4.

[84] Ibid., f. 62, op. 1, d. 3, p. 15; f. 670, op. 1, d. 11, ll. 4, 15–17. One Soviet source indicates that Atabaev lost his job over his conciliatory approach to the Basmachi in 1922; I have not been able to confirm this. Rosliakov, *Sredazbiuro TsK VKP*, p. 28.

[85] GARF, f. 3316, op. 19, d. 855, ll. 101–2.

[86] RGASPI, f. 62, op. 3, d. 42, l. 24.

This was not true of Nadïrbai Aitakov, chairman of the TsIK and Atabaev's closest associate. Although he was a long-standing communist and had a "correct" class background (unlike Atabaev, he was born into a poor family), Aitakov came to be profoundly mistrusted by Iakov Popok, the KPT first secretary who replaced Aronshtam and served from 1930 to 1937. In a letter sent to his superiors in Moscow on December 20, 1933, Popok compared Aitakov unfavorably with Atabaev and indicated that he had questioned Aitakov's loyalty for some time:

> Working with them over a period of more than three years, I have frequently had to call them to order for their political errors. The TsK of Turkmenistan has repeatedly noted these errors in its decisions, marking down rather strongly Atabaev and especially Aitakov. But I have become firmly convinced that comrade Atabaev will never betray us, that he wants to become and is capable of becoming a Bolshevik and gradually, with the help of the TsK, freeing himself from his petit bourgeois and nationalist burden. I said this to comrade Kaganovich in a private conversation. I remain convinced of this even now. I have a completely different impression of Aitakov. Observing him over a number of years, I have come to the conclusion that it is almost impossible to correct him.[87]

Aitakov's most serious transgressions had occurred during the violent uprising against the collectivization of agriculture that shook many regions of Turkmenistan in 1931. In Feburary 1931, while Popok was absent from Turkmenistan, Aitakov convinced the Central Committee to ship fifty thousand puds of grain to the famine-threatened Dashhowuz region.[88] According to Popok, the grain and the camels carrying it fell almost entirely into the hands of the rebels. Popok blamed Aitakov and implied that he had intentionally betrayed the Soviet regime by allowing supplies to go to the rebels.[89] Aitakov had committed other suspicious acts during the 1931 uprising. As the Central Committee's representative in the nomadic Krasnovodsk and Gazanjïk regions in 1931, he had inexplicably ordered the release of a band of forty armed rebels who had surrendered to Soviet authorities. He had criticized the forces of the Red Army and the secret police for excessive cruelty in the military assault on the rebels. Moreover, before military operations began, Aitakov had pleaded with the Central Committee to try to resolve the conflict by means of peaceful negotiations, offering to serve as the envoy from the Soviet

---

[87] Ibid., op. 2, d. 3086, l. 233.

[88] A pud is a unit of weight measurement equivalent to a little more than thirty-six pounds. See chapter 7 for more on the resistance to collectivization.

[89] RGASPI, f. 62, op. 2, d. 3086, l. 234. The OGPU had noted at the time of the rebellion that its causes were mainly economic and famine-related. Thus, Aitakov had reason to think his action might defuse tensions while avoiding a mass slaughter.

side.[90] These acts, which could be read as trying to prevent the mass starvation and slaughter of Turkmen nomads, were sufficient to cast doubt on Aitakov's loyalty to the regime.

Popok's comments about Atabaev and Aitakov reveal a highly condescending attitude toward both of these men. Atabaev, after fourteen years of membership in the Communist Party, was described as still trying to "become a Bolshevik." Yet Atabaev and Aitakov had forged rather different relationships with the party leadership in Moscow. For all his outspokenness, Atabaev had somehow managed to persuade his superiors that he would always put the interests of the party first. Aitakov, by his unauthorized actions during the 1931 rebellion, had led Soviet authorities to wonder where his true loyalties lay.

TURKMEN COMMUNISTS AND "COUNTERREVOLUTIONARY NATIONALISM"

In May 1932, the OGPU claimed to have uncovered a "bourgeois nationalist" organization fighting for the Turkmen republic's independence from Soviet rule. The organization, Türkmen Azadlïgï (Turkmen Independence), was allegedly plotting an uprising against the Soviet government with the aid of Turkmen emigrants in Persia.[91] In May 1933, some three dozen officials were convicted of membership in Türkmen Azadlïgï and sentenced to five years imprisonment. Most of the accused were officials working for cultural and educational institutions such as the press, the education commissariat, and the Institute for Turkmen Culture. They included K. A. Böriev, a former commissar of education who later became head of the Turkmen state publishing house; Bäshim Perengliev, another former education commissar; Begjan Nazarov, head of the indigenization commission and deputy chair of the TsIK; the poets K. Burunov and O. Vepaev; A. Gulmuhammedov, the former deputy editor of the newspaper *Türkmenistan*; and Berdi Kerbabaev, the writer and editor of *Tokmak*. (Kerbabaev was later released, but Gulmuhammedov was reportedly shot while attempting to flee to Iran.) The linguist Muhammet Geldiev was also described as a leading figure in the organization, although he had died in 1931.[92] Other accused conspirators included Ak-Murad Orazov, commissar of trade and later permanent representative of the Turkmen republic

[90] RGASPI, f. 62, op. 2, d. 3086, ll. 234–35.
[91] Ibid., d. 3084, l. 127; d. 3086, l. 236; Palvanova, *Tragicheskie 30-e*, p. 63.
[92] T. Tächmïradov, *Muhammet Geldieving ömri we döredidzhiligi*, pp. 10, 30. Geldiev's official obituary says that he died of a stomach ulcer. *Turkmenovedenie*, no. 1–2 (January-February 1931): 36; on Gulmuhammedov, see *Türkmen arhivi*, no. 1 (1993): 52.

in Moscow, and Seidmïrad Övezbaev, a member of the presidium of Gos-plan.[93] The purge of 1933 was not unique to Turkmenistan; similar campaigns of persecution against cultural and educational officials took place in other republics, including Russia, at approximately the same time.[94]

While it was long unclear whether there was any truth to the allegations of a counterrevolutionary plot, it is now virtually certain that Türkmen Azadlïgï was an invention of the secret police.[95] Apart from their involvement in culture and education, it is not clear exactly how individuals were identified as members of the fictitious counterrevolutionary organization. Unlike the terror of the later 1930s, which struck Turkmen and Russians alike within the Turkmen republic, this purge affected mainly Turkmen. Yet those arrested were from a variety of regional and tribal backgrounds: Nazarov was from Khiva; Gulmuhammedov was from Bukhara; Geldiev was a Yomut; Övezbaev was a Teke. Some, like Nazarov, Böriev, and Orazov, were party members; others were not. There was clearly a class factor in their selection, as some of them came from prominent prerevolutionary families. However, this in itself does not explain why they were chosen, since other Turkmen officials with similar backgrounds were not arrested.[96]

Perhaps the most obvious characteristic shared by all the "conspirators" was their strong belief in Turkmen national autonomy. They were the ones who most vehemently insisted on full implementation of nativization and maintained that the Turkmen republic should exist primarily for the benefit of the Turkmen. They insisted that local conditions be taken into account in the formulation of policy. They demanded, in short, that the regime make good on the promises of nationality policy. Many of the accused conspirators were the very people who had been identified as "nationalists" by the OGPU in 1920s. They included Perengliev, who blamed Russian colonialism for holding back Turkmen development and education; Böriev, who had proposed harsh punishment for Russians who failed to learn Turkmen; Nazarov, who incessantly complained about the inade-

[93] RGASPI, f. 62, op. 3, d. 3086, l. 12

[94] See RGASPI, f. 62, op. 2, d. 2794, l. 29; F. D. Ashnin and B. M. Alpatov, *Delo Slavistov: 30-e gody* (Moscow: Nasledie, 1994); Simon, *Nationalism*, pp. 80–88.

[95] Gerhard Simon considered it quite plausible that such counterrevolutionary organizations existed in the national republics, given the political climate of the time. However, NKVD agents who had worked in Turkmenistan in the 1920s and 1930s admitted in 1956 to the commission charged with rehabilitating Stalin's victims that they had never seen any actual evidence of the existence of Türkmen Azadlïgï. Simon, *Nationalism*, p. 80; I. G. Ivanchenko, "Turkmen Azatlygy—Tragicheskii final mistifikatsii," *Izvestiia Akademii Nauk TSSR, seriia gumanitarnykh nauk*, no 2 (1990): 29–30. Ivanchenko examined files on Turkmenistan in the central KGB archive in Moscow around 1990. These materials are not currently open to researchers.

[96] RGASPI, f. 62, op. 2, d. 3086, ll. 12–13.

quate implementation of indigenization; and Kerbabaev and Gulmu-hammedov, who edited the Turkmen-language periodicals that contained "anti-Russian" commentaries and articles in the late 1920s. While it was not Moscow's official policy to consider such people "counterrevolution-ary nationalists," negative attitudes toward Russians seem to have played a role on the local level in determining who would be targeted in the purge.

The accusations of the early 1930s did not topple any of the leading party figures in Turkmenistan, but they came dangerously close.[97] Popok told his superiors in Moscow that Atabaev and Aitakov were friends or relatives of many of the top conspirators, and that the two Turkmen com-munists had sought to hinder the investigation.[98] In late 1930 or early 1931, Popok claimed, the counterrevolutionary organization sent two of its members—the poet Vepaev and the linguist Geldiev—to Persia to re-quest assistance from Turkmen emigrants in organizing an anti-Soviet up-rising. According to Popok, both were close relatives of Aitakov. Vepaev was arrested, and after fifteen months in detention, began to name names. He claimed (no doubt after some prodding by the secret police) that the nationalist organization Türkmen Azadlïğï had been formed at the time of the national delimitation of Central Asia. He said that Aitakov had been recruited early on by his cousin Böriev, who was one of the organiza-tion's leaders. Vepaev claimed that he never attempted to recruit Atabaev, the Turkmen official who was most loyal to the party, since he feared the latter would denounce him to the police.[99]

The fact that a number of such "counterrevolutionary organizations" sprang up in various republics at around the same time indicates that they were probably invented in Moscow, not by a rogue local branch of the secret police. In light of this, it is not clear how we should understand Popok's statements about Atabaev and Aitakov. Did Popok believe what he was writing to Moscow about the two Turkmen leaders? Was he duped by the secret police, or was he simply writing what he thought the Politburo wanted to hear? Were people fingered as members of the fictitious Türkmen Azadlïğï simply because they were perceived as being insufficiently loyal to the Soviet state? It is impossible to know with the available evidence. Despite the serious accusations, Aitakov was not arrested at this time.

During the terror of 1937–38, the Commissariat for Internal Affairs (NKVD), successor to the OGPU, revived the fictitious organization Türk-men Azadlïğï. Turkmen and European communists alike fell victim to the terror, but the accusations they faced varied according to their nationality; Turkmen communists were most often accused of counterrevolutionary

[97] Ibid., d. 3084, l. 127; d. 3086, l. 236; Palvanova, *Tragicheskie 30-e*, p. 63.
[98] RGASPI, f. 62, op. 2, d. 3086, l. 233.
[99] Ibid., ll. 235–36.

nationalism, while Europeans were generally accused of being Trotskyists or foreign spies. The NKVD represented Türkmen Azadlïgï as a hierarchical organization with branches throughout the republic. Its goal was allegedly to overthrow Soviet rule in Turkmenistan with the aid of capitalist governments.[100] In July 1937, eight officials of the all-union Central Committee arrived to carry out investigations in the Turkmen republic under the leadership of Ia. A. Chubin. Chubin, who reported directly to Moscow, had the power to question and arrest even the highest party officials in the republic.[101] The Turkmen republic's commissar of internal affairs, Iu. L. Zverev, was removed for his alleged lack of vigilance against spies and counterrevolutionaries. He was replaced by O. Ia. Nodev in August 1937. (Zverev was arrested and later shot.)[102]

The NKVD claimed that Türkmen Azadlïgï was controlled by a group of high-ranking Turkmen party officials that included Atabaev, Aitakov, Sähetmïradov, Vellekov, Annamuhammedov, and Gurban Sähedov. All of them were arrested in 1937, and they all confessed (probably under torture) to membership in the counterrevolutionary organization.[103] On July 2, 1937, Atabaev and Aitakov traveled to Moscow for a session of the all-union TsIK. Atabaev was arrested in Moscow; Aitakov was picked up shortly after his return to Ashgabat. Aitakov and Sähedov were condemned as "enemies of the people" by the executive bureau of the KPT Central Committee on July 21, 1937. On August 3, the Bureau expelled Atabaev from the party, the TsK, and the Sovnarkom.[104]

Those arrested as "enemies of the people" in Turkmenistan during the Terror included the deputy chair of the Central Executive Committee; the heads of the KPT Central Committee departments of agriculture, agitprop, press, and trade; the first secretaries of the Dashhowuz and Kerki provincial party committees and of the Young Communist League; the people's commissars of agriculture, state farms, social welfare, education, trade, industry, finance, justice, and internal affairs; and the republican prosecutor. Employees of publishing and cultural institutions were also hard hit. As in other republics, the terror ensnared relatives of the accused. Aitakov's brother Begjan was expelled from the party for concealing the counterrevolutionary activities of his brother and for holding a ceremony to mourn his brother's arrest.[105] He and another brother, Tajimïrad, were subsequently executed.[106] The wives of Aitakov, Halmïrad Sähetmïradov, and Gurban

---

[100] Ivanchenko, "Turkmen Azatlygy," p. 29.
[101] Palvanova, *Tragicheskie 30-e*, pp. 36–37.
[102] Ivanchenko, "Turkmen Azatlygy," pp. 31–32.
[103] Ibid., pp. 31–33.
[104] RGASPI, f. 17, op. 30, d. 121, l. 2; Palvanova, *Tragicheskie 30-e*, pp. 71–73.
[105] RGASPI, f. 17, op. 30, d. 121, l. 136.
[106] Palvanova, *Tragicheskie 30-e*, pp. 73–76, 96–99.

Sähedov were arrested, along with other female relatives of leading officials.[107] A number of European party officials who currently worked or had
previously worked in the Turkmen republic were also arrested and shot,
including Paskutskii, Popok, Aronshtam, and Mezhlauk.[108] At the February 1938 party plenum, only twenty-two members and thirteen candidates
remained out of the ninety-three members and thirty-five candidates who
had been elected at the sixth KPT congress in January 1934.[109]

The purges of the 1930s eliminated most of the Turkmen communists
who had been in power since 1924 and who had ideas of their own about
nationhood and socialism in Turkmenistan. The growth of Turkmen-Euro-
pean conflict within the upper levels of the party in the late 1920s and early
1930s was a reflection of the rising expectations and self-confidence of this
group of Turkmen. Before the creation of the Turkmen republic, the small
number of Turkmen party members relied on European communists to
protect them from the "oppression" of other Central Asian ethnic groups.
After the delimitation, however, Turkmen officials found themselves in direct competition for jobs and political power with Europeans. The sense
of being treated as second-class citizens within their own republic fueled
Turkmen resentment and strengthened their identification as Turkmen. The
division between Turkmen and European communists was sharpened by
the campaign against "counterrevolutionary nationalists" within the republic in 1932–33, which targeted only Turkmen communists. Yet the distinction between who was trusted and who was not became moot in 1937,
when everyone became a suspect. Ironically, the KPT became a unified,
internationalist party only in destruction, as Stalin's terror brought imprisonment and death to communists of all nationalities.

---

[107] Jamilia Poltaeva, "Doroga byla dolgoi," *Komsomolets Turkmenistana*, April 28,
1990, p. 8. I am grateful to Eduard and Zelili Aitakov, the twin sons of N. Aitakov, for
sharing this information about their mother.

[108] Khudaiberdyev, *Obrazovanie*, p. 193; Palvanova, *Tragicheskie 30-e*, pp. 53–54.

[109] Palvanova, *Tragicheskie 30-e*, p. 106. Mass repressions also extended far beyond the
party leadership. Nodev, the new commissar of internal affairs, launched "mass operations"
in the countryside, sending groups of NKVD investigators to outlying regions with lists of
former kulaks, merchants, and other class aliens. They carried specific orders as to whether a
given individual should be shot or sent to labor camp. Using torture and fabricated investiga-
tory materials, the NKVD got confessions from many of its victims. A new round of "operations" in early 1938 targeted for arrest all males of Iranian and Armenian nationality, regardless of citizenship, all migrants from other countries, all Turkmen "reemigrants" (Soviet
Turkmen who had emigrated and later returned) who had relatives across the border, all Ba-
hais, and all Iranian citizens. TsA KGB SSSR. f. 2, d. No. P. 23.693, l. 276, cited in Ivanchenko,
"Turkmen Azatlygy," pp. 32–34. Palvanova estimates the number of the "repressed" in the
TSSR at about twenty thousand. *Tragicheskie 30-e*, p. 106. On the mass terror in Turkmenistan, see also Oleg Khlevniuk, "Les mècanismes de la 'grande terreur' des années 1937–1938
au Turkménistan," *Cahiers du Monde Russe* 39, no. 1–2 (January–June 1998): 197–208.

Chapter Five

DUELING DIALECTS

THE CREATION OF A TURKMEN LANGUAGE

IN 1933, the Turkmen-language newspaper *Shuralar Türkmenistan*
published a poem entitled "Fisherman" by the Yomut poet M. Saralï.
In response to these seemingly innocuous verses, the Teke writer Berdi
Soltannïyazov fired off a critical article, accusing Saralï of fostering lin-
guistic anarchy by using "made-up words" that were unknown in the
Turkmen language. Saralï responded with an angry letter of his own, in-
sisting that his poem employed seafaring terms that were common to the
Caspian coastal regions of Turkmenistan. A poet, he added sanctimo-
niously, had a duty to use indigenous terminology when writing about
daily life; by refusing to acknowledge the validity of these Yomut words,
Soltannïyazov was trying to "promote the hegemony of the Teke dialect."
In the end, the editors of *Shuralar Türkmenistan* apologized for having
published Soltannïyazov's article, noting that the Teke writer was clearly
seeking to "put tribalism on the agenda."[1]

Heated disputes over arcane questions of linguistic usage were common
in Turkmenistan in the 1920s and 1930s, showing the tremendous importance of language as a symbolic arena for working out the meaning of
Turkmen nationhood. The Turkmen passion for linguistic issues was a bit
surprising, given that genealogy rather than language was the primary
basis of Turkmen identity; traditionally, people who spoke Turkmen dialects were not considered Turkmen unless they also claimed Oguz ancestry.
Yet language was important to the Turkmen in another sense. In Turkmen
communities, where historical traditions and legends were passed down
orally through songs and poetry, eloquence had long been a source of
prestige and honor. The idea that language was a critical aspect of national
identity was first introduced by Russian colonizers in the late–nineteenth
century—a time when linguistic nationalism was relatively new even to
Russia.[2] The Bolsheviks reinforced this idea, making the promotion of indigenous languages a cornerstone of their nationality policy.

[1] B. Soltannïyazov, "Saralï M. goshularï barada bir iki agïz söz," *Shuralar Türkmenistan*,
March 21, 1933; M. Saralï, "Shuralar Türkmenistanïng redaktorïna hat," *Shuralar Türkmenistan*, July 10, 1933.

[2] Even in Europe, linguistic criteria for defining nationality became dominant only in the
late-nineteenth century. Hobsbawm, *Nations and Nationalism since 1780*, pp. 101–20.

In the 1920s, Turkmen intellectuals adopted the Soviet emphasis on language as a key component of nationhood. Just as they had welcomed the idea that the Turkmen deserved a territorial republic of their own, Turkmen elites embraced the notion of a Turkmen "national language." Yet this shift did not imply an abandonment of genealogical considerations. On the contrary, language and genealogy became inextricably linked in Turkmen debates of the 1920s, as the need to create a standardized literary language inevitably raised the question of which tribe's dialect would form the basis for this language. One proposition on which virtually all Turkmen agreed was that the Turkmen language should be used as widely as possible in schools, government offices, and the press. The overwhelming support for linguistic indigenization helped to solidify a sense of shared Turkmen interests, particularly in the face of Russian intransigence. More contentious among Turkmen was the precise shape of the Turkmen literary language to be created. In debates over this question in the 1920s and 1930s, Turkmen elites symbolically worked through their own internal divisions and their complex attitudes toward non-Turkmen. When Turkmen linguists discussed the need to merge the various tribal dialects into a single, "supratribal" Turkmen language, they were indirectly addressing the sensitive issue of regional and tribal divisions within the republic. Similarly, debates about the incorporation of foreign loan words into the Turkmen language addressed in an oblique way the Turkmen nation's proper place in the world. What was, or should be, its relationship to other Turkic peoples, the Islamic world, Russia, and Europe?

The changing relationship of Turkmen elites to ethnic "others" in the linguistic sphere paralleled similar shifts in the political arena. Just as Turkmen viewed other Central Asians as their primary rivals at the republic's inception, they initially saw other Turkic languages as posing the greatest threat to Turkmen linguistic distinctiveness. In order to differentiate themselves as a nation, Turkmen elites sought to create impermeable linguistic boundaries against other forms of spoken Turkic; in similar fashion, they had argued for formal territorial boundaries that would separate them from other Central Asians. At first, Turkmen elites relied on Moscow as an ally in their quest for national autonomy. As time went on, however, they found that the greatest threats to their linguistic and political autonomy came from Europeans. Within the Soviet elite, as we have seen, conflict between Turkmen and Europeans arose in the late 1920s as indigenization faltered and the increasing centralization of the party underscored the second-class status of Turkmen communists. Similarly, the institutions of Soviet language policy became increasingly centralized in the early 1930s, even as purges of non-Russian intellectuals deprived Turkmenistan of its most experienced linguists. By the late 1930s, Turkmen had been relegated to a supporting role in discussions about the future of their language.

The Need for a "National Language"

The Bolsheviks believed that language was an essential attribute of nation-hood. Language, moreover, was the cornerstone of many aspects of Soviet policy in non-Russian areas. The spread of mass secular education, the recruitment of native elites, the administration of local government, and the publication of newspapers and textbooks all depended on the exis-tence of standardized vernacular languages. Each national territory re-quired its own language, uniform and universally understandable to its own citizens but distinct from that of neighboring republics. Where such languages did not exist, they would have to be created.[3]

Written vernacular languages are always in some sense artificial, the product of "attempts to devise a standardized idiom out of a multiplicity of actually spoken idioms."[4] In Central Asia, however, the process of cre-ating national languages faced special problems. Before the Russian Revo-lution, literate Central Asians generally did not write in their vernacular tongues; rather, they used Persian, Arabic, or the Eastern Turkic literary language known as Chaghatai.[5] Many sedentary and urban Central Asians were bi- or trilingual, and the idea that each territory and popula-tion group should have its own language was unfamiliar. Nor was it al-ways easy to determine which dialects should be included in a republic's "national language." Central Asia was dotted by a multitude of locally spoken Turkic dialects with subtle variations in pronunciation, vocabu-lary, and grammar, each shading into the next in a way that confounded any attempt to draw national borders between them.[6] In some cases, the creation of a "national language" meant arbitrarily grouping together related dialects and calling them by a single name.[7]

[3] On Soviet policies toward non-Russian languages, see Michael Kirkwood, ed., *Lan-guage Planning in the Soviet Union* (London: Macmillan, 1989); Isabelle T. Kreindler, ed., *Sociolinguistic Perspectives on Soviet National Languages* (New York: Mouton, 1985); Wil-liam Fierman, *Language Planning and National Development: The Uzbek Experience* (Ber-lin and New York: Mouton de Gruyter, 1991); Michael G. Smith, *Language and Power in the Creation of the USSR, 1917–1953* (Berlin and New York: Mouton de Gruyter, 1998). On language and nation-making more generally, see Joshua Fishman, Charles A. Ferguson and Jyotirindra Das Gupta, eds., *Language Problems of Developing Nations* (New York: John Wiley and Sons, 1968).

[4] Hobsbawm, *Nations and Nationalism since 1780*, p. 54.

[5] Khalid, *Politics of Muslim Cultural Reform*, p. 188.

[6] Schoeberlein-Engel, "Identity in Central Asia," pp. 19–23; Roy, *The New Central Asia*, pp. 3–5; Khalid, *Politics of Muslim Cultural Reform*, pp. 187–90. See also Edward A. All-worth, *The Modern Uzbeks: From the Fourteenth Century to the Present, A Cultural His-tory* (Stanford, CA: Hoover Institution Press, 1990), pp. 176–79.

[7] Shirin Akiner, "Uzbekistan: Republic of Many Tongues," in Kirkwood, *Language Plan-ning in the Soviet Union*, p. 100; Fierman, *Language Planning and National Development*, pp. 69–71.

In contrast to the lack of linguistic clarity in the settled regions of Uzbekistan and Tajikistan, it was relatively easy to determine which dialects should be included in the Turkmen "national language." By definition, the Turkmen language was whatever was spoken by those who identified themselves genealogically as Turkmen. The dialects spoken by Turkmen tribes, moreover, were for the most part distinct from those of nearby non-Turkmen. They belonged to the southwestern branch of the Turkic language family, and were therefore more closely related to Azerbaijani and Anatolian Turkish than to the Turkic dialects of the Turkmens' closest Central Asian neighbors.[8]

Soviet Russian writers sometimes claimed that the Turkmen, like many other "backward" peoples of the Soviet Union, lacked a written language before the Russian Revolution.[9] This assertion, which served to underscore the benefits of Soviet rule in non-Russian regions, obscured a more complex reality. In the centuries before the Russian conquest, the tiny number of literate Turkmen participated in the broader Chaghatai-based literary culture of Central Asia.[10] At the same time, some of these Turkmen began to write in a form of literary Western Turkic that was closer to their native vernacular. Prerevolutionary Turkmen poets, the most famous of whom was the eighteenth-century bard Magtïmgulï, fused Turkmen vernacular speech with Western Turkic literary forms and Arabic and Persian loan words in their poetry.[11] Thus, the basis for a written language rooted in the Turkmen vernacular existed before the arrival of the Bolsheviks.

What is clear is that there was no standard way of writing Turkmen prior to the Soviet era. Nor was there any need for one under conditions of mass illiteracy. Before the Russian conquest, manuscripts were produced by hand in small quantities, and individual authors and copyists wrote as they saw fit. There were not only many spoken dialects, but a variety of written forms based on those spoken dialects.[12] It was only under Russian colonialism that the Turkmen language encountered the printing press. The first Turkmen-language newspaper, a Russian government-issued periodical called "The Transcaspian native's newspaper,"

---

[8] Larry Clark, *Turkmen Reference Grammar* (Wiesbaden: Harrassowitz Verlag, 1998), pp. 12–21.

[9] A. M. Annanurov, *Razvitie turkmenskogo iazyka za sovetskii period* (Ashgabat: Ylym, 1972), p. 5.

[10] Clark, *Turkmen Reference Grammar*, p. 12.

[11] A. P. Potseluevskii, *Dialekty turkmenskogo iazyka* (Ashgabat: Turkmengosizdat, 1936), pp. 28–29; Annanurov, *Razvitie turkmenskogo iazyka*, pp. 4–5; Feldman, "Interpreting the Poetry of Mäkhtumquli," p. 169.

[12] Tagangeldi Tächmïradov, "Razvitie i Normalizatsiia Turkmenskogo literaturnogo iazyka v Sovetskuiu epokhu" (avtoreferat dissertatsii, Ashgabat, 1974), p. 11.

was published from 1914 to 1917.[13] Written in Turkmen and Farsi using the Arabic script, the newspaper was edited by Russian officials and published government decrees and military news, along with materials on Turkmen literature, history, and ethnography. The first Turkmen-language books were published in the late-imperial period as well.[14]

After the Bolshevik revolution, the new regime's determination to promote mass literacy and native-language education made it essential to standardize and codify written Turkmen. In the early 1920s, new commissions under the auspices of the all-union commissariats of education and nationalities were charged with studying, developing, and standardizing the non-Russian languages of the Soviet periphery.[15] In April 1922, the Turkmen Academic Commission was formed in Tashkent under the leadership of the Yomut scholar Muhammet Geldiev. The commission was charged with reforming the Turkmen Arabic script, producing the first textbooks for Turkmen-language schools, facilitating the publication of Turkmen-language newspapers and journals, organizing literacy courses, and assisting in the development of Turkmen literature.[16] In the early 1920s, the number of Turkmen-language publications began to grow. In 1920, the daily newspaper *Türkmenistan* was established in Ashgabat. A Turkmen-language journal devoted to questions of language and culture, *Türkmen ili* (the Turkmen people), began to come out in 1922. A satirical magazine, *Tokmak* (the mallet), was established in 1925. A Turkmen grammar text in the Turkmen language, written by Geldiev and the Tatar linguist G. Alparov, was published in 1924.[17]

With the formation of the Central Asian national republics in 1924–25, the pace of language construction accelerated. A newly formed Turkmen state publishing house (Turkmengosizdat) began to publish Turkmen-language books, newspapers, and journals, as well as prerevolutionary poetry

[13] A. Iazberdyev, *Izdatel'skoe delo v dorevoliutsionnom Turkmenistane* (Ashgabat: Ylym, 1993), pp. 30–33. The first printing press was introduced in Central Asia in 1868 by the tsarist colonial regime; only handwritten manuscripts had been produced locally prior to that. Akiner, "Uzbekistan: Republic of Many Tongues," p. 101; Khalid, *Politics of Muslim Cultural Reform*, pp. 117–18.

[14] A. Nazarov, "Is istorii turkmenskogo literaturovedeniia," *Izvestiia Akademii Nauk TSSR, seriia gumanitarnykh nauk*, no. 3 (1991): 46–51; Iazberdyev, *Izdatel'skoe delo*, pp. 32–33.

[15] Smith, *The Bolsheviks and the National Question*, p. 163; see also Simon Crisp, "Soviet Language Planning since 1917–1953," in Kirkwood, *Language Planning in the Soviet Union*, p. 25.

[16] K. Böriev, "Türkmen dili," *Türkmen medenieti*, no. 3–4 (July–August 1931): 40. On Geldiev, see Victoria Clement, "The Politics of Script Reform in Soviet Turkmenistan: Alphabet and National Identity Formation" (M.A. thesis, Ohio State University, 1999), pp. 47–51.

[17] Tächmïradov, "Razvitie," p. 11.

and folklore.[18] Within the republic, several new institutions had responsibility for language reform. The Turkmen Central Committee for the New Turkic Alphabet (TsKNTA), which was under the supervision of the republican Central Executive Committee (TsIK), was charged with the implementation of alphabet reform in the 1920s and 1930s.[19] Research on the Turkmen language was initially centered in the national culture section of the State Academic Council (GUS) of the Turkmen Commissariat of Education. Beginning in 1928, this responsibility shifted to the language and literature department of the Institute of Turkmen Culture (Turkmen-kul't), which published frequent articles on language and culture in its two journals: the Russian-language *Turkmenovedenie* (Turkmenology) and the Turkmen-language *Türkmen medenieti* (Turkmen culture).

In the republic's early years, native intellectuals led the movement to create a unified and standardized Turkmen language. They used Soviet-sponsored institutions—research institutes, newspapers, and publishing houses—as venues for conducting intense discussions on the future of the Turkmen language. The one point on which they agreed overwhelmingly was that there was—and should be—a distinct Turkmen literary language. There were good reasons for the Turkmen embrace of this idea. Some educated Turkmen had been exposed to Western notions about the relationship between language and group identity through their contact with Russians during the colonial period. Some were also familiar with the ideas of Ottoman Turkic nationalists and the jadid reformers of the Russian empire, who began to promote notions of linguistic identity in the early twentieth century. However, Turkic nationalists in the Ottoman and Russian Empires generally did not favor the creation of written languages based on locally spoken vernaculars; instead, they called for a single Turkic written language to facilitate communication among the Turkic peoples. Central Asian jadids, while rejecting the idea of a pan-Turkic language, favored the creation of a single pan-Turkestani language for all Central Asians.[20] Turkmen elites, who had a sense of distinct identity based on their genealogical traditions, viewed all such proposals as outright linguistic imperialism. They welcomed the idea that Turkmen should be developed as a distinct written vernacular and joined Soviet propagandists in condemning those who argued for a pan-Turkic or pan-Turkestani language. Just as many Turkmen resisted the idea of a Turkestani territorial republic in which they would be an underprivileged minority, they rejected the notion of an official Turkestani language that

[18] Ibid.
[19] Potseluevskii, *Dialekty*, p. 17; D. Chersheev, *Kul'turnaia revoliutsiia v Turkmenistane*, p. 188.
[20] Khalid, *Politics of Muslim Cultural Reform*, pp. 211–14.

would relegate Turkmen to the status of a spoken dialect. The xenophobic sentiments expressed against "brother Turks" in the 1920s indicate that neither a pan-Turkic nor a pan-Turkestani identity figured prominently in the thinking of most Turkmen intellectuals.

In December 1925, a blistering attack by an outsider on the Turkmen language galvanized the small community of Turkmen intellectuals in defense of their mother tongue. The author, Ferid Effendizade, was an instructor at the Ashgabat pedagogical academy and the Communist Party school. (His surname indicates that he was one of the many Azerbaijani teachers then working in Ashgabat.)[21] In an article published in the newspaper *Türkmenistan*, Effendizade argued that Turkmen was nothing but a subsidiary dialect of Turkish, destined to become extinct in the natural order of things. It would be a waste of time and effort to try to turn this primitive and provincial dialect into a language suited for the modern world. As he put it, "If you're constructing a house, you won't get good building material out of straw." The Turkmen, as "Turkic sons," would do better to abandon their own "weak and corrupted" language, which was "perishing in the burning desert," and adopt one that was already fully developed. This would represent "cultural progress" and allow the Turkmen people to develop more rapidly. Ideally, the Turkmen should switch to a proper language such as Ottoman Turkish. To do otherwise would be "stupid chauvinism" and a "crime." Effendizade pointed to the example of the Azerbaijanis, who, he said, had eliminated some of the "crude-sounding words" in their own language and replaced them with more "pleasant and elegant-sounding" terms drawn from Turkish.[22]

Effendizade's comments could not have been more carefully calculated to unleash a passionate defense of the uniqueness of the Turkmen language. The linguist Muhammet Geldiev wrote that Effendizade's call on the Turkmen to give up their language was about as likely to be effective as a group of Christian priests telling Muslim faithful: "You, Muslims! Don't stick with your Muslim religion. One day Jesus Christ is going to descend from the heavens and you'll be forced to abandon your religion. You might as well just abandon it now."[23] The poet and deputy editor of *Türkmenistan*, Abdïlhekim Gulmuhammedov, also spoke out against Effendizade's "mistaken" ideas. There was absolutely no reason, he wrote, for Turkmen to abandon their own language and adopt Ottoman Turkish or Azerbaijani. In fact, most Turks and Azerbaijanis would regret

---

[21] M. Söyegov, "O iazykovoi politike v Turkmenistane v 20-e gody (po rabotam K. Sakhatova)," *Izvestiia Akademii Nauk TSSR, seriia obshchestvennykh nauk*, no. 2 (1987), p. 52.

[22] F. Effendizade, "Shivechie," *Türkmenistan*, December 30–31, 1925. See also K. Sakhatov, "O turkmenskom iazyke i ego 'druziakh,' " *Za partiiu* no. 1 (January 1928): 67–69.

[23] M. Geldiev, " 'Shivechie' adïnda gaitargï baryan yoldasha gaitargï," *Türkmenistan*, January 4, 1926, p. 2.

the disappearance of the Turkmen language, since they knew that Turkmen was "their own former mother tongue."[24] (Gulmuhammedov was expressing the view of many Turkmen that their language represented Turkish in its original, pristine form, before it had been sullied by Persian, Arabic, and European influences.) In their attacks on Effendizade, the insistence of Turkmen intellectuals on maintaining the distinctiveness of the Turkmen language corresponded perfectly to the goals of Moscow's nationality policy. A similar criticism of Effendizade was published for a Russian-speaking audience in the Central Asian party journal *Za partiiu*, accusing him of "pan-Turkism" and "petit-bourgeois nationalism."[25]

Turkmen intellectuals were hostile not just toward foreigners who rejected the Turkmen language altogether, but also toward those who meddled in its development. Initially, the outsiders who aroused the greatest concern were not Russians but speakers of other Turkic languages. Because the number of literate Turkmen was so small, numerous individuals from "more advanced" Turkic republics such as Azerbaijan and Tatarstan were brought in to help staff Turkmenistan's cultural and educational institutions in the 1920s.[26] Yet Turkmen intellectuals showed little gratitude toward these visiting "Turkic brothers"; instead, they expressed concern about the negative influence of outsiders on the embryonic Turkmen national culture. Azerbaijanis and Tatars aroused the ire of Turkmen intellectuals when they expressed views on Turkmen language reform or—worse yet—attempted to use the Turkmen language in their own work. These outsiders did not know the Turkmen language sufficiently well to participate in its development, Turkmen intellectuals maintained; moreover, they were heedlessly "polluting" it with words from their own languages.[27] Gulmuhammedov wrote in early 1926 that outsiders were "destroying" the Turkmen language. Individuals who scarcely knew Turkmen at all were translating literary and scientific works and government decrees into Turkmen, introducing numerous errors in the process.[28] Geldiev equated the fate of the Turkmen with the fate of their language: "For many years, we Turkmen have been held in captivity, and our language has also been a prisoner." Now, he said, just when the Turkmen had a chance to build their own language and literature with their own

[24] A. Gulmuhammedov, "Shive chekishmesi yekebar diling bozulmasï meselesi?" *Türkmenistan*, January 19, 1926, pp. 2–3.

[25] Sakhatov, "O turkmenskom iazyke," pp. 68, 70. Some Uzbeks also favored the creation of a literary language based on their own Turkic dialect and opposed plans for a single Turkic language. Fierman, *Language Planning and National Development*, pp. 71–74.

[26] Tächmïradov, *Razvitie*, p. 13; Chersheev, *Kul'turnaia revoliutsiia*, p. 46.

[27] Tächmïradov, *Razvitie*, p. 10; *Tokmak*, no. 21 (1925): 3.

[28] Gulmuhammedov, "Shive chekishmesi"; see also K. Böriev, "Türkmen dili," p. 40.

hands, "comrades who don't know two words of Turkmen are already cutting the cloth for its shroud."[29]

Resentment against the interference of their Turkic brethren did not mean that Turkmen were unconcerned about the dangers of Russian language use within the republic. Some Turkmen objected to the decree of the first all-Turkmen Congress of Soviets in February 1925, which had declared Russian and Turkmen to be the two official languages of the republic. They argued that Turkmen should be the "sole state language" of the Turkmen republic.[30] There were also numerous complaints in the 1920s about the tendency of government institutions to use Russian instead of Turkmen in their work. However, while the use of Russian within the republic may have constituted an offense to Turkmen pride, the use of Azerbaijani and Tatar posed a different kind of threat. Few Russians spoke Turkmen or were interested in learning it. Individuals from neighboring Turkic republics, on the other hand, could easily learn to speak and understand Turkmen (if imperfectly) and participate in debates about its future. Moreover, because of the close relationship of other Turkic languages to Turkmen, their use threatened to undermine the integrity and very existence of Turkmen as a separate language.

These concerns were evident in a 1926 debate over the language of secondary school instruction within the Turkmen republic. Because of the extreme shortage of Turkmen-speaking teachers and Turkmen-language textbooks, some of the republic's educational officials considered temporarily introducing Russian or Azerbaijani as the language of instruction in secondary and vocational schools. A relative abundance of instructional materials existed in Russian and Azerbaijani, and there were numerous teachers of both nationalities present in the republic. Geldiev, whose primary concerns were linguistic rather than pedagogical, was categorically opposed to using anything but Turkmen in the schools.[31] More pragmatically inclined officials favored the use of Azerbaijani because it was closely related to Turkmen and therefore easy for Turkmen students to learn. Yet K. Böriev, the head of the Institute of Turkmen Culture who was soon to become Commissar of Education, opposed Azerbaijani for precisely the same reason. He maintained that making Russian the language of instruction would pose less of a threat to the integrity of the Turkmen language. "The Russian language, since it is not related to Turkmen, will not hinder

---

[29] M. Geldiev, "Türkmenistan gazetining dili ya ki bizde adalga (istilah) meselesi?" *Türkmenistan*, April 14, 1925, p. 2.

[30] K. Sakhatov, "Anti-proletarskie vylazki na fronte ideologii i zadachi partii," *Za partiiu*, no. 5 (May 1928): 41; TsIK Sovetov TSSR, *Pervyi vseturkmenskii s"ezd sovetov rabochikh, dekhkanskikh, i krasnoarmeiskikh deputatov (14–24 fev., 1925 g.): stenograficheskii otchet* (Poltoratsk, 1925), p. 12.

[31] Tächmïradov, *Razvitie*, p. 14.

and negatively affect the normal development of our tongue if it is used in our schools and in public affairs," he argued. If Azerbaijani were used, by contrast, "thanks to the closeness of the Turkmen and Azerbaijani languages," students "will involuntarily seek to create some sort of inter-mediate language by combining these two closely related dialects. The boundary between them will be erased."[32]

Turkmen intellectuals expressed fear of other kinds of foreign influence as well. They accused foreign teachers, especially "individual Azerbaijani pedagogues," of spreading pan-Turkic propaganda among their students and teaching them to sing pan-Turkic nationalist songs. Some Turkmen demanded the dismissal of all non-Turkmen teachers (except Russians) within the Turkmen republic, since their efforts were leading to "linguistic pan-Turkism."[33] There were also concerns about Tatar influence on the Turkmen language. Geldiev, the father of Turkmen linguistic studies, was accused of allowing Tatar elements to creep into his textbook of Turkmen grammar published in 1924. (Since the coauthor of the text was a Tatar philologist, this was not altogether implausible.)[34]

There was general agreement among Turkmen intellectuals and cultural figures, then, that Turkmen was a distinct and unique language. At the same time, it was clear that this "Turkmen language" was to some extent a fiction. Instead of a single language, there were a number of different dialects, each with its own peculiarities of grammar and vocabulary. With the emergence of a print culture that would include newspapers and school textbooks, the need for a standardized language became urgent. The discussions about creating a standardized Turkmen literary language revolved around three primary issues: the choice of an alphabet, the incorporation of foreign terminology into the Turkmen language, and the consolidation of Turkmen dialects into a single literary language. Each of these issues had important symbolic implications for Turkmen national identity and unity.

THE POLITICS OF SCRIPT

In the relatively brief period between the 1917 revolutions and the Second World War, the Turkmen language used three different alphabets. Origi-

---

[32] K. Böriev, "O iazyke srednei shkoly," *Turkmenskaia iskra*, April 5, 1926, p. 1. Böriev was still expressing concern about this issue several years later, when he claimed that there was a great deal of "Azerbaijani Turkish" influence in the language used by Turkmen newspapers. Böriev, "Türkmen dili," p. 40.

[33] Sakhatov, "Antiproletarskie vylaski," pp. 39–41.

[34] Tächmïradov, *Razvitie*, p. 15. Geldiev's early efforts at Arabic script reform also relied on Tatar models. Clement, "The Politics of Script Reform in Soviet Turkmenistan," p. 57.

nally written in Arabic characters, Turkmen shifted to the Latin script in 1928 along with the other Turkic republics of the Soviet Union. In 1940, Turkmen again followed the other Soviet republics and adopted the Cyrillic script. In addition to these major shifts there were frequent smaller changes in the Turkmen writing system, as attempts were made to revise both the Arabic and Latin scripts before abandoning them entirely. Taken singly, each reform had the goal of simplifying the writing of Turkmen and making it easier for the masses to become literate. Collectively, however, the changes did little to stabilize the written language or simplify the acquisition of literacy. With each alphabet reform, the few published materials that existed in Turkmen were rendered obsolete and the small number of people who had managed to "liquidate their illiteracy" were thrown back into the ranks of the illiterate.

Even before the Soviet regime became involved in promoting language reform in Central Asia, local elites sought to improve the Arabic script so that it would correspond more closely to the phonetic requirements of Turkic languages. The jadid reformers regarded the Arabic script as poorly suited for native-language education because it did not fully convey the vowel sounds of Turkic languages. Turkic languages have a greater variety of vowel sounds than Arabic; in addition, many Turkic languages, including Turkmen, feature a system of "vowel harmony" under which vowels of different types ("front" and "back" vowels, for example) may not appear in the same word. The Arabic script has only three actual vowel characters, representing the long vowels "a," "i," and "u," along with a set of diacritical marks used to indicate short "a," "i," and "u." (The diacritical marks are hardly ever used.) Thus, without significant modifications Arabic is incapable of conveying phonetically the many different shadings of Turkic vowel sounds.[35]

Reform of Turkmen orthography was undertaken in 1922, 1923, and 1925 under the auspices of the newly formed Turkmen Academic Commission in Tashkent. The main goals of the reform were to allow the Arabic script to convey Turkmen vowels phonetically and to reflect vowel harmony.[36] A secondary effect of Arabic script reform was that by conveying Turkic vowels more accurately, it would make the Central Asian written languages more distinct from one another. Since many of the differences between the Central Asian Turkic dialects were in the vowels used, the Arabic script with its limited repertoire of vowels had tended to conceal differences in pronunciation.[37] Thus, the move toward more

[35] Fierman, *Language Planning and National Development*, pp. 59–61.

[36] Tächmïradov, *Muhammet Geldieving*, pp. 14–15; K. Böriev, "Türkmenistan ïlmï konferentsiasïna degishli," *Türkmenistan*, April 25, 1930, p. 2; Clement, "The Politics of Script Reform in Soviet Turkmenistan," chap. 2.

[37] Fierman, *Language Planning and National Development*, pp. 59–60.

phonetic writing in the early 1920s helped to pave the way for separate standardized written languages after the national delimitation.

Reform of the Arabic script was preempted in the second half of the 1920s by the mass movement for Latinization of the languages of the Soviet Union. In the 1920s and early 1930s, some seventy Soviet nationalities adopted the Latin script as the basis for their written language. Many of these switched from the Arabic script, but others were abandoning Cyrillic or creating an alphabet for the first time. The movement for Latinization originally arose in the Azerbaijani republic, where the first Committee for the New Turkic Alphabet was established in 1922. By 1924, Azerbaijan had adopted the Latin script, and its proponents began agitating for Latinization in other Turkic republics. In 1926, representatives of all the Soviet Union's Turkic nationalities endorsed Latinization at the first Turkological Congress in Baku, and other republics began to implement the transition to Latin script. The Soviet leadership in Moscow, after some prodding from Latinization activists, eventually decided to support the movement and to give state funding to the all-union Commitee for the New Turkic Alphabet, created in 1927. By mid-1928, all the Soviet Turkic republics had declared themselves in favor of Latinization. In August 1929—after the republics had already begun to implement the change—the all-union Central Executive Committee and Council of People's Commissars banned the Arabic script and made the adoption of the Latin alphabet mandatory in all Turkic republics and regions of the Soviet Union.[38]

The reasons given for the shift were both practical and ideological. In strictly technical terms, reformers argued that the Arabic script was unsuited to Turkic languages, since it contained superfluous consonants while lacking the vowels needed to express the complex Turkic vowel system. Moreover, the Arabic writing system was said to be extraordinarily complex, using 128 different symbols instead of the 33 to 36 found in most European languages. (The large number of symbols was due to the fact that Arabic letters took different forms depending on their position in the word.)[39] The reformers also argued that reading from right to left, as one does in Arabic, was inherently more difficult than reading from left to right. These factors allegedly made it much more time-consuming to learn to read in the Arabic script and complicated the use of modern technology such as typewriters and printing presses.[40]

---

[38] Martin, *The Affirmative Action Empire*, pp. 185–89, 194–95.

[39] The argument about the simplicity of European alphabets neglected the existence of capital letters and divergent cursive and printed forms.

[40] "Obrashchenie TsIKa TSSR ko vsem trudiashchimsia TSSR," reprinted in *Turkmenovedenie*, no. 9 (1928); 16; Arkhiv Rossiiskoi Akademii Nauk (henceforth ARAN) f. 676, op. 1, d. 40, ll. 6–7; Fierman, *Language Planning and National Development*, pp. 74–81;

The technical arguments for Latin were to some extent a screen for a more compelling motivation: the rise of secularism and the shift to a Western orientation. Advocates of Latin argued that the Arabic script, considered sacred by Muslims because of its association with the Koran, was hindering the cultural development of the "backward" Turkic peoples and preventing them from learning from the West. They pointed out that the Arabic alphabet was not indigenous to the Turks but had been imposed on them, along with Islam, during the Arab conquest. The reformers considered Latin to be the script of progress, internationalism, and the future—in short, of Europe. Cyrillic, which might have seemed a logical choice for the Soviet Turkic peoples, was less favored because it was associated with tsarist colonialism and russification. Idealistic Latinists also argued that the Latin alphabet, unlike Cyrillic, had the potential to become universal. Soon all humanity would communicate using the same symbols.[41]

The Latinization movement was truly impressive in the number of languages it encompassed and the speed of its adoption throughout the Soviet Union. As a result, it has featured more prominently than any other aspect of language reform in the Turkic republics in most discussions of the subject. What is less often noted is that the very speed of the triumph indicates a lack of serious opposition. The success of Latinization can be instructively compared to the fate of other policies to which the Soviet regime was far more committed from the start, such as indigenization, where overt and covert opposition hindered the attainment of Soviet goals. Latinization was a highly visible movement that represented an important change for the peoples concerned, but other aspects of language reform were often more bitterly contested.[42]

One of the striking things about Latinization in Turkmenistan was just how little controversy it seemed to provoke. Most Turkmen cultural workers and intellectuals seemed to take it for granted that the shift to Latin was desirable and necessary. In Turkmenistan, officials were convinced that introducing the new alphabet would be exceptionally easy. The low rate of literacy (estimated at somewhere between 1 and 4 percent of the population) and the small size of the Turkmen intelligentsia meant that few people had a vested interest in the Arabic script. As Begjan Na-

---

F. Agazade and K. Karakashly, *Ocherk po istorii razvitiia dvizheniia novogo alfavita i ego dostizheniia* (Kazan: Izdanie VTsK NTA, 1928), pp. 13–16.

[41] Fierman, *Language Planning and National Development*, pp. 74–81; Agazade and Karakashly, *Ocherk po istorii*, pp. 13–16; Martin, *The Affirmative Action Empire*, pp. 193–95.

[42] Even William Fierman, who sees Latinization as "the most tangible way in which the Bolsheviks attempted to undermine the Uzbek language's ties with Islam in the 1920s" and says that "the hidden hand of Moscow" was probably the decisive factor in the triumph of Latinization, concedes that there was little opposition to the shift in Uzbekistan. Fierman, *Language Planning and National Development*, pp. 74–84.

zarov, an official of the Turkmen TsIK, said in 1927: "The population itself does not object to the introduction of the Latin alphabet. To them it's a matter of indifference whether we use Arabic or Latin, since they don't know either one." Proponents argued that the relatively small amount of literature written in the Turkmen language could easily be translated into the new alphabet. Because Islamic clerical influence was relatively weak among the Turkmen, reformers expected little religiously based opposition to the change.[43] As Böriev told an all-union alphabet committee plenum in 1930, "We had nothing to lose from [giving up] the former Arabic alphabet."[44]

One might imagine that the strongest opposition to Latinization would come from the Turkmen linguists who had invested a great deal of effort in reforming the Arabic alphabet. Surprisingly, there is no record of such opposition. On the contrary, the main architects of Arabic script reform— Geldiev, Böriev, and Gulmuhammedov—were among the leading members of the new Turkmen alphabet committee. This committee was created on April 7, 1927 by the republican Central Executive Committee to oversee the creation and introduction of a new Latinized Turkmen alphabet. Aitakov, chair of the TsIK, was named chair of the committee. Its members included the heads of most of the leading cultural and educational institutions within the republic.[45]

On September 1, 1927, a special meeting of the Turkmen Sovnarkom issued a decree declaring the Arabic alphabet to be "one of the greatest obstacles to popular education and the development of national culture" and calling for the introduction of a new Latin alphabet in the Turkmen republic by September 1, 1928. The decree required all government institutions and public organizations to conduct their business in the new Turkmen alphabet by this date. All employees of such organizations were required to learn the Latin alphabet or face dismissal. The Commissariat of Education was asked to shift instruction in literacy and the Turkmen language to the new alphabet by September 1, 1928, and all periodicals were required to switch at the beginning of the 1928–29 fiscal year.[46] The Turkmen Committee for the New Turkic Alphabet quickly devised a new Latin Turkmen script, based in large part on the scripts adopted by other republics such as Azerbaijan. The new alphabet was confirmed by the Turkmen TsIK on January 3, 1928.[47] The transition to the new script went

[43] ARAN, f. 676, op. 1, d. 40, ll. 6–8; d. 3, l. 26; GARF, f. 3316, op. 20, d. 156, ll. 12–13; *Turkmenovedenie*, no. 9 (September 1928), pp. 15–18; K. Böriev, "Latinizatsiia turkmenskogo alfavita," *Turkmenovedenie*, no. 9 (September 1928), p. 13.

[44] Stenograficheskii otchet 4. plenuma VTsKNA (Alma-Ata, 1931), p. 128.

[45] ARAN, f. 676, op. 1, d. 3, ll. 21, 14.

[46] Ibid., ll. 24–26.

[47] Ibid., d. 86, l. 32.

remarkably quickly. By October 1, 1929, periodicals, book publishers, and Soviet schools had all begun using the new alphabet. Only religious schools and certain national minority languages continued to use the Arabic script.[48]

While muted opposition to the reform was reported among conservative segments of the population, most Turkmen, including "workers in cities, the intelligentsia, teachers, [and] students" were said to have "an entirely sympathetic attitude" toward the reform.[49] Still, the change was not easy for those who were accustomed to the Arabic script. Teachers who were marginally literate in the old script now had to learn a new script and teach it to their charges. The alphabet change also exacerbated the existing shortage of Turkmen-language books, since Arabic-script publications had to be withdrawn and replaced by those in Latin script. Delays in learning the new script were reported even among some Turkmen Communist Party officials, who were expected to be in the vanguard on such matters. Those who were already bilingual in Turkmen and Russian now found that they had to learn a third alphabet. Some Turkmen communists preferred to use Russian instead of Latinized Turkmen, raising the question of whether *latinizatsiia* was compatible with *korenizatsiia*.[50]

To Borrow—Or Not to Borrow?

Far more controversial than alphabet reform was the question of how to expand and modernize the Turkmen vocabulary. Turkmen spoken dialects had been formed in a rural culture focused mainly on livestock herding and agriculture, and they lacked many of the terms needed by a modern socialist state. As one of the two official languages of a Soviet republic with its own newspapers and government administration, Turkmen needed new words for everything from socialism and class struggle to more concrete phenomena such as tractors and village soviets.

Controversy erupted over how to create these new words. Should linguists form neologisms based on Turkmen roots, or should Turkmen speakers simply borrow wholesale from other languages? When borrowing from other languages, should Turkmen rely on Arabic and Persian (sources of much borrowing in the past), on "more advanced" Turkic languages such as Azerbaijani, or on European languages, including Russian? Most Turkmen linguists considered it essential to come up with rules

[48] Stenograficheskii otchet 4. plenuma VTsKNA, pp. 18, 128–30, 239–40.
[49] ARAN, f. 676, op. 1, d. 3, l. 19.
[50] K. Iunusov, "Sostoianie latinizatsii v Turkmenii," *Revoliutsiia i pis'mennost'*, no. 4–5 (1932): 70.

to govern borrowing and word creation, since multiple influences and redundant synonyms violated the very notion of a unified, standardized language. It was considered highly problematic in the 1920s that the all-important Russian word *sovet* (council) was represented in Turkmen by three different words: *sovet*, taken directly from the Russian; *shura*, an Arabic word that had long ago been adopted into Turkmen; and *gengesh*, a Turkic word with the same meaning.[51] Linguists argued that this sort of "anarchy" would make Soviet newspapers inaccessible to the newly literate masses.

Most Turkmen linguists agreed that whenever possible, words with Turkmen or Turkic roots should be used to represent new concepts. Beyond this point of consensus, however, there was a wide range of opinion. Some believed that foreign words should be avoided at all costs; others argued that Turkmen should continue to borrow terms from Persian and Arabic when an appropriate Turkic word could not be found; still others advocated closer linguistic ties with Europe. These questions were controversial precisely because they represented in a symbolic way Turkmenistan's relationship with various "others."

Some Turkmen intellectuals were opposed to foreign borrowing on principle because it threatened Turkmen linguistic purity. One commentator writing in the newspaper *Türkmenistan* in March 1925 argued that the Turkmen language already had a rich vocabulary and that adopting foreign words would result in the "destruction" of the language.[52] Others argued against incorporating words of foreign origin into Turkmen for the seemingly unassailable reason (in Soviet terms) that this would make written Turkmen harder for the masses to learn and understand. Rapid gains in literacy could be achieved only if the written language were kept as close as possible to spoken Turkmen. A student of the Soviet-party school, Sh. Khalï, objected to the virtual inundation of the republic by foreigners and foreign influence. He noted that Turkmen students began to stutter whenever they tried to pronounce difficult foreign words such as feudalism, capitalism, socialism, and communism. Incorporating too many foreign words, Khalï maintained, "will not only cause difficulties but will make our language incomprehensible to our people and others."[53]

Other Turkmen were not opposed to all borrowing, but favored taking loan words only from specific sources. A minority wanted to maintain the Turkmen language's close historical relationship with Arabic and Persian. One commentator used the principle of the greatest good for the greatest

[51] Tächmïradov, *Razvitie*, p. 11.

[52] B., "Dil düzetmegi," *Türkmenistan*, March 3, 1925.

[53] Sh. Khalï, "Türkmen dili, imlasï hem metbugatïmïz," *Türkmenistan*, February 20, 1927, p. 1.

number to argue that Turkmen should take loan words from Arabic and Persian rather than from Russian. He noted that those Turkmen who had lived in Bukhara and Khiva prior to the national delimitation had absorbed some knowledge of Arabic and Persian, due to the strongly Islamic character of government and education in those states. Those Turkmen from Transcaspia who had been under Russian colonial rule, by contrast, had little exposure to Arabic and Persian. However, the vast majority of Transcaspian Turkmen were equally unfamiliar with Russian. Thus,

> If we take terms from Arabic and Persian, correcting them according to the rules of the Turkmen language, people in Chärjew, Kerki, and Dashhowuz [parts of the Turkmen republic formely in Bukhara and Khiva] will understand well. But if we use Russian terms, none of our Turkmen in any province will understand.[54]

The leading Turkmen linguists were more eager to leave behind the Islamic-Arabic orientation. Geldiev argued that the Turkmen should primarily exploit the internal resources of their own language to create new terminology. Writing in April 1926, he criticized the tendency to adopt foreign words when perfectly good Turkmen words already existed. When Turkmen sources proved unfruitful, Geldiev wrote, linguists should turn first to Turkic "brother languages" to expand the Turkmen vocabulary. "If there isn't a word for something in our language, in the very first place we must take from our brothers such as Kazakhs, Uzbeks, and Azerbaijanis. In their languages we will find not foreign words but pure Turkic words." If modern Turkic languages lacked the necessary words, Geldiev argued that Turkmen linguists should turn next to old Turkic languages such as Chaghatai and Uighur. If none of these Turkic sources were able to provide the necessary words, it would be best to borrow from European languages rather than from Persian and Arabic, since, he noted pragmatically, "Europe is the master of the past century and the basis for our culture in the future."[55] The resolutions on terminology adopted by the Baku Turkological Congress later that year were quite close to Geldiev's views. The congress declared that new terminology in all the Soviet Turkic republics should be based primarily on Turkic-language sources, but that it would be acceptable to borrow European words in certain cases. While there was no need to eliminate Arabic and Persian

[54] A. Kh., "Edaralarï yerlileshdirmek we termin meselesi," *Türkmenistan*, October 31, 1926, p. 3. For another writer who advocated primarily borrowing terms from Persian and Arabic, see Abdulla, "Bizde dil meselesi," *Türkmenistan*, April 10, 1925.

[55] Geldiev, "Türkmenistan gazetining dili yaki bizde adalga (istilaah) meselesi." One commentator favored taking terms only from Latin-based European languages. (This would pointedly exclude Russian.) See Nasïrlï, "Dil meselesindaki düshünishimiz," *Türkmenistan*, April 12, 1925.

terms that were already well integrated into Turkic languages, no new words from these languages should be incorporated.[56]

The question of terminology was not conclusively settled in the 1920s, in part because there was no official venue for standardizing the literary language prior to the creation of the republican alphabet committee in 1927. Individuals proposed rules for terminology and usage and discussed them in the press, but their suggestions were not binding. In the first two years after the creation of the committee, linguists were preoccupied with carrying out Latinization within the republic. By 1929, the alphabet reform was fully launched and the linguistic community was ready to move on to questions of vocabulary and usage. Planning began for a 1930 republican language conference that would decide these matters once and for all.

In the period leading up to the conference, there were extensive discussions in the Turkmen-language press about the content of the new literary language. Böriev, head of the Institute of Turkmen Culture, opened these debates in a series of articles published in April 1930. Böriev had a highly eclectic approach to the use of loan words in Turkmen, although he gravitated linguistically toward Europe rather than toward the Turkic nations. He criticized those who hoped to maintain the "purity" of the Turkmen language by refusing to use foreign words. The Turkmen language should not only borrow such terms, but borrow them from anywhere and everywhere. Whenever possible, of course, Turkmen sources should be used. Böriev gave an example of how Turkmen roots could be used to form new words. Rather than adopt the alien-sounding Russian word *perchatka*, one could add the common suffix "lik" to the Turkmen word "el" (hand) to create a new word, *ellik*, meaning "glove"—an article of clothing unfamiliar to desert dwellers and hence absent from the Turkmen vocabulary. When this sort of word creation was impossible, Böriev said that linguists should turn freely to foreign sources.[57] Since modern scientific and technical terms mainly came from Europe via Moscow, "from now on we should take mostly terms from Western Europe." Yet it would be a mistake to borrow words only from peoples with "higher culture" such as Europeans, since loan words "from our Turkic brothers" would in many cases be more comprehensible to Turkmen than their Russian equivalents. For example, it made more sense to incorporate Uzbek words relating to cotton and silk cultivation than to use the corresponding Russian terms.[58] Finally, Böriev argued that there should not be

---

[56] Fierman, *Language Planning and National Development*, p. 155.

[57] K. Böriev, "Türkmenistanïng birinji ïlmï konferentsiasï," *Türkmenistan*, April 6, 1930, pp. 2–3.

[58] Ibid.; also K. Böriev, "Türkmenistan ïlmï konferentsiasïna degishli," *Türkmenistan*, April 25, 1920, p. 2.

a hard and fast rule against borrowing from Arabic and Persian, if there happened to be useful terms that existed in those languages alone.[59]

Another contentious issue relating to foreign loan words was whether such words should be modified in accordance with Turkmen linguistic and orthographic rules, especially the rules of vowel harmony. The resolutions of the 1926 Baku Turkological Congress had emphasized that orthography should follow the phonetic rules of each language. This made sense, since a primary goal of Soviet language policy was to ensure that written languages would be close to popular speech and hence accessible to the masses.[60] Thus, Böriev argued that the "Turkmenization" of foreign words would allow the masses to assimilate them more easily.[61] "When we take an originally French word we should not use it in its Russian or French form, but should adapt the root to Turkmen forms, corresponding to the rules of the Turkmen language, so that these words will be understandable to all Turkmen working people."[62]

An article published in the Russian-language republican newspaper the day before the conference opened made it clear that this view was not universally accepted. The author, Mezhnun, was critical of the tendency to clothe foreign loan words in "national dress" by making them look and sound more like Turkmen words. He also criticized the tendency of some Turkic peoples to adopt the French version of "international" words instead of the Russian version. Instead, the author argued, since most foreign words "entered Turkmen usage through the October revolution and the aftermath of October," the Turkmen should use the unaltered Russian versions of foreign terms.[63] This seemingly arcane matter acquired enormous significance just a few years later, when changing the form of a Russian word came to be seen as a rejection of the great language of Lenin and October.

These debates culminated in the first Turkmen scientific conference on the literary language, terminology, and orthography, which took place May 19–23, 1930. Along with Turkmen linguists, the conference was attended by representatives from neighboring Turkic and Central Asian republics and from Russia. (It was scheduled to coincide with a meeting of the all-union alphabet committee in Almaty on May 5, 1930, so that the peripatetic Soviet linguists could move on to Ashgabat immediately afterward.)[64] The delegates adopted decisions on terminology that were in-

[59] Böriev, "Türkmenistanïng birinji ïlmï konferentsiasï," pp. 2–3.

[60] Crisp, "Soviet Language Planning since 1917–1953," p. 33.

[61] Böriev, "Türkmenistan ïlmï konferentsiasïna degishli," p. 2.

[62] Böriev, "Türkmenistanïng birinji ïlmï konferentsiasï," pp. 2–3.

[63] *Turkmenskaia iskra*, May 16, 1930, p. 2.

[64] Gurban Gulïev, "Birinji ïlmï konferentsiasïnïng ehemietli hïzmatlarï nämeden ïbarat?" *Türkmen medenieti*, no. 6–7 (June-July 1930): 5; Böriev, "Türkmenistan ïlmï konferentsia-

tended to be definitive. They declared that Turkmen would not borrow any more Arabic and Persian words, but that Arabic and Persian words that had long ago become part of the Turkmen language's patrimony could remain. Ignoring the hints of changing official priorities contained in Mezhnun's article, the conference declared that all foreign words brought into the Turkmen language must observe Turkmen rules of vowel harmony.[65]

DEALING WITH DIALECTS

One of the most important issues discussed at the 1930 language conference was the merging of the diverse Turkmen dialects into a single literary language. At the time of the national delimitation, there was not a single Turkmen spoken language, but a collection of related dialects spoken by the different groups that identified themselves as Turkmen. Because of the mobility of the major Turkmen groups in the several centuries prior to the Russian conquest, these dialects were more closely associated with descent groups than with regions; in other words, they were genealogically rather than territorially defined.[66]

For the linguists of the new Turkmen republic, the obvious question was how to create a single literary language out of such a variety of dialects. One easy route (and one that has often been taken historically when forming literary languages out of a host of regional dialects) would have been to take the dialect of the strongest and most numerous Turkmen group as the basis for the literary language.[67] In the Turkmen case, the obvious candidate would have been the Teke dialect. However, this was vehemently opposed by the leading language officials in Turkmenistan. The general consensus was that the Turkmen literary language would have to be an "intermediate form" combining features of all the dialects.[68] Just as the Turkmen national republic had united all the Turkmen tribes, so the Turkmen national language would unite their spoken dialects. It was easier to declare such a high-minded aim than to achieve it in practice,

---

sïna degishli," p. 2. See also Mezhnun, "Turkmenskaia nauchnaia konferentsiia po voprosam literaturnogo iazyka, terminologii i orfografii," *Turkmenovedenie* no. 6–7 (1930): 7.

[65] Guliev, "Birinji ïlmï konferentsiasïnïng ehemietli," p. 5; K. Böriev, "Türkmen dilining esasï yagdailarï: Birinji Türkmenistan ïlmï konferentsiasïna khödür edilen tezis,"*Türkmen medenieti*, no. 4–5 (April–May 1930): 3.

[66] Potseluevskii, *Dialekty*, p. 27; Potseluevskii, "Iazykovoe stroitel'stvo Turkmenii i ego osnovnye problemy," *Revoliutsiia i natsional'nosti*, no. 67 (September 1935): 42–43.

[67] On dialect choice in constructing European literary languages, see Hobsbawm, *Nations and Nationalism since 1780*, pp. 54–55.

[68] Böriev, "Türkmenistanïng birinji ïlmï konferentsiasï," pp. 2–3.

however. Political competition among the major tribes was a serious problem within the republic, and tensions naturally spilled over into the arena of language reform. Linguists found that it was difficult to satisfy everyone, no matter how careful their efforts to incorporate words and grammatical forms from all the dialects.[69]

By all accounts, the major Turkmen dialects were mutually intelligible, with many shared grammatical features and a great deal of overlap in vocabulary. However, the differences between the tribal dialects were noticeable enough to make an individual's origins identifiable by his or her speech. Even common words such as "father" had a number of different variants (*kaka, ata, däde, aba, eke,* and *akga*). Some words had different meanings in different tribal dialects; for most Turkmen, for instance, the word *derya* meant "river," but among the western Yomuts who lived near the Caspian it meant "sea."[70] The linguist A. P. Potseluevskii, who devoted most of his career to the study of the Turkmen language, divided Turkmen dialects into two main groups. The first, which was by far the larger of the two, included the dialects of all the major Turkmen tribes: Yomuts, Tekes, Göklengs, Salïrs, Sarïks, and Ersarïs. The dialects of the major tribes were distinguished from each other by small phonetic differences and by lexical differences that "did not hinder mutual comprehension, being limited to a relatively small group of words differing in their roots." One of the most obvious grammatical differences involved the formation of the verbal present tense, for which the tribes used slightly different endings. For example, in forming the present tense of the verbs *almak* and *gelmek* ("to take" and "to come," respectively), the Yomuts said *alyar* and *gelyer* ("he/she/it takes/comes"), the Tekes and Salïrs dropped the "r" and said *alya* and *gelye*, and the Saryks said *alor/gelor*. The dative case of the verbal infinitive in Yomut and Teke was *almage/gelmege*, while in other dialects it was *almana/gelmene*.[71]

The second group included the dialects of a number of smaller tribes, in particular those living near the borders of Iran and Uzbekistan. These were mostly groups of dubious genealogical provenance, from the Turkmen point of view. The small tribes living near the Iranian border were culturally "Turkmenized" groups who called themselves Turkmen but were believed to be descended from the original Persian inhabitants of the area. The groups living along the border with Uzbekistan were of unknown (presumably non-Turkmen) genealogical origin, sometimes calling

[69] Böriev, "Türkmenistan ilmï konferentsiasïna degishli," p. 2.
[70] Tächmïradov, *Razvitie*, pp. 8–9.
[71] Potseluevskii, *Dialekty*, pp. 28–30.

themselves Turkmen and sometimes Uzbeks.[72] The dialects of the second group diverged in significant ways from the main Turkmen dialects. They were more prone to violate vowel harmony, which was generally observed in the dialects of the first group. They also failed to observe one of the most obvious distinguishing features of Turkmen speech—the pronunciation of "s" and "z" as hard and soft "th," respectively. The dialects of the second group pronounced them simply as "s" and "z," like neighboring non-Turkmen peoples. There were also fairly large differences in vocabulary between the second group of dialects and those of the first group, especially along the Iranian border where it was common to hear many Farsi words.[73]

The individuals engaged in constructing a modern Turkmen literary language were from various regions and tribes. Geldiev was a Yomut from western Turkmenistan; Gulmuhammedov was an Ersarï from Bukhara; Allagulï Garahanov was a Teke. The early years of language reform were dominated by Geldiev, with Böriev as his closest collaborator and main supporter. Geldiev wrote the earliest textbooks and learning aids for the Turkmen language, and the alphabet reforms of the early 1920s carried out by the Turkmen Academic Commission in Tashkent were largely his handiwork. Some claimed, perhaps inevitably, that the early attempts to create a Turkmen literary language were biased toward Geldiev's own Yomut dialect. A group led by the Teke linguist Garahanov was highly critical of the linguistic work of Geldiev and Böriev throughout the 1920s and early 1930s, accusing them of seeking to make the Yomut dialect the basis of the literary language.[74]

Geldiev and his supporters denied having such intentions. In his public statements, Geldiev consistently campaigned for the creation of a common Turkmen literary language that would include elements from the spoken language of all tribes. Geldiev and other experts affiliated with Turkmenkul't and GUS made linguistic expeditions to various parts of the republic between 1927 and 1930, studying the dialects spoken in Krasnovodsk, Esengulï, Gïzïletrek, Garrïgala, and Lebap. Geldiev made a point of incorporating his new findings about these dialects into his Turkmen grammar text published in 1929.[75] Böriev, Geldiev's closest collaborator on language matters, similarly argued for a "supratribal" Turkmen written language fashioned from elements common to all Turk-

[72] Ibid., pp. 28–29; Karpov, "Turkmeniia i Turkmeny," p. 39; RGASPI, f. 62, op. 2, d. 102, l. 62; d. 100, l. 15, l. 27.

[73] Potseluevskii, *Dialekty*, pp. 29–31, 37.

[74] Tächmïradov, *Muhammet Geldieving*, p. 31.

[75] Ibid., p. 36; M. Geldiev and G. Alparov, *Türkmen dilining grammatikasï* (Ashgabat, 1929), pp. 3–9; see also A. P. Potseluevskii, "Lingvisticheskaia ekspeditsiia GUS'a," *Turkmenovedenie*, no. 2 (1928): 25–28.

men dialects. Words specific to a single dialect should be excluded from this common language, he argued, unless they described unique aspects of a group's way of life that did not have equivalents in other regions. Thus, the western Yomut Turkmen who made their living from the Caspian Sea could provide maritime and fishing terms for all Turkmen speakers.[76] Böriev noted in 1930 that the written language currently in use was based mainly on the Teke and western Yomut dialects, since these groups lived in the central regions of Transcaspia and provided most of the republic's officials, journalists, and educators. The "Amu Darya dialects" spoken in the eastern portions of the republic (including those of the Ersarï and Salïr), were poorly represented, largely because few Turkmen from those regions were involved in publishing newspapers and writing textbooks. He argued that it was important to involve the eastern Turkmen in language work and to incorporate their vocabulary and grammatical forms into the literary language. Eventually, Böriev maintained, linguistic elements used exclusively by one group would gradually disappear and the dialects would merge into a single literary language understandable to all.[77]

There is no reason to believe that Geldiev and Böriev were insincere in their calls for a literary language incorporating elements from all Turkmen dialects. However, these unobjectionable proposals for linguistic inclusiveness also happened to be an effective way of countering the threat of Teke "linguistic hegemony" within the republic. Since Tekes were the largest tribe and comprised the majority of Turkmen educators and journalists, in the natural course of events their dialect might have come to dominate. Some Tekes clearly believed that their dialect should be the basis of a common literary language, although for the most part they concealed this conviction behind more politically acceptable arguments that the "language of the capital," "the language of the most economically developed parts of the republic," or the "language of the cultural *aktiv*" should predominate. Böriev pointed out that since the majority of "culturally active" Turkmen were Tekes, such arguments were tantamount to calling for Teke hegemony in language construction.[78]

Non-Teke linguists maintained that Tekes were undermining the effort to devise an "intermediate" Turkmen literary language, using their weight in publishing and education to promote their own dialect. Böriev and Gulmuhammedov claimed that new editions of Mägtïmgulï's poetry published in the 1920s had been translated into the Teke dialect from the poet's original Gökleng. Similarly, the Commissariat of Health had trans-

[76] Böriev, "Türkmenistan ïlmï konferentsiasïna degishli," p. 2.
[77] Ibid.; see also Böriev, "Türkmenistanïng birinji ïlmï konferentsiasï," pp. 2–3.
[78] Böriev, "Türkmen dili," p. 41.

lated public health brochures from Russian into the Teke dialect and sent them to Kerki province, where the local Turkmen were allegedly unable to understand them.[79] Böriev's claim that Tekes were deliberately striving for "linguistic hegemony" may have been exaggerated. However, non-Tekes clearly had reason to worry that their dialects would be pushed aside, even without any deliberate Teke efforts in that direction.

The problem of reconciling the diverse Turkmen dialects was a primary focus of the 1930 Turkmen linguistic conference.[80] Declaring that the written language of the press must be understandable to a majority of Turkmen workers and peasants, the conference adopted detailed decisions on which elements from each of the major dialects would be incorporated into the literary language.[81] The main principle behind the decisions appeared to be that of linguistic inclusiveness; as Böriev said, the conference tried to adopt "intermediate forms" that would incorporate elements from all dialects and be understandable to all Turkmen.[82] The conference thus officially adopted a form of the present tense ending in "r" (*alyar, gelyer*) that was characteristic of Yomuts, although not used by Tekes or Salïrs. It adopted the Teke "thin vowel" form of certain words, as opposed to the "fat vowel" form common in some other dialects (for example, *hiil* rather than *hïïl*). The conference adopted the common Yomut and Teke form of the dative infinitive (*gelmege, almaga*) and incorporated certain forms of verb negation characteristic of the Amu Darya dialects. It adopted demonstrative pronouns in the form used by Sarïks and Ersarïs (*shöile, böile*), rather than those used by most Tekes and Yomuts (*sheile, beile*).[83]

Some Turkmen intellectuals considered the conference's efforts to draw on all the major Turkmen dialects to be a great success.[84] However, not everyone was pleased. The difficulty of finding "intermediate forms" that would satisfy everyone became clear in the controversy that resulted from the decision to use present-tense forms ending in "r." Geldiev was accused of favoring the Yomut dialect in this decision. He responded that the conference had adopted the forms ending in "r" not because they were Yomut, but because the majority of Turkmen dialects used an "r" to construct the present tense. The Teke dialect was one of the few that did not.[85]

[79] Ibid.; A. Gulmuhammedov, *Materialy po sredne-aziatskim literaturnym pamiatnikam* (Ashgabat: Turkmengosizdat, 1931), p. 48.

[80] Guliev, "Birinji ïlmï konferentsiasïnïng ehemietli," p. 5; Böriev, "Türkmenistan ïlmï konferentsiasïna degishli," p. 2.

[81] Böriev, "Türkmen dilining esasï yagdailarï," p. 3.

[82] Böriev, "Türkmen dili," p. 43.

[83] Böriev, "Türkmen dilining esasï yagdailarï," p. 3.

[84] Guliev, "Birinji ïlmï konferentsiasïnïng ehemietli," p. 5.

[85] Tächmïradov, *Muhammet Geldieving*, p. 37.

The 1930 conference did not end the controversy over the dialect basis of the literary language. Writers, journalists, and teachers felt free to disregard rules with which they disagreed. Instead of abiding by the official orthography, vocabulary, and grammar of the "intermediate" literary language, they continued to write in their own dialects. While the newspapers *Türkmenistan* and *Daihan* were written in a widely understandable form of Turkmen, the journal *Tokmak*, satirical mouthpiece of the Teke intelligentsia, continued to use the Teke dialect. The Teke linguist Garahanov, who was highly critical of the conference decisions, issued a new grammar textbook that contradicted its resolutions. The failure of many Turkmen to use the official literary language provoked many complaints about linguistic "tribalism, clanism, and anarchy."[86]

THE DESTRUCTION OF THE TURKMEN CULTURAL ELITE

The decisions of the 1930 conference were soon discredited in a more serious way. Between 1930 and 1936, control of language reform passed from Turkmen linguists and intellectuals in Ashgabat to Russian linguists and centralized committees in Moscow. The role of local elites was greatly diminished, and their public debates about the place of language in Turkmen national identity largely ceased. Three main developments underscored the centralization of language policy. One was the shift of the all-union alphabet committee from Baku to Moscow. Another was the rise of Marrist linguistics and stringent new demands that all local linguists conform to a set of centrally decreed dogmas. Finally, the most prominent Turkmen linguists all passed from the scene in the purge of the early 1930s, resulting in a virtual collapse of indigenous work on language reform.

The All-Union Committee for the New Turkic Alphabet (often referred to by its Russian acronym, VTsKNTA) was initially based in Baku, the center of Turkic language reform in the 1920s. As we have seen, the initiative for Latinization originated in Azerbaijan. Russian linguists and scholars were very much involved in Turkic language reform, attending the 1926 Turkological congress in Baku and providing scholarly and technical assistance. However, their role was mostly advisory. In fact, linguists from Moscow and Leningrad occasionally complained that the Baku alphabet reformers did not consult enough with their Russian colleagues. The all-union committee, moreover, lacked the authority to compel local and republican alphabet committees to abide by its deci-

[86] Böriev, "Türkmen dili," p. 42; Iunusov, "Sostoianie latinizatsii v Turkmenii," pp. 72–73; A. Begjanov, "Garara garshï garar," *Türkmenistan*, January 9, 1931, p. 2.

sions.[87] This meant that language reform efforts were relatively decentralized in the 1920s.

The situation changed around 1930, when the VTsKNTA moved to Moscow and was placed under closer central supervision.[88] Around the same time, the linguistic theories of N. Ia. Marr were elevated to the level of official Marxist-Leninist dogma. Marr rejected the "elitist" concern of most linguists with linguistic "purity" and the literary language, calling instead for greater attention to the colloquial speech of the masses. He also criticized the tendency of conventional linguists to focus primarily on Indo-European languages. Not only were these "Indo-Europeanists" guilty of a haughty disregard of other languages, but their work was based on a false assumption, in Marr's view—namely, the belief that languages could be grouped into "families," each descended from a common ancestor tongue. Marr maintained that all languages were related, with different languages representing distinct stages of human development. Eventually, all would merge into a single universal tongue under communism. Moreover, since language was part of the superstructure and controlled by the dominant class, it evolved along with the class structure and economic basis of society.[89] By 1933, all linguists had to pay homage to Marr and preface their works with treatises on his theories. Linguists in non-Russian republics began studying the speech of "advanced" portions of the population, such as industrial workers and collective farmers, in an attempt to document class-based linguistic changes and movement toward the merger of languages.[90] Older, "bourgeois" linguists were criticized as "Indo-Europeanists" and "elitists" for neglecting non-Indo-European languages and for privileging the speech of the dominant classes and cultural elites over the speech of the masses.

As these changes in central language policy were occurring, an attack on the cultural elite in Turkmenistan swept up a large number of the leading writers, poets, linguists, journalists, and educators who had been prominent in the 1920s. This campaign was launched shortly after the appearance of a letter from Stalin in the journal *Proletarskaia revoliutsiia* in the autumn of 1931, which criticized scholars for political errors and for taking an excessively academic approach to their subjects.[91] Those

[87] Fierman, *Language Planning and National Development*, pp. 218–21.

[88] The committee also underwent a name change in 1930, becoming the All-Union Committee for the New Alphabet.

[89] Fierman, *Language Planning and National Development*, pp. 222–25; Yuri Slezkine, *Arctic Mirrors: Russia and the Small Peoples of the North* (Ithaca and London: Cornell University Press, 1994), pp. 250–252; Yuri Slezkine, "N. Ia. Marr and the National Origins of Soviet Ethnogenetics," *Slavic Review* 55, no. 4 (Winter 1996), pp. 826–62.

[90] Fierman, *Language Planning and National Development*, p. 225–27.

[91] See G. Vesel'kov, "Pis'mo tov. Stalina i bor'ba za proletarskuiu khudozhestvennuiu literaturu v Turkmenistane," *Turkmenovedenie*, no. 10–11 (October–December 1931): 44–

who came under attack from the KPT leadership included employees of
Turkmenkul't, the state publishing concern, the education commissariat,
the Turkmen-language press, and the pedagogical institute. Leading Turkmen cultural figures such as Böriev, Geldiev, Kerbabaev, Burunov, Perengliev, and Gulmuhammedov were accused of a variety of sins, from pan-
Turkism and national chauvinism to propagating "feudal" or "bourgeois" ideologies.[92] The linguists who had dominated the 1920s debates
and the 1930 language conference were attacked for their "pan-Turkism," "pan-Islamism," and "narrow tribalism." Turkmen "nationalists"
within the state publishing house were accused of "sabotage" in their
translations of Marxist-Leninist works into Turkmen. Böriev was said to
have translated the *Communist Manifesto* in such a way as to imply that
communists were in favor of communalizing wives.[93]

The flood of criticism was not aimed solely at Turkmen. Writers and
scholars of European background came under attack as well. The linguist
A. P. Potseluevskii's 1926 Turkmen-language textbook was suddenly
found to be so riddled with "political deviations" that he was accused of
being simultaneously a pan-Turkist, a great-Russian chauvinist, and a
supporter of feudalism.[94] The ethnographer and historian G. I. Karpov
was criticized for his 1930 work, *The Khivan Turkmen and the End of
the Kungrad Dynasty*, which allegedly failed to emphasize class struggle
and idealized both the Russian colonial rulers and the Yomut rebel leader
Junaïd Khan.[95] The head of the Turkmen state publishing house apologized publicly for allowing the publication of works by Gulmuhammedov, Potseluevskii, and Karpov, as well as a collection of proverbs
edited by the "nationalist" Geldiev and the works of the "reactionary
poet" Mägtïmgulï.[96]

While Europeans such as Karpov and Potseluevskii generally kept their
positions and regained their reputations after the furor of the cultural
revolution died down, many of the Turkmen writers and educators did

47, continued in no. 1–2 (January–February 1932): 25–29. Stalin's letter appeared in *Proletarskaia revoliutsiia*, no. 6 (1931). On the effects of this letter on Russian scholars, see
George M. Enteen, "Marxist Historians during the Cultural Revolution" in *Cultural Revolution in Russia, 1928–1931*, ed. Sheila Fitzpatrick (Bloomington: Indiana University Press,
1978), pp. 164–66.

[92] RGASPI, f. 62, op. 2, d. 3200, l. 124; f. 17, op. 30, d. 46, l. 146.

[93] Ibid., f. 62, op. 2, d. 3084, l. 128.

[94] An attack on Potseluevskii by KPT secretary Popok was published in *Turkmenskaia
iskra*, January 10, 1932, pp. 2–3. The book in question was Potseluevskii's *Rukovodstvo
dlia izucheniia turkmenskogo iazyka* (Ashgabat: Turkmengosizdat, 1929). See also I. L-i,
"Za bol'shevistskuiu podgotovku kadrov: ob odnom uchebnike turkmenskogo iazyka i ego
avtore," *Turkmenovedenie*, no. 1–2 (January–February, 1932): 44–50.

[95] *Turkmenskaia iskra*, January 10, 1932, p. 2.

[96] RGASPI, f. 17, op. 30, d. 46, ll. 146–47.

not. When the OGPU claimed to have uncovered a Turkmen nationalist organization in May 1932 (see chapter 4), some of the leading Turkmen linguistic and literary figures were accused of membership.[97] The poet K. Burunov was arrested in the spring of 1932. Böriev was expelled from the party and arrested in March 1932.[98] The poet and literary scholar Gulmuhammedov, the writer and editor Kerbabaev, the poet Vepaev, the former education commissar Perengliev, and the Teke political and cultural figure Övezbaev were also implicated. Geldiev was described as a leading figure in the organization, although he had died in 1931.[99]

The results of all this upheaval were devastating for language reform within the Turkmen republic. The disappearance of Geldiev, Böriev, Gulmuhammedov, and others from the scene was a particularly severe blow in view of the small size of the cultural intelligentsia in Turkmenistan. The Turkmen alphabet committee ceased to exist during the cultural revolution, and virtually all formal work on language reform came to a halt. The journals *Turkmenovedenie* and *Türkmen medenieti*, leading venues for scholarly discussions of Turkmen language and culture, ceased publication. K. Iunusov, a representative of the presidium of VTsKNA who was sent to Turkmenistan in the summer of 1932, could find no one who knew anything about language reform. He could not locate any of the Turkmen alphabet committee members, several of whom had been arrested. Iunusov was never able to find out exactly what had happened to the committee; Turkmen officials claimed it had been dissolved by the TsIK as "superfluous," but the relevant decree was never found.[100]

After an abortive attempt by Iunusov to revive linguistic work within the republic, the republican Central Executive Committee finally reestablished the Turkmen Central Committee for the New Alphabet in early 1933. The new committee had twenty-two members, including the leading officials of most of the republic's major cultural and educational institutions and periodicals. The major focus of Turkmen language reform would now be the standardization of orthography and the adoption of foreign terminology. The committee made plans to publish subject-specific Russian-Turkmen terminological dictionaries in math, physics, anatomy, military science, language and literature, biology, and political economy. The committee's responsibilites also included the creation of Latin alphabets and textbooks for small national minorities within the republic.[101]

[97] Ibid., f. 62, op. 2, d. 3084, l. 127; d. 3086, l. 236; Palvanova, *Tragicheskie 30-e*, p. 63.
[98] RGASPI, f. 62, op. 2, d. 3084, l. 128.
[99] Tächmïradov, *Muhammet Geldieving*, pp. 10, 30. RGASPI, f. 62, op. 3, d. 3086, l. 12.
[100] ARAN, f. 676, op. 1, d. 1015, ll. 27–28, 201, 213.
[101] Ibid., ll. 24–26; d. 350, ll. 50–51; d. 618, ll. 14–15; d. 479, ll. 1–2, 5–6.

Two years later, the all-union alphabet committee in Moscow was still concerned about the state of "language construction" in Turkmenistan. The committee's presidium invited A. P. Potseluevskii to Moscow in April 1935 to report on the work of the revived Turkmen language committee. In a resolution adopted following Potseluevskii's report, the presidium acknowledged the need for fundamental reform in Turkmen orthography and terminology and called for the convening of a new linguistic congress. The committee's presidium also sent a representative, M. I. Bogdanova, to the republic to evaluate the situation. Bogdanova ultimately stayed in Turkmenistan and became the leading full-time official working on language policy.[102]

Bogdanova reported to her superiors in Moscow that at the time of her arrival in Turkmenistan in 1935 there was complete chaos on the "language front." The "counterrevolutionary nationalists and pan-Turkists" had been exposed and purged, she wrote, but the negative effects of their work in language construction had not yet been overcome. Little had been done to standardize terminology, and there was incessant fighting among the different tribes for hegemony over the literary language. At the same time, linguistic reform focused not on the language of the "working masses" but on the worn-out linguistic norms of the feudal epoch.[103] Bogdanova oversaw the reorganization and restaffing of the Turkmen alphabet committee, and was appointed temporary deputy head of the committee on November 28, 1935.[104] With this she effectively became the highest-ranking linguistic official within the republic, since Aitakov's position as committee chair was honorary. Bogdanova and Potseluevskii now supervised almost all linguistic projects, calling in leading Turcologists and linguists from Moscow and Leningrad as consultants, while the native Turkmen staff were relegated for the most part to secondary roles. Whereas Turkmen intellectuals such as Geldiev and Böriev had represented Turkmenistan at all-union linguistic meetings in the 1920s, the Europeans Bogdanova and Potseluevskii were the Turkmen TsKNA's delegates at the all-union alphabet committee plenum in Moscow in January 1936.[105]

With the arrival of Bogdanova and new control from Moscow over language policy came a conclusive rejection of all the linguistic work that had gone before, including the results of the 1930 conference. Potseluevskii, who had narrowly survived being labeled a feudal pan-Turkist and

---

[102] Ibid., d. 479, l. 37; d. 932, l. 21. It is not clear what Bogdanova's scholarly credentials were as an expert on the Turkmen language. Clearly, her most important qualifications were her mastery of Marrist rhetoric and her willingness to carry out central policies.

[103] Ibid., d. 932, l. 21.

[104] Ibid., d. 742, l. 5.

[105] Ibid., ll. 25–26, ll. 31–35; d. 932, l. 27.

great-power chauvinist during the cultural revolution, now condemned
the linguistic work of the 1920s intellectuals:

> In the first stage of language construction in Turkmenia, when cadres of
> Marxist linguists did not yet exist, this work was in the hands of the bourgeois
> and feudal-bureaucratic intelligentsia. The class background of this intelli-
> gentsia could not help but affect the character of its work in the sphere of
> language.[106]

Potseluevskii, Bogdanova, and other linguists of the new breed now
described all previous language work as a battleground between two tendencies: "Geldievism" and "Garahanovism." These "nationalists" had allegedly failed to struggle for a "unified all-Turkmen, proletarian-collective
farm language," instead seeking supremacy for their own tribal dialects—
in Geldiev's case, that of the Mangïshlak Yomuts, and in Garahanov's, that
of the Marï Tekes.[107] Moreover, while Geldiev tried to revive the "obsolete
written language of the feudal epoch," Garahanov had sought to impose
on Turkmen the orthography of Ottoman Turkish. Geldiev defended the
bourgeois Indo-European theory of language and regarded language as
a "national, above-class" phenomenon with its own structure and rules
separate from the social and economic base. Geldiev was also said to have
engaged in "linguistic sabotage," by, for example, introducing characters
into the new Turkmen alphabet that differed from those of other Turkic
alphabets, thereby making the printing of Turkmen language books more
difficult.[108] Others accused the Geldiev-Böriev "counterrevolutionary nationalist" group of "a pan-Islamic orientation toward Arabo-Iranian elements in the language" and a "nationalist deviation" that strove to create
all new words from Turkmen roots, instead of adopting the Russian equivalent. They had brought about the phonetic and orthographic distortion
of Russian and "international" terms, "under the pretext of bringing them
closer to popular pronunciation."[109] Finally, Gulmuhammedov, Böriev,
Vepaev, Geldiev and other linguists and writers were guilty of both "ignoring and disregarding popular culture and the living conversational language" and "fighting against the absorption of the riches of Russian, Soviet, and international literature."[110]

Responding to the initiatives of the VTsKNA, the executive bureau of
the KPT Central Committee in November 1935 adopted a resolution de-

---

[106] Potseluevskii, "Iazykovoe stroitel'stvo," pp. 45–46.

[107] Ibid., p. 46; ARAN, f. 676, op. 1, d. 1197, l. 6.

[108] Potseluevskii, "Iazykovoe stroitel'stvo," p. 46.

[109] M. I. Bogdanova, *Osnovnye voprosy terminologicheskoi raboty v Turkmenii* (Ashgabat: Turkmengosizdat, 1936), p. 6.

[110] O. Tashnazarov, *Iazyk turkmenskoi khudozhestvennoi literatury* (Ashgabat: Turkmengosizdat, 1936), p. 4.

manding renewed attention to language policy. The bureau called for intensified study of Marxist-Leninist (i.e., Marrist) theories of language; an expansion of the permanent research staff of the Turkmen TsKNA; reform of orthography and syntax; and a greater number of expeditions to study the speech of workers and collective farmers in the republic. It also asked the Turkmen TsIK and Turkmen alphabet commitee to convene a republican language conference in May 1936.[111]

On December 4, the newly reinvigorated Turkmen TsKNA issued a long statement of purpose outlining a series of ambitious new goals. It would perfect and promote the new Latin alphabet, create new terminology, solve problems of grammar and orthography, prepare linguistic cadres, supervise the translation of all government records into the new alphabet, and oversee the publication of grammar texts, dictionaries, and scholarly works on language. The committee now had subcommittees devoted to alphabet, orthography and the literary language, terminology, and national minority languages.[112] In early 1936, the Turkmen party leadership created a new research institute on language and literature within the Turkmen State Scientific Research Institute (TGNII), the successor to Turkmenkul't, to provide scientific support to the alphabet committee. Bogdanova was named as its head.[113] The alphabet committee and the research institute made plans to conduct joint linguistic expeditions to study the spoken dialects of "advanced portions of the population" such as the industrial proletariat and collective farmers. By comparing the speech of such "advanced Turkmen" with that of the "backward strata of the population," scholars would be able to analyze the evolution of the Turkmen language under socialism.[114]

The institutional reorganization and reinvigoration of language work in the republic culminated in an all-Turkmen linguistic congress during the week of May 18–24, 1936, which was intended to supersede the work of the 1930 conference. Some three hundred delegates attended, including many from Moscow, Leningrad, and neighboring Turkic republics.[115] The 1936 congress showed the heightened level of central and party involvement in the minutiae of language development. The 1930 conference had been a relatively low-key affair that mostly involved Turkmen linguists and cultural figures and received little attention in the Russian-language press. The 1936 congress, by contrast, featured speeches by major party figures and was covered extensively in the repub-

[111] RGASPI, f. 17, op. 30, d. 85, ll. 147–49; ARAN, f. 676, op. 1, d. 932, ll. 21–22.
[112] ARAN, f. 676, op. 1, d. 742, ll. 2–4.
[113] Ibid., d. 932, l. 21; RGASPI, f. 17, op. 30, d. 102, l. 54.
[114] ARAN, f. 676, op. 1, d. 670, ll. 2, 6–7.
[115] Ibid., d. 934, ll. 3–4.

lic's main Russian-language newspaper.[116] At the 1930 conference, decisions on language reform were taken unilaterally by Turkmen delegates and subsequently approved by the all-union alphabet committee. In 1936, the Turkmen alphabet committee, already run by an official handpicked by central language authorities in Moscow, was required to request the approval of the all-union committee in advance for any changes in Turkmen orthography. The basic principles of the proposed 1936 reforms were presented and discussed long before the May 1936 congress at a January 1936 VTsKNA plenum in Moscow and by a special commission of leading Soviet turcologists.[117]

The organizers of the 1936 congress made a point of denouncing the previous cohort of Turkmen linguists. On May 14, 1936, the Turkmen Central Committee's executive bureau instructed the congress not to exempt any of these linguists from criticism, saying that it was

> essential to subject open and hidden proponents of tribal dialects in language construction to sharp criticism at the congress, and, especially in view of the fact that the theoretical positions of Böriev and Geldiev have been exposed and fully defeated in the press, to concentrate special emphasis at the congress on the less familiar nationalist positions of Garahanov.[118]

The organizers of the 1936 congress conceded that some progress in Turkmen language development had occurred since the founding of the republic, mainly because of the emergence of "a new army of people" made up of kolkhoz chairs, brigade leaders, tractor drivers, and Stakhanovites, who had "enriched their native language with new international and Soviet terms and freed the language from a number of concepts and remnants of the feudal epoch." However, "the rules of orthography, syntax, and terminology still have not been completely worked out," and the language of Turkmen newspapers and textbooks was therefore not yet completely understandable to the masses. These delays in language construction were blamed on the activities of "counterrevolutionary nationalists and great power chauvinists" who tried to prevent the formation of a unified literary language.[119]

---

[116] Reports on the conference and the texts of the speeches delivered at its sessions appeared in the leading Russian-language republican newspaper *Turkmenskaia iskra* on May 18, 20, 21, 22, 23, 24, 26, 27, 1936. Only one article (the above-mentioned commentary by Mezhnun) was published in *Turkmenskaia iskra* in connection with the 1930 language conference.

[117] ARAN, f. 676, op. 1, d. 932, l. 22; *Iazyk i pis'mennost' narodov SSSR. Stenograficheskii otchet 1. vsesoiuznogo plenuma nauchnogo soveta VTsK NA (15–19 fev. 1933)* (Moscow, 1933), p. 218.

[118] RGASPI, f. 17, op. 30, d. 103, l. 72.

[119] ARAN, f. 676, op. 1, d. 934, ll. 50–52.

Since the published resolutions of the 1930 conference had spoken explicitly of the need to overcome tribalism and create a unified literary language based on popular speech, the new linguists did not attack these resolutions directly. Instead, they claimed that the Geldiev/Böriev group had concealed its true intentions at the time of the 1930 conference. A resolution of the 1936 congress declared that "Böriev's nationalist group" had "succeeded in the declarative portion of the conference decisions in masking their platform with innocent phraseology." Nevertheless, the 1936 linguists claimed, the official decisions of the 1930 conference belied the verbal commitment to a supratribal language: "The rules of grammar adopted established the dominance of the Yomut dialect and retained archaic forms of the old literary language, in which our language has remained enmeshed until the present day." Garahanov, the leading critic of the Geldiev/Böriev group, was said to have opposed the nationalists in words while supporting them in deeds. Although he called rhetorically for "making the literary language close to the living conversational language in all possible ways," in his practical linguistic work, especially his own grammar text, "he included unchanged archaic forms of the old literary language, and even introduced rules characteristic of the grammar of caliphal Turkey." In addition, instead of the "Geldievite orientation toward the Yomut tribal dialect," Garahanov "oriented the rules of orthography toward the Teke tribal dialect."[120]

The main differences between the 1936 and 1930 conferences had to do with the shift in the locus of control from local cultural elites to committees in Moscow, but there were also shifts in the substance of language policy. While the policies adopted on two of the most controversial questions—foreign terminology and tribal dialects—bore many similarities to the policies worked out by the earlier group of Turkmen linguists, there were subtle but important differences.

On the question of foreign terminology, the congress harshly criticized the numerous "deviations" that had allegedly surrounded the issue in the past: a "pan-Islamist orientation" toward Islamic and Persian words, a "nationalist deviation" calling for the exclusive use of words of Turkmen origin, and a "Great Russian chauvinist deviation," which demanded the indiscriminate introduction of Russian terms into the Turkmen language. It condemned the absence of unified rules for the adoption of new terminology, which had led to "chaos" and "distortions." The Congress declared, much like the 1930 conference, that when an "international" term or concept could be completely and accurately translated into Turkmen, the Turkmen term should be used. While no new Arabic and Persian words should be adopted, those Arabic and Persian words completely

120 Ibid., l. 51.

internalized by the Turkmen masses should be used on an equal footing
with Turkmen words.[121] However, the congress declared—and here it
parted company with the architects of the 1930 conference—that "international" and Soviet terms lacking exact equivalents in Turkmen (*aktiv*,
Bolshevik, *partiia*, and so forth) should be used in their original form,
without adapting them to the phonetic and orthographic requirements of
the Turkmen language. Since these "international" terms generally en-
tered the Turkmen language through Russian, their spelling and pronunciation should be based on Russian forms. The congress criticized the "nationalists" for "oversimplifying" by "replacing international or Soviet
terms with Turkmen words that did not have the same meaning." Also,
by adapting "international" words to make them correspond to Turkmen
rules of vowel harmony, they had "distorted" borrowed words under the
pretext of making them closer to popular pronunciation.[122]

   On the question of tribal dialects, the 1936 congress similarly continued
the basic approach taken by Böriev and Geldiev, calling for the formation
of a unified national literary Turkmen language based on "the living spoken popular language" and "a concentration of the tribal dialects." The
literary language, the Congress declared, should use the forms and words
that were most widespread among all the Turkmen dialects. Echoing the
earlier words of the "counterrevolutionary nationalists," the Congress declared that "it would be completely incorrect from a scientific point of
view and deeply wrong in political terms to adopt a policy of exclusive
orientation toward one or another major dialect. . . . The resources of all
dialects without exception must be fully used." The economic specificities
of individual regions should also be taken into account; thus, Turkmen
terms for shipbuilding and seafaring should be based on the dialects of
those Turkmen who commonly engage in these occupations.[123]

   Up to this point, the 1936 principles were similar to the Geldiev and
Böriev position on creating an "intermediate literary language," but there
was one important difference. The 1936 congress also declared that when
two or more competing "linguistic facts" were approximately equally
widespread, preference should be given to those common in economically
developed regions or among the "most advanced" portion of the population, such as the Turkmen proletariat and "advanced" collective farmers.
The speech of such groups should have a disproportionate weight in the
literary language, not because it was spoken by a majority of the popula-

   [121] Ibid., ll. 75–80.
   [122] Ibid., ll. 53, 75–76, 80, 86. This shift with regard to "international" terms took place
in other republics as well. See Fierman, *Language Planning and National Development*, pp.
128–29, 157–60.
   [123] ARAN, f. 676, op. 1, d. 934, ll. 52–53, 56–57.

tion, but because it represented linguistic "progress." In this, the 1936 congress was following the instructions of the Scientific Council of the all-union alphabet committee, which had stipulated that the orthography of the literary language should reflect the development of the conversational speech of the broad masses, led by the proletariat and the progressive portion of the collective farmers.[124]

The Turkmen linguists purged in 1932–33 had been vilified for their "elitism" and "narrow tribalism." Yet the principles of the central Committee for the New Alphabet, when applied to language reform in Turkmenistan, were far more likely to produce elitism and tribalism in practice. Geldiev and Böriev had argued for basing the literary language on all dialects and using forms common to the majority of Turkmen. They had rejected suggestions that the literary language be based on the language of the capital, the central regions of the republic, or the "cultural activists." By favoring the language used by the most "advanced" part of the Turkmen population—the "proletariat and advanced collective farmers"—the 1936 congress gave official sanction to the dominance of the speech of the "economically developed" central regions close to the capital. In practice, this was most likely to be the Teke dialect.[125] The new policy on terminology similarly undermined the stated goal of making the Turkmen literary language comprehensible to the masses. Böriev and Geldiev had insisted on using as many Turkmen and Turkic words as possible and adapting foreign loan words to the rules of the Turkmen language. While this may have been partly due to a "nationalist" drive for linguistic "purity," as their critics claimed, the two linguists had also argued convincingly that "Turkmenizing" foreign vocabulary would make it more accessible to the population. The 1936 congress's decisions requiring the use of "international" words whenever there was no exact Turkmen equivalent and decreeing that these words should be kept in their original Russian form, even if this violated Turkmen vowel harmony, were likely to render much of the new Turkmen vocabulary incomprehensible and unpronounceable for the majority of the population.[126] The congress's resolutions were con-

[124] Ibid., ll. 57, 59–60.
[125] According to one Turkmen scholar, some non-Teke linguistic elements adopted by the pre-1932 linguists in an attempt to include elements from all dialects were subsequently replaced by Teke forms later in the 1930s. Tächmïradov, *Muhammet Geldieving*, p. 37. Other scholars have noted that contemporary literary Turkmen is based primarily on the Teke dialect. See Clark, *Turkmen Reference Grammar*, p. 12. In similar fashion, Uzbek shifted its dialect base in the 1930s to the "more progressive" urban dialects, rather than the more "purely Turkic" rural dialects that had preserved vowel harmony to a greater extent. Fierman, *Language Planning and National Development*, pp. 129–31.
[126] Simon Crisp has noted that this aspect of Soviet language policy created a gap between spoken and written languages in many republics. Crisp, "Soviet Language Planning since 1917–1953," p. 34.

firmed by the Turkmen Central Executive Committee on October 1, 1936. The TsIK obligated all government institutions and public organizations to observe the new rules adopted by the congress. The seventh plenum of the VTsKNA also approved the congress's decrees and praised the work of the Turkmen alphabet committee.[127]

The 1936 linguistic congress put the final seal on the centralization of language policy that had occurred during the first half of the 1930s. Instead of freewheeling debates about language in the pages of the Turkmen press, there would now be dutiful implementation of measures decreed in Moscow. If the linguistic debates of the 1920s had symbolically represented Turkmen attempts to define their place in the world, the silencing of those voices symbolized not just a loss of linguistic autonomy, but a curtailing of the role of indigenous intellectuals in debating and defining Turkmen identity. In the new linguistic environment, the ideal Turkmen language was one that carried visible marks of its "progressive" class content and its closeness to Russian. The centralization of language policy and discrediting of the founding fathers of Turkmen linguistics paved the way for the centrally decreed adoption of the Cyrillic script in 1940 with a minimum of fanfare and debate.

[127] ARAN, f. 676, op. 1, d. 934, l. 41; f. 952, l. 4.

PART II

CONSTRUCTING SOCIALISM

Chapter Six

A NATION DIVIDED

CLASS STRUGGLE AND THE ASSAULT ON "TRIBALISM"

IN EARLY 1924, the deputy head of the Communist Party's Central
Asian Bureau, O. Ia. Karklin, warned that "tribal conflict" was hindering the spread of Soviet influence among the Turkmen population
of Central Asia. Turkmen recruited to work for the regime were seeking
to enlist Soviet support in disputes with rival lineages, often by falsely
accusing their opponents of anti-Soviet activity. Since entanglement in
local conflicts could only discredit Soviet rule, Karklin argued that the
authorities should treat rival Turkmen groups with complete evenhand-
edness: "If we promote someone from one tribe into an administrative
post, we have to make sure that we give a similar promotion to the others.
If we give an award to someone from one tribe, we have to do the same
for the others as well."[1]

Karklin's prescription for a perfectly equitable "tribal policy" may have
been utopian, but he had nonetheless put his finger on a problem that
was to confound Soviet officials for years to come. In Turkmenistan, the
Bolsheviks encountered a population for whom genealogically defined
groups—not classes or nations—were the primary units of social organization. The persistence of genealogical identities inhibited the emergence
of a broader sense of nationhood within the Turkmen republic. Even more
seriously, from the Soviet point of view, kinship loyalties complicated the
promotion of class consciousness among the Turkmen. Just as class was
of overriding importance to the Bolsheviks, so kinship was virtually all-
embracing in its significance for many Turkmen. The stage was set for a
clash between these two apparently incompatible discourses of identity.

Soviet officials in Turkmenistan were well aware that welding the fragmented and fractious Turkmen into a unified nation would require the
formulation of a successful "tribal policy."[2] The correct outlines of such
a policy were not immediately obvious, however. Should the Soviet regime
launch a head-on assault on "tribal-clan structures," seeking to destroy
them along with other vestiges of prerevolutionary backwardness such as

---

[1] RGASPI, f. 62, op. 1, d. 20, ll. 46–48.
[2] Turkmenskoe Natsional'noe Buro, "Gde byt' stolitse Turkmenii?" p. 2.

the blood feud and child marriage? Or did tribes, like nations, warrant a more sensitive approach to avoid inflaming their particularist feelings? Specifically, should Soviet "tribal policy" be modeled on nationality policy, fostering tribal elites and territories with the aim of diminishing kinship-based conflict and winning support for the Soviet regime?

Although the distinction between "tribe" and "nation" was essentially arbitrary, Soviet officials soon decided that tribes were not nations and did not deserve to be treated as such. Unlike nations, subnational groups were not expected to have a long-term future as building blocks of the Soviet state, and kinship was not allotted even a circumscribed place in the range of acceptable Soviet identities. Instead, the goal was to eliminate these archaic affiliations as quickly as possible so that the native masses could enter the mainstream of Soviet society. Nevertheless, official policy toward Turkmen genealogical identities remained ambiguous and contradictory during the 1920s and 1930s. On the one hand, the Soviet regime sought to undermine the economic basis of descent group affiliation by dismantling the existing system of collective land tenure and creating a class of poor peasants dependent on the Soviet regime. On the other hand, republican authorities followed the strategy of political appeasement suggested by Karklin, attempting to provide equitable treatment to all genealogical groups. The underlying logic of this policy of "tribal parity" closely resembled that of Soviet nationality policy. Just as all Soviet nationalities were to be treated with scrupulous fairness, so that they would have no reason to nurse nationalist grievances, the regime would win support and suppress "tribal-clan conflict" by refusing to favor one descent group over another.

Neither of these approaches was effective in doing away with kinship-based identities. For a population buffeted by constant, often violent upheaval, genealogical structures remained one of the few sources of stability and continuity. Moreover, as was often the case with the regime's ambitious efforts at social engineering, Soviet "tribal policy" produced results that were virtually the opposite of what was intended. Instead of allowing class consciousness to supplant genealogical loyalties, Soviet rule tended to increase the salience of distinctions based on genealogy and ethnicity. Through land reform and other ambitious programs aimed at transforming Turkmen rural life, the regime broadened the scope for descent group competition and reinforced the rationale for kin-based solidarity. At the same time, "tribal parity" implicitly recognized and sanctioned the very genealogical categories that the regime was determined to eradicate. Finally, because of the close linkage between genealogy and socioeconomic standing in Turkmenistan, Soviet attempts to foment class conflict worked against the policy of "tribal parity," inadvertently exacerbating descent group conflict. Instead of creating new social fissures in the Turkmen countryside, Soviet policies simply deepened existing ones.

GENEALOGY AND SOCIAL STRATIFICATION

For the Bolsheviks, it was axiomatic that class struggle was the driving force of human history. The Turkmen masses would never progress toward socialism without developing class consciousness and learning to struggle against their economic exploiters. The most important conflicts and inequalities in Turkmen society, however, were between groups defined by genealogy and history. Rather than identifying with others who shared their economic status, the Turkmen identified primarily with those who shared their ancestry—in a real or imagined sense. Since nomadic mobility made long-term identification with a particular territory impractical, genealogical forms of conceptualizing identity were common among historically pastoral nomadic groups in Central Asia and the Middle East.[3] While most Turkmen had become settled or semisettled in the period preceding the Russian revolution, their social structure remained heavily influenced by their nomadic history.[4]

Soviet authorities seeking to undermine "tribal and clan structures" tended to forget that Turkmen identity was itself rooted in genealogy. "Turkmen-ness" was understood in terms of patrilineal descent, with all those who called themselves Turkmen claiming origin in a single mythical ancestor. On this tree of lineal descent, only the smallest branches tended to represent "real" or biological kinship; most Turkmen knew their own genealogy and their relationships to other individuals going back five or seven generations.[5] Among larger groups, kin relationships were likely to be vague or even mythical, with distant ancestors remembered—or invented— only to the degree necessary to explain current political relationships.[6]

---

[3] Khazanov, *Nomads and the Outside World*, pp. 138–39. John Armstrong has discussed the crucial role of the "genealogical principle" in the emergence of ethnicities in the Middle East and Central Asia. See his *Nations before Nationalism*, chap. 2. See also Andrew Shryock, *Nationalism and the Genealogical Imagination*, pp. 311–28.

[4] In the Soviet Turkmen republic of the mid-1920s, about 15 percent of the population was fully nomadic. GARF, f. 3316, op. 20, d. 392, l. 25.

[5] Irons, *The Yomut Turkmen*, pp. 40–44. I will use the term "tribe" to mean the largest subset of the genealogical category Turkmen (Teke, Yomut, and so forth). I will use "lineage" to refer to smaller, local groups and "descent group" as a general term for all genealogically defined groups.

[6] Ibid., pp. 43–44. See also G. I. Karpov, "Rodoslovnaia turkmen," *Turkmenovedenie*, no. 1 (January 1929): 56–70; G. I. Karpov "Iomudy: Kratkii istoricheskii ocherk," *Turkmenovedenie*, no. 7–9 (July–September 1931): 69–70. This distinction between "real" or "effective" kinship and mythical kinship has been observed in other genealogically orga-

The identification with one's lineage was not just sentimental, but was of vital practical importance. The descent group was the primary economic unit as well as the ultimate source of political protection for the individual in a stateless society. Among both pastoralists and agriculturalists, land and other natural resources were owned collectively by the lineage. Before the Turkmen came under the effective control of neighboring states, much of political life was regulated genealogically as well. In the event of a murder, for example, Turkmen customary law required the victim's close relatives through the male line—those who traced their common descent back no more than seven generations—to avenge the crime.[7] Presumed patrilineal kinship was not the only foundation for mutual aid; matrilineal ties, residence in the same village or encampment, and patron-client relationships all brought obligations of cooperation and support. Nevertheless, when other commitments clashed with obligations to patrilineal kin, the latter took priority.[8]

European anthropologists have historically characterized pastoral nomadic societies as highly egalitarian, noting that they lack social stratification, occupational specialization, or a hereditary aristocracy. Nomadic communities have often been portrayed in idealized terms as rough-and-ready democracies in which every man (women were seldom included) was simultaneously a herder, warrior, politician, and poet.[9] More recently, however, scholars have argued that genealogy may be used to mark prestige and legitimate inequality among nomads. Some groups have high-status lineages that dominate leadership positions, while many distinguish sharply between insiders and outsiders based on genealogy.[10]

nized societies as well. See Thomas J. Barfield, "Tribe and State Relations: The Inner Asian Perspective," in *Tribes and State Formation in the Middle East*, ed. Philip S. Khoury and Joseph Kostiner (Berkeley: University of California Press, 1990), pp. 156–57; Lois Beck, "Tribes and the State in Nineteenth and Twentieth Century Iran," in Khoury and Kostiner, *Tribes and State Formation in the Middle East*, pp. 197–98; Fathi, *Jordan: An Invented Nation?* pp. 52–53. See Shryock, *Nationalism and the Genealogical Imagination*, pp. 21–25, for a dissenting view on the mythical nature of tribal genealogies.

[7] A. Lomakin, *Obychnoe pravo turkmen* (Ashgabat, 1897), p. 52; Irons, *The Yomut Turkmen*, pp. 61, 113–15.

[8] Irons, *The Yomut Turkmen*, pp. 46–53, 112–15.

[9] On Western views of nomadic and tribal groups, see Eickelman, *The Middle East and Central Asia*, pp. 128–34; Lila Abu-Lughod, "Anthropology's Orient: The Boundaries of Theory on the Arab World," in *Theory, Politics, and the Arab World: Critical Responses*, ed. Hisham Sharabi (New York and London, 1990), pp. 99–101; Fathi, *Jordan: An Invented Nation?* pp. 55–56. Anthropologists have noted that pastoral nomads often adhere to an ideology of equality despite the persistence of economic and political stratification within the group. See, for example, Jacob Black-Michaud, *Sheep and Land: The Economics of Power in a Tribal Society* (London: Cambridge University Press, 1986).

[10] Tapper, *The Conflict of Tribe and State in Iran and Afghanistan*, p. 47; Khazanov, *Nomads*, pp. 142–43; also A. Hammoudi, "Segmentarity, Social Stratification, Political Power, and Sainthood: Reflections on Gellner's Theses," *Economy and Society* 9, no. 3

Although they were no longer exclusively nomadic in the early-twenti-eth century, the Turkmen corresponded more closely to the pastoral egali-tarian ideal than did many of their Central Asian neighbors. In contrast to Kazakh society, which featured an aristocratic stratum claiming a he-reditary right to rule, Turkmen leaders lacked coercive authority and were chosen by group consensus.[11] Nevertheless, there were clear hierarchies of status within the Turkmen population. On the individual level, the most obvious distinctions were based on age and sex, with younger people and females deferring to males and older individuals. A distinction was also made between "pure-blooded" Turkmen (*ig*), who enjoyed consider-able prestige, and those of "mixed blood" (*yarïmcha*) or "slaves" (*gul*), who were descendants of non-Turkmen captives. These "pure-blooded" Turkmen formed an elite that preferred not to intermarry with Turkmen of the other two categories.[12]

In relations between groups, status distinctions were based on real or mythical legacies of history and genealogy. Within each locality one Turk-men lineage claimed predominance, usually because its ancestors had con-quered the region from its previous inhabitants. Other Turkmen groups were allowed to settle in the area only with the dominant group's permis-sion. Members of the dominant group claimed to be the "real Turkmen" in the area, commanding first rights to all natural resources and looking down on other Turkmen and non-Turkmen groups as interlopers. These attitudes remained potent in the Soviet period. As the Turkmen Commu-nist Party official K. A. Böriev noted in 1930, "In Krasnovodsk the Yo-muts consider themselves to be the indigenous Turkmen population, and consider all other small peoples, like the Shikhs and so forth, to be insig-nificant." A similar situation prevailed in the Ahal and Marï regions, where the Tekes claimed preeminence. This, he added, "produces a hostile attitude on the part of every tribe toward every other."[13]

(August 1980): 279–303. On inequalities in Bedouin Arab society, see Fathi, *Jordan: An Invented Nation?* pp. 55–57. One anthropologist has distinguished between the "nonstra-tified" tribal structure found in the Middle East and the stratified Inner Asian type, although others have questioned the existence of such a dichotomy. See Barfield, "Tribe and State Relations: The Inner Asian Perspective," pp. 157–60; Beck, "Tribes and the State in Nine-teenth- and Twentieth-Century Iran," p. 219.

[11] Bregel, *Khorezmskie turkmeny*, pp. 122–44; Paul Georg Geiss, "Turkman Tribalism," *Central Asian Survey* 18, no. 3 (1999): 347–49. On genealogy and social stratification among Kazakhs, see Esenova, "Soviet Nationality, Identity, and Ethnicity in Central Asia," pp. 13–14.

[12] The ethnographer Georgii Karpov estimated in 1925 that only 10 or 15 percent of the Turkmen in the Ashgabat region were "pure-blooded" Tekes. RGASPI, f. 62, op. 2, d. 286, ll. 13, 144. See also Bode, "O turkmenskikh pokoleniiakh yamudakh i goklanakh," p. 224; Lomakin, *Obychnoe pravo turkmen*, pp. 33–34; König, *Die Achal-Teke*, p. 79.

[13] RGASPI, f. 62, op. 3, d. 513, l. 121.

In some areas, non-Turkmen ethnic groups such as Kurds and Persians were part of the demographic mix, generally occupying the lowest rung on the status ladder. Some were remnants of the indigenous population who had lived there before the conquest of the area by Turkmen tribes. Others had migrated into the area recently from Persia or Afghanistan or were descendants of slaves who had been captured by Turkmen during the nineteenth-century Teke wars with Persia.[14] There were also groups that lived among the Turkmen and resembled them in language and way of life, but were thought to be genealogically distinct. These included Turk-menized groups of Persian origin as well as "saintly" tribes popularly believed to be of Arab descent.[15]

Interaction among the diverse groups within each locality took place according to a complex system of of precedence and deference, in which the dominant group claimed first right of access to resources.[16] Thus, the "indigenous" Turkmen group within a region was the economic and polit-ical elite. Sacred tribes and "nonindigenous" Turkmen groups that had been allowed to settle there were next in the hierarchy, possessing a sec-ondary claim to social prestige and economic resources, while non-Turk-men ethnic groups were the lowest on the ladder. In the words of a Soviet ethnographer, "the rich and middle peasants are the indigenous inhabi-tants of this or that village, who arrived on the land before the others, conquered it, and consider themselves the only ones to have full rights in the matter of land tenure. The poor consist mostly of alien [prishlye] elements, who don't have the right to land and water."[17] The non-Turk-men poor often worked as servants or sharecroppers for the dominant Turkmen elite.[18] These social hierarchies were reflected in stark economic terms on the bridal market, where a "pure-blooded" Turkmen woman was worth two to three times as much in bridewealth as one of "mixed blood" and ten times as much as a Kurdish bride.[19]

While distinctions based on descent and historical-political relation-ships were enduring, wealth differences between individual households were more fluid. Among those who mainly practiced livestock herding,

[14] Ibid., op. 2, d. 286, ll. 13–16, 19–21, 42, 182–85, 264.

[15] Ibid., ll. 13–16, 19–21; Karpov, "Turkmeniia i Turkmeny," p. 39; Mikhailov, *Tuzemtsy Zakaspiiskoi oblasti*, pp. 38–39; Basilov, "Honour Groups in Traditional Turkmenian Soci-ety," pp. 220–43; A. P. Potseluevskii, "Plemia Nokhurli (po materialiam ekspeditsii Turk-menkul'ta)," *Turkmenovedenie*, no. 5–6 (May–June 1931): 30–35.

[16] RGASPI, f. 62, op. 2, d. 286, ll. 42, 182–85, 264.

[17] Ibid., l. 42.

[18] Ibid., ll. 182–85, 164.

[19] Ibid., ll.144, 264. On stratification and oppression of "outsiders" in other nomadic societies, see *Pastoral Production and Society: Proceedings of the International Meeting on Nomadic Pastoralism, Paris, 1976* (Cambridge: Cambridge University Press, 1979) pp. 58–59, 443.

herds were subject to frequent losses due to disease, changes in climate, and availability of pasture. Moreover, certain large but essential expenses could also nearly wipe out a family's wealth—for example, the payment of *galïng*, or bridewealth, when a son married. A household might go from comfortable circumstances to virtual destitution within a single year. It was also possible for a family to rebuild its wealth quickly, provided it possessed a pool of able-bodied workers. A large family with many grown sons was the best guarantee of prosperity for both nomads and agriculturalists. Among nomads, sons could work as shepherds for neighbors or relatives; the animals they received in payment would allow the family to rebuild its capital in livestock within a few years. Among predominantly agricultural Turkmen, too, it was relatively easy to convert labor into capital. Even in the early Soviet period, many regions had surplus arable land that could be cultivated by anyone willing to invest the necessary labor.[20] Because the most important inequalities in Turkmen communities were not between individuals but between groups, a "poor peasant" and a "rich peasant" of the same lineage or tribe had reciprocal obligations that far outweighed any potential common interests between two "poor peasants" of different groups. Thus, for most Turkmen Soviet exhortations to struggle against local "exploiters" were unpersuasive; it made little sense to engage in conflict with members of one's own group based on possibly ephemeral distinctions in individual wealth.

Russian travelers and military officers who wrote about Central Asia in the nineteenth and early-twentieth centuries tended to stress the absence of social stratification among the Turkmen. Like their Western European counterparts, many Russians were impressed by the independence, rough democracy, and military prowess of nomadic and seminomadic groups. They were also fascinated by the political structure of the stateless Turkmen, in which conflict was regulated without an overarching political authority. Fëdor Mikhailov, an officer in the Russian military administration of Transcaspia at the beginning of the twentieth century, argued that "all Turkmen, rich and poor, live almost completely alike," and that the Turkmen "put the principles of brotherhood, equality, and freedom

---

[20] Irons, *The Yomut Turkmen*, pp. 2–3, 155–58. Some Russian scholars in the 1920s argued that cyclical wealth fluctuations based on the size of the household labor pool were features of the Russian countryside as well. Sheila Fitzpatrick, *Stalin's Peasants: Resistance and Survival in the Russian Village after Collectivization* (Oxford: Oxford University Press, 1994), p. 29; a similar argument is made in Teodor Shanin, *The Awkward Class: Political Sociology of Peasantry in a Developing Society, Russia 1910–1925* (Oxford: Clarendon Press, 1972), pp. 63–65. On cyclical wealth fluctuations elsewhere in Eurasia, see Caroline Humphrey, *Marx Went Away, But Karl Stayed Behind* (Ann Arbor: University of Michigan Press, 1998), pp. 280–81; Khazanov, *Nomads*, p. 157.

into practice more completely and consistently than any of our contemporary [European] republics."[21]

Early Soviet writers on the Turkmen generally agreed that nomadic Turkmen life in its "pure" form—before the tsarist conquest in the 1880s—had been a classless, egalitarian society.[22] Like their imperial predecessors, Soviet ethnographers in the 1920s were well aware of the importance of genealogical consciousness among the Turkmen. Expeditions to Turkmen regions routinely collected information on the "tribes, clans, and lineages" represented in each area. Interviewers for the 1926 census in Turkmenistan were instructed to determine not only the nationality (*narodnost'*) of each individual, but also his or her "tribe, clan, lineage, and sub-lineage."[23] Soviet scholars were also aware of the absence of anything even remotely resembling European class consciousness among the Turkmen; as one ethnographer wrote, Turkmen society featured a "strongly tribal way of life and an absence of specific class differentiation."[24] However, Soviet ethnographers and economists also argued that things had changed under colonial rule. The Turkmen were no longer footloose steppe warriors, unbeholden to any authority. A majority had settled and taken up some form of agriculture, with many growing cotton and other crops for the market.[25] Some Soviet ethnographers maintained that Russian colonialism had led to the rise of private property in land and class stratification.[26] This was a positive development, in the view of Bolshevik theorists, since it would allow the Turkmen to move beyond their "tribal-clan structure" and develop class consciousness.

For the Bolsheviks, Soviet society was divided into two antagonistic camps: "class friendly" groups that could be expected to support the Soviet regime, such as factory workers and poor peasants; and "class aliens" such as the capitalist bourgeoisie, feudal landlords, and well-to-do peasants.[27] Since this analysis was of dubious applicability even in Russia, it was far from clear how the party would apply Marxist class catego-

---

[21] Mikhailov, *Tuzemtsy Zakaspiiskoi oblasti*, pp. 34, 50.

[22] See Tumanovich, *Turkmenistan i Turkmeny*, pp. 94, 90–91.

[23] RGAE, f. 1562, op. 336, d. 26, l. 157; *Materialy po raionirovaniiu Srednei Azii*, pp. 13–14.

[24] M. A. Nemchenko, "Agrarnaia reforma v Turkmenii," *Novyi vostok*, no. 19 (1927): 123.

[25] The 1897 Russian census showed that nearly two-thirds of Turkmen in the Transcaspian province engaged in agricultural cultivation at least part of the time. Juma Dovletov, *Turkmenskii aul v kontse XIX–nachale XX veka* (Ashgabat, 1977), pp. 56–61, 66–67; Nemchenko, *Dinamika*, pp. 6–10.

[26] Nemchenko, *Dinamika*, pp. 19–27; Nemchenko, "Agrarnaia reforma," pp. 126–27, 134.

[27] See Sheila Fitzpatrick, "Ascribing Class: The Construction of Social Identity in Soviet Russia," *Journal of Modern History* 65 (December 1993), pp. 749–50.

ries to "backward" peoples such as the Turkmen. In Turkmenistan, the tiny industrial proletariat and the urban population were almost exclusively composed of Russians and other Europeans. The overwhelming majority of Turkmen lived in the countryside, practicing agriculture or livestock-herding.[28]

In the absence of a native proletariat, party theorists argued that the rural population would provide the main support for the Bolshevik regime. Turkmen peasants (and Soviet theorists generally included nomads as part of the peasantry) were expected, with the help of Soviet theorists and agitators, to recognize that they were being exploited by rich landowners and "feudal tribal leaders" and to support Soviet power wholeheartedly. Beginning in 1925, the regime sought to classify the Turkmen population according to categories imported directly from the Russian context. Like the Russian peasantry, Turkmen agriculturalists and nomads would be divided into three groups: poor peasants (*bedniaks*), middle peasants (*seredniaks*), and rich peasants (*kulaks*). The rich peasant was regarded as a class enemy and budding capitalist; the poor peasant was the ally of the proletariat; and the middle peasant was the object of a fluctuating and ambivalent policy, sometimes regarded as a proletarian and sometimes as a petty capitalist. Finally, there was the *batrak*, or landless agricultural laborer, presumed to be the Soviet regime's most reliable ally.[29] As in Russia, all members of "nonlaboring" classes—those who exploited the labor of others, made a profit from trade or speculation, or practiced other "socially harmful" professions such as the priesthood—would be deprived of the right to vote and subject to discrimination. At the same time, the regime adopted policies designed to foster class consciousness among the poor. "Bedniaks" and "batraks" were recruited into special organizations for the poor and given preferential access to agricultural credit, government jobs, and education.[30]

THE LAND-WATER REFORM OF 1925–1926

The first large-scale effort to promote class conflict and undermine "tribalism" among the Turkmen population was the land-water reform of 1925–26. In Central Asia as a whole, the reform was intended as an agrarian revolution from above that would remake rural society and render it

[28] Vareikis and Zelensky, *Natsional'no-gosudarstvennoe razmezhevanie*, p. 72.

[29] Moshe Lewin, *Russian Peasants and Soviet Power: A Study of Collectivization* (New York, 1968), pp. 41–78.

[30] See Fitzpatrick, "Ascribing Class," pp. 752–53, for a discussion of these policies in Soviet Russia.

amenable to socialist transformation. It would strike a blow at "feudal elements . . . tribal remnants, and the village bourgeoisie," which were seen as blocking the extension of Soviet power.[31] The all-union Communist Party Central Committee ordered Central Asian party organizations to bring an end to "feudal" and "tribal" patterns of land use, distribute the holdings of large landowners among the poor, and confiscate all "kulak" lands above a certain limit.[32] In Turkmenistan, where land was owned communally and large landowners were rare, the primary goal was to eliminate the genealogical basis of land tenure, which reinforced loyalty to the descent group and complicated Soviet efforts to make political inroads into the Turkmen village.[33]

Soviet officials impatient to carry out land reform assumed that land tenure was the most important economic fact in the Turkmen countryside, as in Russia, and that major social change would follow any redistribution of land. Yet peasant land hunger was not a driving political force in the Turkmen republic. Turkmenistan had not witnessed anything similar to the "black repartition" of 1917 in Russia, where peasants spontaneously seized and redistributed the land of landlords. In fact, many parts of Turkmenistan actually had a surplus of land; the problem, in this arid part of the world, was water with which to irrigate it. Moreover, land was not equally important to all Turkmen. Among those who were wholly or partially nomadic, agriculture—and hence land—played a secondary role.

In the agricultural villages of Transcaspia, the use of land and water with which to irrigate it was most commonly regulated by a system known as *sanashïk*. Under this system, land and water were owned collectively by the descent group. Every married man within the lineage received an equal share of land and water for the use of his household.[34] Households in each village were divided into groups, which would take turns diverting the common flow of water from the local *arïk*, or canal, onto their fields for a specified period of time. Every autumn, lands were redistributed from those who had died or moved away to the newly married. Because there was generally plenty of land, the Turkmen practiced extensive agriculture, moving from plot to plot so as not to exhaust the soil's fertility.[35]

---

[31] A. Vel'tner, "Minuia kapitalisticheskuiu stadiiu razvitiia," *Turkmenovedenie*, no. 10 (October 1930): 4. See also V. Vorshev, "Osnovnye etapy razvitiia partorganizatsii Turkmenistana," *Revoliutsiia i natsional'nosti*, no. 12 (December 1934): 69.

[32] Park, *Bolshevism in Turkestan*, pp. 336–37.

[33] *Ves' Turkmenistan* (Ashgabat, 1926), p. 220.

[34] *Ves' Turkmenistan*, p. 219; Lomakin, *Obychnoe pravo turkmen*, pp. 108–9. This system was also used by some of the neighboring peoples of Iran and Afghanistan. See Tapper, *The Conflict of Tribe and State*, pp. 48–49.

[35] Nemchenko, *Dinamika*, p. 8; Lomakin, *Obychnoe pravo turkmen*, p. 119; *Ves' Turkmenistan*, p. 219. See also Ch. Iazlyev, *Turkmenskaia sel'skaia obshchina* (Ashgabat, 1992).

In areas with elaborate irrigation works, the system for distributing
land and water was highly complex. In Marï province, numerous lineages
cooperated in the building and maintenance of large-scale irrigation systems. Land was categorized according to its fertility and degree of irrigation, with every village receiving an equal amount of land and water in
each category. Thus, each village, and each household within it, had plots
of land in several different locations.[36] Just as land and water ownership
was collective, much of the agricultural work was also accomplished
jointly. Sowing and harvesting took place collectively. The village as a
whole often practiced an informal division of labor, with some residents
taking the entire village's livestock out to pasture, while others tended the
fields of the absent ones. All villagers who received a share of land and
water were obligated to help maintain the irrigation system (a custom
known as *hoshar*), or to provide a substitute if unable to perform this
work themselves.[37] Under the sanashïk system, the most significant inequalities tended to be between groups rather than between individuals.
The poor were those who belonged to groups without access to land and
water—often, members of non-Turkmen ethnic minorities.[38]

• After the tsarist conquest of Transcaspia, the system of land tenure
began to change. With the opening of Transcaspia to the world market,
many Turkmen began to grow cash crops, especially cotton. By the beginning of World War I, 38 percent of the cultivated area of Turkmenia was
devoted to cotton.[39] The rise of cash crops brought about the expansion
of a form of tenure known as *mülk*. Although *mülk* meant slightly different things in different regions, the basic principle was the same; land remained in the hands of a single household and was not subject to annual
redistribution.[40] This form of land tenure was more suitable for growing
cotton and other intensive crops, which required a greater long-term in-
vestment in improving the land.[41] Under tsarist rule, there was also a
growth in the practice of renting land. Many Turkmen households lacked
the resources to cultivate all their sanashïk plots in different locations.
Instead, they concentrated their efforts on their mülk plots, leaving the
sanashïk lands unused or renting them to others.[42] Despite the rise of mülk
and rented land, certain basic principles of customary law did not change;

---

[36] *Ves' Turkmenistan*, p. 218.

[37] Nemchenko, *Dinamika*, p. 8.

[38] RGASPI, f. 62, op. 2, d. 286, ll. 42, 182–85, 264.

[39] Dovletov, *Turkmenskii aul*, p. 88; Nemchenko, *Dinamika*, p. 12.

[40] Lomakin, *Obychnoe pravo turkmen*, pp. 107–8; Nemchenko, "Agrarnaia Reforma,"
p. 122.

[41] Nemchenko, *Dinamika*, p. 9; Dovletov, *Turkmenskii aul*, pp. 156–58; *Ves' Turkmenistan*, p. 219.

[42] *Ves' Turkmenistan*, p. 219; Lomakin, *Obychnoe pravo turkmen*, p. 108.

only a member of the lineage could be a mülk holder, land could not be bought and sold, and the tribe retained the sovereign right to decide on land usage. The tsarist regime, which viewed the tribal collective as a source of stability and a convenient way of collecting tax revenues, encouraged the maintenance of this system.[43]

With the rise of mülk, wealth differentials increased in the regions that had been incorporated most rapidly into the capitalist market. According to Soviet writers, the number of landless peasants in Transcaspia tripled between 1914 and 1917, In 1914, the poorest 80.5 percent of all households in Transcaspia owned 49.9 percent of the land, while the wealthiest 2.9 percent owned 12.4 percent of land. Ashgabat province had gone furthest in the direction of "capitalist" development, with many villages abandoning the sanashïk system entirely. Fifteen percent of households had no land. In other regions, sanashïk remained the dominant form of land tenure, and Soviet investigators found little class differentiation or concentration of land in the hands of the well-to-do.[44] In Marï province, 60 percent of all land remained under the sanashïk system at the time of the land reform, and Soviet analysts reported that wealth differentiation was not yet highly developed.[45] In the Tejen, Saragt, and Yölöten regions, sanashïk was still virtually the only form of land tenure.[46]

The result of the tsarist-era changes was a highly complex land tenure system, still primarily based on sanashïk but rapidly being modified to meet the needs of a cash economy. While economic inequality was clearly on the rise in some regions, there was nothing approaching the peasant dissatisfaction and gross inequalities that had led to "black repartition" in Russia. The Soviet ethnographer Georgii Karpov noted that "well-off people and middle peasants"—in other words, the majority of the Turkmen population—were generally satisfied with the existing system.[47] The purpose of land reform, therefore, was not primarily to redress inequalities and win the support of the peasantry by redistributing land. Instead, it was to destroy traditional economic and landholding patterns, break the link between genealogy and economic interest, and open the countryside to class struggle and Soviet influence.[48] Through land reform in Turk-

[43] Nemchenko, "Agrarnaia reforma," p. 122; Dovletov, *Turkmenskii aul*, pp. 50–51, 158–59, 179.

[44] Nemchenko, "Agrarnaia reforma," pp. 126–27, 133–34; RGASPI, f. 62, op. 2, d. 849, l. 38.

[45] Nemchenko, "Agrarnaia reforma," pp. 126–27, 134.

[46] RGASPI, f. 62, op. 2, d. 849, l. 38. Nevertheless, Soviet investigators claimed that there was "hidden class differentiation" in these regions.

[47] Ibid., d. 286, ll. 41–42.

[48] See Park, *Bolshevism in Turkestan*, pp. 335–36; Vel'tner, "Minuia kapitalisticheskuiu stadiiu," p. 4; Vorshev, "Osnovnye etapy," p. 69.

menistan and elsewhere in Central Asia, the Soviet regime would create a group of peasants dependent on Soviet patronage, instead of on their lineage, for land and economic benefits.[49]

In most of their public pronouncements, however, party officials did not emphasize the destruction of the tribal landholding system. Instead, they justifed the reform by arguing that the existing system of land tenure was "confusing" and "inefficient." Allotting equal shares of land and water to every village, lineage, and household, regardless of size, was said to be both inefficient and inequitable, since it did not reflect the relative growth and decline of lineages and families over time. Moreover, in an argument that echoed criticisms of the Russian peasant commune, Soviet officials claimed that the yearly redistribution of land under sanashïk hindered the development of agriculture, since peasants had no incentive to improve their lands. Finally, they maintained that the scattering of each village's and each household's plots in a number of different places, often miles apart, prevented peasants from concentrating and maximizing their agricultural efforts.[50]

On September 24, 1925, the Turkmen republic's Central Executive Committee decreed that land reform would be conducted in portions of Marï province (Tagtabazar, Yolöten, and Bairamalï districts) and Poltoratsk province (Ginzburg, Gïzïlarbat, and Poltoratsk districts). Several districts in Poltoratsk province (Krasnovodsk, Gazanjïk, and Etrek) were excluded from the reform because they were almost completely nomadic. The Turkmen agricultural areas that had been part of the Bukharan and Khivan republics were also excluded, because they were not deemed "politically ready" for such a step. These regions had a much smaller network of Soviet officials and institutions than Transcaspia; moreover, little was known about their social and economic systems because they had never fallen under direct Russian colonial rule.[51]

The TsIK decree nationalized all land in the republic, banning sanashïk and mülk. Land was allotted to individual households—in the preferred terminology of the Soviet regime, "given to those who till it." The decree established norms, which differed from region to region, for the maximum

---

[49] *Ves' Turkmenistan*, p. 220.

[50] Nemchenko, "Agrarnaia reforma," p. 129–30; *Ves' Turkmenistan*, pp. 218, 221.

[51] RGASPI, f. 17. op. 69, d. 20, l. 102; *Ves' Turkmenistan*, p. 213; Nemchenko, "Agrarnaia reforma," p. 137. The Poltoratsk and Marï provinces correspond to the present-day Ahal and Marï wilayets. Among the Turkmen of Khiva, land and water were owned collectively by the lineage and distributed equally among tribal subsections, as in Transcaspia. In Bukhara, according to Soviet ethnographers, individual land ownership was the rule among the Turkmen population. Bregel, *Khorezmskie turkmeny*, pp. 96–107; N. V. Briullova-Shaskolskaia, "Na Amu Dare: Etnograficheskaia ekspeditsiia v Kerkinskii okrug TSSR." *Novyi Vostok*, no. 16–17 (1927): 297.

amount of acreage a household was permitted to own. Those who had more land than the norm saw the surplus confiscated. Land was confiscated entirely from "merchants who earned their living from trade," from "clergy who did not work the land themselves," and from "nomads who did not take any part in the agricultural economy." Central, provincial, and village land reform commissions were created to implement the decrees.[52]

The land-water reform was a massive effort. In Poltoratsk province, the reform affected 121 villages containing a total of 24,834 households. Of these, 40 percent were "landless" or "land poor" peasants who received land, while 19 percent saw some or all of their land confiscated. In Marï, 22,211 households were affected.[53] The redistribution of lands also entailed large-scale population movements, as thousands of peasants were shifted onto sanashik and mülk lands confiscated from their previous owners.[54] The Turkmen republic's leadership painted a rosy picture of the results of land reform in its official accounts. In published articles and in a presentation to the all-union Communist Party Central Committee, Sovnarkom chair Atabaev maintained that local party cells and the Koshchi Union (the Soviet-sponsored organization of poor peasants) had provided strong leadership for the land reform commissions, "bedniaks" had stood united against their exploiters, and the masses had supported the reform. However, investigators sent by the all-union Central Committee to the Marï region in April 1926 told a different story, describing a process that was chaotic, poorly planned, and corrupt. The reform was accomplished in extreme haste, with thousands of households going before the land-water reform commissions in the course of only a few days. Under these circumstances, accuracy and fairness were nearly impossible.[55]

There was considerable opposition to the reform in the countryside. Villagers argued that the land reform "contravenes Muslim law and custom," and that it was a way for Russians to "register the entire population so that later they can control us." In direct contradiction to the claims of the Turkmen party leadership, the investigators found that "the party, the Komsomol and especially Koshchi played no role in land reform." On the contrary, many rural members of Koshchi and the Communist Party faced confiscation of their lands and vigorously opposed the reform.[56]

People engaged in subterfuge to prevent the confiscation of their lands. Heads of households divided their property among their sons and other relatives to make themselves less vulnerable to the reform. As a result of

[52] *Ves' Turkmenistan*, pp. 212, 334–35; RGASPI, f. 17, op. 69, d. 20, l. 102.

[53] *Ves' Turkmenistan*, pp. 213, 217, 224–25.

[54] Ibid., pp. 220–22, 224–25.

[55] RGASPI, f. 17, op. 69, d. 20, l. 103.

[56] Ibid., f. 62, op. 2, d. 630, ll. 46–47; f. 17, op. 69, d. 20, l. 103; GARF, f. 374, op. 28c, d. 1474a, l. 22.

such maneuvers, the number of households in the Marï region increased from 18,683 to 24,134 virtually overnight.[57] Meanwhile, those who were subject to confiscation as "merchants," "clergy," or "nomads" tried to present themselves as dedicated, full-time agriculturalists.[58] Seeking to retain their plots of land, speculators and traders hastened to close their shops or sell their businesses.[59] Poor peasants failed to stand firm against the wealthy in their villages, instead helping them to conceal their land holdings.[60] Rural residents provided erroneous information to Soviet officials in order to aid their own relatives, "hiding many lands belonging to wealthy peasants and clan leaders."[61] The land reform commissions, full as they were of influential people and members of dominant tribes, did their best to undermine land reform and exempt their kin and supporters from dispossession. Often, an investigator noted, "a member of the commission would protect the rich peasants who were members of his own clan. Subsequently, another member of the commission from a different clan would retaliate by protecting the rich of his own clan."[62]

As a result of such maneuvers, the required transfers of land sometimes failed to take place or took place only fictitiously. In the Yolöten region, for example, dominant Turkmen descent groups were able to resist dispossession and keep more land than the allotted norm, while the poor—mainly members of the Baluchi ethnic minority—remained landless or received less than the standard allotment. In the aftermath of the land-water reform, Soviet institutions reported that "rich peasants" were attempting to undo the reform and "restore old land-water relations." In 1928 and 1929, the Central Asian Economic Soviet and the secret police (OGPU) noted a number of instances of "restoration" throughout the republic. In some cases, "poor peasants" had voluntarily returned land to the original owners; in others, "rich peasants" had continued to use land that had technically been taken away from them, had bought land cheaply from the "poor peasants" to whom it had been given, or had pressured "bedniaks" to return land to its original owners.[63]

Since land was held by the group and divided equally among its members, it was the group, not the individual member, whose economic posi-

[57] Ves' Turkmenistan, p. 214; GARF, f. 374, op. 28c, d. 1474a, l. 22.

[58] GARF, f. 374, op. 28c, d. 1474a, l. 22; Ves' Turkmenistan, p. 214.

[59] Ves' Turkmenistan, p. 214.

[60] GARF, f. 374, op. 28c, d. 1474a, l. 25; RGASPI, f. 17, op. 69, d. 20, l. 103.

[61] RGASPI, f. 17, op. 69, d. 20, l. 103. See also GARF, f. 374, op. 28c, d. 1474a, l. 23; RGASPI, f. 62, op. 2, d. 1811, l. 191.

[62] GARF, f. 374, op. 28c, d. 1474a, l. 23; RGASPI, f. 62, op. 2, d. 1811, l. 191; f. 17, op. 69, d. 20, l. 103.

[63] RGASPI, f. 62, op. 2, d. 1494, ll. 5–6, 31; d. 1811, l. 190, ll. 284–85; d. 1350, l. 86; GARF, f. 374, op. 28c, d. 1474a, l. 23.

tion was harmed or enhanced by the reform. Those who received land often belonged to different descent groups or ethnicities from those who lost land. In the village of Gökcha, members of the Kuvash lineage kept all their holdings, while members of the Kel lineage saw their lands confiscated.[64] In the Yolöten and Saragt regions of Marï province, Baluchis were given the land of Turkmen groups. Often with the collusion of village and district authorities, the former owners of the land plotted to reverse this "unnatural" state of affairs. In the village of Ata in the Saragt district in May 1928, the OGPU reported that "the Turkmen who lost their lands are trying to squeeze the Baluchis out of the village, accusing them of theft and smuggling."[65]

However mixed its results in practice, the land-water reform was the first major intervention in the Turkmen countryside by the Soviet government. In contrast to Russia, where the years of the New Economic Policy (NEP) were a time of relative peace in the countryside, the mid-1920s were a time of upheaval in the villages of central Turkmenistan, as the regime tried to drive a wedge into the heart of Turkmen social and economic organization.[66] The land-water reform was also the first large-scale effort by the Soviet regime to obtain information about the economic and social structure of the Turkmen countryside. On the basis of information obtained during the reform, individuals were classified as "poor peasants," "kulaks," "clergy," and so forth—classifications that had major political consequences for years to come. At the same time, it is clear from the haste, corruption, and opposition involved in the land reform process that much of the information obtained about land ownership and "class" status was tainted and unreliable. Moreover, the reform hardly produced the desired effect of diminishing descent-based loyalties and solidarities. If anything, the rationale for descent group solidarity was increased by Soviet attempts to dispossess some groups in favor of others.

The Commitment to "Tribal Parity"

The attempt to undermine the economic basis of Turkmen descent group affiliation through land reform was just one aspect of Soviet "tribal policy." At the same time, Soviet authorities pursued a second, more concilia-

---

[64] RGASPI, f. 121, op. 1, d. 42, ll. 30.

[65] Ibid., f. 62, op. 2, d. 1350, l. 86; d. 1494, ll. 5–6, 31.

[66] This was true of Central Asia as a whole. See Carrère d'Encausse, *The Great Challenge*, pp. 201–2. On NEP in Russia, see Fitzpatrick, *Stalin's Peasants*, p. 26. For a somewhat less benign view of Russian peasants' lot under NEP, see Vladimir Brovkin, *Russia after Lenin: Politics, Culture, Society* (London and New York: Routledge, 1998), especially pp. 60–66.

tory approach, seeking to diminish the importance of kinship through equitable treatment for all tribes and lineages. This policy of "tribal parity" was not explicitly spelled out in party declarations or publicized in the party press; since "tribal-clan remnants" were supposed to disappear as the Turkmen socialist nation was built, party officials were unwilling to appear to endorse them through an official system of preferences. Rather, it was an informal system of preferences, carried out without fanfare within the republic as a logical extension of the policy of *korenizatsiia*.

In Central Asia, as we have seen, indigenization was intended to help "backward" peoples become Soviet nations. In the view of the Bolsheviks, the promotion of national territories with their own elites and languages would speed the historical development of the non-Russians, mitigate ethnic conflict, and "clear the arena for class struggle."[67] In areas such as Turkmenistan where prenational forms of social structure still prevailed, fair and equal treatment for all descent groups would undercut the basis for "tribalism" and allow the natives to move more quickly to the stage of full Soviet nationhood. Just as national oppression strengthened national identification, genealogical conflict would be exacerbated if some groups believed they were being shortchanged by Soviet rule. Such conflict could be mitigated by assurances that all would have an equal claim on Soviet jobs, education, and political representation.

"Tribal parity" proved difficult to carry out in practice. It was impossible to guarantee all descent groups equal access to administrative positions and economic benefits, given the hierarchical relations among groups within each locality. Soviet authorities were unable to prevent stronger groups from dominating weaker ones. More fatally, the attempt to mitigate descent group conflict through "tribal parity" was at odds with the simultaneous campaign to foment class conflict among the Turkmen. Because "poor peasants" and "kulaks" frequently belonged to different descent or ethnic groups, the Soviet attempt to single out certain classes for preferential treatment or persecution resulted in the inadvertent reinforcement of distinctions based on genealogy and history.

In their ambitious attempts to achieve tribal parity, Soviet authorities set themselves the thankless task of balancing the interests of rival groups at all levels of the genealogical structure. The primary large-scale division within the republic was between the Turkmen of Transcaspia, Bukhara, and Khiva. These three population groups, which had been exposed to different historical experiences and influences over a period of several centuries, were united for the first time by the 1924 "national delimitation" of Central Asia. The Transcaspian regions of Ahal and Marï were

---

[67] Vareikis and Zelensky, *Natsional'no-gosudarstvennoe razmezhevanie*, p. 60; Martin, *The Affirmative Action Empire*, pp. 5–6.

home predominantly to Teke Turkmen and had been under direct Russian colonial rule since the 1880s. The Tekes, as the largest and most powerful Turkmen tribe, had dominated neighboring Turkmen groups prior to the Russian conquest and had been at the forefront of the military resistance to Persian and Russian incursions in the nineteenth century. More recently, the Tekes' proximity to the centers of colonial power had given them some familiarity with Russians and the Russian language. The Turkmen regions of the former Khivan republic, home mostly to Yomut Turkmen, and of Bukhara, inhabited by Ersarïs and other groups, had not experienced direct Russian rule and were more distant from the centers of Soviet power. For all these reasons, Tekes tended to see themselves as "first among Turkmen" and to assume they should dominate the new republic.[68] They were dismissive of other tribes, regarding the Ersarïs, for example, as Turkmen who had been "uzbekified" through long submission to Bukharan rule.[69]

In appointing the leading officials of the new republic, the Central Asian Bureau tried to avoid the impression of Teke or Transcaspian domination and to ensure that government institutions included representatives from each of the three major constituencies. The six appointed members of the Turkmen National Bureau (the committee responsible for drawing the borders of the Turkmen republic during the delimitation) included Turkmen from Transcaspia, Bukhara, and Khiva, as well as a single Russian. The first chair of the republican Central Executive Committee, Nadïrbai Aitakov, was a Yomut from western Transcaspia, while his two deputies were from Khiva and Bukhara. The chair of the Council of People's Commissars, Gaigïsïz Atabaev, was a Teke from the Tejen region of the former Transcaspian oblast. His two deputies were Paskutskii, a Russian, and Mamedov, a Khivan.[70]

The authorities went beyond balancing the interests of the three largest population groups, committing themselves to providing equal treatment to rival subsections of a single tribe. Frequently, one party leader recalled, "promotion of people into this or that post was based not on the professional qualifications of a given employee, but on whether he was from the Utamïsh or Togtamïsh, Atabai or Jafarbai clan." (The Utamïsh and Togtamïsh were subgroups of the Teke tribe; the Atabai and Jafarbai were subgroups of the Yomuts.) At the local level, one Soviet official argued that executive organs of village soviets should include a representative of

[68] RGASPI, f. 62, op. 1, d. 22, ll. 209–12; op. 3, d. 513, ll. 121–22. According to 1927 figures, there were 270,254 Tekes, 157,483 Ersarïs, 103,729 Yomuts, 32,729 Sarïks, 35,541 Salïrs, 20,899 Göklengs, and 24,077 Chaudïrs in the Turkmen republic. Karpov, "Turkmeniia i Turkmeny," pp. 39–40.

[69] RGASPI, f. 62, op. 3, d. 513, ll. 121–22.

[70] Ibid., f. 17, op. 67, d. 206, l. 11.

every lineage in the village; otherwise, local government would be dominated by the strongest descent group. Even the agents of the OGPU became involved, recommending to authorities in Ashgabat that underrepresented lineages be given a greater presence in local government.[71]

With the addition of the "tribal factor," Soviet-style affirmative-action policies had become extraordinarily complicated. Soviet agencies were now required to employ an adequate number of Turkmen, national minorities, women, workers, poor peasants, and members of underrepresented descent groups. Even when officials made genuine efforts to conform to these demands, the policy was not entirely successful at ameliorating group conflict. Non-Tekes continued to complain about "Teke hegemony," maintaining that members of the Teke tribe held a disproportionate number of responsible jobs at high levels of the state and party bureaucracy. Because figures on recruitment generally did not include information on the individual's tribal origins, it is difficult to evaluate these claims.[72] Whatever the reality, the impression of Teke dominance caused resentment among non-Tekes. Teke officials were frequently sent from the capital to work in party and soviet organs in non-Teke regions. As outsiders who were not enmeshed in local kinship obligations, they were more willing to carry out central policies that impinged on the interests of the local population. As a result, Teke officials encountered hostility and suspicion from local Turkmen, who associated them with Russians and the central republican government.

In Gazanjïk, a predominantly Yomut region in western Turkmenistan, a visiting party investigator in April 1932 found bitter mistrust between Teke officials sent from Ashgabat and local Yomut officials. Among the Tekes "there is a kind of fear of appointing local people. They usually hope the center will send someone, therefore there is a real shortage of cadres." The Tekes claimed that the Yomuts could not be trusted to carry out Soviet policies in a disinterested fashion; lacking sufficient "class vigilance" and linked to the local population through ties of kinship, local Yomut officials were reluctant to unmask "kulaks" in the countryside. Meanwhile, the Yomuts pushed for the promotion of local people, sometimes even saying of a candidate, "he can't handle the work, but we have to promote him anyway, otherwise they'll send us a Russian or a Teke."[73]

Soviet authorities were firmly resolved to avoid favoritism toward any segment of Turkmen society, associating such divisive policies with colo-

---

[71] Popok, O likvidatsii sredne-aziatskikh organov, p. 6; RGASPI, f. 62, op. 2, d. 286, ll. 166–68; d. 1494, l. 75.

[72] Statistics are scarce, but an impressionistic survey of the biographies of leading party officials in the 1920s and 1930s indicates that a majority were Tekes from the Ashgabat and Marï regions.

[73] RGASPI, f. 62, op. 2, d. 2818, l. 20.

nial rule by the Russian Empire and the bourgeois European countries. Nevertheless, the regime was forced to rely on whichever local people seemed most capable of carrying out central policies effectively.[74] In practice, this could mean favoring Tekes in conflicts with non-Teke officials in the Turkmen periphery. A bitter conflict erupted in 1927 in Chärjew province, a predominantly Ersarï region, after the young Teke communist Charï Vellekov was appointed first secretary of the provincial party committee. Vellekov's appointment was intended in part to serve as a counterweight to local Ersarï leaders, who viewed the province as their personal fiefdom.[75] It was not long before Vellekov had aroused the wrath of these leaders. In May 1927, local officials in Chärjew launched a petition drive demanding the ouster of the young party secretary and two of his Russian colleagues, Zhukov and Mikhailov.[76] Complaining that the provincial party leadership was undermining local officials and ignoring local concerns,[77] they accused Vellekov of squeezing out Ersarï officials in order to replace them with less-qualified Tekes.[78] District governments, village soviets, and students at the local technical institute all sent anti-Vellekov petitions to the republican TsIK. A leader of the anti-Vellekov movement told one group of supporters that the Chärjew, Dashhowuz, and Kerki provinces of Turkmenistan would secede and join the Uzbek republic if their concerns were not met.[79] Vellekov denied that locals were being removed without good reason, arguing that the Ersarï officials involved were all guilty of drunkenness, venality, corruption, and consorting with "class aliens." After mediation by party leaders in Ashgabat, the matter was settled in favor of Vellekov, who soon afterward became first secretary of the republican party central committee.[80]

Just as it was difficult to maintain "tribal parity" among the largest genealogical subgroups, efforts to ensure equal treatment on the local level were hindered by existing Turkmen social hierarchies. Among the Turkmen, the strongest descent groups had always been able to accumu-

---

[74] European colonial states frequently attempted to bolster their own control by cultivating local minorities who would be dependent on the European rulers for their own power. A prime example is the Levant, where French rulers promoted the Maronites in Lebanon and the Alawites in Syria in order to counter the traditional dominance of Sunni urban elites. See Philip Khoury, *Syria and the French Mandate: The Politics of Arab Nationalism, 1920–1945* (Princeton: Princeton University Press, 1987), pp. 5, 28, 57, 630. The French also supported Berbers against the Arab majority in Morocco. See Tibi, "The Simultaneity of the Unsimultaneous," p. 148.

[75] RGASPI, f. 62, op. 2, d. 874, l. 24.

[76] Ibid.

[77] Ibid., l. 31.

[78] Ibid., ll. 19–21.

[79] Ibid.

[80] Ibid., l. 23; f. 17, op. 67, d. 382, l. 100.

late more social, political, and economic capital than their rivals. Under
Soviet rule, this capital came in the form of Communist Party membership, access to higher education, and control of village election committees. Within specific localities, the influential citizens and elders of high-
status Turkmen lineages tended to control Soviet institutions and the best
jobs. Local cells of Koshchi, the government-sponsored union of poor
peasants, were dominated by the influential people of each community,
rather than the poor and the dispossessed. The Turkmen elite was often
singularly unwilling to allow the poor and landless to participate in local
soviet or party organs, regarding them as "foreigners" and interlopers
who had no right to make decisions about Turkmen affairs. In the village
of Bagïr, near Ashgabat, the Koshchi cell consisted entirely of leaders of
the "saintly" Mahtum tribe and influential members of the dominant Be-
kevül lineage, while "the Kurdish residents of the village, who make up
the poorest part of the population—hired hands, sharecroppers—are not
considered worthy of joining Koshchi and participating in public affairs
along with their employers."[81]

A 1928 investigation of village Communist Party cells in the Poltoratsk
and Marï provinces found a similar situation. In contrast to Russia, where
it was initially the poorest and least powerful peasants who joined the
party, Turkmen village cells were usually dominated by *aksakgals* ("white
beards," or elders)—well-off and influential local leaders. These local
communists refused to accept "batraks" into party cells despite the urging
of party leaders, saying that they are not "our people," and accusing them
of being thieves and opium addicts. In one village in the Gökdepe region,
the party cell secretary explained the absence of "batraks" thus: "There
aren't any batraks in our village, and if there are, they're foreigners, and
we don't bother with them. There aren't any landless people at all." In
the village of Yarïgala, members of the party cell said, "We're afraid of
batraks, they'll eavesdrop in the cell and then tell their own leaders." In
the village of Keshi, one leading party member reported, "There is no
information about the number of batraks in the village. No special meetings of the poor have been called, as the majority of batraks are Persians
and Kurds."[82] The Turkmen republic was not the only place where the
"batraks" and "bedniaks" patronized by the Soviet regime were regarded
as good-for-nothings by other peasants, but in Turkmenistan this alienation was exacerbated by the fact that the poor generally belonged to
different ethnic or descent groups.[83]

---

[81] Ibid., f. 62, op. 2, d. 286, l. 107.
[82] Ibid., op. 3, d. 293, ll. 18–20, 26.
[83] On attitudes toward "bedniaks" in Russia, see Brovkin, *Russia after Lenin*, p. 165;
Fitzpatrick, *Stalin's Peasants*, p. 31.

If poor and landless peasants were members of certain genealogically defined groups, the same was true of the "class aliens" persecuted by the Soviet regime. The well-off peasants stigmatized as "kulaks" generally belonged to the formerly dominant, most prestigious Turkmen lineage in a region, which had naturally been able to accumulate more resources than other groups. Other "class aliens," such as the clergy, also tended to come from specific descent groups. Unlike the settled and urban areas of Central Asia, Turkmen-inhabited regions had little in the way of a professional clergy. Among the indigenous population, the clerical role was most often played by members of the "saintly" tribes. Because Turkmen feared divine retribution if they harmed a member of a saintly tribe, these groups served as neutral mediators in conflicts between descent groups. The saintly tribes also cared for shrines and cemeteries and served as religious folk healers, or *tabibs*.[84] Because of their historical role, the Soviet assault on the Muslim clergy singled these groups out for persecution. In Dashhowuz, when educational institutions were purged of "class-alien elements" in the late 1920s, boys from the saintly Mahtum tribe were classified as sons of clerics and expelled from school.[85]

The examples above show the extent to which Soviet class policy served to harden existing divisions along genealogical lines. Historians have argued that late-nineteenth and early-twentieth-century colonialism resulted in a reification of the "traditional" in many colonized societies, as European rulers codified and institutionalized their own interpretations of local social structures.[86] In similar fashion, Soviet attempts at "tribal parity" and the promotion of class conflict inadvertently perpetuated the distinctions they were designed to eliminate.

Against a backdrop of intensifying class rhetoric, the establishment of Soviet institutions offering villagers access to political and economic power likewise provided compelling new reasons for descent group solidarity.[87] In Turkmenistan, along with conflicts over land and water that

[84] Basilov, "Honour Groups in Traditional Turkmenian Society," pp. 222–30; Irons, *The Yomut Turkmen*, pp. 65–66; König, *Die Achal-Teke*, pp. 82–84. Such religious strata were a common feature among the tribal populations of Central Asia. See also Tapper, *The Conflict of Tribe and State*, pp. 49–50.

[85] RGASPI, f. 62, op. 3, d. 513, l. 121.

[86] Some scholars have argued that British colonialism actually created "traditional" Indian society. For an overview of this literature, see Niels Brimnes, *Constructing the Colonial Encounter: Right- and Left-Hand Castes in Early Colonial South India* (Richmond, Surrey, UK: Curzon, 1999), pp. 5–9. See also Nicholas Dirks, "Castes of Mind," *Representations* 37 (1992): 56–78.

[87] Studies of ethnicity have shown that incorporation into a modern polity often results in a strengthening of particularistic loyalties, at least in the short term. See Eriksen, *Ethnicity and Nationalism*, pp. 67–68; Milton J. Esman and Itamar Rabinovitch, *Ethnicity, Pluralism, and the State in the Middle East* (Ithaca, 1988), pp. 14–15.

predated the Russian revolution, groups came to struggle over who would control the village soviet, whose sons would be conscripted into the Red Army, and who would be deported as a "kulak" (a rich peasant and exploiter). Frequently, a single group would gain control of a region's party and soviet organs, allowing only its own members to reap the benefits of association with the Soviet regime.

In the Tagtabazar region, the Soviet and party apparatus was completely dominated in 1928 by the Sugtï section of the Sarïk tribe. The OGPU reported that whenever there was an attempt to promote a member of a rival group, "you hear endless statements to the effect that he's an opium addict, he has ties with kulaks, and so forth."[88] In the Marï region, the Utamïsh and Togtamïsh branches of the Teke tribe battled over control of Soviet institutions. Having gained control of the government in the Gökdepe district, the Utamïsh succeeded in allotting a larger share of water to their own group during the land-water reform of 1925–26. Moreover, with an Utamïsh at the head of the district executive committee, Togtamïsh candidates had little chance of finding jobs in the local bureaucracy.[89] In 1927, the republican commissariat of education sent a Togtamïsh, a member of the KPT Central Committee, to serve as its representative in Gökdepe. Because of his descent group affiliation, the Utamïsh-led presidium of the district executive committee refused to confirm his appointment.[90] In the village of Büzmeyin in the Ashgabat region, on the other hand, it was reportedly the Togtamïsh who were in charge. As one man lamented at a meeting of nonparty peasants, "In the provincial executive committee there are no Utamïsh. Every official who heads an organization promotes his own relatives, and puts Utamïsh in lower-level jobs."[91] Similar cases were reported throughout the republic. Regional governments neglected villages inhabited by people belonging to the "wrong" descent group, refusing to build schools or provide medical and veterinary assistance. Chairs of village soviets exempted their own kin from military training, conscripting only members of opposing groups.[92]

Village soviets were a prime focus of rural descent group competition. Only by dominating the soviet could one ensure that members of one's own group were classified as "bedniaks" and freed from taxes, while members of opposing groups were classified as "kulaks" and subjected to discrimination.[93] One effective way of achieving this was to dominate

[88] RGASPI, f. 62, op. 2, d. 1494, ll. 67–68.
[89] Ibid., d. 882, l. 169.
[90] Ibid.
[91] Ibid., d. 545, l. 56.
[92] Ibid., d. 1494, ll. 67–68; d. 1349, ll. 154, 159.
[93] On village soviets in Russia, see Lewin, *Russian Peasants and Soviet Power*, p. 81–84; Brovkin, *Russia after Lenin*, p. 164.

the village election committee, which determined who could vote and who would be disenfranchised as a "class alien." In the process of struggling over the village soviets, Turkmen rural residents learned to use Soviet rhetoric to promote the interests of their own descent groups. In this, they were similar to peasants elsewhere in the Soviet Union, who also used Marxist class categories to pursue animosities based on local history, political affiliation, or personal dislike.[94] The difference was that such conflicts in Turkmenistan tended to have a genealogical basis. The Soviet state, by offering political and economic benefits to its "class allies" while meting out punishments to its enemies, had created a strong incentive for Turkmen to express kin conflict in class terms.

Local elections to soviets in 1928 and 1929 featured stepped-up class rhetoric and efforts to recruit more poor and landless peasants as candidates. Between 1928 and 1932, the end of NEP and the acceleration of the Soviet industrialization drive brought a more radical approach to class. Stalin introduced the idea—which quickly became dogma—that as socialism approached, "class enemies" would escalate their desperate resistance and class struggle would intensify. In Turkmenistan, as in all parts of the Soviet Union, there were new efforts to mobilize "bedniaks" and "batraks" in support of the Soviet regime. At the same time, discrimination against disenfranchised "class aliens" intensified; they were purged from mass organizations, fired from jobs, and expelled from educational institutions.[95] However, heightened "class struggle" in Turkmen villages most often manifested itself as heightened descent group struggle.

In 1929, published accounts of the elections in Turkmen villages stressed the growing involvement of the poor, "sharpening class tensions," and the efforts of "rich peasants, clergy, and disenfranchised individuals" to influence the election campaigns in their own interests.[96] However, astute communists recognized that class conflict was not the real story in the Turkmen countryside. Secret accounts of the election campaigns submitted by the OGPU and party investigators indicated that the outcome of local elections was determined almost exclusively by the logic of descent group rivalry. In village after village, the same picture emerged; a single descent group would gain control of the local election committee and deprive members of rival groups of their right to vote by declaring them to be "class-alien elements." Having ensured that its members alone could vote, the dominant group could count on an easy victory for its own candidates. As one OGPU analyst reported:

[94] On the use of "kulak" allegations in village feuding, see Fitzpatrick, *Stalin's Peasants*, p. 260.

[95] Fitzpatrick, "Ascribing Class," pp. 757–59; RGASPI, f. 62, op. 2, d. 1811, ll. 74–75.

[96] "Perevybory sovetov 1929 g. po Turkmenskoi respublike," *Sovetskoe stroitel'stvo*, no. 6 (1929): 64–68.

During the election campaigns, there were many cases in which clans strove to get only their own members onto the election committees and to block representatives of opposing clans. As a result, in a number of districts (Bäherden, Ashgabat, Saragt, Bairamalï, etc.) the election committee was made up of members of only one clan. These clan election committees deprived members of other clans of their voting rights, while restoring the rights of their own rich peasants.[97]

Weaker and smaller descent groups did not submit quietly to their own disenfranchisement. In the Saragt region, four smaller lineages united against the dominant group, which had the support of the district executive committee. In the Bäherden region, the Bek Mamed lineage threatened to emigrate to Persia if its members' voting rights were not restored. In the village of Keshi in the Ashgabat district, where the Gule lineage had controlled the soviet for a number of years, disenfranchised descent groups demanded that the soviet include representatives of all groups in proportion to their numbers within the village.[98]

Tensions between lineages frequently erupted when village soviets held meetings (otchetnye sobraniia) to report on their activities. In a number of mixed-lineage villages in the Ashgabat region, meetings were held separately for each group in order to avert conflict. At these gatherings, one descent group (the one dominating local government) would invariably declare the work of the village soviet to be entirely satisfactory, while the other groups would criticize it with equal vehemence. Rival groups would accuse each other of protecting "kulaks," consorting with "criminal elements," and illegally depriving others of their voting rights.[99] In the village of Sünche in the Bäherden region, members of the Hoja and Shikh lineages complained that the chairman of the village soviet had deprived several members of their groups of their voting rights, while leaving intact the voting rights of "opium addicts and kulaks" among the the locally dominant Arab lineage. The village election committee, it turned out, was made up exclusively of members of the Arab group. In the village of Mürche, the Dekyash lineage accused the village soviet, which consisted solely of members of the Bayakchi-Yüzbashï lineage, of providing agricultural loans to its own well-off kin and refusing to give credit to the poor.[100]

Beginning in 1928, there were accelerated efforts to root out the "exploiters" of the Turkmen masses, especially the "kulaks" who were allegedly seeking to reverse land reform. The secret police played a leading

[97] RGASPI, f. 62, op. 2, d. 1349, ll. 83, 153; on the misuse of electoral commissions in Russia, see Brovkin, Russia after Lenin, p. 164.
[98] RGASPI, f. 62, op. 2, d. 1349, ll. 83, 153.
[99] Ibid., l. 154.
[100] Ibid., ll. 154, 84.

role in urging a tougher policy toward supporters of the pre-reform status quo. A 1928 report submitted by Karutskii, head of the Turkmen OGPU, to his superiors in Tashkent urged a crackdown on "rich peasants" and "large landowners" in the Marï district. Karutskii noted that the liquidation and resettlement of "non-laboring households" had not been properly carried out, and that land taken from "rich peasants" had not actually been given to the poor. The district executive committee, after confiscating land from those presumed to be well-to-do, in many cases allowed it to fall into the hands of "class-alien" elements. Karutskii recommended that Marï officials be put on trial for neglect of duty and distortion of the class line. He also advocated the arrest and deportation of a number of leading Marï landowners. These individuals were considered extremely dangerous not because they were openly opposing Soviet policies, but because they were seeking to influence local Soviet institutions through their supporters and relatives. One of those slated for deportation was Emir Berdiev, a leader of the Togtamïsh who had been a prominent political figure in tsarist times. A large landowner whose lands had been worked by hired hands and sharecroppers before the revolution, Berdiev continued his efforts to control local government under Soviet rule, ensuring that his sons and supporters occupied top jobs in the local administration. The OGPU also targeted Övezmïrad Klïch Mïrad, a former tsarist district administrator who reportedly used hired labor to work his extensive lands. Despite losing a portion of his property in the land-water reform, he had retained some land and one thousand head of sheep. Moreover, by arranging for his nephew to be elected secretary of the village soviet, Övezmïrad was able to influence the local administration.[101]

The OGPU noted that many "poor peasants" continued to lack class consciousness and remained subject to the influence of "kulaks." In Chärjew, "poor peasants" responded negatively to a decree exempting them from labor conscription on hoshar (public works), calling it a "sin" and saying, "How can we eat bread and drink water, without working? For centuries everyone has worked on the hoshar, we are obliged to, if only for fairness' sake." In the village of Agar, Dänew region, peasants identified as poor and landless spoke out in 1929 in favor of restoring voting rights to the well-to-do.[102] "Rich peasants," too, naturally rejected the attempt to divide villagers by class. At meetings in the Kaka region, peasants identified as kulaks demanded that representatives of all social groups be included in village soviets. In Chärjew, they declared that "all people are equal and should have the right to attend meetings. The Soviet authorities

[101] Ibid., ll. 6–8, 10, 12–13, 15–17, 20–21.
[102] Ibid., d. 1884, l. 75.

are sowing conflict among the peasants, inviting some of them to meetings and chasing away others."[103]

The policy of promoting class struggle and exposing "exploiters" reached a climax in 1930 and 1931 with the campaign for the collectivization of agriculture and the "liquidation of kulaks as a class." In Turkmenistan, as in Russia, the absence of a clear-cut definition of "kulak" meant that the category was applied in an arbitrary manner, often to those perceived as enemies of the Soviet state.[104] Moreover, the close intertwining of the categories of class and kinship that had taken place in the 1920s meant that many of those repressed as "kulaks" belonged to specific genealogically defined groups. At the same time, this unprecedented assault on the Turkmen countryside led much of the population to unite in opposition to the Soviet regime. Protests were mostly peaceful in the central agricultural regions of the republic, but in the more remote nomadic and desert regions, they swelled into a massive violent uprising and led to large-scale emigration in the spring of 1931. Turkmen pastoralists burned and looted collective farms and other Soviet institutions, killed European officials, and poured over the border into Afghanistan along with their flocks. (See chapter 7 for more detail on this uprising.) Even Soviet officials admitted that this violent rejection of Soviet policy knew no class boundaries: "poor" and "middle" pastoralists rioted, looted, and emigrated along with "kulaks."[105]

One result of the intensification of class struggle was a changing view of nomads and nomadism. If the Turkmen tribal system was one of the most egregious manifestations of Turkmen backwardness, nomads were thought to be the most devoted adherents of the tribal structure and all the archaic customs that went along with it. Moreover, they represented a segment of the Turkmen population that was highly mobile and hard to "sovietize." When Soviet ethnographers stressed the classless nature of Turkmen society in the 1920s, they placed special emphasis on the poverty and primitive egalitarianism of the Turkmen nomads. Visitors to nomadic encampments noted how poor and "backward" they were, citing their monotonous diet, the prevalence of poor sanitation, disease, and superstition, and the lack of formal education among the desert dwellers.[106] Offi-

[103] Ibid., l. 22.

[104] On arbitrariness and the intrusion of political factors in defining kulaks elsewhere in the Soviet Union, see Fitzpatrick, *Stalin's Peasants*, p. 54; Lewin, *The Making of the Soviet System*, pp. 124–28; Viola, *Peasant Rebels under Stalin*, pp. 33–35.

[105] RGASPI, f, 62, op. 1, d. 888, l. 65; op. 2, d. 2140, ll. 3–4; d. 2740, ll. 24–25; d. 2793, l. 93. On resistance to collectivization in Russia, see Viola, *Peasant Rebels under Stalin*, pp. 68–69, 82–83.

[106] See, for example, RGASPI, f. 62, op. 2, d. 801, ll. 124–25; Tumanovich, *Turkmenistan i Turkmeny*, pp. 90–91, 94.

Figure 10. Nomadic encampment in the Karakum desert, 1928. (From the collection of the Russian State Archive of Film and Photographic Documents at Krasnogorsk.)

cial sources mentioned the frequent and great fluctuations in herd size and estimated that the average income of nomadic households was lower than that of sedentary agriculturalists.[107] Although ethnographers in the 1920s did observe inequalities among the present-day nomads, they argued that these were deformations introduced by Russian colonialism, not inherent features of nomadic society. In any case, ethnographers prior to 1928 were just as likely to emphasize the nomads' love of equality and freedom as the gap between rich and poor—or to argue that this gap was not terribly significant because rich and poor were kin.

During the late 1920s and early 1930s, however, some party officials came to see nomads as an intransigent and uniquely anti-Soviet part of the Turkmen population. Not only were they elusive and hard to control, but they were also the most likely to flee across the border to Iran and Afghanistan in response to unpopular Soviet policies, and the most likely to take

[107] GARF, f. 3316, op. 20, d. 392, l. 24.

up arms against the Soviet regime in extremis. In the logic of Soviet thinking, those who opposed Soviet power tended to be defined as "class enemies." Gradually, nomads came to be defined more and more as "kulaks,"
a "nonlaboring" part of the population that should be "liquidated." By
1932, party officials were arguing that the nomadic lifestyle itself required
great wealth; hence nomads were "kulaks" by definition. Only wealthy
individuals could afford to move their livestock, families, and possessions
from place to place in search of fodder for their animals.[108]

Despite the Soviet discovery of a class hierarchy among nomads, kinship
showed no sign of disappearing as the main ideology structuring nomadic
social solidarities and animosities. On the contrary, the violent campaign
to transform society had only increased the need for the safe harbor of
genealogical affinity. Thus, in the "livestock collective farms" established
in nomadic regions, conflict along genealogical lines was widespread in the
1930s. Often the farm's administration would be dominated by a single
descent group, which would exempt its own kin from the required communalization of livestock. Work would be distributed inequitably, with members of the dominant descent group assigning their relatives the best paid
and least arduous tasks. On livestock collectives, as elsewhere in Turkmenistan, class conflict was transformed into kin rivalry.[109]

At the same time, Soviet theorists were attempting a reverse feat of
conceptual alchemy: the transformation of kinship into class. Fired by the
cultural revolution's impatience with lingering forms of backwardness,
ethnographers did their best in the early 1930s to define the Turkmen
kinship problem out of existence. "Tribes" and "clans" were declared to
be relics of an era that had already been left behind by a fully collectivized
Central Asia. Fewer articles in the Turkmen press now exhorted Turkmen
to overcome their anachronistic "tribal-clan structure," since to do so
was to imply that the heroic upheavals associated with the "great turn"
had failed to transform the Turkmen. Some scholars concluded that kinship had already ceased to exist as the main principle of Turkmen social
structure, even among nomads, where the "tribal order" was thought to
be strongest. The ethnographer P. F. Preobrazhenskii argued that tribal
solidarity had become largely a fiction among Yomut Turkmen, since kin-
based relationships had given way to territorial allegiances. Another
scholar, A. Bernshtam, argued that the Turkmen had moved from primitive communism to feudalism, leading to the disintegration of kinship
relations and the concentration of wealth in a few hands. Instead of acting
in the interests of tribal solidarity, descent group leaders had now become

---

[108] RGASPI, f. 62, op. 2, d. 2793, ll. 114–15.
[109] K. Lapkin, "Kollektivizatsiia i klassovaia bor'ba v kochevykh raionakh Turkmenii,"
Sotsialisticheskoe khoziaistvo Turkmenii, no. 1 (1934): 23–26.

"kulaks" who used slogans about solidarity to exploit their kin.[110] With this new view of Turkmen society, Soviet theorists had found a convenient way of reconciling the contradictions between class and kinship. Genealogy and class were no longer competing conceptions of social organization; in reality, class alone existed, and kinship relations were merely a front for class exploitation.

In the rhetoric of Soviet theorists and Turkmen villagers, then, class and kinship had become one and the same thing. What accounts for the striking ease with which each side adopted and manipulated the other's categories? The explanation may lie in the conceptual similarities between class and kinship ideology. Each followed a rigid, dichotomous logic of exclusion and inclusion, which provided a mechanism for distinguishing "insiders" from "outsiders" and determining who would have access to political and economic power. Turkmen villagers were familiar with the idea that society was divided into mutually exclusive—and often mutually antagonistic—groups. Instead of "class allies" and "class enemies," however, Turkmen communities were divided between *ig* and *gul*, conquerors and conquered, dominant lineages and "aliens," and these were the distinctions Turkmen villagers had in mind when they employed the Soviet rhetoric of class warfare. Such conceptual affinities help to explain why the promotion of class conflict tended to reinforce genealogically based distinctions. Among the Turkmen, genealogy was to some extent destiny, playing a significant role in determining one's social status, choice of marriage partner, and economic opportunities. In a sense, then, kinship *was* class—or the closest thing to class Turkmen society had to offer—and eliminating the one while promoting the other was next to impossible.

[110] P. F. Preobrazhenskii, "Razlozhenie rodovogo stroia i feodalizatsionnyi protsess u turkmenov-iomudov," *Etnografiia*, no. 4 (1930): 11–15; A. Bernshtam, "Problema raspada rodovykh otnoshenii u kochevnikov Azii," *Sovetskaia etnografiia*, no. 6 (1934): 86–115. On the new impatience with "backwardness" during the cultural revolution, see Slezkine, *Arctic Mirrors*, pp. 259–63; Hirsch, "Empire of Nations," pp. 208–9.

Chapter Seven

COTTON AND COLLECTIVIZATION

RURAL RESISTANCE IN SOVIET TURKMENISTAN

O N JUNE 24, 1931, a band of Turkmen guerrilla fighters invaded the "International" collective farm in Dashhowuz province. More than 150 of the kolkhoz's members, including the chairman and party cell secretary, joined forces with the attackers. Fortified with the farm's supplies of money and weapons, the rebels headed for the nearby town of Köneürgench. Along the way, the mob grew as it was joined by villagers and rural soviet members from the surrounding area. In Köneürgench, the rebels went on a rampage, looting government offices and Russian homes and lynching a number of Soviet officials. Finally, they burned down the buildings housing the key institutions of Soviet power in the countryside—the local office of the OGPU, the district executive committee (*raiispolkom*), and the district party committee (*raikom*).[1]

The assault on Köneürgench was not an isolated incident, but part of a massive uprising that shook the Turkmen republic in the spring and summer of 1931. Along with ordinary peasants and nomads, rural officials and even Communist Party members took part in the looting, burning, and killing. What had happened in the six short years since the founding of the Turkmen republic to produce such violent opposition to the Soviet regime among the rural population? Although policies such as land reform had antagonized many rural Turkmen in the mid- and late 1920s, the real impetus for the 1931 uprising was the Soviet campaign for agricultural collectivization launched in 1929–30. The revolt in Turkmenistan, one of the worst outbreaks of anticollectivization violence in the Soviet Union, showed that the promises of Soviet "nationality policy" meant little to rural people facing an unprecedented assault on the foundations of their economic and social life. While there was intense resistance to collectivization throughout the Soviet Union, it took its most violent form in the "national republics," especially those of the Muslim periphery.[2]

---

[1] RGASPI, f. 62, op. 2, d. 2541, ll. 229–30, 224–25.

[2] On resistance in different parts of the Soviet Union, see Viola, *Peasant Rebels under Stalin*, pp. 159–60; Martin, *The Affirmative Action Empire*, pp. 293–95.

The Bolsheviks had sought to distance themselves from tsarist colonialism by pledging support for the national autonomy and equality of all Soviet peoples. Indigenization, the centerpiece of Soviet nationality policy, was popular with Turkmen elites, who were not only ideologically disposed toward nationalism but also enjoyed the practical benefits of preferential access to jobs and education. Yet the rhetoric of national autonomy was lost on most rural Turkmen. They cared little about the location of national borders, the number of university places reserved for Turkmen, or the content of the national literary language; their concerns and interests were overwhelmingly local. Moreover, the rural population's illiteracy and unfamiliarity with Russian limited the Soviet regime's ability to communicate its supposedly benevolent intentions. While elites in Ashgabat embraced the goals of nationality policy as their own, villagers were more openly suspicious of Soviet initiatives.

In the early years of Soviet rule, building socialism in Turkmenistan meant above all the eradication of backwardness and the introduction of a "civilized"—read European—way of life. Yet villagers who welcomed the practical benefits of modernity such as electricity and medical care were understandably less enthusiastic about Soviet efforts to engineer radical social change within their communities and families. The rural population sought in various ways to evade and undermine Soviet campaigns against "backwardness," whether these targeted land tenure, marital practices, or kinship loyalties. With the adoption of the first Five-Year Plan in 1928, the construction of socialism in the Soviet Union came to mean a headlong rush toward a centrally planned, industrialized economy. This, in turn, required the forcible restructuring of the rural sphere. The Stalinist regime used naked coercion to push recalcitrant peasants into collective farms controlled by the state, a policy designed to ensure a steady supply of grain at low prices and provide the regime with the capital needed for industrialization. In Turkmenistan, collectivization was accompanied by a campaign to force the rural population to grow cotton instead of food crops. Despite the rhetoric of national equality, Central Asia was to play a subordinate role within the industrialized Soviet economy as a supplier of raw materials.

Between 1928 and 1932, large numbers of Turkmen peasants and nomads made it clear that they wanted nothing to do with the Soviet regime, which they regarded as a hostile and alien power. They understood collectivization as an effort by outsiders—"Russians" or "infidels"— to destroy the Turkmen way of life. Faced with all the coercive resources of the Soviet state, Turkmen villagers sought to evade government control through subterfuge, selective cooperation, and passive resistance. When these strategies failed, the rural population turned to more overt forms of opposition: demonstrations, armed rebellion, and flight across the borders of the Soviet Union.[3]

MOBILIZATION AND MISTRUST

From the outset, Turkmen peasants and nomads had good reason to be suspicious of their new Bolshevik rulers. The decades of Russian colonial rule had left a bitter legacy of violence and mistrust between Turkmen and the authorities of the Russian state—a legacy recent enough to be vivid within the memories of older people in the 1920s. On several occasions in the late-nineteenth and early-twentieth centuries, Russian troops had massacred Turkmen populations who resisted colonial rule. In 1873, the Russians sent a punitive expedition against the Khivan Yomuts, killing people and livestock and burning their nomadic encampments.[4] In 1881, Russian forces killed thousands of Ahal-Teke Turkmen, including many women and children, who had barricaded themselves in the Gökdepe fortress in a last-ditch attempt to resist Russian conquest.[5] More recently, Russian troops brutally put down a 1916 uprising in response to World War I labor conscription. Even after the 1917 revolutions, officials interested in appeasing the urban Russian population ignored Turkmen sufferings in famine and war, while the Red Army suppressed native attempts to achieve self-governance. Turkmen peasants and nomads had little reason to think that the Russians—even in their new "Soviet" incarnation—had the best interests of the indigenous population at heart.

The wariness of Turkmen villagers toward the new regime manifested itself in several ways. One was a reluctance to provide information to government representatives. Like all modern states, the Soviet regime was keen to collect data about its population, obsessively mapping, surveying, and classifying the peoples and territories under its rule.[6] Just as rural Turkmen had little understanding of the new regime and its goals, Russian officials knew little about Turkmen customs and beliefs. Study of the Turkmen by European anthropologists and linguists had begun relatively late, since Transcaspia was not considered safe for European travelers

[3] On the many forms taken by resistance among rural populations, see Scott, *Weapons of the Weak*.

[4] Pierce, *Russian Central Asia*, p. 33; Karpov and Batser, *Khivinskie turkmeny i konets kungradskoi dinastii*, pp. 6, 23, 31.

[5] Saray, *The Turkmens*, pp. 210–12; Karpov, *Ocherki po istorii turkmenii i turkmenskogo naroda*, p. 22; Pierce, *Russian Central Asia*, pp. 40–41.

[6] James Scott, *Seeing Like a State: How Certain Schemes to Improve the Human Condition Have Failed* (New Haven and London: Yale University Press, 1998), pp. 2–3; Holquist, "To Count, to Extract, and to Exterminate," pp. 112–14.

prior to the establishment of Russian control in the 1880s. Before then, only a handful of intrepid souls had ventured into Turkmen territory and reported back on the ways of the "wild, half-savage" inhabitants.

After the conquest of Transcaspia, Russian geographers and ethnographers began collecting information on the ethnic composition and economic activities of the population.[7] The Soviet regime built on the efforts of the Russian colonial administration. The pursuit of information was hardly motivated by idle curiosity, since the data collected would provide an essential basis for carrying out Soviet policies. Before the national delimitation of Central Asia, Soviet scholars traveled throughout Central Asia collecting ethnographic and demographic data that would facilitate the drawing of borders between the republics. In 1925, "brigades" of ethnographers traveled to a number of Turkmen regions in order to study village social structure and land tenure in anticipation of the upcoming land-water reform. In 1926, the republican Central Committee formed a Committee on Livestock Herding, which was charged with studying the republic's nomadic pastoralists and recommending ways to bring them under Soviet influence and control. This committee organized numerous expeditions to nomadic regions between September 1926 and January 1927. The year 1927 saw the creation of the Institute for Turkmen Culture and its journal *Turkmenovedenie*, which were charged with researching all aspects of Turkmen society and culture.[8]

Fearing that the information gathered could be used against them, some rural residents undermined the regime's efforts. Members of an ethnographers' brigade investigating Ashgabat province in 1925 reported that villagers had intentionally provided the investigators with false information about social and economic conditions.[9] During the 1925–26 land reform, peasants lied about their landholdings, seeking to protect the property of their kin from confiscation. Exploiting the regime's concern with "class aliens," villagers falsely accused members of rival groups of being kulaks. Villagers also concealed basic information about their age and nationality if it was in their interest to do so. A commission seeking to determine the tribal composition of village party cells in 1926 encountered numerous Turkmen party members who claimed not to know their own tribe or lineage—an ignorance that seemed highly suspicious in light of the Turkmen obsession with genealogy. When rumors circulated during the 1926 census

[7] Daniel Brower, "Islam and Ethnicity," pp. 122–30.

[8] M. Pravda, "Sovetizatsiia turkmenskikh kochevii," *Turkmenovedenie*, no. 10–11 (October–November 1929): 53–55; SPF ARAN, f. 135, op. 1, d. 18, ll. 1, 4–5, 36–37; RGASPI, f. 62, op. 2, d. 102, l. 62; on the relationship between Soviet ethnographers and the state, see Hirsch, "Empire of Nations," pp. 34–38; on ethnographic "brigades" studying Turkmen regions, see RGASPI, f. 62, op. 2, d. 286.

[9] RGASPI, f. 62, op. 2, d. 286, ll. 4–5.

that non-Turkmen would lose their land allotments, members of minority groups simply told census takers that they were Turkmen.[10] Young women lied about their age in order to make themselves legally eligible for marriage, while young men lied about their age in order to make themselves ineligible for military service. When the army called up all men born in 1907 for military training, numerous villages reported the astonishing news that not a single male child had been born to their residents that year.[11] In the absence of official records and sources of information apart from the villagers themselves, it was difficult for government representatives to check or correct the erroneous information they were given.

Turkmen villagers were similarly cautious in their response to Soviet efforts to mobilize the population. The authorities urged peasants and nomads to participate in the Soviet enterprise by joining village soviets, Communist Party cells, the alliance of poor peasants known as the Koshchi Union, and women's groups. Party leaders hoped that villagers who joined these organizations would form a rural elite that could be counted on to support Soviet policies. Many Turkmen did sign up for the various village organizations sponsored by the Soviet regime, but their involvement was often fictitious or half hearted. While propagandists claimed that the poor and landless were "spontaneously organizing in support of the Soviet regime," more candid sources acknowledged that local village organizations were most often created by visiting officials and agitators from the city. A party investigator noted in 1925 that the village branches of the Koshchi Union in Marï were "artificially grafted" onto village society and not "a natural result of the population's striving to organize itself." Poor peasants were incapable of organizing on their own, Soviet investigators wrote, because they were unaware of their exploitation at the hands of well-to-do peasants.[12] Village soviets and party cells met only when ordered to do so by higher-ups from Ashgabat, passing resolutions that echoed verbatim the instructions of their superiors.[13]

While officials in Ashgabat hoped that Turkmen who joined Soviet organizations would form a pillar of support for the regime in the countryside, many Turkmen expected that their participation would bring immediate and tangible benefits such as government salaries, political influence, and the ability to protect their kin from intrusive state policies. Because they joined for practical reasons rather than out of sympathy with the ideological basis of the Soviet regime, Turkmen peasants were quick to

---

[10] Ibid., d. 881, ll. 10, 27. On land reform, see RGASPI, f. 17, op. 69, d. 20, l. 103. See also GARF, f. 374, op. 28c, d. 1474a, l. 23; RGASPI, f. 62, op. 2, d. 1811, l. 191. On Turkmen concealing their tribal affiliation, see RGASPI, f. 121, op. 1, d. 42, ll. 89, 103–4.

[11] RGASPI, f. 62, op. 2, d. 1810, ll. 51–52.

[12] Ibid., d. 284, l. 198.

[13] Ibid., d. 1494, l. 72.

abandon Soviet organizations when they failed to deliver as promised. In the Tagtabazar region in 1928, for example, peasants rapidly became disillusioned with the Koshchi Union. According to an investigator, the members refused to pay their dues, "declaring openly that the organization does not bring any benefits and that the Soviet authorities had tricked the peasantry, promising members of Koshchi all sorts of benefits and giving them absolutely nothing."[14] In 1928, when mandatory military training was instituted exclusively for "organized youth"—in other words, those belonging to the party, Komsomol, and other Soviet organizations—villagers found that participation in Soviet organizations could actually be a liability. In response, young men left these organizations in droves. In the Etrek and Tagtabazar regions, people warned their neighbors, "Don't join any sorts of organizations. Today they're taking Komsomols and party members, but tomorrow they'll mobilize everybody who belongs to any kind of social organization. Give back your membership cards."[15]

COLLECTIVIZATION AND MASS REBELLION

The attitude of the rural population toward the state was wary but not overtly antagonistic prior to 1928. With the exception of the vocal male opposition to female emancipation in the mid-1920s, discussed in the next chapter, villagers did not openly oppose Soviet initiatives in the countryside; instead, they favored passive resistance such as the withholding of information, surreptitious undermining of Soviet policies, and superficial compliance with Soviet decrees. At the same time, they made opportunistic use of Soviet organizations such as village party cells and soviets. With the launching of the first Five-Year Plan and the campaign for rapid industrialization in 1928, accommodation gave way to overt resistance as Turkmen peasants and nomads came under growing pressure from the Soviet regime. The campaign for the collectivization of agriculture infuriated many Turkmen, who just three or four years earlier had been forced to scrap their collective land-holding system for a system of individual land tenure that was supposedly more "progressive."

At the same time, the Soviet regime's efforts to force Turkmen peasants to plant cotton evoked painful memories of the famine in Central Asia between 1917 and 1921, which was caused in part by an overreliance on cotton at the expense of grain and other food crops. In the Turkmen countryside, tensions over collectivization and cotton erupted in the early

14 Ibid., ll. 71–72
15 Ibid., d. 1351, l. 171.

Figure 11. Turkmen men attending a Soviet trade union meeting in Dashhowuz, 1930. (From the collection of the Russian State Archive of Film and Photographic Documents at Krasnogorsk.)

1930s into forms of resistance reminiscent of the late-imperial and revolutionary periods. Villagers demonstrated against Soviet demands and vented their rage in physical assaults on local officials; bands of Basmachi-style rebels launched attacks on the institutions and representatives of Soviet power in the countryside; nomads packed up their tents, families, and flocks and fled beyond the borders of the Soviet Union. As Moscow's demands came into direct conflict with the economic interests of Turkmen villagers, the relationship between center and periphery became one of acute mutual hostility.

The move toward mass collectivization of agriculture in the Soviet Union took place in the winter of 1929–30. After several years of conflict between state and peasantry that had begun with the "grain crisis" of early 1928, the party became convinced that large-scale collectivization was the only way to control the peasantry and ensure an adequate supply of grain at state-determined prices. The need for rapid and total collectivization was proclaimed at the end of 1929 and launched in the first two months of 1930. At the same time, Stalin declared a stepped-up effort to root out the "class enemies" of the Soviet state, including the wealthy peasants known as "kulaks"; in December 1929, he called for the "liqui-dation of the kulaks as a class."[16]

In Turkmenistan, the crop in question was cotton rather than grain, but the policy and pattern of execution were similar. As in Russia, the growth of collective farms (*kolkhozes*) in the Turkmen republic began in the fall of 1929. Between October 1, 1929, and January 1, 1930, the proportion of collectivized households rose from 6.8 percent to 14.8 per-cent. A decree of the executive bureau of the republican Central Commit-tee on January 1, 1930, called for the complete collectivization of all ag-ricultural households in Turkmenistan by the end of the first Five-Year Plan. In early February 1930, three districts (Farap, Sayat, and Dänew) were declared regions of "100 percent collectivization." As tempos accel-erated, other districts, including Marï, Gïzïlayak, Kaka, and Kerki, also declared themselves zones of 100 percent collectivization; Chärjew prov-ince declared its intention to be totally collectivized by spring of 1931. The authorities in some districts declared a goal of total collectivization even without pressure from Ashgabat, assuming, as did the deputy chair of the district executive committee in Yolöten, that "if we don't declare 100 percent collectivization, the center won't give us tractors, money, or people." By February 1930, 38 percent of all households in the republic were collectivized.[17]

Though collectivization was officially voluntary, in practice, as else-where in the Soviet Union, peasants in Turkmenistan were threatened, cajoled, and coerced into signing up. In the village of Shordepe in the Marï region, the chair of the village soviet told peasants that their land allotments would be confiscated and they would be exiled from the region if they refused to join the kolkhoz. In the village of Araki, Chärjew prov-ince, a visiting government representative declared, "If you don't sign up for the kolkhoz, they'll force you to plant cotton. They won't allow you to plant even one pound of grain, and you'll die of hunger." In the village of Büzmeyin in the Ashgabat region, authorities told peasants that those who refused to join the kolkhoz would lose their land and water allot-ments and would not be allowed to buy cooking oil or train tickets.[18]

The forcible communalization of peasants' livestock during the collec-tivization drive led to the loss of many animals through negligence and poor planning. In Chärjew province, "livestock was gathered into com-mon bases, but there was nothing to feed it with, so the animals could

---

[16] Lewin, *Russian Peasants and Soviet Power*, pp. 19–20; Fitzpatrick, *Stalin's Peasants*, pp. 3–4, 54.

[17] Central State Archive of Turkmenistan (henceforth TsGAT), f. 1, op. 7, d. 200, ll. 2–16, excerpted in *Türkmen arhivi*, no. 1 (1993): 54, 59–60.

[18] Ibid., pp. 57–58.

hardly drag their legs behind them and were completely unfit for work, especially heavy work in the fields." In the Kaka district, three collective farms lost all their animals due to the authorities' failure to provide fodder for communalized livestock. In many regions, people began to sell off and slaughter their livestock, believing it would be taken away from them in any case.[19]

As a result of these "crude errors and distortions of the party line," a groundswell of opposition to collectivization emerged in Turkmenistan in March and April 1930. Nearly every part of the republic witnessed demonstrations by peasants who harassed and beat up particularly detested Soviet officials and demanded the disbanding of collective farms. People condemned collectivization at meetings and demonstrations in Kaka, Farap, Marï, and Dashhowuz. In Marï, peasants invited to attend "educational" meetings about collective farms announced, "We don't need kolkhozes, we live worse than dogs. Having joined the kolkhoz, we forgot the taste of plov [rice pilaf with meat]. The kolkhoz is a noose placed around our neck." In Dashhowuz, well-to-do peasants in the village of Ketli warned others that they would go hungry as a result of joining the kolkhoz. Some villagers viewed the conflict over collectivization as a life-or-death struggle between the Turkmen and Russian ways of life, warning that

> by joining the kolkhoz, Muslims will take on the Russian way of life and become infidels. We have to save our lands from Russians and destroy all those who support kolkhozes and Soviet power, all those who are connected to the Russians. Previously, under the khans, the peasants lived better than they do now.[20]

Mass demonstrations against collectivization took place in many parts of Kerki and Dashhowuz provinces, while smaller protests occurred in Marï, Saragt, Bairamalï, Ashgabat, and other regions. On March 4, 1930, a demonstration in the village of Beshir in the Hojambaz district of Kerki province drew around eight hundred participants. The protesters, led by women, demanded the dissolution of the kolkhozes and the expulsion of all Europeans from the area. Finally, the protesters demanded that the secretary of the local party cell and the local OGPU agents be handed over to them in order to "settle scores." On March 6, a crowd of four hundred made up of members of four kolkhozes descended on the Hojambaz district executive committee. They demanded the dissolution of the collective farms. When the district officials explained that joining the kolkhoz was strictly voluntary, the crowd burst into delighted applause. Around five

[19] Ibid., p. 55; RGASPI, f. 62, op. 2, d. 2140, l. 4; d. 2793, l. 93.
[20] TsGAT, f. 1, op. 7, d. 200, excerpted in *Türkmen arhivi*, no. 1 (1993): 60, 63.

hundred people from the village of Ketli in the Dashhowuz region marched on the city of Dashhowuz to demand a halt to collectivization. The crowd, made up mostly of women, destroyed their village school and beat up several Soviet officials. They dispersed only after a meeting with Sovnarkom chair Gaigïsïz Atabaev, who happened to be visiting Dashhowuz.[21] The drive for collectivization slowed temporarily after Stalin's "dizzy with success" letter of March 1930, in which he accused local officials of artificially accelerating the tempo of collectivization and failing to abide by the principle that joining the kolkhoz should be voluntary. The percentage of collectivized households in Turkmenistan dropped to 18 percent after Stalin's letter, then began to rise again slowly.[22]

Soviet policies mandating the planting of cotton aroused equally strong opposition. In Central Asia, the expansion of cotton cultivation was closely linked to collectivization, since the Soviet regime believed that the heavy irrigation required for cotton production could be accomplished most efficiently on large collective and state farms.[23] Before 1928, the state had encouraged but not required the planting of cotton. The rise of the crop in Turkmenistan had its roots in the tsarist period, when high prices for cotton encouraged many Turkmen peasants to shift from subsistence agriculture to growing cotton for the market. The opening of the Central Asian railway in 1896 accelerated the trend toward cultivating cash crops.[24] After the devastation of agriculture in Central Asia in the revolution and Civil War, the importance of textiles in Soviet plans for developing light industry made the revival of cotton production an urgent priority. The ultimate goal was to free the Soviet Union from dependence on imported cotton. As part of an efficient division of labor, Central Asia would concentrate on supplying cotton for Soviet industry while receiving food and manufactured goods from other Soviet republics. Thus, despite the Bolsheviks' harsh criticism of the tsarist regime for turning Central Asia into a "cotton colony," Soviet economic interests ultimately forced the same role on Central Asia.[25]

During the NEP period, cultivators were encouraged to plant cotton by means of benefits such as preferential access to seed, agricultural implements, credit, and tax breaks. The relative prices fixed in 1922 favored cotton producers over grain producers, making it attractive for peasants

[21] Ibid., pp. 64–65.
[22] Fitzpatrick, *Stalin's Peasants*, pp. 62–63; TsGAT, f. 1, op. 7, d. 200, excerpted in *Türkmen arhivi*, no. 1 (1993), p. 54; RGASPI, f. 62, op. 2, d. 2549, l. 15.
[23] "Postanovlenie plenuma Sr.-Az. Biuro TsK VKP o razvitii khlopkovodstva," *Za partiiu*, no 7–8 (July–August 1929): 95.
[24] Dovletov, *Turkmenskii aul v kontse XIX–nachale XX veka* (Ashgabat, 1977), p. 88; Nemchenko, *Dinamika*, p. 12.
[25] Park, *Bolshevism in Turkestan*, p. 320.

to grow cotton. But as supplies of cheap grain disappeared in the mid-to-late 1920s, it became unprofitable for Turkmen peasants to grow cotton. Increasingly, the state resorted to coercion to induce peasants to plant cotton.[26] A decree of the all-union Central Committee called on the Central Asian republics, including Turkmenistan, to ensure the "cotton independence" of the Soviet Union. The first Five-Year Plan set extremely high goals for cotton, calling for an increase in annual production from 18 million puds to 32 million by 1932. This goal was revised upward to 48 million in a Politburo decree of July 18, 1929. The decree noted the exceptional importance of cotton production for the industrialization of the Soviet Union and in particular as the basis for the textile industry. The Politburo called for "maximal acceleration" of the expansion of cotton acreage, declaring that all suitable irrigated lands should be put under cotton instead of food crops.[27] In Turkmenistan, local authorities began pressuring peasants to grow cotton, telling them that they would be deprived of their voting rights if they refused to do so.[28]

In the face of criticism for continuing to use Central Asia as a "cotton colony," Soviet leaders argued that cotton production in the Soviet Union was actually a progressive form of agriculture, since peasants now dealt directly with the government rather than with native "exploiters" and middlemen.[29] Such arguments did not persuade Turkmen peasants, who for perfectly rational economic reasons resisted the pressure to plant exclusively cotton. Remembering the famine of the Civil War years, they did not want to rely on distant government authorities to provide food in a crisis. At conferences organized by the Soviet regime in 1926, Turkmen peasants expressed opposition to the Soviet push for cotton. They pointed out that while Soviet propaganda encouraged peasants to plant cotton, the regime paid such a low price for the crop that cultivators could not afford to buy the food and other goods they required. "Give us a good price for cotton or we won't plant it," they declared.[30] Peasants were also angry over the regime's failure to provide enough grain and other essential goods—tea, sugar, butter, and kerosene—in exchange for their cotton.[31]

[26] Ibid., pp. 311–16.
[27] *Istoriia sovetskogo Turkmenistana, Chast' pervaia. 1917–1937 gg.* (Ashgabat: Ylym, 1970) p. 293; "Postanovlenie TsK VKP(b) o razvitii khlopkovodstva," *Za partiiu*, no 7–8 (July–August), 1929: 90–91.
[28] RGASPI, f. 62, op. 2, d. 1808, l. 135.
[29] See "Postanovlenie TsK VKP(b) o razvitii khlopkovodstva," p. 91. Some Central Asians opposed the attempt to impose a cotton "monoculture" on Central Asia. The exiled dissident Mustafa Chokaev argued in 1927 that cotton production was a kind of corvée labor imposed on peasants by the Bolsheviks. Nodel', "Menshevistskie spletni v srednei azii," p. 58.
[30] RGASPI, f. 62, op. 2, d. 630, ll. 38, 41, 43.
[31] TsGAT, f. 1, op. 7, d. 200, excerpted in *Türkmen arhivi*, no. 1 (1993): 56.

Although these views were widespread, the Soviet regime officially attributed anticotton sentiment to "class-alien elements." In April 1929, the OGPU reported that "rich peasants" were spreading rumors that the cotton crop would fail because of insufficient water, and that the peasants would starve. In Dashhowuz, "kulaks" said that it was better to sow wheat, because a part of the cotton crop might fail. In Marï, people said, "Don't trust the authorities who say you should plant cotton instead of wheat. If the peasants plant cotton, they'll end up hungry." The supposedly imminent fall of Soviet power was cited as a reason not to plant cotton. In the Yïlanlï region, a peasant said, "Soviet power is now at war with England. Soon there won't be a single Russian left, so we should hold off on planting cotton."[32]

As food became more scarce, resistance to cotton grew. Despite a 30 percent expansion of cotton acreage in Turkmenistan in 1931—an expansion that came at the expense of food crops—the supply of grain to the republic was reduced. Deliveries of grain to the republic began to fall short in November 1930, and the shortages grew much worse in December and January. Between January 1 and June 1, 1931, only 262,625 centners of grain were delivered to cotton growers, compared with the 325,474 called for in the economic plan. (During the same six-month period in 1930, 309,720 centners had been distributed.) The population was soon forced to subsist on remnants of grain from the previous year. Turkmen women began to bake bread using flour "substitutes." In the Garrïgala region, there were reports of deaths from starvation.[33]

In these difficult circumstances, Turkmen accused the Soviet regime of practicing "robbery and deception" against the rural population. Peasants spoke openly at meetings in the spring of 1931, saying that if the regime did not distribute grain they would join the Basmachi rebels.[34] In 1931, mass protests erupted in Chärjew province when the republican Central Committee ordered a number of fields already planted with grain to be plowed under and replanted with cotton.[35] At a meeting on March 19 in the village of Gularïk, three hundred men and women demanded that the government issue a written order to stop the planting of cotton and distribute grain. The demonstrations grew larger every day and often ended in beatings of district and village officials. Twenty-eight demonstrations took place in Chärjew region in March, with the number of participants each time ranging from forty to three hundred people. At these protests, rural residents demanded the distribution of grain and the can-

---

[32] RGASPI, f. 62, op. 2, d. 1809, l. 11; d. 1808, l. 135; TsGAT, f. 1, op. 7, d. 200, excerpted in *Türkmen arhivi*, no. 1 (1993): 60.

[33] RGASPI, f. 62, op. 2, d. 2549, ll. 12–13. A Soviet centner was equal to 100 kilograms.

[34] Ibid., l. 14.

[35] Ibid., op. 1, d. 888, ll. 72–73.

cellation of orders to replant grain fields with cotton. There were similar demonstrations in Dashhowuz, Köneürgench, and Yïlanlï.[36]

In predominantly nomadic desert regions, resistance to cotton and collectivization took more violent forms. In some nomadic areas, the herders were organized into agricultural collective farms and forced to grow cotton or wheat, despite the inadequacy of water supplies in these arid regions. Their livestock, traditionally the property of individual households, was communalized.[37] These policies resulted in a massive loss of livestock due to inadequate fodder, deliberate slaughter, and emigration. The number of heads of livestock in the republic declined by nearly 12 percent between 1929 and 1930, and by another 30 percent between 1930 and 1931.[38] Meanwhile, the regime's inability to provide grain resulted in malnutrition, especially among children. To make matters worse, the nomads were required to make mandatory deliveries of milk to the state even as their food and fodder supplies were disappearing.[39] In the Gökdepe area, women reportedly said, "Our children are swelling up from hunger, we've barely saved them thanks to milk, and now they're taking that away too." The Soviet regime had no goods to offer the nomads in exchange for their milk, meat, and wool; in many rural cooperative stores, there was nothing for sale but sugar.[40]

In late 1930, demonstrations and protests began to give way to armed resistance. Toward the end of the year, the OGPU noted a rise in "bandit" activity in the nomadic regions of the Karakum desert and neighboring areas. Groups of "bandits" moved in armed cells on horseback through the desert, attacking Soviet collective farms and officials, looting and burning kolkhozes and administration buildings, and even making guerrilla-style assaults against Soviet troops and OGPU special forces. The threat posed by the Soviet regime brought together groups that had often had tense relations in the past. In the Krasnovodsk and Gazanjïk regions of western Transcaspia, Yomut Turkmen pastoralists united with Kazakh nomads to attack the eighty-fifth Division of the OGPU forces. The Mïradali rebel band united about three hundred fighters from the Togtamïsh and Utamïsh segments of the Teke tribe; led by the former chairman of a livestock-herding collective farm, it operated in the Gïzïlarbat, Bäherden, and Gökdepe regions.[41] By the spring of 1931, OGPU reports were referring to an "armed uprising against Soviet authority" in Turkmenistan.[42]

[36] Ibid., op. 2, d. 2542 (part 2) ll. 315–16; d. 2549, l. 10.

[37] TsGAT, f. 1, op. 7, d. 200, excerpted in *Türkmen arhivi*, no. 1 (1993): 59.

[38] RGASPI, f. 62, op. 2, d. 2836, l. 26. See also RGAE, f. 399, op. 2, d. 1680, ll. 79–80.

[39] RGASPI, f. 62, op. 2, d. 2549, l. 51.

[40] Ibid., ll. 29–32, 77.

[41] Ibid., ll. 9, 57, 67.

[42] Ibid., ll. 47–48

Entire districts, such as Krasnovodsk and Gazanjïk in western Turk-menistan, were taken over by rebel bands. In all, fourteen of the republic's thirty-eight districts were affected by the revolt. In many areas, local So-viet and party officials panicked and fled, leaving the population to fend for themselves. Elsewhere, Turkmen Soviet officials themselves partici-pated in the raiding and looting. The attack on Köneürgench was led by Tächmïradov, a member of the all-union and Turkmen Central Executive Committees; Ashïr Orazov, chairman of a village soviet and a former member of the Red Army Cavalry; and Ata Nur, chairman of a village soviet.[43] Under conditions of famine and forced collectivization, local of-ficials were forced to choose between loyalty to the regime and to the Turkmen population, and many chose in favor of their own communities. Previously, Turkmen who worked for the regime had been able to use their positions to benefit their relatives and friends. As the relatively be-nign NEP period gave way to forcibly imposed, desperately resisted change, it was no longer possible to straddle the middle.

Soviet officials explained the desperate resistance to collectivization in various ways. Some blamed it on a failure to properly educate the pop-ulation about the aims of Soviet power. In nomadic regions, especially, there was little communication between the regime and the populace. Prior to the extension of collectivization into the desert, most nomads knew little about the nature of the new Soviet state of which they were citizens. Some were blissfully unaware of the regime's very existence; when two Turkmen pastoralists on horseback were stopped in the desert in 1925 and asked their citizenship, one replied that he was the subject of the Bukharan emir, and the other that he owed allegiance to Nicholas II, tsar of Russia.[44] An OGPU investigator reporting on the nomadic re-gions of Turkmenistan in May 1932 noted the "complete absence of polit-ical mass work among the population" and declared that "Soviet power does not exist there at all."[45] Even rural officials recruited from among the Turkmen population often had no real understanding of the Soviet enterprise, let alone ideological commitment to it. After his capture, a former village soviet chairman who participated in the 1931 rebellion blamed his involvement on ignorance:

I am a poor peasant. Recently I was appointed chair of village soviet X. I don't know what Soviet power is, what its tasks are, or who it defends. I always understood that Soviet power is based in the cities and along the railroad. When Soviet officials came to us, they just took our wool and sheep and forced us to subscribe to the state loan. They explained these matters, but no one ever

[43] Ibid., ll. 57–59; d. 2541, ll. 228–29; op. 1, d. 888, l. 65.
[44] Ibid., op. 2, d. 1803, l. 18.
[45] Ibid., d. 2740, l. 24.

explained what Soviet power is and where it is located. I don't know what the party is, or what a party cell is—I never heard about it. I never heard who Lenin was, but once I saw his portrait and someone told me that he's an important person.[46]

For all his professed ignorance, the repentant rebel demonstrated a keen understanding of how to win clemency from the Soviet regime; by presenting himself as a poor peasant, inadequately educated about the benefits of Soviet power, he might avoid blame for his misguided actions. Communists believed that poor peasants, like the deluded village soviet chairman-turned-rebel, would naturally gravitate toward the regime if they knew what it really stood for. For this, education and patient explanations were crucial. As one sympathetic party official argued, "In a number of places we need to start from the beginning, explaining what Soviet power is and showing how it works, rather than simply carrying out procurements, taking wool, and so forth."[47]

In the absence of Soviet education efforts, rumor filled the information gap. In a predominantly nonliterate culture, orally transmitted information had always played an important role, spreading easily among the Turkmen because of the mobility of the population. Under Soviet rule, rumors of war, famine, the imminent fall of the government, and impending invasion by foreign powers raced through the republic in times of crisis. In August 1929, just before the launching of mass collectivization, rumors spread that the Soviet government was planning to create a universal commune and force the entire population to join. Their property and livestock—even their wives—would be taken away and distributed among the collective.[48] In early 1930, Turkmen villagers passed the word that collectivization had already caused a famine in Russia. Apocalyptic rumors predicted an end to the Soviet regime: "Soviet power has fallen," "Aitakov has shot himself."[49] Superstition and natural catastrophes fed the rumors. After an earthquake rattled the Ashgabat and Gökdepe regions in early 1929, villagers warned that the earthquake meant that "God was punishing the peasants for listening to Bolshevik ideas."[50]

Some Soviet officials acknowledged that the 1931 rebellion was fueled not just by kulak malevolence and popular ignorance, but by legitimate economic grievances. As evidence for the fundamentally economic roots of the unrest, they noted that tensions diminished whenever grain was

[46] Ibid., d. 2792, l. 2.
[47] Ibid.
[48] Ibid., d. 1811, l. 193.
[49] TsGAT, f. 1, op. 7, d. 200, excerpted in *Türkmen arhivi*, no 1 (1993): 63; RGASPI, f. 62, op. 2, d. 2140, l. 3, l. 46.
[50] RGASPI, f. 62, op. 2, d. 1809, ll. 10–11.

distributed to the population. OGPU reports on the popular mood in early 1931 revealed that villagers believed that the Soviet regime was taking a great deal from them and giving little in return. "The government," Turkmen villagers said, "looks on us as a cow to be milked. It can't or won't help us." "It is better to join a [rebel] band than to suffer like this," some concluded.[51] One OGPU analyst condemned the "complete failure of central and local organizations to provide economic services to livestock herders and agriculturalists."[52] Mïradalï, leader of one of the rebel bands, expressed the frustration of the pastoralists in a letter to Soviet officials on April 23, 1931:

> The taxes imposed by the Soviet regime, the procurements of wool and livestock, the mobilization of camels, the transporting of wood, and so forth, all rest on our shoulders. The tea, sugar, and flour distributed by the Soviet regime are not worth what is being taken from us. There was a tsar, but under him we never saw such things. Now we have placed our trust in God. Whatever he does is agreeable to us.[53]

The uprising in the desert was ultimately put down by a massive show of military force. At the same time, the Soviet regime adopted a more conciliatory policy toward the nomads designed to stave off further unrest. In early 1932, KPT first secretary Iakov Popok declared in a letter to officials in border areas that "leftist distortions" and "administrative" techniques of dealing with the nomadic population—in particular, the forcible planting of cotton in nomadic livestock areas—were responsible for many of the problems.[54] A KPT Central Committee resolution of April 20, 1932, deplored the forcible collectivization of livestock and the rush to form *artel'* collective farms among nomads. (The artel' in this case was a radical form of collectivization that entailed complete communalization of all livestock.) Blaming overly zealous regional party organizers for this error, the TsK declared that the looser collective form known as the TOZ (Association for Joint Working of the Land) was more appropriate for nomadic and seminomadic areas. It decreed that all artels should become TOZes and that communalized livestock should be put back into the hands of individual households. The decree also called for an end to all attempts to force nomads to settle and practice agriculture.[55]

[51] Ibid., d. 2549, l. 76.
[52] Ibid., d. 2740, l. 24.
[53] Ibid., d. 2549, l. 67.
[54] Ibid., d. 2740, l. 14.
[55] The decree is reproduced in *Sotsialisticheskoe khoziaistvo Turkmenii*, no. 1 (1934): 3–4.

FIGHT OR FLIGHT? THE POLITICS OF EMIGRATION

With protests and armed rebellion producing at best a temporary respite from Soviet demands, many rural Turkmen turned to another strategy of resistance: emigration beyond the borders of the Soviet republic. The level of migration was an accurate barometer of rural attitudes toward Soviet policies at any given time. Whenever the Soviet regime began to enforce a particularly unpopular measure, masses of Turkmen would pack up their families and belongings and pour across the border, offering armed resistance if border guards attempted to stop them. The most common destinations were Persia and Afghanistan, although Turkmen sometimes migrated to neighboring Soviet republics based on rumors that conditions were better there than in their own republic.

Emigration was a relatively simple matter for many Turkmen. Nomadic households were accustomed to frequent treks in search of pasture. Moreover, flight from the demands of intrusive states had a long history among the Turkmen, who traditionally escaped such pressures by fleeing to remote desert regions or to the territory of more accommodating states. During World War I, Turkmen nomads fled to Persia to avoid Russian labor conscription; in 1920, thousands of Turkmen fled to Afghanistan when the Bukharan emirate fell and was replaced by a Soviet republic.[56] As a result of these earlier migrations, many inhabitants of the Turkmen republic had relatives on the other side of the Soviet border. The Turkmen republic's foreign border was the longest of any of the Soviet Central Asian republics—2,370 kilometers—offering many potential crossing points. Moreover, the border was relatively sparsely guarded.[57]

Flight came as a response to many kinds of grievances. The economic crisis caused by Soviet rural policies was the main impetus for emigration in the late 1920s and early 1930s, but Soviet rule gave rise to other concerns as well. In the Halach region, rumors that Turkmen girls would be forced to marry Russians resulted in mass preemptive marriages and the emigration of many peasants with marriageable daughters. In Gïzïlayak, a number of families moved to Afghanistan after they were forced to place their children in government nurseries. In the Kerki region, the mere rumor that women would be forced to give up their children to nurseries induced some households to emigrate in September 1929. In the village of Chekpete, a young boy was snatched while playing in front of his house and taken to study at the Soviet boarding school in Halach. Villagers said that the boy's mother, a widow, "went to the district capital to look for

[56] Pierce, *Russian Central Asia*, pp. 286–89; RGASPI, f. 62, op. 2, d. 1342, l. 4.
[57] RGASPI, f. 62, op. 2, d. 2740, l. 1.

him, weeping, and if she gets him back, they're definitely going to leave for Afghanistan."[58] The prospect of serving in the Soviet military pushed many young men to flee. When a new law required some Turkmen to report for preconscription military training in 1927, a number of potential draftees headed for the border. In the village of Gökcha, the prominent local leader Anna Durdï Khan offered assistance to young men seeking to escape to Afghanistan, declaring that a young man who served in the Red Army would "forget about God and stop respecting his parents."[59] A broader military training requirement in September 1929 similarly caused large numbers to flee to Persia from the nomadic regions of Gïzïletrek, Esengulï, Gazanjïk, and Garrïgala.[60]

For the Soviet authorities, emigration was a scandalous secret. It cast doubt on the Soviet claim to be a benefactor and protector of the non-Russians, while depriving the state of much-needed labor power. It reduced the number of head of livestock available to provide the Soviet economy with milk and wool, since departing households took their flocks with them. Emigration also damaged the Soviet state's reputation in neighboring countries. Instead of praising the Soviet Union as a beacon of cultural development and self-determination for minority nationalities, emigrants spoke of the indignities they had suffered at the hands of the Soviet regime. Soviet authorities were determined to move aggressively to address the problem. Within the Turkmen republic, a reemigration commission was established to study the reasons for emigration and to seek ways to bring back the departed Soviet citizens.

The reemigration commission initially focused its efforts on luring back those Turkmen who had fled the Bukharan emirate in 1920, when the emir was deposed in favor of a "people's republic." Soviet records showed that 11,376 Turkmen households had emigrated to Afghanistan from Bukhara. This included 4,230 pastoral nomadic households and 7,146 mixed agricultural and livestock-herding households. Most of them settled in the Andhai region of Afghanistan, close to the Soviet border.[61] Some of these emigrants began to trickle back after the establishment of the Turkmen republic, but the majority remained in Afghanistan.[62] The reemigration commission operated on the assumption that emigration, especially among the less well-to-do, was caused by a lack of education and information. If only they were properly informed, Turkmen emi-

[58] Ibid., d. 2206, ll. 4–5; d. 1811, l. 194.
[59] Ibid., d. 882, ll. 89–90, 120.
[60] Ibid., d. 1810, ll. 51–52.
[61] Ibid., d. 1342, l. 4; d. 1803, l. 6. According to one party official's estimate, sixty thousand Turkmen had emigrated to Afghanistan after the fall of the Bukharan emir. RGASPI, f. 17, op. 67, d. 382, l. 19.
[62] Ibid., f. 62, op. 2, d. 628, l. 4; d. 1342, l. 7; d. 1803, l. 16.

grants would realize that they would be better off in the Soviet Union. Poor Turkmen, in particular, were thought to have an instinctive sympathy toward the Soviet regime. Surely, most would return voluntarily if they were not being prevented from doing so by "kulaks," reactionary tribal leaders, and the false promises of authorities in neighboring states.[63]

The Soviet scholar M. Nemchenko, a specialist on the Turkmen economy and an official of the republic's Commissariat of Internal Affairs, demolished these arguments in a report written in 1928. He maintained that it was futile to expect the return of the majority of Turkmen who had left during the Civil War. Nemchenko pointed out that many of the emigrants had found better economic conditions on the other side of the Afghan border. They enjoyed more abundant land and water, including land allotments provided by the Afghan government, good seasonal pasture land for their flocks, and exemptions from taxes. These people were permanently settled in Afghanistan, and were unlikely to come back.[64] Moreover, Soviet policies such as military conscription and land reform were highly unpopular and were likely to cause a new surge of emigration. Nemchenko was critical of Soviet officials who believed that emigrants could be induced to return through coercive and punitive measures, such as the denial of access to Soviet pastureland. (Many Turkmen emigrants to Afghanistan continued to claim rights to land and wells on Soviet territory and to pasture their livestock in Soviet pastures part of the year.) Nemchenko maintained that the only way to reverse the flow of emigration was to improve the economic well-being of the Soviet Turkmen population.[65]

As Nemchenko had predicted, emigration began to rise again in 1928 and 1929, due to unpopular Soviet policies and poor economic conditions on the Soviet side of the border. In March and April 1928, the OGPU reported a flurry of emigration from the Tagtabazar region. Peasants in Tagtabazar approached the residents of a nearby Afghan village in April 1928, asking them for armed protection and assistance during their planned border crossing.[66] In July 1928, a number of nomadic pastoralists in the Yölöten, Kerki, and Tagtabazar regions attempted to cross into Afghanistan. In the summer of 1928, about three hundred Turkmen households in the Tagtabazar region wrote to the governor of Herat in Afghanistan. Saying that the Soviet government was "oppressing them and not allowing them to live in peace," the peasants expressed a desire to migrate to Afghanistan if the Afghan government would give them

---

[63] Ibid., d. 1342, ll. 1–2.
[64] Ibid., ll. 5–6.
[65] Ibid., ll. 8–10.
[66] Ibid., ll. 27–28, 41.

land. In April 1929, the OGPU reported that proemigration sentiments in Kerki and Chärjew provinces were on the rise.[67]

Secret police reports confirmed Nemchenko's claim that emigration was largely due to unfavorable economic conditions on the Soviet side of the border, many of which stemmed directly from Soviet policies.[68] A March 1929 OGPU report on the situation in the southern Karakum desert noted that conditions for Turkmen pastoralists were much better in Afghanistan than in the Soviet Union. In particular, the relative price of agricultural and animal products there favored the pastoralists. In Afghanistan, one pud of wheat cost one ruble and 75 kopecks; the same amount of wheat in Soviet Turkmenistan cost between 3.5 and 4 rubles. A high quality black karakul sheep fetched 10 rubles in Soviet Turkmenistan; the same animal brought the much higher price of 22 rubles in Afghanistan. Because of these differences, the income of a poor pastoralist household in Afghanistan was 92 percent higher than in the Turkmen republic. The tax burden was also lower in Afghanistan than in the Turkmen republic, even for relatively poor pastoralists with only one hundred head of sheep—those who paid the lowest taxes under Soviet rule.[69] The only advantage Soviet pastoralists had over their counterparts in Afghanistan was that the pasturelands of the Karakum desert, which they customarily used for three to four months of the year, were located on Soviet territory.

Between 1928 and 1932, the Soviet attempt to radically transform Turkmen rural society brought about a massive upsurge in emigration. In early 1930, the push for "100 percent collectivization" in Kerki and Chärjew provinces induced many to emigrate.[70] However, the real explosion in emigration came in 1931, when the assault on the "kulaks" in the desert and attempts to collectivize nomads and communalize their livestock coincided with a severe grain shortage. During 1931, Soviet officials reported that a total of 6,263 households emigrated from six of the republic's districts: Gïzïlayak, Halach, Kerki, Hojambaz, Charshangï, and Karluk.[71] The Etrek and Esengulï districts lost an estimated 50 percent of their population to emigration. The urge to flee involved all segments of the population, from the wealthiest to the poorest, and included many Soviet officials, Komsomols, and Communist Party members. In Etrek, for example, the emigrants included the chair of the district executive committee, the chair of the district kolkhoz union, the chief of police, and a number of kolkhoz chairmen.[72] Gorbunov, head of the OGPU in Turkmenistan, cited a virtual

[67] Ibid., d. 1351, l. 16; d. 1342, l. 111; d. 1808, ll. 136–37.
[68] Ibid., d. 1808, l. 137.
[69] Ibid., d. 1803, ll. 7, 10, 14.
[70] Ibid., d. 2740, l. 66; d. 2140, ll. 3–4.
[71] Ibid., d. 2740, l. 66.
[72] Ibid., ll. 24–25.

laundry list of reasons for the mass flight: grain shortages, coercive collectivization, the compulsory planting of cotton, "distortions" in livestock
and wool procurements, the arbitrary application of tax policy, illegal arrests, the failure of Soviet authorities to provide medical care and other
services, the failure to conduct political agitation among the population,
the continuing strength of "feudal leaders," and "agitation" from across
the border by those who had already emigrated. Moreover, those collective
farmers who remained were being forced to pay off the debts of those who
had departed; this, in turn, was leading to further emigration.[73]

State policies toward Turkmen emigrants fluctuated between coercion
and concessions. Some local officials in high-emigration regions favored
aggressive policies to pressure Turkmen emigrants to return by taking advantage of their need for Soviet pastureland. The district party committee
and local border guard division in Kerki proposed charging a pasture tax
to emigrants who wished to use Soviet pastures, nationalizing the wells
owned by emigrants, denying pasture rights to "leaders of anti-Soviet
movements," and lowering taxes on sheep for Soviet citizens in border
regions.[74] A Turkmen Central Executive Committee decree of October 30,
1928, adopted some of these suggestions, nationalizing wells and forbid-
ding the pasturing of sheep on Soviet territory by emigrants who had led
"Basmachi" bands. Visiting emigrants were also required to pay 30 kopecks per head of livestock to pasture their herds on Soviet territory. The
goal of these decrees was to force emigrants to return by making it excessively costly for them to use Soviet pastures while maintaining a home base
in Afghanistan. The effectiveness of such measures was limited, however,
especially since many of the pastoralists remaining in Afghanistan belonged to the most intransigently anti-Soviet part of the population and
had taken part in the armed resistance to Soviet rule; it was said that such
people would rather let their herds perish than return to Soviet territory.[75]

The harsh policies pursued by Turkmen republican authorities conflicted with a more conciliatory policy toward border populations advocated by communist party leaders in Tashkent and Moscow. Border areas
had long been a special concern for the Bolshevik leadership, since they
provided a conduit for Soviet influence on the populations of neighboring
states as well as a channel for foreign influence on Soviet populations. In
1923, the Soviet regime had designated the territories immediately adjacent to the Soviet Union's international borders as special "border regions" subject to close monitoring by the OGPU's border guard service.
At the same time, Soviet policies established special privileges and eco-

[73] Ibid.
[74] Ibid., d. 1803, ll. 14, 19–20.
[75] Ibid., ll. 14–16, 19.

nomic benefits for border areas in an attempt to win the support of border populations and impress the residents of neighboring countries.[76]

The Turkmen republic had eleven districts of the "first zone"—that is, located directly on the border—and eight districts of the "second zone," adjacent to first-zone border regions.[77] In decrees of February 11 and April 22, 1929, the executive commission of the Central Asian Bureau ordered a number of measures designed to improve conditions for the population living in border areas and thereby make emigration less attractive.[78] The Bureau also hoped to appeal to Turkmen emigrants in Afghanistan and Persia who were "socially close" to the Soviet regime and thereby encourage them to return to the Turkmen republic. A special border commission of the KPT Central Committee ordered various measures in accordance with the Central Asian Bureau decree, such as a reduction of the agricultural tax in border areas.[79]

But measures to improve conditions on the border conflicted with other Soviet policies associated with the "great transformation"—the promotion of class struggle among the nomads, the maximization of cotton production, and the "liquidation of the kulaks as a class." The KPT Central Committee under first secretary Iakov Popok was most concerned with meeting Moscow's demands on collectivization, cotton production, and kulaks; the foreign policy implications of conditions in border regions were of secondary importance to communists in Ashgabat. Thus, there were disagreements between KPT officials, on the one hand, and the Central Asian Bureau and the OGPU, on the other, about which policies should have precedence—the uncompromising attack on "class enemies" or the more conciliatory attempts to placate the population of border regions. The OGPU border guard service reported in 1930 that it was having trouble enforcing the more conciliatory decrees of the Central Asian Bureau due to the obstructionism of local and republican officials. Emigration was taking place, the OGPU noted, "exclusively because of the inadequacy of our work among bedniaks, batraks, and seredniaks, because of excesses and distortions in the localities." Republican organs were "in no hurry" to implement measures to appease public opinion in border regions. As a result, even the poorest peasants and nomads were continuing to emigrate in many regions.[80]

A KPT Central Committee resolution of early 1932 downplayed the economic reasons for emigration and insisted on the need for a harder

[76] Martin, *The Affirmative Action Empire*, pp. 313–15.
[77] RGASPI, f. 62, op. 2, d. 2828, ll. 37–38.
[78] Ibid., d. 2140, ll. 6, 13.
[79] Ibid., l. 6.
[80] Ibid., d. 2205, ll. 6, 13–16.

line. Although the KPT admitted that "leftist errors" and excesses had taken place, such as "violation of the voluntary principle" in collectivization, it stressed the need for a firmer class policy and a more uncompromising attack on the "kulaks" who were allegedly organizing emigration. The Central Committee declared the main task of border regions to be "the practical realization of the liquidation of the kulaks as a class, on the basis of 100-percent collectivization." The Central Committee canceled all previous benefits given to "kulaks" in border regions, ordering district party committees and the Commissariat of Finance to root out concealed "kulaks" and subject them to the individual tax and "firm [work] assignments." Emigration to Afghanistan and Persia could be halted, the KPT Central Committee maintained, if only regional party committees would do more "explanatory work" among poor peasants and nomads.[81]

The KPT was forced to adopt a more conciliatory approach to the border regions after an April 1932 conference sponsored by the Central Asian Bureau. Among other things, the conference called for the cancellation of some peasant debts and decreed that cotton cultivation should be limited to 75 percent of the land in a given area, with the rest reserved for grain and fodder.[82] Just as the KPT had been forced by nomadic unrest to halt the forcible collectivization of livestock, the Turkmen Central Committee now confirmed the new policy on cotton and adopted other measures designed to placate residents of border regions, such as writing off some peasant debts.[83] The decision on cotton was particularly important, since efforts to enforce the planting of cotton had been a disaster in predominantly nomadic regions.

On April 22, KPT first secretary Popok sent a letter to all district party committees in the republic in which he retreated from his previous hardline stance toward emigrants. In this letter, Popok blamed the high levels of emigration to Persia and Afghanistan partly on the coercive tactics of officials who had used threats, beatings, and arrests to force peasants to plant cotton in predominantly livestock-herding areas.[84] Local party organizations in the Kerki, Gïzïlayak, Halach, Hojambaz, Charshangï and Karluk districts had failed to take into account the specificities of these regions, which had highly developed livestock herding economies:

Party organizations, instead of mobilizing the masses, frequently conducted the struggle for cotton with naked coercion and heedless neglect of food and fodder crops. This led to 100-percent cotton sowing in a number of villages and collec-

[81] Ibid., op. 3, d. 738, ll. 74–75.
[82] Ibid., op. 2, d. 2740, ll. 66–67.
[83] Ibid., l. 15, ll. 18–21; *Sotsialisticheskoe khoziaistvo Turkmenii*, no. 1 (1934): 3–4.
[84] RGASPI, f. 62, op. 2, d. 2740, l. 14.

tive farms, inexcusably endangering the local food and fodder base of the peasant collective-farm household.[85]

In May 1932, the KPT made additional concessions to stop emigration.
A new decree freed most rural dwellers in border areas from the agricultural tax and reassured nomads currently pasturing flocks in Persia that
their livestock would not be confiscated if they returned permanently to
Soviet territory. At the same time, the KPT prohibited emigrants from
making temporary use of Soviet pastures.[86] By the end of 1932, the worst
of the emigration surge seemed to be over. KPT officials reported that the
rate of emigration had declined sharply as a result of the policies adopted
earlier in the year, and that some emigrant households were even returning
from Afghanistan.[87] For any Soviet officials who still had doubts on this
score, this showed clearly that emigration was directly related to economic conditions in the Turkmen countryside.

The rural resistance of the early 1930s did not succeed in throwing off
Soviet rule or dramatically changing the course of Soviet policy. Nevertheless, the actions of Turkmen peasants and nomads had a discernable impact. Emigration aroused a great deal of government concern and led to
concessions to popular sentiment in the republic's border regions. The
intense opposition to collectivization among nomads produced a hasty
retreat to the looser form of collective farm known as the TOZ. With the
decision to return collectivized livestock to its owners, the Soviet regime
tacitly permitted Turkmen pastoralists to return to their precollectiviza-
tion way of life.[88] Overall, the main effect of the "great leap forward" of
1928–32 was to produce a great leap backward in the regime's relationship with the rural population. The tentative steps toward mobilizing the
masses came to a halt, as rural communists and village soviet officials
declared that their allegiance lay with their kin and communities against
the Soviet regime. As the population turned to flight and violent resistance, the original goals of Soviet nationality policy—winning the support
of non-Russians and hastening their development into "socialist nations"—seemed to recede into an ever more distant future.

---

[85] Ibid., ll. 14–15.
[86] Ibid., ll. 29–30.
[87] Ibid., ll. 67–68.
[88] Ibid., d. 3290, ll. 1–6, 9–10; Lapkin, "Kollektivizatsiia i klassovaia bor'ba," pp. 23–26.

Chapter Eight

EMANCIPATION OF THE UNVEILED

TURKMEN WOMEN UNDER SOVIET RULE

IN THE SOVIET CAMPAIGN to abolish "backwardness" in Central Asia, some of the fiercest battles were fought over the fate of Muslim women. The Bolsheviks believed that it was impossible to build a socialist society without freeing women from their subordinate status and recruiting them into Soviet collective farms, mass organizations, and schools. By doing away with "archaic" and "degrading" gender relations, the Soviet regime hoped to transform Central Asian women into free individuals and active Soviet citizens.

In much of Central Asia, the effort to transform the lives of women centered on the campaign against female seclusion and the veil. Yet the unveiling campaign—and indeed, the veil itself—was generally limited to the urban and sedentary agricultural areas of what are today Uzbekistan and Tajikistan. In Turkmenistan, as in other parts of Central Asia with a recent history of pastoral nomadism, women were not secluded and did not wear the heavy veil and cloak that were the focus of Soviet activists' attention.[1] As a result, Soviet officials initially believed that the task of emancipating women would be easier in Turkmenistan. Yet they soon found that Turkmen women, too, were enmeshed in a web of tradition and custom that hindered their full participation in Soviet life. Early efforts to persuade women to "liquidate their illiteracy," speak at public meetings, or join the Communist Party met with little success. In the absence of the veil, officials of the Communist Party women's department (*zhenotdel*) blamed Turkmen women's reticence on a host of "backward" marital customs that were seen as degrading to women. Thus, the campaign for women's emancipation in Turkmenistan concentrated on legal reform to change women's status within marriage and the family. Through the adoption of new laws facilitating divorce and outlawing tra-

---

[1] Marianne Kamp, "Unveiling Uzbek Women: Liberation, Representation and Discourse, 1906–1929" (Ph.D. dissertation, University of Chicago, 1998), pp. 253–58. Throughout the Islamic world, veiling is generally less common in rural areas, especially among nomadic and tribal populations. Nikki Keddie, "Introduction: Deciphering Middle Eastern Women's History," in Nikki R. Keddie and Beth Baron, eds., *Women in Middle Eastern History: Shifting Boundaries in Sex and Gender* (New Haven: Yale University Press, 1991), p. 4.

ditional marital practices such as bridewealth and polygamy, Soviet authorities hoped to free Turkmen women from the constraints of custom and draw them into Soviet public life.

The campaign to emancipate women was in many ways an extension of the campaign to undermine Turkmen kinship structures. Like the descent group or lineage, the Turkmen family was relatively impervious to penetration by outsiders, demanding internal solidarity and imposing behavioral norms on its members that even Turkmen communists could ill afford to ignore. The Soviet battle for the hearts and minds of the Turkmen masses could not be won as long as loyalty to the family and kin group overrode all else. Marriage and gender roles, which are at the heart of the family and kinship network, were natural targets for Soviet modernizers keen to undermine any social institutions that competed with the influence of the state. Thus, policy on the "woman question" was meant to work together with other Soviet measures such as land reform and "tribal policy" to reweave the fabric of Turkmen family and community life, allowing the emergence of a modern socialist society.

But just as the Soviet attempt to do away with "tribes and clans" conflicted with the attempt to promote class struggle among the Turkmen, the effort to liberate women threatened to undermine the regime's relationship with its "class allies" in the Turkmen countryside. There was strong opposition to female emancipation among many male Turkmen, especially among the poor rural dwellers who were supposed to form the primary constituency of the Soviet state. Opponents of far-reaching gender reform in Turkmenistan pointed to this fact, arguing that the assault on traditional gender relations would antagonize the very social groups whose support the regime needed. In an influential 1974 work, Gregory Massell suggested that the Soviet regime sought to enlist Central Asian women as a "surrogate proletariat"—in other words, the primary social basis for Soviet power in a region that lacked an indigenous proletariat.[2] In Turkmenistan, however, there is little evidence that the local communist authorities viewed women as their most important constituency. Instead, Soviet officials were inclined to tread cautiously in attempts to undermine the patriarchal social system, for fear of alienating what they saw as the regime's true basis of support—poor and landless male peasants.

If a conflict existed between female emancipation and Soviet class priorities, there was an equally fundamental contradiction between the transformation of family life and the construction of a Turkmen nation. Even as the Soviets sought to promote Turkmen nationhood, they were determined to expunge the very social and cultural practices that were most

---

[2] Massell, *The Surrogate Proletariat*, pp. 128–82.

closely identified with being Turkmen. Soviet authorities did not see any contradiction here, since they viewed nationhood as a neutral container for socialist content. Turkmen national sentiments would be satisfied by the existence of a territorial republic and the use of the native language, while the practices and institutions of daily life would be generically "Soviet."[3] In any case, there was no room in a Soviet nation for archaic customs left over from the feudal past. Yet for most Turkmen, language and territory were not what made them Turkmen. Instead, their identity was bound up with distinctive Turkmen genealogical structures and the customary law that regulated family and community life. Many Turkmen therefore strenuously resisted the campaign to remake their families and communities, perceiving this as an attempt to "Europeanize" Turkmen private life and deprive Turkmen of the basis of their identity.[4] The more the Turkmen were transformed into something resembling a modern nation, the more consciously they rejected the idea that their "ancient traditions" should be thrown onto history's rubbish heap.

THE TURKMEN WOMAN: VICTIM OF OPPRESSION OR MAN'S "BEST FRIEND"?

The absence of the veil in Turkmenistan did not mean that women enjoyed all the rights and privileges of men. Turkmen women faced a variety of economic and social disadvantages, some deriving from Islamic law and some from the customs of a patriarchal society. Women were expected to play a smaller public role than men, show modesty before strangers, and obey their fathers and husbands. As in many premodern societies, the needs of the family and extended kinship group came before those of the individual. Marriages were arranged not on the basis of romantic love, but to produce children and further the interests of the family or lineage. Various aspects of Islamic law observed by the Turkmen were disadvantageous to women; for example, men were permitted to practice polygamy and had

[3] Slezkine, "The USSR as a Communal Apartment," p. 418.
[4] In colonized regions of the Middle East, women's emancipation similarly came to be associated with European rule and therefore seen as a betrayal of national values. Elizabeth Thompson, *Colonial Citizens: Republican Rights, Paternal Privilege, and Gender in French Syria and Lebanon* (New York: Columbia University Press, 2000), pp. 138–39; Leila Ahmed, *Women and Gender in Islam: Historical Roots of a Modern Debate* (New Haven: Yale University Press, 1992), pp. 129, 164. In colonized India, nationalists came to define women's role as an interior sphere of culture in which colonizers did not have the right to intervene. Partha Chatterjee, *The Nation and Its Fragments: Colonial and Postcolonial Histories* (Princeton: Princeton University Press, 1993), pp. 116–17, 120–21. On the "nationalization" of tradition in Uzbekistan, see Northrop, "Uzbek Women and the Veil," p. 6.

the sole right to initiate divorce. In some spheres, such as inheritance law, Turkmen custom was even less favorable to women than Islamic law.[5]

Women's status was determined in part by a social structure in which the well-being of each family and lineage depended on the presence of sons. Sons formed a permanent labor pool, brought wives and future children into the family, cared for their parents in their old age, and provided political support to their relations in conflicts with outsiders. A daughter, by contrast, was a "guest" who was lost to the family when she married; her future offspring belonged to the husband's lineage. However much daughters might be cherished as individuals, they contributed nothing to the future growth and prosperity of the family.[6] For all these reasons, the birth of a daughter was greeted with less overt joy than that of a son. Yet Turkmen women were highly valued in their roles as wives and mothers. Bearing and nurturing children was very important in Turkmen culture; moreover, women's labor was crucial to the functioning of the extended family household, the basic unit of Turkmen society. Traditionally, men cultivated the land, pastured the livestock, and cared for the horses, while women took care of all the household work—setting up and taking down the yurt, cooking, cleaning, making clothes, milking the animals, bearing and caring for the children, and weaving the carpets that decorated the yurts and brought additional income to the family.[7]

Europeans had long seen the condition of the Muslim woman as a unique sign of the backwardness and depravity of Muslim civilization. Not only did they point to female seclusion and veiling as evidence that Islam was inherently antagonistic toward women, but they cited oppressive gender relations as justification for colonial efforts to transform indigenous societies. Thus, in British and French colonies in the late nineteenth and early twentieth centuries, the attack on veiling became the "the spearhead of the assault on Muslim societies."[8] Pastoral nomads formed an

[5] Islamic inheritance law stipulates that daughters inherit a share of family property, although this share is smaller than those of their brothers. Among the Turkmen, as among many other tribal groups, women were generally excluded from inheriting. Keddie, "Deciphering Middle Eastern Women's History" p. 5; Irons, *The Yomut Turkmen*, p. 93. On the role of women in Turkmen society, see Sharon Bastug and Nuran Hortacsu, "The Price of Value: Kinship, Marriage, and Meta-narratives of Gender in Turkmenistan," in *Gender and Identity Construction: Women of Central Asia, the Caucasus, and Turkey*, ed. Feride Acar and Ayşe Günes-Ayata (Leiden: Brill, 2000), pp. 117–40; Carole Blackwell, *Tradition and Society in Turkmenistan: Gender, Oral Culture, and Song* (Richmond, Surrey, UK: Curzon, 2001), pp. 35–85.

[6] Bastug and Hortacsu, "The Price of Value," pp. 118–21; Irons, *The Yomut Turkmen*, pp. 163–64.

[7] B. Belova, "Zhenotdely v Turkmenii," *Turkmenovedenie*, no. 12 (December 1928): 36.

[8] Ahmed, *Women and Gender in Islam*, pp. 151–52. In India, too, native "barbarism" in the treatment of women was used as justification for British colonial rule. See Chatterjee, *The Nation and Its Fragments*, pp. 118–19.

exception to the bleak view of women's condition under Islam. In part because they were unveiled, women of historically nomadic groups were thought to enjoy greater freedom and higher social status than women in sedentary Muslim societies. Imperial Russian officials and ethnographers noted that Kazakh and Turkmen women had considerable freedom of movement and were allowed to become acquainted with their future husbands before marriage, unlike the secluded women of neighboring settled regions.[9] Some Russians went even further, arguing that nomadic women were the equals of men. The Russian orientalist P. S. Vasiliev, who visited the Teke Turkmen shortly after the Russian conquest of Transcaspia in the 1880s, was impressed by the high status of Teke women. He attributed this to the challenges of the nomadic lifestyle, in which survival demanded all the skill and energy both sexes could muster:

> The Teke woman does not resemble other Muslim women, who do not have the right to show themselves to a male stranger and who know no life but that of the harem. Nor does she resemble the European woman. She has equal rights. The Teke does not regard his wife as a slave or solely as a source of household labor, but sees in her a friend, a person equal to himself.[10]

This favorable view of nomadic women was based in part on observable differences between their behavior and that of sedentary women, such as the absence of veiling. It also arose out of an idealized perception of nomadic life that prevailed among Russians and other Europeans, who were deeply impressed by the apparent freedom and rough democracy enjoyed by steppe nomads.[11] Finally, the belief in the high status of nomadic women was closely related to a conviction that nomadic and tribal peoples were less intensely devoted to Islam than their settled neighbors. As the tsarist colonial administrator Fëdor Mikhailov wrote in 1900:

> The Turkmen are not fanatical and not very religious. They have a very murky understanding of the Koran and of the essence of Muslim doctrine, limiting themselves, with few exceptions, to a highly imprecise performance of the Muslim rituals of fasting, prayer, and almsgiving.[12]

Since Islamic doctrine and Muslim clerics were assumed to be inherently hostile to women, their diminished influence among the Turkmen

---

[9] Mikhailov, *Tuzemtsy*, p. 51; Lomakin, *Obychnoe pravo turkmen*, p. 32; P. S. Vasiliev, *Akhal-tekinskii oazis: Ego proshloe i nastoiashche* (St. Petersburg, 1888), p. 17.

[10] Vasiliev, *Akhal-tekinskii oazis*, p. 17.

[11] On European idealization of pastoral nomads, see Abu-Lughod, "Anthropology's Orient," pp. 94–102.

[12] Mikhailov, *Tuzemtsy*, pp. 49–50. See also Mikhailov, "Religioznye vozzreniia," pp. 95–96; Sev, "Zametki o turkmenskom dukhovenstve," *Turkmenovedenie*, no. 2 (February 1928): 8–9.

was thought to account for women's relative freedom. Among the Turk-men, a complex unwritten code of customary law known as *adat* played the primary role in regulating social relations and behavior. When adat contradicted Islamic law, customary law prevailed.[13]

Early Soviet writers continued to maintain that unveiled nomadic women were "less oppressed" than other Muslim women. According to O. Tumanovich, author of a popular 1926 ethnography of the Turkmen, the Turkmen love of equality and freedom was reflected in the high status of women. Echoing P. S. Vasiliev, Tumanovich wrote that men respected their wives and consulted with them on everything: "The Turkmen woman is not the concubine of her husband or a decoration for his house, but rather his best friend."[14] The Russian-born Turkmen scholar Karash-khan Yomutskii argued that Turkmen women had more power within the family and kin group than was generally recognized: "The official head of the family is always the oldest man, but women have a huge influence on the life of the family and frequently even the entire tribal collective."[15] Even the activists of the zhenotdel, ever the vigilant guardians of women's rights, initially believed that their task would be easier in Turkmenistan than elsewhere in Central Asia. A 1925 zhenotdel report on the status of women in Central Asia noted that "the woman question in Turkmenia is not as prominent" as in neighboring Muslim regions; the "relative free-dom of the Turkmen woman," the author declared, "is linked to the reten-tion of remnants of tribal life."[16]

"Unheard-Of Impudence": Female Political Activism

Because Turkmen women were considered less oppressed than their Mus-lim sisters, they were expected to move quickly to take advantage of the new opportunities afforded by Soviet rule. The effort to mobilize women was led by the zhenotdel, the women's section of the Communist Party created in 1919 to fight for changes in women's status throughout the Soviet Union. The twelfth all-union Communist Party Congress in 1923

[13] Islamic law, or *sharia*, held sway to varying degrees among the Turkmen. The stateless Turkmen in Transcaspia applied it only in limited spheres of activity, such as marriage and inheritance law, and even then in a modified form, while the Bukharan Turkmen were more likely to apply Islamic law and resort to religious (*qazi*) courts. See Lomakin, *Obychnoe pravo Turkmen*, pp. 1, 56–58, 93–94; Sev, "Zametki o turkmenskom dukhovenstve," p. 10; Mikhailov, *Tuzemtsy*, pp. 57–59.

[14] Tumanovich, *Turkmenistan i Turkmeny*, p. 96.

[15] Yomutskii, "Bytovye osobennosti turkmen Turkmenskoi SSR," p. 200.

[16] RGASPI, f. 62, op. 2, d. 440, ll. 106–7.

had emphasized the "special significance" of work among Muslim women, as part of a larger Soviet strategy of exploiting the revolutionary potential of the "peoples of the East." The zhenotdel carried out this party policy by focusing a considerable amount of attention and resources on Central Asia in the mid- and late 1920s, aided by the establishment of women's sections within the Communist Parties of each Central Asian republic.[17]

The mostly European activists of the zhenotdel sought to involve Central Asian women in public life by encouraging them to join mass organizations, attend political meetings and literacy classes, and run for election to village soviets. Political activism would eventually pave the way for some women to join the party and perhaps be tapped for administrative jobs within the Soviet bureaucracy. Literacy classes, meanwhile, would enable the overwhelmingly illiterate female population to attend training programs and institutions of higher education. The zhenotdel also promoted the economic mobilization of women in the 1920s, with initiatives designed to foster economic self-sufficiency such as the establishment of state-supported handicraft-production workshops.

The effort to transform Turkmen women into political activists enjoyed limited success in the early years of Soviet rule. Women were far less likely than men to become involved with Soviet institutions, since public activism violated cultural norms of appropriate behavior for women and threatened to weaken the patriarchal control of men. Women who did engage in political activity in the early years were considered something akin to prostitutes and risked estrangement from their families and communities.[18] As in many other societies, women in Turkmenistan were viewed as the most important keepers and transmitters of traditional culture and values.[19] The prospect that they would absorb the individualistic and atheistic values of the Soviet regime was almost as alarming as the

[17] Carol Eubanks Hayden, "Feminism and Bolshevism: The Zhenotdel and the Politics of Women's Emancipation in Russia, 1917–1930" (Ph.D. dissertation, University of California, Berkeley, 1979), pp. 140–44, 289–97. Hayden has argued that involvement in Central Asia may have been a way of boosting the zhenotdel's revolutionary credentials at a time when it was no longer defending women's interests in an uncompromising fashion within Russia.

[18] RGASPI, f. 62, op. 2, d. 1234, l. 67.

[19] On the role of women in reproducing and symbolizing ethnic and national differences, see Nira Yuval-Davis and Floya Anthias, eds., *Woman-Nation-State* (New York: St. Martin's Press, 1989), pp. 6–10. See also Nayereh Tohidi, "The Intersection of Gender, Ethnicity and Islam in Soviet and Post-Soviet Azerbaijan," *Nationalities Papers* 25, no. 1 (1997): 147–67.

Figure 12. "Episode from the New Life": A Turkmen civil servant rocks his infant while waiting for his wife to return from a political meeting. (*Tokmak*, no. 11 [1927]: 3.)

possibility that they would marry Russian men.[20] Because of the dangers involved in exposing women to contact with foreigners, many men—even communists and Soviet officials—were unenthusiastic about allowing their wives and daughters to join Soviet organizations.[21] Turkmen-language periodicals depicted men with politically active wives as ridiculous, emasculated creatures. In a 1927 cartoon captioned "Episode from the New Life," a Turkmen civil servant is shown rocking his hungry infant while his wife attends a meeting: "Sleep, little one," he murmurs. "The meeting will be over soon, and you can drink like a calf when your mother gets home."[22]

Women themselves also had solid practical reasons for reticence; already overworked within their households, they were not eager to take on the additional commitment of attending meetings and literacy classes. Those who did get involved in the 1920s were often older women, who faced fewer cultural constraints and were less burdened by housework than their young daughters-in-law. At a conference of Muslim women in May 1923, there were just five Turkmen women in attendance, most of

[20] In the late 1920s, some Turkmen families fled to neighboring Afghanistan because of rumors that Turkmen would be forced to marry Russians. RGASPI, f. 62, op. 2, d. 2206, l. 5.

[21] Ibid., f. 121, op. 1, d. 42, l. 19; *Tokmak*, no. 11 (1927): 10.

[22] *Tokmak*, no. 11 (1927): 3.

them spoken of dismissively by zhenotdel organizers as "decrepit old women." However decrepit they may have been, they still had to be bribed to attend. In 1923, three Turkmen women were elected to village soviets. Once again, they were older women and material inducements had to be used: "This was considered a great achievement, even though once again they were all old women, and moreover they had been bribed, as later became clear; they each got two puds of flour or five rubles for agreeing to be elected to the soviet."[23]

The reference to "decrepit old women" reveals an important area of friction between Bolshevik and Turkmen values. The revolutionary ethos of the Bolsheviks idealized the vigor and iconoclasm of youth, but Turkmen society valued age and experience above all.[24] Young women, more than any other group, faced restrictions based on requirements of modesty and respect for their elders. Only older women were gradually able to shed some of these constraints, appear in public, and interact more freely with others. Those younger women who did heed the call of the zhenotdel and take on public roles faced severe difficulties. In particular, they were burdened by requirements of modesty that prevented them from speaking out in front of strangers or older relatives. Ene Gulïeva, one of the first female Turkmen party members and the very picture of the emancipated Turkmen woman, had to overcome a great fear of speaking in public. One of her zhenotdel mentors recalled: "It took great effort to convince Comrade Gulïeva to speak for the first time at a large meeting, and only after many such appearances, once again with great effort, did we succeed in convincing her to speak at the provincial Congress of Soviets, where her father-in-law was present." Since Turkmen tradition did not permit a young woman to speak in the presence of her older in-laws, "this was unheard of impudence from the point of view of custom." Similarly, a Turkmen woman who spoke at the founding congress of the union of poor peasants in November 1925 "completely lost her head during her speech when her eyes met those of one of her relatives."[25]

When young women became involved, they were often the wives of Communist Party members, pushed into Soviet activities by their husbands in order to satisfy state demands for visible female participation. In the Ginzburg region, singled out by the zhenotdel in 1927 as "a particularly bright example of a party organization's serious approach to the question of female liberation," village party cells were praised for their

[23] P. P. Perimova and L. Ya. Belova. *10 let na fronte bor'by za raskreposhchenie zhenshchin* (Ashgabat: Turkmengosizdat, 1929), pp. 10–11.

[24] Many of the individuals appointed to high positions in the republic were extremely young. For example, Charï Vellekov was twenty-six when he was appointed first secretary of the KPT Central Committee.

[25] RGASPI, f. 62, op. 2, d. 440, l. 102.

successful recruitment of women into Soviet activities. In the village of
Yüzbashï, the zhenotdel noted, the fifteen members of the local party cell
had "drawn their wives into public life, regularly taking them along to
meetings of the party cell, enrolling them in the literacy school, and signing them up for delegates' meetings."[26]

The busy women of Yüzbashï may have been exceptional. Many women
were unenthusiastic about Soviet activities, regarding political meetings
and literacy classes as a waste of their valuable time. Faisulina, a schoolteacher, noted in 1927 that the women in her village refused to attend
literacy classes because they had nowhere to leave the children or simply
no spare time.[27] In the village of Bagïr, a woman declared her objection to
attending pointless meetings when there were other, more pressing problems facing women: "The zhenotdel comes and does nothing but hold
meetings. . . . All the women and children are ill here, but it's too far to
go to the doctor in Bezmen and the doctor never comes here. So we're not
going to go to meetings anymore."[28] Most Turkmen women seemed more
interested in practical economic and medical assistance that would improve their daily lives than in the mobilization touted as "emancipation"
by the Soviet regime. In a predominantly nomadic Yomut area near the
settlement of Jebel, an ethnographer in 1929 found women to be "more
interested in the economic/practical than in the cultural/educational under-
takings of women's organizations." Not a single girl was enrolled in the
area's Soviet schools, and the women's movement was regarded with
"veiled hostility by the men and timid alienation on the part of the
women."[29] In meetings with Soviet officials, rural women most often expressed concern about the health of their families, asking the regime to
provide medical care and to install running water in their villages.[30]

Official statistics showed rising female participation in political life during the second half of the 1920s. At election meetings, the proportion of
women in attendance increased from 1.5 percent in 1926–27 to 38.7 percent in 1928–29. The proportion of female village soviet members rose
from 6.2 percent in 1926–27 to 20 percent in 1928–29. Between 1925
and 1928, an estimated twenty-five hundred women "liquidated their illiteracy" at Soviet literacy points.[31] Yet these numbers did not necessarily
provide a meaningful gauge of women's own interest in these activities;

[26] Ibid., d. 1237, l. 7.
[27] Ibid., ll. 33–35.
[28] Ibid., l. 34
[29] S. Morozova, "K etnograficheskim kharakteristikam raionov Turkmenii," *Turkmenovedenie*, no. 1 (January 1929): 80.
[30] RGASPI, f. 62, op. 2, d. 1237, l. 40.
[31] G. Karpov, "Raskreposhchenie zhenshchiny-turkmenki," *Za partiiu*, no. 3–4 (March–
April, 1929): 81, 84.

often, they reflected falsification or outright coercion by local officials faced with demands that they show evidence of women's participation. In July 1929, women were physically dragged to meetings in the village of Kïrk-Ujlï.[32] In the village of Ashïkalï, a woman named Nele Gün Yakshïrova was called into court after she failed to show up at an election meeting during the campaign for local soviets. "After that," the villagers said, "all the women started going wherever the authorities asked them to."[33]

Men were threatened with sanctions if they failed to make their womenfolk available for "emancipatory" activities. A 1927 decree of the Turkmen TsK called for the dismissal of any communist official who refused to send his wife to literacy classes. The rationale for penalizing men was made clear by KPT secretary Halmïrad Sähetmiradov at a meeting of zhenotdel activists in 1927; since Turkmen women were obedient wives, he declared, they would attend school if ordered to do so by their husbands.[34] In the Garabekevül district, the regional inspector of education announced to all villagers that "it was mandatory for women to enroll in school, and that if anyone failed to send his wife to be educated, he would be deprived of his voting rights, taken to court, and fined." In the village of Islam, the village soviet repeatedly sent a policeman to harass a peasant who failed to send his wife to school. In the village of Chekpete, the peasant Gurban Hojerek Oglï explained that his wife had not attended a meeting sponsored by the village soviet because she had recently had a miscarriage. In response, "the chair of the village soviet grabbed him by the collar and declared, 'I command you to bring your wife, even if she is lying on her death bed.' "[35] In the Yölöten region, local authorities announced in 1928 that men whose wives failed to attend meetings would pay a fine of three rubles. In this manner, wrote an OGPU investigator, "they herd all the women to the meeting . . . and after all this they say in their report that nearly 100 women came to the meeting."[36] Such methods may have had dubious emancipatory potential, but they did have the desired effect of producing impressive figures on female mobilization for use in reports to higher-ups.

In the long term, Soviet authorities recognized that the best way to mobilize the female half of the population was to inculcate a new generation of girls with Soviet ideas. Yet the expansion of primary school education for girls got off to a slow start in the 1920s. Parents were reluctant to expose their daughters to Soviet values, and particularly reluctant to

[32] RGASPI, f. 62, op. 2, d. 1811, l. 194.
[33] Ibid., d. 2206, ll. 3–4.
[34] Ibid., d. 1234, ll. 37, 49.
[35] Ibid., d. 2206, l. 4.
[36] Ibid., d. 1494, ll. 35–36.

send them to schools with male students and teachers. During the 1926–27 school year, only 5.2 percent of all Turkmen children between the ages of eight and seventeen in the republic were enrolled in Soviet schools.[37] Among Turkmen school-aged girls, the figure was closer to 1 percent.[38] The republican Communist Party tried to remedy this by offering benefits to parents who sent their daughters to school, recruiting young Turkmen women into the teaching profession, and building separate schools for girls.[39] These efforts did eventually increase the numbers of schoolgirls in Turkmenistan, but progress was slow; in 1930, girls still made up only 9 percent of the schoolchildren in rural Turkmen villages.[40]

The area in which Turkmen women were most receptive to zhenotdel initiatives was the establishment of cooperative workshops for carpet- and silk-weaving. Turkmen women were skilled weavers of carpets, which traditionally furnished and decorated nomadic homes.[41] The production of carpets for sale was also a highly lucrative source of cash income, since the striking traditional patterns were prized by non-Turkmen as well. One source estimated that 30 percent of the income in Turkmen households came from the sale of carpets.[42] The value of this female economic contribution was recognized by male villagers, one of whom told the zhenotdel official Anna Aksentovich, "If it weren't for our wives, our village economy would not be very profitable."[43] Because of the obvious practical benefits of cooperative rug production and marketing, women who balked at attending Soviet meetings and literacy classes were extremely interested in the zhenotdel workshops. When zhenotdel activists visited Turkmen villages, they were approached by women eager to learn whether the cooperatives would give advances for carpets and provide high-quality dyes.[44]

By 1929, there were 21,500 women involved in carpet-weaving workshops and 4,187 in silk-weaving workshops in Turkmenistan—many times the number of women who served on village soviets or attended literacy classes.[45] The promotion of economic self-sufficiency was popular among women because it enhanced their lives and the economic prospects of their families, instead of making unproductive demands on their time.

[37] GARF, f. 3316, op. 20, d. 156, l. 13.
[38] RGASPI, f. 17, op. 60, d. 814, l. 88; f. 62, op. 2, d. 545, l. 24.
[39] Ibid., f. 62, op. 2, d. 1237, l. 15.
[40] Karpov, "Raskreposhchenie zhenshchiny-turkmenki," p. 84; GARF, f. 6983, op. 1, d. 139, l. 11.
[41] RGASPI, f. 62, op. 2, d. 440, l. 116.
[42] Ibid.; d. 1234, l. 6.
[43] Ibid., d. 1218, ll. 40–41.
[44] Morozova, "K etnograficheskim kharakteristikam," p. 80.
[45] Karpov, "Raskreposhchenie zhenshchiny-turkmenki," p. 83.

Figure 13. Turkmen village children, Ashgabat region, 1920s. (From the collection of the Russian State Archive of Film and Photographic Documents at Krasnogorsk.)

Moreover, unlike political activism, female participation in weaving coop-eratives did not alienate male villagers or drive a wedge between women and their families. Men even helped to recruit their wives and daughters into the workshops, recognizing that this would benefit the household and village economy.[46] As a result of these successes, a few zhenotdel offi-cials argued that the promotion of craft workshops was the best way to reach Turkmen women; this would be a first step toward their "sovietiza-tion," which would lead them to become "allies" of the Soviet regime and eventually to participate in political and social activity.[47]

THE SEARCH FOR A VEIL SUBSTITUTE

It was not long before zhenotdel officials realized that the expectation of easier "emancipation" among women in Turkmenistan had been overly optimistic. With the growing intensity of the campaign to mobilize women throughout Central Asia in the late 1920s, Soviet women's activ-ists reconsidered the notion of nomadic exceptionalism and found it want-ing. Turkmen women, after all, were not full participants in public life. They attended Soviet schools and joined Soviet organizations in much smaller numbers than men. Their destinies were still controlled by their fathers, husbands, and brothers. Zhenotdel officials came to believe that Turkmen women, even in their unveiled state, were oppressed and in need of deliverance by Soviet law.

Soviet advocates of gender reform now tried to separate the issues of Islam and women's oppression, claiming that Turkmen customary law denigrated women just as much as the sharia. Turkmen women would have to be released from the cruel constraints of tribal custom before their energies could be exploited by the Soviet regime. By the end of the 1920s, the official view of Turkmen women could scarcely be distinguished from the more general propaganda literature on Muslim female oppression. The Turkmen woman came to be seen as a hapless victim of male domina-tion, her status only marginally better—if at all—than that of her heavily veiled Uzbek sisters.[48] She was a piece of property to be bought and sold at will, a slave subject to the whims of her husband and male relatives, a drudge who worked night and day in the household while her husband relaxed with his friends, drank tea, or went hunting.[49] The contrast with

[46] RGASPI, f. 62, op. 2, d. 1234, ll. 78, 82.
[47] Ibid., d. 440, ll. 116, 121. See also d. 1234, l. 78.
[48] On Bolshevik views of the oppressed condition of Muslim women, see Massell, *The Surrogate Proletariat*, pp. 93–123; Northrop, "Uzbek Women and the Veil," pp. 28–32.
[49] For depictions of Turkmen women as victims of gender oppression, see D. G. Yomud-skaia-Burunova, *Zhenshchina v staroi Turkmenii: Bytovoi ocherk* (Moscow and Tashkent,

the earlier view of Turkmen women as free, equal consorts of men could hardly be greater.

Nevertheless, the campaign for women's emancipation in Turkmenistan was hindered by the lack of a potent symbol around which to rally women's activists. In neighboring Central Asian republics, this role was played by the veil—specifically, the *paranji* and *chachvon*, a heavy veil and cloak that hid women's faces and bodies from the eyes of the world. The Bolsheviks viewed the veil as an appalling manifestation of female inferiority, and the veiled woman herself as a potent symbol of Central Asian backwardness. Soviet propaganda vividly and indignantly described Muslim women who were covered from head to toe with heavy fabric, secluded in the female quarters of their houses, and prohibited from speaking to men who were not their relatives.

In Uzbekistan, the campaign to promote unveiling culminated in the *hujum* (onslaught) of 1927, in which thousands of women tore off and burned their veils in public squares.[50] Discarding the veil came to symbolize conversion to the Soviet way of life. After unveiling, women would be free to attend literacy classes and meetings, run for the village soviet, and work outside the home. The mass unveilings of 1927 helped to crystallize both support for and opposition to the regime's efforts at social transformation. As Douglas Northrop has written, the Soviet narrative of female liberation depended heavily on the act of unveiling—a "public, even theatrical act of individual emancipation."[51] Moreover, the veil was an important symbol for male party members, who could prove their commitment to the Soviet regime by unveiling their wives and daughters.[52] In Turkmenistan, the absence of the veil not only deprived zhenotdel activists of a potent symbol of oppression and conversion, but also gave local officials an excuse to dismiss the need for work among women. As a group of Turkmen Communist Party members in the Gïzïlayak region noted laconically in 1927, "Our women don't wear the veil and therefore we can't emphasize the question [of women's emancipation] very much."[53]

The response of some women's activists in Turkmenistan was to seek a local substitute for the veil, a visible symbol of Turkmen women's oppression that could become a focus of propaganda and action. The most

---

1931); Briullova-Shaskol'skaia, "Na Amu Dare," pp. 298–99; Belova, "Zhenotdely v Turkmenii," p. 34; Morozova, "K etnograficheskim kharakteristikam," p. 79; RGASPI, f. 62, op. 2, d. 801, l. 125.

[50] On the *hujum* and the unveiling campaign in Central Asia, see Massell, *The Surrogate Proletariat*; Northrop, "Uzbek Women and the Veil"; Kamp, "Unveiling Uzbek Women."

[51] Northrop, "Uzbek Women and the Veil," p. 91.

[52] Douglas Northrop, "Languages of Loyalty: Gender, Politics, and Party Supervision in Uzbekistan, 1927–1941," *Russian Review* 59, no. 2 (April 2000): 179–200.

[53] RGASPI, f. 62, op. 2, d. 1218, ll. 42–43.

obvious candidate was the Turkmen practice known as *yashmak*, which required a woman to cover her mouth with a scarf in certain circumstances. Some zhenotdel officials viewed the practice as functionally equivalent to the veil, a form of symbolic seclusion that prevented women from participating fully in public life. The problem was that yashmak was very different from veiling in its social significance. It was not simply a form of female seclusion, but part of a cultural system revolving around notions of shame and respect for seniority.

Extremely complex rules of deference and avoidance regulated relations within a Turkmen household. Family members behaved in ways that were considered necessary to show respect or to avoid feelings of shame. These rules fell most heavily on young daughters-in-law. A new bride was required to avoid all direct contact with in-laws, both male and female, who were older than her husband. In their presence, she covered her mouth with the end of a headscarf and did not speak or eat. With time, and after the birth of children, some of the strictures were relaxed, but with more senior individuals (especially older males) the rules of avoidance remained inflexible. Thus, a woman might experience a lifetime of marriage without ever speaking directly to her father-in-law.[54] Young bridegrooms faced a similar prohibition on speaking to their elder in-laws. Nevertheless, the burden on women was greater, since the young married couple customarily lived with the husband's family.[55]

Zhenotdel officials fell upon yashmak as the solution to the problem of Turkmen exceptionalism, arguing that it was a heinous manifestation of Turkmen women's subordinate status and equivalent in its purpose to the veil. After a visit to Turkmenistan, the leading zhenotdel official Anna Aksentovich declared that "the covering of the mouth made just as strong an impression on me as the wearing of the veil. . . . If we want to change the conditions of daily life, we must begin by simply untying this scarf."[56] Some advocates for women even tried to argue that yashmak was worse than the veiling practiced in Uzbekistan. Uzbek women, they contended, at least had the right to behave freely in their own homes, where they were not required to veil. A Turkmen woman, on the other hand, was not even allowed to converse with her husband in her own home if her mother-in-law was present. Because of this, one official argued, a Turkmen woman was made aware of her "slavelike position, moral oppres-

---

[54] Irons, *The Yomut Turkmen*, pp. 104–7; Yomudskaia-Burunova, *Zhenshchina v staroi Turkmenii*, pp. 30–33; Bastug and Hortacsu, "The Price of Value," pp. 133–35. Similar avoidance practices have been documented among other Turkic peoples. See Bastug and Hortacsu, "The Price of Value," p. 34.

[55] Irons, *The Yomut Turkmen*, pp. 109–11.

[56] RGASPI, f. 62, op. 2, d. 1218, l. 51; see also d. 2438, l. 101.

Figure 14. Young Turkmen woman with *yashmak* scarf, Ashgabat, 1930. (From the collection of the Russian State Archive of Film and Photographic Documents at Krasnogorsk.)

sion, and absolute lack of rights" every moment of the day.[57] Despite these efforts, zhenotdel officials did not succeed in sparking a mass campaign against yashmak. Indigenous male communists argued that yashmak was not nearly as onerous as the paranji, since women were not required to cover their faces.[58] A few desultory articles appeared in the press, and there were periodic proposals to make it a crime to force a woman to practice yashmak, but little more. There were no mass burnings of yashmak cloths and no public conversions to a yashmak-free life. Perhaps because the practice was so much more subtle and flexible than veiling—and because, unlike the veil, it blurred the boundaries between the public and private spheres—yashmak was poorly suited to serve as a rallying symbol for women's emancipation.

The Assault on Custom

In the absence of a Turkmen equivalent to the veil, zhenotdel activists in Turkmenistan concentrated their efforts on crafting legislation designed to transform Turkmen marital and family life. European Bolsheviks considered many aspects of Turkmen customary law and family life to be demeaning to women, since they violated progressive Western notions of individual autonomy, equality of the sexes, and freely chosen relationships between men and women. Legislation was one of the most important ways of righting these wrongs. Through legal means, women's lives were to be remodeled along the most progressive European lines, with an emphasis on personal autonomy rather than submission to the needs of the family. They would have the right to marry and divorce at their own pleasure, and to attend school or work outside the home without obtaining the permission of their parents and husbands.

The Soviet belief in the necessity of radical intervention to change family and sexual mores was not limited to Muslim Central Asia. It was an outgrowth of debates within Russia about the fate of family, marriage, and gender relations under socialism. From 1917 through the mid-1930s, the Bolsheviks moved rapidly to emancipate women from the legal and economic constraints that tied them to the household and made them dependent on men, preventing them from realizing their individual potential and participating in the larger society. Soviet authorities sought to do away with the patriarchal family and with marriage as an economic and legal relationship, making it instead a free union based on mutual feeling and equality. Eventually, they envisioned the "withering away of the fam-

---

[57] Ibid., d. 2696, l. 144; d. 2438, l. 101.
[58] Ibid., d. 2696, l. 144.

ily"—a society in which children would be raised by the state and household drudgery such as cooking and laundry would be accomplished communally, while women joined men in working outside the home. This vision was not only light years away from domestic reality in Turkmenistan but also from peasant family life within Russia proper.[59]

Early Soviet legislation called for radical changes in marital and sexual practices and the status of women. The 1918 Russian Federation Code on Marriage, the Family, and Guardianship ended the religious sanction of marriage and provided for civil registration of marital unions. The new code declared the legal equality of men and women, guaranteeing women equal pay for equal work. It equalized the status of children born within and outside of wedlock, set the minimum marriage age at eighteen for males and sixteen for females, and required the consent of both parties to marriage.[60]

In Turkmenistan, perhaps the most controversial aspect of the new Soviet marriage and family legislation was the policy on divorce. The Russian Federation family code adopted in 1918 allowed a marriage to be dissolved at the request of either partner, without any grounds.[61] The Soviet regime's liberalization of divorce, and particularly the granting of equal rights to women in this sphere, was perceived by men as a direct assault on the Turkmen family. Ultimately, the rising rate of female-initiated divorces aroused the impassioned defense of tradition that the veil had aroused elsewhere. At the same time, the conflict underscored the difficulty of freeing Turkmen women from the constraints of custom while winning the support of Turkmen men.

Under Koranic guidelines, only men were permitted to initiate divorce. In theory, a Turkmen man could divorce his wife unilaterally by pronouncing "I divorce thee" three times, as prescribed by Islamic law. In practice, the Turkmen frowned upon divorce except in cases of impotence, a husband's refusal to support his wife, or incurable disease in one of the partners. It was unheard of for a woman to initiate a divorce.[62] A Turkmen

[59] For a detailed discussion of the evolution of Bolshevik ideas on women and family, see Wendy Z. Goldman, *Women, the State, and Revolution: Soviet Family Policy and Social Life, 1917–1936* (Cambridge: Cambridge University Press, 1993), chap. 1. See also Gail Warshovsky Lapidus, *Women in Soviet Society: Equality, Development, and Social Change* (Berkeley and Los Angeles: University of California Press, 1978), chap. 2. On the status of women in Russian villages, see Goldman, *Women, the State, and Revolution*, pp. 146–50.

[60] On the 1918 Russian Federation code, see Goldman, *Women, the State, and Revolution*, pp. 50–52; Massell, *The Surrogate Proletariat*, pp. 201–2.

[61] Russian federation laws at the time applied to Turkestan, including the Turkmen oblast'. Massell, *The Surrogate Proletariat*, p. 202.

[62] Tumanovich, *Turkmenistan i Turkmeny*, p. 96; Irons, *The Yomut Turkmen*, pp. 142–43; GARF, f. 3316, op. 21, d. 100, l. 86.

proverb put it succinctly: "A husband's death is a wife's divorce."[63] Soviet policies posed a head-on challenge to these traditional attitudes. Many Russian zhenotdel officials believed that Muslim marriages were ipso facto oppressive to women, and they sought to deliver as many women as possible from these unequal unions. The zhenotdels spread the news about the new divorce law in the early and mid-1920s, encouraging Central Asian women who were unhappy in their marriages to get divorces and helping them to navigate the Soviet bureaucracy.[64]

Turkmen men vigorously protested the Soviet sponsorship of divorce. In the Kerki and Leninsk/Chärjew regions, formerly part of the Bukharan emirate, peasants protested at nonparty conferences and sent complaints to the provincial party committee. In Kerki, local officials warned in 1925 that the large number of women filing for divorce was threatening to cause a violent uprising.[65] Many local officials claimed that the policy of easy divorce was affecting mostly poor and landless peasants, whose wives were leaving them in order to marry wealthier men. In a number of cases, parents were said to be encouraging or even compelling their daughters to divorce impoverished husbands in order to marry more well-to-do men.[66] A report from Kerki province in late 1927 referred to a new trend involving the "repeat selling" of women by their families, which was resulting in the "collapse of the family among the native population." In some cases, the husbands being divorced were not only poor, but decades older than their wives. Such divorces were "especially tragic," according to the Kerki zhenotdel, because the impoverished husband had often struggled all his life to save enough money to marry.[67]

There was disagreement within the Communist Party over the divorce issue, with opinion dividing to some extent—although not exclusively—along national lines. Many native Turkmen officials believed that divorce should be strictly regulated within the republic. Given the possibility that young women would be forced into divorce by their parents, they argued, a number of restrictions should be introduced to prevent possible abuse. European officials, more influenced by the Bolshevik rhetoric of sexual

[63] Cited in *Turkmensko-russkii slovar'* (Moscow: Isdatel'stvo Sovetskaia Entsiklopediia, 1968), p. 615.

[64] RGASPI, f. 62, op. 2, d. 1234, l. 49.

[65] Ibid., d. 440, ll. 93–94, 109–10. The new freedom to divorce was taken advantage of by other Central Asian women as well; Northrop reports that in Tashkent in 1927, 91 percent of divorce petitions were filed by women. "Uzbek Women and the Veil," p. 391. There was also an upsurge of divorce in Russia in the 1920s, although Russian divorces tended to be initiated by men. See Richard Stites, *The Women's Liberation Movement in Russia: Feminism, Nihilism, and Bolshevism, 1860–1930* (Princeton: Princeton University Press, 1978), pp. 370–71.

[66] RGASPI, f. 62, op. 2, d. 440, ll. 3, 93–94; d. 1237, ll. 68–69.

[67] Ibid., d. 1237, ll. 68–69.

equality, tended to maintain that women's freedom to divorce should not be restricted for any reason. The opponents of divorce in Turkmenistan ultimately won the battle, introducing harsh new restrictions at a time when women elsewhere in the Soviet Union had unprecedented freedom to end their marriages.

At a session of the Turkmen Central Executive Committee on October 4, 1926, Turkmen Sovnarkom chair Gaigïsïz Atabaev argued that Soviet-style free divorce was against the interests of poor peasants. In the view of the local population, he said, the new divorce laws were bringing about the destruction of the family and the household economy. Moreover, they were giving rise to new practices of questionable legality. Atabaev described cases in which the wife of a poor man would ask an acquaintance to help her obtain a divorce. The acquaintance would then arrange her "sale" to a new husband for bridewealth, and the woman and her acquaintance would split the proceeds. Atabaev also claimed that some parents had become "repeat resellers," marrying off their daughters five or six times in the course of two or three years.[68]

In Atabaev's view, the upsurge in divorce could be explained by the typical Turkmen woman's flightiness and lack of class consciousness:

The Turkmen woman is not yet a mature individual; her understanding is extremely limited and she is still ignorant and benighted. It is not at all difficult to tempt her with the good life, with jewelry or trinkets. Wealthy men take advantage of these circumstances to lure away the wives of poor men. This is generally why the Turkmen woman asks for a divorce—she imagines better prospects for her personal life, and she marries a wealthy or prosperous man as his second, third, or fourth wife.

Since Turkmen villages were not yet "sovietized" and harbored many opponents of Soviet power, Atabaev continued, the free application of Soviet divorce laws risked provoking anti-Soviet violence. Thus, both class equity and the security of Soviet power in the countryside demanded an end to divorce on demand.[69]

The first steps toward limiting divorce were taken in 1925. A special commission of the Turkmen Central Committee reviewed the work of the zhenotdel in mid-1925. After meeting with leading Turkmen officials, who argued persuasively that the rising divorce rate in Turkmenistan was dangerous, the commission suggested that local courts should be more cautious about approving divorces among the native population.[70] On November 3, 1925, the commissariat of justice sent a circular

[68] GARF, f. 3316, op. 19, d. 855, ll. 103–4.
[69] Ibid., ll. 102–5.
[70] RGASPI, f. 62, op. 2, d. 440, ll. 68, 72–73, 92–94.

to local judicial organs and prosecutors, urging them not to grant divorces unless they were certain that the wife was seeking a divorce of her own free will.[71]

A decree of the Turkmen TsIK adopted on October 6, 1926, imposed even more stringent restrictions on divorce. The decree repeated Atabaev's claims about the repeated "reselling" of brides and the frivolity of Turkmen women who were lured by the promises of rich men. It maintained that easy divorce worked exclusively against the interests of poor peasants, justifying restrictions on divorce as necessary to keep the peace in Turkmen villages, where a woman's demand for divorce often led to bloodshed due to "peculiar notions of honor" among men.[72] The TsIK decree stipulated that divorce suits among the native population must be decided in courts, not in administrative organs or registry offices, as was the practice in Russia. Only in the more formal context of a courtroom could officials ascertain that a petition for divorce reflected the sincere desire of the husband or wife, rather than the influence of others. In cases where there was "insufficient justification" for divorce or a suspicion that parents or other relatives were pushing for dissolution of the marriage, the courts should deny the petition. Anyone forcing a married woman to divorce her husband could go to jail for up to three years.[73] Atabaev insisted that this decree would limit only "groundless" divorces. A Turkmen woman who had a "good reason" for wanting a divorce—for example, one whose husband had taken a second wife or had an incurable disease—would still be eligible.[74] However, local judges tended to interpret both the TsIK decree and the judicial commissariat's instructions to mean that they should deny all petitions for divorce, even those technically considered justified. The era of easy divorce for Turkmen women was over.[75]

Not everyone agreed with the new restrictions. Perengliev, the commissar of education, objected to Atabaev's narrow definition of a valid divorce suit, saying that a husband's neglect or infidelity should be considered sufficient grounds for divorce.[76] More fundamentally, leading Russian advocates for women within the republic took issue with the portrayal of high divorce rates as the product of ignorant women, unscrupulous and greedy relatives, and professional "resellers." The republican branch of the Commission on the Improvement of Daily Life and Labor among Women (KUBT), a women's advocacy organization under the auspices of the TsIK, disputed the claim that divorce was mostly affecting the

---

[71] Ibid., l. 92; d. 1237, l. 270; d. 800, ll. 8–9.

[72] Ibid., d. 1234, l. 124.

[73] GARF, f. 3316, op. 21, d. 100, l. 84.

[74] Ibid., op. 19, d. 855, ll. 100–101.

[75] Ibid., op. 21, d. 100, ll. 44–45; RGASPI, f. 62, op. 2, d. 1237, l. 270.

[76] GARF, f. 3316, op. 19, d. 855, l. 90.

poor. According to 1928 KUBT statistics on divorce petitions, only 25 to 30 percent were from the wives of "poor peasants." The most common reasons for divorce were not the desire for "trinkets" cited by Atabaev but much more serious complaints: polygamy, "sexual deviancy," abusive treatment and beatings, a large age difference between the spouses, or a husband's refusal to allow his wife to pursue an education. Only an insignificant number of divorces were instigated by outsiders, according to G. I. Karpov, head of the KUBT, and in such cases the outside influence on a woman most often came from a "more cultured" Turkmen man who wished to marry her. The view of many Turkmen officials that divorces were affecting exclusively poor peasants was not a reflection of reality, but was based on "prejudices rooted in custom." The reason why most divorce petitions were from women, Karpov added, was that men did not bother using Soviet legal mechanisms—they simply threw their wives out the old-fashioned way.[77]

Karpov maintained that Turkmen men were falsely claiming to be poor peasants in order to block their wives' perfectly legitimate divorce suits. In one case investigated by the Ashgabat provincial procuracy, a divorce was granted to the wife of a man named Durdïev. Durdïev appealed the decision, and the chair of the district party committee provided an affidavit stating that Durdïev was a poor peasant. Twelve citizens also provided affidavits testifying to Durdïev's excellent treatment of his wife. However, an investigation found that Durdïev was a well-to-do middle peasant, and that he had made several violent assaults on his wife. His illiterate fellow villagers had been coerced into signing the declaration (which they did by making marks with their thumbs). According to Karpov, "Three of the signers candidly admittted that although they knew about Durdïev's crude treatment of his wife, they had signed 'so as not to set a bad example for other women.' "[78]

In the absence of comprehensive statistics on divorce in 1920s Turkmenistan, it is hard to know which side's views more closely reflected reality.[79] Was there really a "mass divorce" problem, or was there merely mass hysteria among Turkmen men who saw their control of their wives and daughters threatened? Did divorce really affect the poor disproportionately? The European officials of the KUBT spent much of their time advising Turkmen women on their rights and helping them to navigate the Soviet legal system. They were advocates for women seeking to escape the constraints of custom, and they naturally tended to impute the most

[77] Ibid., op. 21, d. 100, ll. 43–45.

[78] Ibid., l. 44.

[79] The Turkmen state archives, which may contain this information, are closed to foreign researchers.

noble motives to their protégées. Turkmen officials such as Atabaev, on the other hand, had themselves been shaped by Turkmen gender and family norms and were more sensitive to the popular reception of Soviet policies. These officials believed that the liberal divorce policy would undermine support for the Soviet regime in the countryside, and they knew how to make the case against divorce in terms that European Bolsheviks could understand. This meant shifting the debate from the terrain of gender oppression onto that of class conflict. By claiming that women's desire for divorce was harming the poor, they could force the regime to choose between support for women and support for "class-friendly" elements. The effectiveness of this tactic became clear almost immediately; the measures adopted by Turkmen republican authorities in 1925 and 1926 restricted divorce even as other Soviet women were enjoying unprecedented freedom in this sphere.[80]

The retreat on divorce shows the limitations of the "surrogate proletariat" argument when applied to Turkmenistan. According to Gregory Massell, the Bolshevik leaders believed that they would make women into the strongest supporters of the Soviet project by breaking down traditional family structures and freeing women from the constraints of custom.[81] In Turkmenistan, however, the requirements of women's emancipation were carefully weighed against the larger imperatives of class policy. Soviet officials within the republic indicated unambiguously that they intended to rely on the poorer segments of the peasantry—that is, poor men—as the regime's main social basis. In this scheme, women were at best a "supplementary proletariat." As the first secretary of the Turkmen Communist Party, Halmïrad Sähetmïradov, told a gathering of zhenotdel officials in 1927, communists should not seek to appeal to women through policies that antagonized poor and landless male peasants. Instead, the party had to reconcile its mandate to liberate women with its task of winning the loyalty of poor men.[82] The zhenotdel's efforts to achieve women's emancipation received the party's support as long as they did not conflict with efforts to win the allegiance of *male* peasants. In cases where the two

---

[80] At about the same time as the promulgation of the Turkmen TsIK decree limiting divorces, the new RSFSR code made divorce easier by transferring authority over it from courts to civil registry offices. Goldman, *Women, the State, and Revolution*, p. 212. Moreover, the Uzbek Commissariat of Justice insisted in March 1926 that all female-initiated divorces be processed expeditiously. Massell, *The Surrogate Proletariat*, p. 211. Massell argues that there was a general retreat on the promotion of divorce in Central Asia in the late 1920s; however, all of his examples of antidivorce legislation come from the Turkmen republic. See *The Surrogate Proletariat*, pp. 296–98. Only in 1936 did the Soviet regime reintroduce restrictions on divorce throughout the country, as part of a new campaign to promote stable families and increase the birth rate. Goldman, *Women, the State and Revolution*, pp. 331–32.

[81] Massell, *The Surrogate Proletariat*, chap. 4.

[82] RGASPI, f. 62, op. 2, d. 1234, l. 82.

imperatives conflicted, as with the new divorce law, women's advocates were forced to yield.

In addition to the changes in divorce legislation, a number of laws were passed in the 1920s banning Turkmen customs relating to marriage and the family. In Central Asia, women's activists believed that the new 1918 Russian Federation family code in itself would not be adequate to improve the status of women. It would also be necessary to explicitly outlaw certain customary practices—"crimes of custom"—believed to be hindering women's entry into Soviet life. In the Soviet view, "crimes of custom" were practices that deprived women of the autonomy and dignity they deserved. Some of the "crimes" targeted for eradication in Turkmenistan were common throughout Muslim Central Asia—the payment of bridewealth (known as *kalym* to Russians and *galïng* to Turkmen), polygamy, and underage marriage.[83] Others, such as *gaitarma* (the bride's return to her parents' house for an extended period immediately after her marriage) were not widely practiced elsewhere. The Bolsheviks believed that these customs were the main impediments to women's progress in Muslim regions where women were not veiled or secluded; they were "remnants of the past," "socially dangerous," and likely to "hinder the economic, political, and cultural growth of the republic."[84]

Most Soviet officials of European descent believed that the eradication of "crimes of custom" was an essential precondition for the mobilization of women. But some leading Turkmen officials, led by Sovnarkom Chair Atabaev, argued that the assault on tradition should not be the main focus of Soviet policy toward women. They pointed out that such an ancient and deeply rooted way of life could not be done away with by decree. Moreover, like the liberalization of divorce law, the banning of bridewealth and other practices risked alienating the poor peasants and nomads upon whose support the regime depended. Instead of adopting a punitive policy that penalized people for following their customary way of life, the regime should try to appeal to the rural population by offering educational and economic programs that would benefit their families and villages.

Galïng, or bridewealth, was the central target of the Soviet assault on "crimes of custom" in Turkmenistan. Galïng was the payment given by the groom's family to the bride's relatives when a marriage agreement was concluded. By all accounts the exchange of bridewealth was universal among the Turkmen, and marriages were not considered to be valid without it. Upon marriage, a young woman left her father's household and moved to her husband's family's household, taking her labor and repro-

[83] On legislation against "crimes of custom" elsewhere in Central Asia, see Northrop, "Uzbek Women and the Veil," chap. 7; Massell, *The Surrogate Proletariat*, pp. 192–12.
[84] GARF, f. 3316, op. 21, d. 100, l. 90.

ductive power with her. As in many patrilineal societies, marriage involved a payment from the groom's family to the bride's family, representing compensation for their loss of rights over their daughter and her future children. Anthropologists have argued that the bridewealth reflected the high value placed on women in their roles as wives and mothers.[85]

Bridewealth served other functions in Turkmen society as well. The custom not only created economic linkages between the families of bride and groom, but also served to solidify kinship obligations and authority relationships within the groom's family. The cost of bridewealth was so high that families had to begin saving for this expense soon after their sons' births; as a result, young men were financially dependent on their parents and could not marry without their approval. Moreover, the father's relatives generally contributed to the bridewealth expenses, thus creating reciprocal obligations among patrilineal kin. The bridewealth money was used to provide the bride's trousseau or dowry (known in Turkmen as *atkulak*)— a set of household furnishings, rugs, and other items given to the bride by her family and taken with her to her new home. Thus, much of the money actually returned to the groom's household and helped the young couple to begin their new life together.[86]

The amount of bridewealth varied according to the circumstances of the marriage. Among the Yomuts, there were fairly rigid conventions determining the size of the bridewealth payment, based on the age and previous marital status of bride and groom, whether the bride had a "pure" Turkmen pedigree, and other factors. If the bride was to be a second or third wife in a polygamous household, the payment was three times as high as for a first wife. Sometimes families would "exchange" daughters, thus avoiding the need for a large bridal payment. The bridewealth would also be reduced if the bride and groom were close relatives such as first cousins, a preferred form of marriage among many Turkmen.[87]

The official Soviet view of bridewealth did not take into account the social context in which it operated or its positive connotations in demonstrating the high value placed on women. A few Soviet commentators were tolerant of the custom, noting that its purpose was to give a bride a

[85] Bastug and Hortacsu, "The Price of Value," pp. 121–22. The anthropologist William Irons has analyzed bridewealth among the Yomut Turkmen as a "leveling institution" that compensates the economically unfortunate (those with many daughters) at the expense of the more fortunate (those with many sons). *The Yomut Turkmen*, pp. 163–64.

[86] Bastug and Hortacsu, "The Price of Value," pp. 129, 130–31.

[87] Irons, *The Yomut Turkmen*, pp. 129, 134–36. RGASPI, f. 62, op. 2, d. 286, l. 144. Marriage between first cousins is permitted in Islam, and anthropologists have reported its occurrence among a number of Middle Eastern groups. See Eickelman, *The Middle East and Central Asia*, pp. 169–71; also Ladislav Holly, *Kinship, Honour, and Solidarity: Cousin Marriage in the Middle East* (Manchester and New York: Manchester University Press, 1989).

certain measure of economic security, pay for her trousseau, and bring honor to her parents.[88] However, the vast majority of European communists and zhenotdel activists condemned the exchange of bridewealth as "selling and buying women" like so much livestock. Bridewealth was also condemned on class grounds, since the expense was said to make marriage the prerogative of the well-to-do. Poor men, Soviet officials claimed, often had to save for years to be able to pay bridewealth, and sometimes could not afford to marry at all.[89]

Along with bridewealth, the customary practices targeted by the Soviet regime in Turkmenistan included polygamy and underage marriage. Because polygamy was considered the prerogative of the wealthy, European Bolsheviks justified banning it on class as well as gender grounds; not only did the practice degrade women, but it also benefited the well-off at the expense of the poor. Soviet authorities also claimed that polygamy stimulated inflation in the cost of bridewealth by increasing the demand for marriageable women, thereby making marriage difficult or impossible for poor men.[90]

Appalled by the tender age at which Muslim girls were married off by their families, European Bolsheviks were also determined to abolish child marriage. Most prerevolutionary sources indicated that Turkmen girls were thought to be ready for marriage as soon as they reached puberty. Girls married most often between the ages of twelve and sixteen.[91] This was typical of premodern societies in which adulthood was not postponed by long years of school attendance. It was considered unwise to allow postpubescent girls to remain unmarried and unoccupied, since premarital sexual activity would dishonor the family. There were also economic reasons for early marriage among the Turkmen. Because only married men had the right to a share of land and water under the traditional sanashïk system, families in need of additional land had an incentive to marry off their sons early. Similarly, poor parents in need of cash had an incentive to find husbands for their daughters as soon as possible.[92] Soviet authorities argued that early marriage deprived women of the right to choose their husbands-to-be, while teenaged childbearing harmed the health of the young mothers and their children.[93]

[88] Tumanovich, *Turkmenistan i Turkmeny*, p. 95; GARF, f. 3316, op. 19, d. 855, l. 92.

[89] RGASPI, f. 62, op. 2, d. 1234, l. 125. See also G. Karpov, " 'Kalym i ego sotsial'nye korni," *Turkmenovedenie*, no. 2–3 (February–March 1930), pp. 29–33; Dosov, "Bor'ba s bytovymi prestupleniami," *Kommunistka*, no. 5 (May 1928): 30.

[90] GARF, f. 3316, op. 21, d. 100, ll. 86–87; RGASPI, f. 62, op. 2, d. 1234, l. 123.

[91] Irons, *The Yomut Turkmen*, p. 128; Yomudskaiia-Burunova, *Zhenshchina v staroi Turkmenii*, p. 24.

[92] GARF, f. 3316, op. 19, d. 855, ll. 90–91.

[93] Ibid., op. 21, d. 100, l. 89; RGASPI, f. 62, op. 2, d. 1234, l. 123.

For several reasons, bridewealth became the centerpiece of the conflict between indigenous Turkmen seeking to defend their customs and the mostly European communists seeking to eradicate them. Among the Turkmen, polygamy was relatively rare and underage marriage, while common, was not required by custom or religion. Bridewealth, by contrast, was a universal and mandatory part of the marriage and kinship system.[94] European officials, for their part, viewed bridewealth as the linchpin of a social and economic system that degraded women and the poor; it prevented poor men from marrying, facilated polygamy among the rich, and perpetuated child marriage by encouraging poor fathers to "sell" their young daughters for a profit. Eradicating the practice, these Soviet officials believed, would make it easier to end other "backward" customs relating to women.[95]

Legislation against "crimes of custom" began in the Turkestani republic in the first half of the 1920s. A January 1923 decree of the Turkestani government banned bridewealth throughout Turkestan, although the law had little effect.[96] An October 1924 addendum to the 1918 Russian federation's criminal code outlawed several customary practices relating to women in Central Asia, including bridewealth and polygamy.[97] A new domestic code adopted by the Russian Federation in November 1926 did not technically apply to Central Asia, since the republics created in the national delimitation were no longer part of the Russian republic. However, the wide discussion of marital and family practices that preceded its adoption had the effect of spurring legislation on crimes of custom in other parts of the Soviet Union.[98]

In 1925, an effort began to formulate laws on "crimes of custom" in the new republics of Central Asia and to circulate them for discussion by native communists and the local population.[99] Party officials in Turkmenistan organized peasant conferences with the dual purpose of publicizing Soviet measures and assessing peasant views. At these meetings, it became clear that of all the activities of the Soviet regime, measures designed to emancipate women and "modernize" Turkmen family life aroused the most passion and controversy. Party officials reported that peasants who were passive throughout the conference proceedings, dozing through dis-

---

[94] On the relative rarity of polygamy among the Turkmen, see Mikhailov, *Tuzemtsy*, p. 52; Briullova-Shaskol'skaia, "Na Amu Dare," p. 299; Tumanovich, *Turkmenistan i Turkmeny*, p. 96.

[95] Karpov, "Raskreposhchenie zhenshchiny-turkmenki," pp. 80–81.

[96] GARF, f. 3316, op. 21, d. 100, ll. 79, 90; op. 19, d. 855, l. 102.

[97] Massell, *The Surrogate Proletariat*, pp. 199, 204.

[98] Ibid., pp. 205–6.

[99] Ibid., p. 206.

cussions of village soviet elections and land reform, "came alive exactly as if shot from a cannon as soon as the woman question came up."[100]

When conferences of Turkmen peasants and nomads were asked to issue formal resolutions approving the government's ban on "crimes of custom," some refused to comply. The proposed ban on bridewealth was particularly controversial. In Farap district, the delegates simply declared they would all continue to give and receive bridewealth because their ancestors had done so.[101] Turkmen peasants said bluntly that they regarded bridewealth as compensation for the expense of raising a daughter, who would contribute nothing to her own family's future growth. As one peasant in Leninsk province defiantly said, "If the authorities want to ban galïng, then let them prepare a place for girls [to live], and we'll send them there from the day of their birth." Another declared, even more dramatically: "From the day of their birth until the age of sixteen, girls are dependent on their parents. It's not possible to give them in marriage without receiving galïng. If we have to give them away without galïng, then our wives will kill their daughters at birth."[102]

In Burdalïk, the peasants objected to a blanket ban on polygamy, saying that a man should be permitted to marry a second wife if the first is ill, "so that the first does not become homeless." Others said that if a man's first wife cannot have children, "he should be allowed to take a second." In Old Chärjew, peasants insisted on adding a stipulation that women should not be allowed to divorce their husbands without good reason.[103] There were also objections to raising the marriage age for girls to sixteen. As one Turkmen peasant commented, "The authorities want to raise the marriage age for girls to sixteen, but will they give parents the means to support them?"[104]

While the official Soviet position maintained that galïng was harmful to the poor and should be abolished on class grounds, resistance to banning the practice was strong among poor peasants, many of whom saw the marriage of a daughter as an opportunity for a financial windfall. As one ethnographer noted, "Every poor man who has daughters looks on them as a unique source of income."[105] Thus, Soviet authorities in Turkmenistan faced a clear conflict between their desire to end a practice viewed as demeaning to women and their aim of appealing to poor rural men.

Given the constraints of public opinion, leading Turkmen communists argued, there were limits to how quickly they could move against Turk-

[100] RGASPI, f. 62, op. 2, d. 440, l. 110.
[101] Ibid., d. 630, ll. 36, 38, 44–45; d. 1237, l. 278.
[102] Ibid., d. 1237, ll. 277–78.
[103] Ibid., d. 630, ll. 36, 38, 44–45; d. 1237, l. 278.
[104] Ibid., d. 1237, l. 278.
[105] GARF, f. 3316, op. 21, d. 100, ll. 79–78.

men customs. The practice of bridewealth, in particular, was so deeply ingrained that an outright ban would be pointless. In a discussion of the proposed legislation at a meeting of the Turkmen Central Executive Committee (TsIK) on October 4, 1926, Sovnarkom chair Gaigïsïz Atabaev paid lip service to the official Soviet view of bridewealth, calling it "the crudest sort of assault on the person and freedom of a woman," but noted that previous experience had shown that a ban on the practice "cannot lead to practical results." Despite the efforts of the former Turkestani republic to outlaw it, the population "continues to exchange bridewealth to the broadest possible extent."[106]

Other Turkmen communists agreed with Atabaev that a ban on bridewealth would be ineffective. The commissar of education, Bäshim Perengliev, noted that the 1923 Turkestani ban had simply caused the practice to go underground. Families began to pay bridewealth in cash, which was more difficult to trace than the traditional payments of livestock. Perengliev predicted:

> Galïng will be banned as such, but it will continue to exist as a secret transaction between two parties in dark corners. You won't find a single peasant who will marry his son without paying. Our judicial organs won't know who is or isn't taking bridewealth, since this affair will take place in a narrow circle between two parties. We will have great difficulty learning who gives or receives bridewealth, even if we have hundreds of agents in the village.[107]

The legislation adopted by the Turkmen Central Executive Committee October 1926 was essentially a compromise, banning polygamy and child marriage while taking a more equivocal position on bridewealth. The TsIK prohibited new instances of polygamy (i.e., the marriage of an already married person) among the native population, but did not invalidate previously contracted polygamous marriages. Violators of the new law could receive a prison term of up to five years. A second decree set the legal marriage age at sixteen for girls and eighteen for boys. It gave both boys and girls the right to refuse a marriage arranged by their parents or relatives before they reached majority, and called for a prison sentence of up to three years for anyone who married a minor. Anyone who arranged the future marriage of a minor (a practice known among the Turkmen as *gudalïk*) could also get a one-year prison term.[108] The TsIK decree on bridewealth did not ban it outright, but merely declared it to be "enrichment at the expense of another person, not sanctioned by law." Individuals who paid bridewealth had the right to sue for its return in a Soviet

---

[106] Ibid., op. 19, d. 855, l. 102.
[107] Ibid., ll. 88–89.
[108] RGASPI, f. 62, op. 2, d. 1234, l. 123.

court. Giving or receiving such a payment would not in itself subject a person to criminal punishment.[109]

Almost immediately, problems emerged with the implementation of the new laws. Peasants, not viewing their customary practices as crimes, naturally failed to report them to Soviet authorities, and few cases were brought to court. Local officials refused to enforce the law and covered up "crimes" in their jurisdiction. The situation with bridewealth, in particular, was just what some Turkmen officials had predicted; the half-hearted declaration that it constituted "enrichment at the expense of another person" did not deter many Turkmen. Most sources indicated that the TsIK decrees were not being enforced.[110] A 1928 report by the KUBT noted that the TsIK decree had been ineffective in the battle against bridewealth and that "the number of demands for the return of bridewealth has been minuscule."[111] One thing the convoluted wording of the law did accomplish, however, was to convince many Turkmen that paying bridewealth was illegal, so that the population began to exchange it surreptitiously.[112]

The law raising the marriage age also posed enforcement problems, leading to frequent disputes between Soviet officials and Turkmen parents over the true age of a young bride. As KUBT official Georgii Karpov observed, "It is a rare Turkmen who knows his age precisely, since births were not registered anywhere." In court cases alleging underage marriage, the authorities would ask a medical expert to determine the age of the bride. In the courtroom, typically, "all the defendants and witnesses usually swear that the victim is 16 or 17 years old, while the expert maintains in his report that she has not attained the legal age for marriage."[113] The law against polygamy, too, could not easily be enforced. Because most Turkmen failed to register their marriages with Soviet authorities, it was difficult to determine who was married to whom without an on-the-spot investigation of family living arrangements.[114]

The leaders of the Turkmen republic soon faced the need to revise the 1926 legislation. In addition to the difficulties involved in enforcing the existing laws, Soviet officials realized that Turkmen society featured other

[109] Ibid., l. 125; GARF, f. 3316, op. 19, d. 855, ll. 101–2. By contrast, Uzbekistan had outlawed bridewealth entirely in July 1926. Massell, *The Surrogate Proletariat*, p. 205.

[110] Sources on the implementation of the laws include materials of the republican zhenotdel, the informational/statistical department of the Turkmen TsK and the Turkmen TsIK's Commission on the Improvement of Daily Life and Labor among Women (KUBT). GARF, f. 3316, op. 21, d. 100, ll. 79–78; RGASPI, f. 62, op. 2, d. 1237, ll. 8–10, 263.

[111] GARF, f. 3316, op. 21, d. 100, ll. 79–78.

[112] RGASPI, f. 62, op. 2, d. 628, l. 69; d. 1237, l. 68; d. 1218, l. 43.

[113] GARF, f. 3316, op. 21, d. 100, l. 43.

[114] RGASPI, f. 62, op. 2, d. 1237, ll. 8–10, 262, 267, 273; GARF, f. 3316, op. 21, d. 100, l. 77.

"crimes of custom" that should be outlawed. Pressure on the Central Asian republics to strengthen the new laws increased in April 1928 when the all-union TsIK enacted a supplement to the Russian federation criminal code entitled "On Crimes Constituting the Relics of the Tribal Order." The supplement prohibited bridewealth, polygamy, child marriage, and other practices sanctioned by religion or custom. At the same time, those within the Turkmen Communist Party who did not favor Atabaev's evolutionary approach to women's emancipation complained to the Central Asian Bureau. These "left communists," led by Sähetmïradov, persuaded the Bureau that the Turkmen law on bridewealth should conform to Moscow's policy.[115] As a result, a new criminal code and a series of decrees adopted by the Turkmen republic during 1928 made existing statutes stricter and added new crimes to the list.[116]

A new decree on bridewealth adopted by the Turkmen TsIK on May 20, 1928, replaced the 1926 TsIK decree and brought Turkmen law into line with the new Russian federation code. The decree ended the ambiguous status of bridewealth, making it a crime punishable by up to three years in prison and confiscation of the amount paid. Both the giver and the recipient of bridewealth were subject to criminal prosecution. The law also encouraged exchangers of bridewealth to inform on each other, decreeing that a person who reported such a payment to the authorities within two weeks would escape prosecution and be entitled to the return of the full amount.[117]

The newly identified "crimes" outlawed in 1928 included *garshlïk* (the exchange of brides between two families), *dakïlma* (leviratic marriage), *gaitarma* (the return of a bride to her parents' house for an extended period after marriage), and bride abduction.[118] The republican authorities viewed garshlïk as a loophole that allowed the Turkmen population to evade the ban on bridewealth. By exchanging daughters as brides for their respective sons, the families concerned were able to avoid paying all but a token bridewealth.[119] To bolster the new antibridewealth legislation, a Turkmen TsIK decree of August 1, 1928, prohibited garshlïk and made its practitioners subject to a three-year jail sentence. The TsIK justified

[115] RGASPI, f. 17, op. 30, d. 10, ll. 18–19.

[116] Ibid., f. 62, op. 2, d. 1237, l. 273; GARF, f. 3316, op. 21, d. 100, ll. 82–83.

[117] GARF, f. 3316, op. 21, d. 100, l. 161.

[118] RGASPI, f. 62, op. 2, d. 1237, l. 273; GARF, f. 3316, op. 21, d. 100, ll. 82–83. See also N. Karaje-Iskrov, "Brachnoe pravo turkmenskoi SSR," *Turkmenovedenie*, no. 2–3 (February–March 1930): 25–30.

[119] In such cases a small symbolic payment was made in order to validate the marriage. See Irons, *The Yomut Turkmen*, p. 136. Among the Yomut studied by Irons, bride exchange was called *chalshïk*.

the ban by saying that garshlïk was yet another way of forcing young women to marry against their will.[120]

The custom of dakïlma, under which a widow was married to one of her late husband's brothers, was also condemned as degrading to women. Soviet women's advocates viewed dakïlma as a self-interested attempt by the late husband's family to retain the widow's labor power and thereby get the most for the bridewealth that had been paid; the woman's preferences were ignored as she was passed like chattel from one brother to the next. A joint decree of the Turkmen Central Executive Committee and Council of People's Commissars of August 1, 1928, forbade dakïlma, declaring that anyone who forced a widow to marry in this fashion was subject to a three-year jail sentence.[121] The reasons for the practice of dakïlma among the Turkmen were more complex than Soviet authorities imagined. The anthropologist William Irons, who studied this practice among the Yomut, has argued that leviratic marriage was primarily a way of ensuring that a woman would not be separated from her young children. Since children belonged to the father's lineage, a mother had no right to take them if she returned to her own relatives or remarried into another family. Irons observed that in cases in which the widow became the wife of an already married brother, such marriages were often fictitious arrangements and remained unconsummated; the purpose was to avoid breaking up the family.[122]

European communists also condemned the custom of gaitarma, which required a new bride to return to her parents' home for an extended period after her wedding. In the stages of marital life mandated by Turkmen custom, a young woman usually did not live full time with her husband until several years after the conclusion of their marriage. Among the Yomut, for example, the bride spent only a few days at the groom's residence after the wedding before returning to her parents' house for an extended period. During this period, the spouses were not permitted to see each other at all. If the groom were caught attempting a secret rendezvous with his bride, he risked a severe beating from her relatives. The period of spouse avoidance was cut short only if the bride became pregnant during the initial wedding visit.[123]

---

[120] GARF, f. 3316, op. 21, d. 100, l. 159.

[121] Ibid.

[122] A widow's blood relatives had the right to give her in marriage again for another bridewealth payment. If the widow did marry one of her brothers-in-law, her in-laws were required to give additional bridewealth to her blood relatives. Irons, *The Yomut Turkmen*, pp. 145–48.

[123] Ibid., pp. 136–41; Yomudskaia-Burunova, *Zhenshchina v staroi Turkmenii*, p. 29; Mikhailov, *Tuzemtsy*, pp. 53–54. According to Irons, among the Yomut Turkmen in Iran the period of spousal avoidance was generally three years. See *The Yomut Turkmen*, p. 8.

This rather unusual practice has been interpreted by outsiders in various ways. Some have seen gaitarma as a way of allowing time for the groom's family to pay off the full amount of bridewealth and for the bride to prepare her trousseau; others have interpreted it as a way of controlling fertility in a harsh environment by allowing women to postpone childbearing.[124] Instead of welcoming gaitarma as an antidote to underage marriage, Soviet officials condemned the practice for allegedly preventing the young couple from getting on with independent married life. "Such a long interruption in marital relations occurs in most cases against the will of both spouses, delays the setting up of their household, and deprives them of their independence," one advocate for women wrote.[125] This argument was based on an urban, European ideal of marriage, since marriage was not exactly an occasion for independence among the Turkmen. A young couple generally lived with the groom's parents for several years, setting up an independent household only after their children were sufficiently grown to contribute to the family economy; even then, the different components of the extended family remained economically interdependent.[126] Nevertheless, the 1928 laws banned gaitarma, prescribing a prison term of up to two years for anyone who prevented a wife from living with her husband.[127]

The 1928 legislation also outlawed the practice of bride abduction, a means of acquiring a wife that was frowned upon by most Turkmen but nevertheless had a place in Turkmen marital tradition. When a girl's parents would not accept a prospective suitor or the two families could not come to an agreement on bridewealth, the groom and his family would sometimes simply kidnap the prospective bride. This rather dramatic action, which sometimes involved the collusion of the bride and sympathetic relatives, usually induced her parents to come to rapid agreement on the terms of the bridewealth. Occasionally, abduction led to violence and permanent feuding between the two families. Ignoring the complexities surrounding the practice, Soviet officials declared it to be "one of the most heinous remnants of tribal life."[128] New laws made the abduction of a woman against her will for the purpose of marriage punishable by up to three years in prison with strict isolation.[129]

[124] Irons, *The Yomut Turkmen*, pp. 3–4, 136–41; Yomudskaia-Burunova, *Zhenshchina v staroi Turkmenii*, p. 29.
[125] GARF, f. 3316, op. 21, d. 100, ll. 82–83.
[126] Irons, *The Yomut Turkmen*, pp. 84–85.
[127] GARF, f. 3316, op. 21, d. 100, ll. 82–83.
[128] Ibid.; RGASPI, f. 62, op. 2, d. 1237, ll. 272–73.
[129] GARF, f. 3316, op. 21, d. 100, ll. 81–83. Among some nomadic and tribal groups, bride abduction is so common that it is viewed as an "alternative mode of marriage." See Daniel G. Bates, *Nomads and Farmers: A Study of the Yörük of Southeastern Turkey* (Ann Arbor: University of Michigan Press, 1973), pp. 59–86.

In the aftermath of the 1928 legislation, the number of "crimes of custom" brought before Soviet courts grew significantly. In the first half of 1928, Soviet courts in Turkmenistan had heard only 162 such cases, with 106 resulting in conviction.[130] In the first seven months of 1929, the courts heard 1,127 cases of customary crimes. Yet this surge in enforcement was hardly grounds for celebration. Nearly half of those convicted of "crimes of custom" were poor and landless peasants, furthering the impression that the campaign was incompatible with the effort to win the support of the "toiling masses."[131] Moreover, there is no evidence that this legislation had any significant impact on popular practice or public opinion, or that the values represented by the new laws had been internalized—or even understood—by the Turkmen population.

In order to enforce the new legislation, the Soviet regime had to persuade the population that the way of life they had followed for centuries was harmful and wrong. Yet little effort was made to explain the reasons for the new laws. The zhenotdel and the KUBT both engaged in agitation and propaganda, but most of their employees were European women incapable of communicating with the overwhelmingly non-Russian-speaking Turkmen population.[132] Meetings and conferences with nonparty peasants affected only a small part of the population, most of them male. There was little opportunity to explain Soviet policy in written form because most Turkmen, especially women, were illiterate; in any case, there was a severe shortage of written material in the Turkmen language.[133] Under these circumstances, the Turkmen rural population must have been somewhat mystified by the sudden legal assault on its way of life.

Convincing the public of the need for the new laws was complicated by the reluctance of many indigenous Soviet officials and Communist Party members to enforce them. Local officials were often unwilling to support the zhenotdel in its work among native women, regarding this as "dirty" work not worthy of serious attention.[134] Turkmen communists themselves, expected to set an example for the rural population, did not always obey the new laws. Communists who paid bridewealth, married young girls, or took more than one wife were periodically reprimanded and expelled from the party. Of those convicted of customary crimes in the second half of 1928, 7.5 percent were party members, candidate members, and Komsomols.[135] Ordinary Turkmen villagers pointedly asked why they should abandon their customs if government officials

[130] GARF, f. 3316, op. 21, d. 100, ll. 188–202.
[131] RGASPI, f. 62, op. 2, d. 2438, ll. 65–66.
[132] Ibid., d. 545, l. 89; d. 1237, l. 274; d. 1234, l. 18.
[133] Ibid., d. 1237, l. 274.
[134] Ibid., l. 3; d. 2696, l. 134.
[135] Karpov, "Raskreposhchenie zhenshchiny-turkmenki," p. 83.

failed to do so. In the village of Hojasofï in the Tejen region, the local judge, a party member, paid 450 rubles for a sixteen-year old bride. As a result, "many peasants have pointed to him saying, 'He, a judge, gives bridewealth, why can't we give and take it?' " Another communist declared, "I have not fed my daughter for nothing and won't sell her for less than 500 rubles." In the village of Gökdepe, the chairman of the village soviet married off his underage child, then issued a false document attesting that the bride and groom had reached legal age. In the village of Chacha in the Tejen region, the chairman of the village soviet gave peasants false certificates attesting that they had married without paying bridewealth. At the third republican congress of Soviets, seven nominees for membership in the TsIK were rejected as polygamists.[136] Turkmen communists were in a difficult bind, facing criticism from the party if they observed custom and ostracism from their neighbors if they did not. The lament of one young communist underscored the hardships of belonging to society's vanguard: "If we don't pay bridewealth, all of us party members are condemned to a bachelor's life. They won't give a single girl to us. We can't practice abduction [of girls], since that will cause us to lose our authority among the peasant masses."[137]

The European activists of the zhenotdel were highly critical of Turkmen communist officials for not living up to Bolshevik principles in their own private lives. At a meeting of women activists in Turkmenistan in January 1927, the head of the Central Asian Bureau zhenotdel, S. Shimko, castigated male communists who lived in a European style "for show" but maintained their "uncivilized" Turkmen customs at home: "We have responsible officials who have given up their former way of life and themselves live in civilized circumstances, but they keep their wife in the old style. . . . they have become 100 percent Europeans, but they don't permit this to their wives."[138]

In 1930, major changes took place in the institutional basis for work among women in Central Asia. The party dissolved the zhenotdel, claiming that the eradication of women's cultural backwardness during the cultural revolution had ended the need for a special organization devoted to women. From now on, mainstream party organs would deal with women's issues. The dissolution of the zhenotdel was part of a general policy of abolishing "special interest" sections of the party in the early 1930s. In practice, it resulted in a downgrading of the institutional emphasis placed on the emancipation of women.[139]

---

[136] RGASPI, f. 62, op. 2, d. 1237, ll. 6, 267, 280.
[137] Ibid., d. 1218, l. 44.
[138] Ibid., d. 1234, l. 8.
[139] Hayden, "Feminism and Bolshevism," pp. 362–74.

Nevertheless, officials in the upper echelons of the Turkmen party organization continued to call for increased enforcement and stronger laws against customary practices in the 1930s. Editorialists wrote that remnants of the feudal past were still oppressing women and that underground exchanges of galïng were still widespread. A July 1935 resolution of the KPT Central Committee noted that "crimes of custom" against women were not being adequately prosecuted and that cases of polygamy, underage marriage, and bridewealth "very often go unpunished."[140] Newspapers in the mid-1930s reported that marriages were still arranged against the will of the prospective bride, with wrenching consequences for young women who were beginning to take advantage of Soviet educational opportunities. One of many examples cited was that of a fourteen-year-old collective farm girl who was forced to leave school in 1935 when her father arranged to marry her to the accountant of a neighboring farm. The report indignantly noted that her father "sold" her for six thousand rubles, eight sheep, eight silk robes, and eight pounds of flour.[141] In October 1935, the executive bureau of the Central Committee called on the republican TsIK and the commissariat of justice to urge central authorities in Moscow to strengthen the laws against these offenses. The Bureau called for supplementing the laws banning bridewealth and underage marriage with laws aimed at "responsible officials who know about this but fail to take any action." It also called for new laws that would prohibit "interfering with a girl's freedom to choose her own husband," forcing a woman to practice yashmak, or preventing women from participating in public life.[142] Despite Soviet efforts, then, there was a remarkable persistence of "crimes of custom" in Turkmenistan. As some Turkmen communist officials had predicted in the 1920s, these practices simply went underground when they were outlawed.

In one of his last speeches before falling victim to the Stalinist terror in late 1937, Atabaev reiterated his view that education, not coercion, was the best way to mobilize Turkmen women: "One can't just have a punitive policy; the fundamental thing is to induce Turkmen women to study."[143] Atabaev and his fellow "national communists" within the KPT understood that education for girls, while it might be opposed by some conservatives, was not viewed by the majority of Turkmen as a fundamental threat to their way of life. Unlike the assault on Turkmen custom, it did not pit men against women; nor did it undermine other goals of Soviet

---

[140] RGASPI, f. 17, op. 30, d. 83, l. 85; "Vytirat' kalym," *Turkmenskaia iskra*, October 14, 1935, p. 4; "Sbroshen rabskii yashmak!" *Turkmenskaia iskra*, October 14, 1935, p. 4;
[141] "Vytirat' kalym," p. 4.
[142] RGASPI, f. 17, op. 30, d. 85, l. 56.
[143] Stenogram from 7th TsK KPT plenum of March 18–23, 1937, published in *Atabaeving Songkï Tutlushïgï* (Ashgabat: Sïyasï Söhbetdesh, n.d.), p. 5.

policy, such as the promotion of class struggle and the construction of a Turkmen nation. Over the long term, moreover, the transformative potential of education was far greater than that of the assault on custom.

In the 1920s and 1930s, the Soviet state was just beginning to mobilize a new generation of young women who—unlike their mothers and grandmothers—would take advantage of higher education, civil service jobs, and other Soviet-sponsored opportunities. By the end of the Soviet period, a number of Turkmen women were university educated and pursuing careers as teachers, doctors, and civil servants. Even women who lived in remote villages attended years of school and had literacy rates vastly higher than in the pre-Soviet era. Their horizons were immeasurably broadened as they read Soviet newspapers, watched Soviet television, and saw their children become Pioneers and Komsomols. Yet galïng, yashmak, and other customs continued to characterize family life among all but a tiny minority of russified Turkmen. The reformers of the 1920s zhenotdel had been wrong; improvements in women's educational and employment prospects were not contingent on the eradication of traditional family life. Scholars of the Islamic Middle East and India have argued that feminism does not require the replacement of indigenous culture with European ways; similarly, Turkmen women made gains in education and increased their participation in public life during the twentieth century without the wholesale Europeanization of marriage and the family.[144]

What was the purpose, then, of the Soviet assault on custom? Was the Soviet attempt to "emancipate" women simply a means of exerting colonial control over the Turkmen? At first glance, the campaign against indigenous traditions appears to be precisely this—a transparent attempt to undermine patriarchal control by interfering in family structures, while spreading a belief in the superiority of European culture over "barbaric" customs. Much like the French rhetoric against the veil in Algeria or the British campaign against the immolation of widows in India, Soviet policies served to justify foreign rule. The response, among Turkmen and other Central Asians, was also classically "colonial," in that traditions linked to women and marriage came to be valorized as symbols of national identity. Adhering to custom became a point of pride even among intellectuals who might have disdained such "backward" customs under different circumstances.

---

[144] In contemporary independent Turkmenistan, bridewealth reportedly enjoys widespread support among the population, including women. Bustag and Hortacsu, "The Price of Value," p. 128. On the persistence of yashmak and galïng in contemporary Turkmenistan, see also Blackwell, *Tradition and Society in Turkmenistan*, chapters 5–6. On the relationship between female emancipation and Europeanization in other colonized regions, see Ahmed, *Women and Gender in Islam*, p. 129; Chatterjee, *The Nation and Its Fragments*, pp. 128–33.

Figure 15. Two Turkmen women and a young boy demonstrating their reading ability, 1933. (From the collection of the Russian State Archive of Film and Photographic Documents at Krasnogorsk.)

Yet there was more to Soviet policy than simply the substitution of Russian imperial control for Turkmen patriarchal control. Unlike other European rulers of non-European populations, the Soviets sought to mobilize Muslim women to pursue education, careers, and political activism.[145] Moreover, while French and British colonizers opposed feminism at home even as they trumpeted the need for the liberation of Muslim women, communists sought to emancipate all Soviet women, including those of the Russian heartland.[146] In its policy toward women, the Soviet Union resembled Kemal Atatürk's Turkey, which pursued gender reform as part of a modernizing project, more than it resembled the French and British empires. Yet Turkey was able to successfully reform personal status laws and promote unveiling precisely because changes in women's status were associated with strengthening the modern nation-state and not with colonial coercion.[147] Because the Soviet regime carried the taint of alien rule, communist authorities were unable to persuade most Turkmen that the emancipation of women was essential to their future as a nation.

[145] The British and French showed little interest in supporting state education for girls in colonized regions. Thompson, *Colonial Citizens*, p. 87; Ahmed, *Women and Gender in Islam*, pp. 137–38, 153.

[146] Ahmed, *Women and Gender in Islam*, pp. 150–52.

[147] This argument has been made by Elizabeth Thompson. See *Colonial Citizens*, p. 289. On gender reform in Turkey, see Nermin Abadan-Unat, "The Impact of Legal and Educational Reforms on Turkish Women," in Keddie and Baron, eds., *Women in Middle Eastern History*, pp. 177–94.

Conclusion

FROM SOVIET REPUBLIC TO INDEPENDENT NATION-STATE

IN THE 1920s and 1930s, the Soviet state sought to transform the Turkmen—a scattered, tribally organized population of mostly illiterate nomads and peasants—into a socialist nation. Nationality policy in Turkmenistan consisted of two distinct projects, which the Soviet authorities saw as mutually reinforcing: the making of a unified Turkmen nation and the construction of a modern, socialist society. In Turkmenistan, however, these two projects proved to be distinct and even contradictory. By the end of the 1930s, Soviet nation-making in Turkmenistan had proved more successful than anyone could have anticipated. Crucial to this success was the receptiveness of an indigenous elite, which yearned for the political unification of a Turkmen nation imagined in terms of genealogy. Turkmen communists and intellectuals rapidly embraced the main tenets of Soviet nationality policy, seeking to unite the perpetually fragmented Turkmen and to free them from the domination of other Central Asian nationalities. Indigenous party members enthusiastically promoted the territorial division of Central Asia and the policy of indigenization, often with more fervor than Moscow had bargained for. Intellectuals threw themselves into the work of Soviet cultural institutions, working to create a standardized literary language and a Turkmen "national culture." After two decades of Soviet rule, Turkmenistan possessed many of the elements of modern nationhood, including a national territory and language, a network of native-language schools and periodicals, and a Turkmen-speaking political elite.

The institutionalization of Turkmen ethnicity within a Soviet republic served to further solidify embryonic national sentiments among the elite. The policy of nativization made a national identity relevant to a growing number of Turkmen, leading them to identify with "Turkmen-ness" rather than with subnational forms of identity. This newfound national consciousness was intensified by the elite's indignation at being treated as inferiors by Russian communists. The rhetoric of Soviet nationality policy created the expectation that native Turkmen and their language would play the leading role within Turkmenistan; when this expectation was not immediately fulfilled, the result was an upsurge in nationalist resentment.

The creation of national institutions also paved the way for the emergence of a broader popular identification with the Turkmen nation. While many peasants and nomads were indifferent to questions of nationhood in the 1920s and 1930s, the spread of mass education and literacy would eventually give rural Turkmen a vested interest in the use of their native language and a sense of belonging to a larger national community.

This study has argued that a Turkmen national identity emerged through a dynamic process of interaction between Bolshevik and Turkmen ideas and practices. Turkmen elites willingly adopted the Soviet emphasis on territory and language as important elements of nationhood, yet they never abandoned the premodern understanding of Turkmen identity based on genealogy. In fact, the discourse of genealogy continued to operate in a variety of contexts in the Soviet era. Ethnographers studied Central Asian tribal genealogies in an effort to determine the boundaries between ethnic groups—essential information for those assigned to draw "national" boundaries between Soviet republics. The role of genealogically based tribal dialects emerged as a central issue in the construction of a Turkmen national language. Genealogy also intruded on the categorization of the Turkmen population by socioeconomic class; as a result, the meaning of categories such as "kulak" and "bedniak" was even more ambiguous in Turkmenistan than in the European parts of the Soviet Union.

The campaign against Turkmen "backwardness," which went hand in hand with the effort to foster Turkmen nationhood, faced a far chillier reception. Neither the indigenous elite nor the population as a whole displayed much enthusiasm for the remaking of Turkmen society. Rural dwellers welcomed certain aspects of the modernity introduced by the Soviets, such as access to medical care, artisan cooperatives, and Soviet government jobs. Many of them did "liquidate their illiteracy," join party cells and village soviets, and learn to speak the Bolshevik language of class struggle and socialism. Yet even among those who were ostensibly most committed to supporting the Soviet regime, there was resistance to radical policies of social transformation. Rural communists went to great lengths to minimize the effects of land reform on their communities. Turkmen party members continued to adhere to customary law in their marriages and kin relationships. In the crisis of 1931, Turkmen rural officials joined demonstrations against collectivization, waged war against the Soviet regime, and emigrated along with their fellow villagers.

Soviet policy was never able to resolve the contradiction between nationhood and socialist modernity, which only sharpened with the passage of time. For Russian Bolsheviks and more russified Turkmen communists, "socialism" was a universal ideal; the Turkmen, like all other Soviet peoples—indeed, like all humanity—would sweep away the detritus of the past in order to build a more modern and equitable society. For rural Turkmen and more nationally oriented communists, however, "socialism" appeared to be an effort to make them less Turkmen, and the "war on backwardness" a means of compelling them to give up the customs and beliefs by which they had lived for centuries. This campaign was being waged, moreover, at a time when a growing sense of national identity made Turkmen customs seem more precious than ever.

The tension between nationalism and socialism was partly due to the radical nature of the transformation to which the communist regime in Moscow aspired. Other modernizing states of the period attempted to mobilize their populations and combat backwardness, but none sought to uproot existing social, economic, and cultural institutions as completely as the Soviets. This was naturally resented by newly minted nationalists who sought their nation's roots and unique glory—as all nationalists do—in the past. Moreover, the need for these dramatic changes was decreed not by an indigenous nationalizing regime, but by the distant government of a large multinational state. As a result, many Turkmen were unpersuaded that Soviet-style modernity was essential to the formation of a strong and cohesive Turkmen nation. On the contrary, Soviet policies of promoting class struggle, emancipating women, and battling bourgeois nationalists could easily be seen as serving Moscow's interests at the expense of Ashgabat's. Moscow sought to counter accusations that its rule was imperial or self-serving through the policy of indigenization, which was designed to elevate indigenous elites and the native language within each national republic. Yet this policy was not particularly effective in Turkmenistan, where its halfhearted implementation only increased the Turkmen elite's resentment of Moscow and its local Russian representatives.

It was not until the end of the Soviet era, when a Turkmen nation-state emerged from the rubble of the Soviet Union, that the tension between national and socialist imperatives was finally resolved. Jettisoning the ideological baggage of the Soviet past, independent Turkmenistan embarked on an unabashedly nationalist course. The new regime made it clear that the primary purpose of the Turkmen state would be to fulfill the national aspirations of the Turkmen. National symbols and holidays proliferated. Turkmen names replaced Russian designations for streets and government offices. A new National Revival Movement, led by President Saparmurat Niyazov, sought to promote a Turkmen cultural renaissance.[1]

[1] Michael Ochs, "Turkmenistan: The Quest for Stability and Control," in Karen Dawisha and Bruce Parrott, eds., *Conflict, Cleavage, and Change in Central Asia and the Caucasus*

Despite the new Turkmen rulers' efforts to distance themselves from the Soviet era, the discourse and institutions of independent Turkmen nationhood were profoundly shaped by the Soviet experience. The state continued to practice affirmative action for the titular nationality and the indigenous language, although the rationale was now nationalist rather than Marxist-Leninist. The Soviet emphasis on language as part of national identity was retained. New laws made Turkmen the official state language and required its use in all official settings.[2] As in the Soviet era, political changes were reflected in state language policy. Thus, the Turkmen government in 1993 abandoned the Soviet-imposed Cyrillic script and decreed that Turkmen would henceforth be written in a new Latin script (one that differed substantially from the Latin alphabet used in the 1930s). Although the shift to the new alphabet was intended as a rejection of Russian cultural domination, the mode of its adoption was eminently Soviet. Another striking example of continuity with the Soviet era was the emphasis on the Turkmen "homeland" in the new state's nationalist ideology. The creation of a national territory under Soviet auspices had brought about a dramatic change in the attitudes of the historically nomadic Turkmen toward territory. Before the Soviet era, a well-known proverb maintained that a Turkmen's home was wherever his horse happened to stand.[3] In the 1990s, Turkmen state officials and historians spared no effort to prove that the Turkmen had inhabited their current territory since time immemorial; some scholars even went so far as to deny the nomadic heritage of the Turkmen.[4]

Along with the emphasis on language and homeland inherited from the Soviet era, genealogy remained an important aspect of identity in post-Soviet Turkmenistan. While the vital role of kin in providing political protection and economic support had diminished as the Turkmen population became more educated and urbanized, genealogical distinctions re-

(Cambridge: Cambridge University Press, 1997), p. 320; Annette Bohr, "Turkmenistan and the Turkmen," in Graham Smith, ed., *The Nationalities Question in the Post-Soviet States*, 2d ed. (London and New York: Longman, 1996), p. 355. On nationalizing policies in the new Central Asian states, see Graham Smith, Vivien Law, Andrew Wilson, Annette Bohr, and Edward Allworth, *Nation-Building in the Post-Soviet Borderlands: The Politics of National Identities* (Cambridge: Cambridge University Press, 1998), pp. 7–19, 139–63.

[2] Ochs, "Turkmenistan," p. 334, Jeren Sawyer, "Turkmen Nationalism and Higher Education," *Central Asia-Caucasus Analyst* (on-line version), Field Reports, November 22, 2000; Turkmenbashï, *Address to the Peoples of Turkmenistan*, p. 14.

[3] Kadyrov, *Turkmenistan v XX veke*, p. 78.

[4] Ibid., p. 70; Akbarzadeh, "National Identity," pp. 280–89. For an example of the Turkmen discourse on the homeland, see, B. O. Shikhmuradov et al., eds., *Türkmen halkïnïng gelip chïkïshïnïng dünye yairaishïnïng we onung dövletining tarïkhïnïng problemalarï* (Ashgabat: Rukh, 1993), pp. 12, 25.

mained socially significant at the end of the twentieth century.[5] Turkmen still took pride in their ancestry and preferred to marry within their tribes. At the same time, tribal differences were viewed as a threat to Turkmen national unity and were not discussed publicly. It was widely known, for example, that Niyazov was of Teke origin, yet the government and official press studiously avoided referring to his tribal affiliation. The president spoke out strongly against those who would elevate tribal loyalties above national patriotism. Niyazov also used genealogy to justify the dictatorial nature of his own rule, arguing that the adoption of democracy and a free press might inflame tribal conflict.[6]

If the discourse of nationhood first implanted under Soviet rule has flourished in post-Soviet Turkmenistan, the same cannot be said for the ideals of socialism. Soon after coming to power, the new regime announced its commitment to introducing a market economy.[7] Niyazov declared that the Turkmen republic must "do away with Marxism-Leninism, which was imposed upon us" and described Soviet dogmas such as the inevitability of class struggle as "notions alien to our people."[8] Moreover, the new state emphatically rejected the decades-long Soviet effort to uproot Turkmen practices based in religion and customary law. Banned marital customs such as bridewealth were legalized and celebrated as part of the national patrimony in independent Turkmenistan. Interest in Islam as a lost aspect of national tradition was also revived, and religious holidays outlawed under the Soviets were once again officially celebrated.[9] The new Turkmen state, unlike its Soviet predecessor, faced no contradiction between its social policies and its national identity. Moreover, in its embrace of nationalism and rejection of Marxism-Leninism, Turkmenistan was in perfect accord with global trends at the end of the twentieth century. The architects of Bolshevik nationality policy envisioned nation-making in the Soviet periphery as the fastest way to bring about the inevitable victory of the global proletariat. They could not have imagined that they were laying the foundations of nation-states that would eagerly seek to join the global capitalist economy.

[5] Kadyrov, *Turkmenistan v XX veke*, 87–88, 230. Some scholars have argued that Soviet rule reinforced kinship-based loyalties throughout Central Asia, in part because all other forms of independent social organization were suppressed. Khazanov, *After the USSR*, p. 128; Roy, *The New Central Asia*, chap. 5.

[6] Ochs, "Turkmenistan," pp. 316–18, 330; Turkmenbashï, *Address to the Peoples of Turkmenistan*, p. 21; Anderson, "Authoritarian Political Development in Central Asia," p. 514.

[7] Ochs, "Turkmenstan," pp. 324, 344–45.

[8] Turkmenbashï, *Address to the Peoples of Turkmenistan*, p. 20.

[9] Kadyrov, *Turkmenistan v XX veke*, pp. 119–20, 232–33; Ochs, "Turkmenistan," pp. 324, 338–39, 344–45.

GLOSSARY OF TERMS AND ABBREVIATIONS

adat — Turkmen customary law

aksakgal — a Turkmen elder, lit. "white beard"

aktiv — the activist core membership (of the Communist Party)

alaman — raid (generally in search of slaves or livestock)

bai — well-to-do peasant, landowner

Basmachi — native rebel against Soviet rule

batrak — landless peasant, hired hand

bedniak — poor peasant

Cheka — Extraordinary Commission to Combat Counterrevolution and Sabotage

daihan — native peasant

dakilma — Turkmen custom in which a widow is married to her late husband's brother

gaitarma — custom in which a bride returns to her parents' home for an extended period after her wedding

galing — bridewealth paid by groom to bride's family

garshlik — exchange of brides between two families

Gosplan — the state economic planning agency

gudalik — agreement on the future marriage of a minor

GUS — state academic council

hujum — "onslaught"—1927 campaign to liberate native women, including mass unveilings

ishan — Sufi leader

ispolkom — executive committee (of a soviet)

jadid — Muslim reformer

kolkhoz — collective farm

Komsomol — Young Communist League

korenizatsiia — indigenization or nativization: a policy of preferences for native personnel and native languages

Koshchi — union of poor peasants in Central Asia

kulak — rich peasant

latinizatsiia — shift of writing system to the Latin script

lishenets (pl. lishentsy) — disenfranchised person

medrese — Muslim secondary school

mekdep — Muslim elementary school

mülk — form of land tenure among Turkmen in which land does not change hands each year

mulla — Muslim cleric (among the Turkmen, usually any literate person capable of reciting prayers)

NKVD — People's Commissariat for Internal Affairs

oba — Turkmen village or settlement (among nomads, the residence group with common rights to natural resources in a certain territory)

oblast' — province

OGPU — Unified State Political Adminstration (the secret police)

okruzhkom — provincial party committee

orgotdel — organization department (of the Communist Party Central Committee)

paranji — veil worn by Uzbek and other women in Central Asia

raion — district

sanashïk — form of property in which every married male receives annual share of common land and water

seredniak — middle peasant

Sovnarkom — Council of People's Commissars

Sredazburo — Central Asian Bureau (regional bureau of the Communist Party Central Committee)

SredazEKOSO — Central Asian Economic Council

TsIK — Central Executive Committee

TsK — Central Committee (of the communist party)

Turkmenkul't — Institute of Turkmen Culture

TsKNTA — Central Committee of the New Turkic Alphabet

vydvizhenets — individual promoted into a government position

yashmak — Turkmen custom in which a wife covers her mouth in the presence of her senior in-laws

zhenotdel — women's department (of the Communist Party Central Committee)

BIBLIOGRAPHY

ARCHIVES

Rossiiskii Gosudarstvennyi Arkhiv Sotsial'no-politicheskoi Istorii (Russian State Archive of Social-Political History, RGASPI), Moscow
    Fond 17 Tsentral'nyi Komitet KPSS
    Fond 62 Sredneaziatskoe Buro TsK VKP
    Fond 121 Upolnomochennyi TsKK VKP (b)-NK RKI v Srednei Azii
    Fond 670 Sokol'nikov, G. Ia.
Gosudarstvennyi Arkhiv Rossiiskoi Federatsii (State Archive of the Russian Federation, GARF), Moscow
    Fond 374 Tsentral'naia Kontrol'naia Komissiia VKP(b)/Narodnyi Komissariat
Raboche-Krest'ianskoi Inspektsii SSSR (TsKK-NK RKI SSSR)
    Fond 3316 Tsentral'nyi Ispolnitel'nyi Komitet (TsIK) SSSR
    Fond 6892 TsIK Komissia po Raionirovaniiu
Rossiiskii Gosudarstvennyi Arkhiv Ekonomiki (Russian State Archive of the Economy, RGAE), Moscow
    Fond 1562 Tsentral'noe Statisticheskoe Upravlenie (TsSU)
    Fond 399 Sovet po Izucheniiu Proizvodstvennykh Sil
Arkhiv Rossiiskoi Akademii Nauk (Archive of the Russian Academy of Sciences, ARAN), Moscow
    Fond 676 Vsesoyuznyi Tsentral'nyi Komitet Novogo Alfavita
Sanktpeterburgskii Filial Arkhiva Rossiiskoi Akademii Nauk (St. Petersburg Branch of the Archive of the Russian Academy of Sciences, SPF ARAN), St. Petersburg
    Fond 135 Komissiia po Izucheniiu Plemennogo Sostava Naselenia SSSR

PERIODICALS

Antireligioznik
Cahiers du Monde Russe
Central Asian Survey
Central Asiatic Journal
Daedalus
Ethnic and Racial Studies
Etnografiia
Isvestiia sredne-aziatskogo komiteta po delam muzeev i okhrany pamiatnikov stariny, iskusstva i prirody
Izvestiia Akademii Nauk TSSR
Journal of Modern History
Journal of Muslim Minority Affairs

Kommunisticheskaia revoliutsiia
Kommunistka
Komsomolets Turkmenistana
Nationalities Papers
Narodnoe khoziaistvo Srednei Azii
Novyi vostok
Prosveshchenie natsional'nostei
Revoliutsiia i natsional'nosti
Revoliutsiia i pis'mennost'
Revolutionary Russia
Russian Review
Shuralar Türkmenistan
Slavic Review
Slavonic and East European Review
Sotsialisticheskoe khoziaistvo Turkmenii
Sovetskaia etnografiia
Sovetskoe stroitel'stvo
Tokmak
Turkestanskaia pravda
Türkmen arhivi
Türkmen ili
Türkmen medenieti
Türkmenistan
Turkmenovedenie
Turkmenskaia iskra
Voennyi sbornik
Za partiiu
Zapiski russkogo geograficheskogo obshchestva

PUBLISHED PRIMARY SOURCES: BOOKS, STENOGRAMS, ARTICLES

Abdulla. "Bizde dil meselesi." *Türkmenistan*, April 10, 1925.
Aborskii, A. *Vremia oglianut'sia: Sapiski literatora.* Moscow: Sovetskii Pisatel', 1988.
Agazade, F., and K. Karakashly. *Ocherk po istorii razvitiia dvizheniia novogo alfavita i ego dostizheniia.* Kazan: Izdanie VTsK NTA, 1928.
Al. "Velikii toi." *Turkmenskaia iskra*, no. 225 (September 28, 1929): 3.
Atabaev, K. "Sovetizatsiia kochevii i voprosy skotovodstva." *Turkmenovedenie*, no. 2–3 (February–March 1929): 29–36.
Atabaeving Songkï Tutlushïgï. Ashgabat: Sïyasï Söhbetdesh, n.d.
B. "Dil düzetmegi," *Türkmenistan*, March 3, 1925.
Bartold, V. V. "A History of the Turkman People." In *Four Studies on the History of Central Asia.* Leiden: E. J. Brill, 1962.
———. *Istoriia turetsko-mongol'skikh narodov.* Tashkent, 1928.
Begjanov, A. "Garara garshï garar." *Türkmenistan*, January 9, 1931, p. 2.

Belova, B. "Zhenotdely v Turkmenii." *Turkmenovedenie*, no. 12 (December 1928): 33–42.

Bernshtam, A. "Problema raspada rodovykh otnoshenii u kochevnikov Azii." *Sovetskaia etnografiia*, no. 6 (1934): 86–115.

Bode, K. "O turkmenskikh pokoleniiakh yamudakh i goklanakh." *Zapiski russkogo geograficheskogo obshchestva*, kn 2 (1847), pp. 203–325.

Bogdanova, M. I. *Osnovnye voprosy terminologicheskoi raboty v Turkmenii.* Ashgabat: Turkmengosizdat, 1936.

Böriev, K. "Latinizatsiia turkmenskogo alfavita." *Turkmenovedenie*, no. 9 (September 1928): 13–14.

———. "O iazyke srednei shkoly." *Turkmenskaia iskra*, April 5, 1926, p. 1.

———. "Türkmen dili." *Türkmen medenieti*, no. 3–4 (July–August 1931): 40–44.

———. "Türkmen dilining esasï yagdailarï. Birinji Türkmenistan ïlmï konferentsiasïna khödür edilen tezis."*Türkmen medenieti*, nos. 4–5 (April–May 1930): 3.

———. "Türkmenistan ïlmï konferentsiasïna degishli." *Türkmenistan*, April 25, 1920, p. 2.

———. "Türkmenistanïng birinji ïlmï konferentsiasï." *Türkmenistan*, April 6, 1930, pp. 2–3.

Briullova-Shaskolskaia, N. V. "Na Amu Darye: Etnograficheskaia ekspeditsiia v Kerkinskii okrug TSSR." *Novyi vostok*, no. 16–17 (1927): 290–303.

The Country of the Turcomans: An Anthology of Exploration from the Royal Geographic Society. London: Oguz Press and the Royal Geographical Society, 1977.

Desiatyi s"ezd RKP, mart 1921 goda: stenograficheskii otchet. Moscow: Gosudarstvennoe Izdatel'stvo Politicheskoi Literatury, 1963.

Dosov. "Bor'ba s bytovymi prestupleniami." *Kommunistka*, no. 5 (May 1928): 29–32.

Dvenadzatyi s"ezd RKP (b): stenograficheskii otchet. Moscow: Izdatel'stvo Politicheskoi Literatury, 1968.

Effendizade, F. "Shivechie." *Türkmenistan*, December 30–31, 1925.

Geldiev, M. "Ishchi-daihan jashgoshgïjï, yazïjïlarïnï üjishdirip, olarïng hünermentliklerin artdïrmagïng hem amalï sunratda Türkmen edebiyatïnï yüze chïkarmagïng diyip yolarï." *Türkmenistan*, December 10, 1929, pp. 2–3.

———. " 'Shivechie' adïnda gaitargï baryan yoldasha gaitargï."*Türkmenistan*, January 4, 1926, p. 2.

———. "Türkmenistan gazetining dili ya ki bizde adalga (istilah) meselesi?" *Türkmenistan*, April 14, 1925, p. 2.

Geldiev, M., and G. Alparov. *Türkmen dilining grammatïkasï.* Ashgabat, 1929.

Guliev, Gurban. "Birinji ïlmï konferentsiasïnïng ehemietli hïzmatlarï nämeden ïbarat?" *Türkmen medenieti*, no. 6–7 (June–July, 1930): 5.

Gulmuhammedov, A. "Garrïgala rayonïnda edebi agtarïshlar." *Türkmen medenieti*, no. 1–2 (1931): 24–26.

———."Shive chekishmesi yekebar diling bozulmasï meselesi?" *Türkmenistan*, January 19, 1926, pp. 2–3.

Iunusov, K. "Sostoianie latinizatsii v Turkmenii." *Revoliutsiia i pis'mennost'*, no. 4–5 (1932): 69–73.

K. "Voprosy natsionalizatsii: Izuchaite turkmenskii iazyk." *Turkmenskaia iskra*, May 15, 1928, p. 2.

Karaje-Iskrov, N. "Brachnoe pravo turkmenskoi SSR." *Turkmenovedenie*, no. 2–3 (February–March 1930): 25–30.

Karpov, G. "Alamany: Nabegi turkmen i ikh sotsial'no-ekonomicheskie prichiny." *Turkmenovedenie*, no. 5–6 (May–June 1931): 28–29.

———. "Iomudy: kratkii istoricheskii ocherk." *Turkmenovedenie*, no. 7–9 (July–September 1931): 69–70.

———. "Kalym i ego sotsial'nye korni." *Turkmenovedenie*, no. 2–3 (February–March 1930): 29–33.

———. *Ocherki po istorii turkmenii i turkmenskogo naroda*. Ashgabat: Turkmengosizdat, 1940.

———. "Perevybory sovetov 1929 g. po Turkmenskoi respublike." *Sovetskoe stroitel'stvo*, no. 6 (1929): 64–68.

———. "Rodoslovnaia turkmen." *Turkmenovedenie*, no. 1 (January 1929): 56–70.

———. "Turkmeniia i Turkmeny." *Turkmenovedenie*, no. 10–11 (October–November 1929): 35–42.

Karpov, G. I., and D. M. Batser. *Khivinskie turkmeny i konets kungradskoi dinastii*. Ashgabat: Turkmengosizdat, 1930.

Karpych, V. "Iz istorii vozniknoveniia Turkmenskoi SSR." *Turkmenovedenie*, no. 10–11 (October–November 1928): 37–52.

———. "Revoliutsionnyi put' Turkmenistana." *Turkmenovedenie*, no. 1 (January 1928): 6–15.

Kerbabaev, Berdi. *Chudom rozhdennyi (Kaigysyz Atabaev): Roman-khronika*. Moscow: Sovetskii Pisatel', 1967.

Kh., A. "Edalaraï yerlileshdirmek we termin meselesi." *Türkmenistan*, October 31, 1926, p. 3.

Khalï, Sh. "Türkmen dili, imlasï hem metbugatïmïz." *Türkmenistan*, February 20, 1927, p. 1.

Khaptaev, P. "O nekotorykh osobennostiakh klassovoi bor'by v natsional'noi derevne." *Revoliutsiia i natsional'nosti*, no. 2 (1933): 47–60.

"Korenizatsiia i natsionalizatsiia apparata—ser"ezneishaia zadacha partorganizatsii." *Turkmenskaia iskra*, June 23, 1937, p. 1.

Krasnovskii, D. "Administrativnoe-khozyaistvennoe raionirovanie Turkestana." *Turkestanskaia pravda*, no. 246 (November 20, 1923): 2.

Kulmuhammedov, A. *Materialy po sredne-aziatskim literaturnym pamiatnikam*. Ashgabat: Turkmengosizdat, 1931.

Kun, Vl. "Izuchenie etnicheskogo sostava Turkestana." *Novyi vostok*, no. 6 (1924): 350–59.

Kuropatkin, A. *Turkmeniia i Turkmeny*. Saint Petersburg, 1879.

Lapkin, K. "Kollektivizatsiia i klassovaia bor'ba v kochevykh raionakh Turkmenii." *Sotsialisticheskoe khoziaistvo Turkmenii*, no. 1 (1934): 19–36.

Lenin, V. I. *National Liberation, Socialism, and Imperialism: Selected Writings by V. I. Lenin*. New York: International, 1968.

L-i, I. "Za bol'shevistskuiu podgotovku kadrov: Ob odnom uchebnike turkmen-skogo iazyka i ego avtore." *Turkmenovedenie*, no. 1–2 (January–February 1932): 44–50.

Liubimova, S. "Uroki 'nastupleniia.' " *Antireligioznik*, no. 2 (1928): 20–26.

Lomakin, A. *Obychnoe pravo turkmen*. Ashgabat, 1897.

Mezhnun. "Turkmenskaia nauchnaia konferentsiia po voprosam literaturnogo iazyka, terminologii i orfografii." *Turkmenovedenie*, no. 6–7 (1930): 7.

Mikhailov, F. A. "Religioznye vozzreniia turkmen Zakaspiiskoi oblasti," in *Sbornik materialov po musul'manstvu*, edited by V. P. Nalivkin, 2: 87–103. Tashkent, 1900.

———. *Tuzemtsy Zakaspiiskoi oblasti i ikh zhizn: Etnograficheskii ocherk*. Ashgabat, 1900.

Mikhailov, M. "VNO i likbez v Turkmenii." *Revoliutsiia i natsional'nosti*, no. 9 (September 1931): 95–98.

Morozova, S. "K etnograficheskim kharakteristikam raionov Turkmenii." *Turkmenovedenie*, no. 1 (January 1929): 71–83.

Nasïrlï. "Dil meselesindaki düshünishimiz." *Türkmenistan*, April 12, 1925.

Nemchenko, M. A. "Agrarnaia reforma v Turkmenii." *Novyi vostok*, no. 19 (1927): 122.

———. *Dinamika Turkmenskogo krest'ianskogo khoziaistva*. Ashgabat: Turkmengosizdat, 1926.

Nodel', V. "Menshevistskie spletni v Srednei Azii." *Za partiiu*, no. 4 (December 1927): 53–65.

Nukhrat, A. "Kul'tpokhod v Turkmenii." *Kommunistka*, no. 9 (1929): 32–35.

O'Donovan, Edmund. *The Merv Oasis: Travels and Adventures East of the Caspian during the Years 1879–1880–1881*. London: Smith, Elder, and Co., 1882.

Obituary of Muhammet Geldiev. *Turkmenovedenie*, nos. 1–2 (January–February 1931): 36.

Obzor Zakaspiiskoi Oblasti za 1900 g. Ashgabat: Izdanie Zakaspiiskogo Oblastnogo Statisticheskogo Komiteta, 1902.

Obzor Zakaspiiskoi Oblasti za 1912–1913–1914. Ashgabat: Izdanie Zakaspiiskogo Oblastnogo Statisticheskogo Komiteta, 1916.

Perimova, P. P., and L. Ya. Belova. *10 let na fronte bor'by za raskreposhchenie zhenshchin*. Ashgabat: Turkmengosizdat, 1929.

Poltaeva, Jamila. "Doroga byla dolgoi." *Komsomolets Turkmenistana*, April 28, 1990, p. 8.

Popok, Ya. A. *O likvidatsii Sredne-Aziatskikh organov i zadachakh kompartii Turkmenii*. Doklad sekretaria TsK KPT na sobranii partaktiva Ashkhabada, 16. okt. 1934. Ashgabat, Turkmenpartizdat, 1934.

"Postanovlenie plenuma Sr.-Az. Biuro TsK VKP o razvitii khlopkovodstva." *Za partiiu*, no. 7–8 (July–August 1929): 95.

Potseluevskii, A. P. *Dialekty turkmenskogo iazyka*. Ashgabat: Turkmengosizdat, 1936.

———. "Iazykovoe stroitel'stvo Turkmenii i ego osnovnye problemy." *Revoliutsiia i natsional'nosti*, no. 67 (September 1935): 42–50.

———. "Lingvisticheskaia ekspeditsiia GUS'a." *Turkmenovedenie*, no. 2 (1928): 25–28.

Potseluevskii, A. P. "Plemia Nokhurli (po materialiam ekspeditsii Turkmen-kul'ta)." *Turkmenovedenie*, no. 5–6 (May–June 1931): 30–35.

———. *Rukovodstvo dlia izucheniia turkmenskogo iazyka*. Ashgabat: Turkmen-gosizdat, 1929.

Pravda, M. "Sovetizatsiia turkmenskikh kochevii." *Turkmenovedenie*, no. 10–11 (October–November 1929): 53–57.

Preobrazhenskii, P. F. "Razlozhenie rodovogo stroia i feodalisatsionnyi protsess u turkmenov-iomudov." *Etnografiia*, no. 4 (1930): 11–13.

Sakhatov, K. "Anti-proletarskie vylazki na fronte ideologii i zadachi partii." *Za partiiu*, no. 5 (May 1928): 38–44.

———. "O turkmenskikh rabotnikakh." *Turkmenskaia iskra*, March 4, 1926, p. 1.

———. "O turkmenskom iazyke i ego 'druziakh.' " *Za partiiu*, no. 1 (January 1928): 67–71.

Saraly, M. "Shuralar Türkmenistanïng redaktorïna hat." *Shuralar Türkmenistan*, July 10, 1933.

Sev. "Zametki o turkmenskom dukhovenstve." *Turkmenovedenie*, no. 2 (February 1928): 5–20.

Soltannïyazov, B. "Saralï M. goshularï barada bir iki agïz söz." *Shuralar Türkmenistan*, March 21, 1933.

SSSR komissiia po raionirovaniiu Srednei Azii. *Materialy po raionirovaniiu Srednei Azii: Kniga 1, territoriia i naselenie Bukhary i Khorezma*. Tashkent, 1926.

Stalin, I. V. *Marxism and the National Question: Selected Writings and Speeches*. New York: International Publishers, 1942.

Stalin, Joseph. *Marxism and the National and Colonial Question* (London: Lawrence and Wishart, 1936).

Stenograficheskii otchet 4. plenuma VTsKNA. Alma-Ata, 1931.

Sultanbekov, B. F., ed. *Tainy natsional'noi politiki TsK RKP: Chetvertoe soveshchanie TsK RKP s otvetsvennymi rabotnikami natsionl'nykh respublik i oblastei v g. moskve 9–12 iunia 1923 g.: Stenograficheskii otchet*. Moscow: Insan, 1992.

Tashnazarov, O. *Iazyk Turkmenskoi khudozhestvennoi literatury*. Ashgabat: Turkmengosizdat, 1936.

TsIK Sovetov TSSR. *Pervyi vseturkmenskii s"ezd sovietov rabochikh, dekhkanskikh, i krasnoarmeiskikh deputatov (14–24 fev., 1925 g.): Stenograficheskii otchet*. Poltoratsk, 1925.

TsIK TSSR. "Obrashchenie TsIKa TSSR ko vsem trudiashchimsia TSSR." *Turkmenovedenie*, no. 9 (1928): 15–18.

Turkmenbashï, Saparmurat. *Address to the Peoples of Turkmenistan*. Ashgabat, 1994.

Tumanovich, O. *Turkmenistan i Turkmeny*. Ashgabat: Turkmengosizdat, 1926.

"Turkmenizatsiia sovetskogo apparata." *Turkestanskaia pravda*, April 25, 1924, p. 2.

Turkmenskoe Natsional'noe Buro. "Gde byt' stolitse Turkmenii?" *Turkestanskaia pravda*, September 9, 1924, p. 2.

"Turkmeny iomudskogo plemeni." *Voennyi sbornik*, no. 1 (January 1872): 65–88.

Vambery, Arminius. *Sketches of Central Asia*. Philadelphia: J. B. Lippincott and Co, 1868. Reprint, New York: Arno Press and the New York Times, 1970.

Vareikis, I., and I. Zelensky. *Natsional'no-gosudarstvennoe razmezhevanie Srednei Azii*. Tashkent: Sredazgosizdat, 1924.

Vasiliev, P. S. *Akhal-tekinskii oazis: Ego proshloe i nastoiashchee*. Saint Petersburg, 1888.

Vel'tner, A. "Minuia kapitalisticheskuiu stadiiu razvitiia." *Turkmenovedenie*, no. 10 (October 1930): 2–6.

Vereshchagin, M. "Balans kadrov narodnogo khoziaistva i kul'turnogo stroitel' stva Turk. SSR." *Revoliutsiia i natsional'nosti*, no. 10–11 (October–November 1931): 101–4.

Vesel'kov, G. "Pis'mo tov. Stalina i bor'ba za proletarskuiu khudozhestvennuiu literaturu v Turkmenistane." *Turkmenovedenie*, no. 10–11 (October–December 1931), pp. 44–47. Continued in *Turkmenovedenie*, no. 1–2 (January–February 1932): 25–29.

Ves' Turkmenistan. Ashgabat: Turkmengosizdat, 1926.

Vladmimirtsov, B. Ya. *Obshchestvennyi stroi mongolov: Mongol'skii kochevoi feodalizm*. Leningrad: Izdatel'stvo Akademii Nauk SSSR, 1934.

Vorshev, V. "Osnovnye etapy razvitiia partorganizatsii Turkmenistana." *Revoliutsiia i natsional'nosti*, no. 12 (December 1934): 68–80.

Yomudskaia-Burunova, D. G. *Zhenshchina v staroi Turkmenii: Bytovoi ocherk*. Moscow/Tashkent, 1931.

Yomut Khan, Karash Khan Ogly. *Mestnyi sud v Zakaspiiskoi oblasti. Istoriko-kriticheskii ocherk*. Tashkent, 1922.

Yomutskii, Karash-Khan Ogly. "Bytovye osobennosti turkmen Turkmenskoi SSR." *Izvestiia sredne-aziatskogo komiteta po delam muzeev, okhrany pamiatnikov stariny, iskusstva i prirody*. Vypusk 3-ii (1928): 191–203.

———. "Turkmeny i revolutsiia: Desiat' let tomu nazad v Turkmenii." Pt. 1. *Turkmenovedenie*, no. 1 (September 1927): 12–18.

———. "Turkmeny i revolutsiia: Desiat' let tomu nazad v Turkmenii." Pt. 2. *Turkmenovedenie*, no. 2–3 (October–November 1927): 14–20.

SECONDARY SOURCES: BOOKS AND ARTICLES

Abadan-Unat, Nermin. "The Impact of Legal and Educational Reforms on Turkish Women." In *Women in Middle Eastern History: Shifting Boundaries in Sex and Gender*, edited by Nikki R. Keddie and Beth Baron, pp. 177–194. New Haven: Yale University Press, 1991.

Abu-Lughod, Lila. "Anthropology's Orient: The Boundaries of Theory on the Arab World." In *Theory, Politics and the Arab World.: Critical Responses*, edited by Hisham Sharabi, pp. 81–131. New York and London: Routledge, 1990.

Ahmed, Leila. *Women and Gender in Islam: Historical Roots of a Modern Debate*. New Haven: Yale University Press, 1992.

Akbarzadeh, Shahram. "National Identity and Political Legitimacy in Turkmenistan." *Nationalities Papers* 27, no. 2 (June 1999): 271–90.

Akiner, Shirin. "Uzbekistan: Republic of Many Tongues." In *Language Planning in the Soviet Union*, edited by Michael Kirkwood, pp. 100–22. London: Macmillan Press, 1989.

Allworth, Edward A. *The Modern Uzbeks: From the Fourteenth Century to the Present: A Cultural History*. Stanford, CA: Hoover Institution Press, 1990.

———, ed. *Central Asia: 130 Years of Russian Dominance: A Historical Overview*. 3d ed. Durham, NC: Duke University Press, 1994.

Anderson, Benedict. *Imagined Communities*. London and New York: Verso, 1983.

Anderson, John. "Authoritarian Political Development in Central Asia: The Case of Turkmenistan." *Central Asian Survey* 14, no. 4 (1995): 509–27.

Annanurov, A. M. *Razvitie turkmenskogo iazyka za sovetskii period*. Ashgabat: Ylym, 1972.

Armstrong, John. *Nations before Nationalism*. Chapel Hill: University of North Carolina Press, 1982.

Ashnin, F. D., and B. M. Alpatov. *Delo slavistov: 30-e gody*. Moscow: Nasledie, 1994.

Barfield, Thomas J. "Tribe and State Relations: The Inner Asian Perspective." In *Tribes and State Formation in the Middle East*, edited by Philip S. Khoury and Joseph Kostiner, pp. 153–82. Berkeley and Los Angeles: University of California Press, 1990.

Barth, Fredrik, ed. *Ethnic Groups and Boundaries: The Social Organization of Culture Difference*. London: George Allen and Unwin, 1970.

Basilov, V. N. "Honour Groups in Traditional Turkmenian Society." In *Islam in Tribal Societies: From the Atlas to the Indus*, edited by Akbar S. Ahmed and David M. Hart, pp. 220–43. London: Routledge, 1984.

Bastug, Sharon, and Nuran Hortacsu. "The Price of Value: Kinship, Marriage, and Meta-narratives of Gender in Turkmenistan." In *Gender and Identity Construction: Women of Central Asia, the Caucasus, and Turkey*, edited by Feride Acar and Ayşe Günes-Ayata, pp. 117–40. Leiden: Brill, 2000.

Bates, Daniel G. *Nomads and Farmers: A Study of the Yörük of Southeastern Turkey*. Ann Arbor: University of Michigan Press, 1973.

Bauer, Henning, Andreas Kappeler, and Brigitte Roth, eds. *Die Nationalitäten des Russischen Reiches in der Volkszahlung von 1897. Band A: Quellenkritische Dokumentation und Datenhandbuch*. Stuttgart: Franz Steiner Verlag, 1991.

Beck, Lois. "Tribes and the State in Nineteenth- and Twentieth-Century Iran." In *Tribes and State Formation in the Middle East*, edited by Philip S. Khoury and Joseph Kostiner, pp. 185–225. Berkeley and Los Angeles: University of California Press, 1990.

Becker, Seymour. "National Consciousness and the Politics of the Bukhara People's Conciliar Republic." In *The Nationality Question in Soviet Central Asia*, edited by Edward A. Allworth, pp. 159–67. New York: Praeger, 1973.

———. *Russia's Protectorates in Central Asia: Bukhara and Khiva, 1865–1924*. Cambridge: Harvard University Press, 1968.

Bennigsen, Alexandre A., and S. Enders Wimbush. *Muslim National Communism in the Soviet Union*. Chicago: University of Chicago Press, 1979.

Black-Michaud, Jacob. *Sheep and Land: The Economics of Power in a Tribal Society*. London: Cambridge University Press, 1986.

Blackwell, Carole. *Tradition and Society in Turkmenistan: Gender, Oral Culture, and Song*. Richmond, Surrey, UK: Curzon, 2001.

Blitstein, Peter. "Stalin's Nations: Soviet Nationality Policy between Planning and Primordialism, 1936–1953." Ph.D. dissertation, University of California, Berkeley, 1999.

Bohr, Annette. "Turkmenistan and the Turkmen." In *The Nationalities Question in the Post-Soviet States*, 2d ed., edited by Graham Smith, pp. 348–66. London and New York: Longman, 1996.

Bregel, Yu. E. *Khorezmskie turkmeny v XIX veke*. Moscow: Izdatel'stvo Vostochnoi Literatury, 1961.

———. "Nomadic and Sedentary Elements among the Turkmens." *Central Asiatic Journal* 25, no. 1–2 (1981): 5–37.

Brimnes, Niels. *Constructing the Colonial Encounter: Right and Left Hand Castes in Early Colonial South India*. Richmond, Surrey, UK: Curzon Press, 1999.

Brooks, Jeffrey. *When Russia Learned to Read: Literacy and Popular Literature, 1861–1917*. Princeton: Princeton University Press, 1985.

Brovkin, Vladimir. *Russia after Lenin: Politics, Culture, Society*. London and New York: Routledge, 1998.

Brower, Daniel. "Islam and Ethnicity: Russian Colonial Policy in Turkestan." In *Russia's Orient: Imperial Borderlands and Peoples, 1700–1917*, edited by Daniel R. Brower and Edward J. Lazzerini, pp. 115–35. Bloomington: Indiana University Press, 1997.

Brubaker, Rogers. *Nationalism Reframed: Nationhood and the National Question in the New Europe*. Cambridge: Cambridge University Press, 1996.

Buttino, Marco. "Politics and Social Conflict during a Famine: Turkestan Immediately after the Revolution." In *In a Collapsing Empire: Underdevelopment, Ethnic Conflicts, and Nationalisms in the Soviet Union*, edited by Marco Buttino. Milan: Fondazione Giangiacomo Feltrinelli, 1993.

———. "Study of the Economic Crisis and Depopulation in Turkestan, 1917–1920." *Central Asian Survey* 9, no. 4 (1990): 59–74.

Caroe, Olaf. *Soviet Empire: The Turks of Central Asia and Stalinism*. New York: St. Martin's Press, 1967.

Carrère d'Encausse, Hélène. *The Great Challenge: Nationalities and the Bolshevik State, 1917–1930*. New York and London: Holmes and Meier, 1992.

Chatterjee, Partha. *The Nation and Its Fragments: Colonial and Postcolonial Histories*. Princeton: Princeton University Press, 1993.

Chersheev, D. *Kul'turnaya Revoliutsiia v Turkmenistane*. Ashgabat: Izdatel'stvo Turkmenistan, 1970.

Clark, Larry. *Turkmen Reference Grammar*. Wiesbaden: Harrassowitz Verlag, 1998.

Clement, Victoria. "The Politics of Script Reform in Soviet Turkmenistan: Alphabet and National Identity Formation." M.A. Thesis, Ohio State University, 1999.

Clement, Victoria. "Vowels: Language Components as Political Symbols. The 1923 Turkmen Alphabet Reform." Paper delivered at the Eleventh Annual Nicholas Poppe Symposium, University of Washington, May 1999.

Colley, Linda. *Britons: Forging the Nation, 1707–1837.* New Haven: Yale University Press, 1992.

Connor, Walker. *The National Question in Marxist-Leninist Theory and Strategy.* Princeton: Princeton University Press, 1984.

Crisp, Simon. "Soviet Language Planning since 1917–1953." In *Language Planning in the Soviet Union*, edited by Michael Kirkwood, pp. 23–45. London: Macmillan Press, 1989.

Conquest, Robert. *Stalin: Breaker of Nations.* New York: Penguin, 1991.

Davidson, Basil. *The Black Man's Burden: Africa and the Curse of the Nation-State.* New York: Times Books, 1992.

Davies, Sarah. *Popular Opinion in Stalin's Russia: Terror, Propaganda, and Dissent, 1934–1941.* Cambridge: Cambridge University Press, 1997.

Devalle, Susana B. C. *Discourses of Ethnicity : Culture and Protest in Jharkhand.* New Delhi and Newbury Park, CA: Sage Publications, 1992.

Dovletov, Djuma. *Turkmenskii aul v kontse XIX–nachale XX veka.* Ashgabat: Ylym, 1977.

Duara, Prasenjit. *Rescuing History from the Nation: Questioning Narratives of Modern China.* Chicago and London: University of Chicago Press, 1995.

Durdyev, Marat. *Turkmeny.* Ashgabat: Kharp, 1991.

Durdyev, T. *Formirovanie i razvitie Turkmenskoi sovetskoi intelligentsii.* Ashgabat, 1972.

———. "Rol' rabfakov v podgotovke kadrov intelligentsii v Turkmenistane," *Izvestiia Akademii Nauk TSSR, seriia obshchestvennykh nauk,* no. 1 (1981): 49–55.

Eickelman, Dale. *The Middle East and Central Asia: An Anthropological Approach.* 3d ed. Upper Saddle River, NJ: Prentice Hall, 1998.

Engels, Dagmar, and Shula Marks, eds. *Contesting Colonial Hegemony: State and Society in Africa and India.* London: British Academic Press, 1994.

Enteen, George M. "Marxist Historians during the Cultural Revolution." In *Cultural Revolution in Russia, 1928–1931*, edited by Sheila Fitzpatrick, pp. 154–68. Bloomington: Indiana University Press, 1978.

Eriksen, Thomas Hylland. *Ethnicity and Nationalism: Anthropological Perspectives.* London and Boulder, CO: Pluto Press, 1993.

Esenova, Saulesh. "Soviet Nationality, Identity, and Ethnicity in Central Asia: Historic Narratives and Kazakh Ethnic Identity." *Journal of Muslim Minority Affairs* 22, no. 1 (2002): 11–38.

Esman, Milton J., and Itamar Rabinovitch. *Ethnicity, Pluralism, and the State in the Middle East.* Ithaca: Cornell University Press, 1988.

Fainsod, Merle. *Smolensk under Soviet Rule.* Reprint, Boston: Unwyn Hyman, 1989.

Fathi, Schirin H. *Jordan, an Invented Nation? Tribe-State Dynamics and the Formation of National Identity.* Hamburg: Deutsches Orient-Institut, 1994.

Feldman, Walter. "Interpreting the Poetry of Mäkhtumquli." In *Muslims in Central Asia: Expressions of Identity and Change*, edited by Jo-ann Gross, pp. 167–89. Durham, N.C.: Duke University Press, 1992.

Fierman, William. *Language Planning and National Development: The Uzbek Experience*. Berlin and New York: Mouton de Gruyter, 1991.

Fishman, Joshua, Charles A. Ferguson, and Jyotirindra Das Gupta, eds. *Language Problems of Developing Nations*. New York: John Wiley and Sons, 1968.

Fitzpatrick, Sheila. "Ascribing Class: The Construction of Social Identity in Soviet Russia." *Journal of Modern History* 65 (December 1993): 745–70.

———. *Education and Social Mobility in the Soviet Union, 1921–1934*. Cambridge: Cambridge University Press, 1979.

———. *Everyday Stalinism*. New York: Oxford University Press, 1999.

———. *Stalin's Peasants: Resistance and Survival in the Russian Village after Collectivization*. New York and Oxford: Oxford University Press, 1994.

Geiss, Paul Georg. "Turkman Tribalism." *Central Asian Survey* 18, no. 3 (1999): 347–57.

Gellner, Ernest, *Muslim Society*. Cambridge: Cambridge Univeristy Press, 1981.

———. *Nations and Nationalism*. Oxford: Basil Blackwell, 1983.

Geraci, Robert. *Window on the East: National and Imperial Identities in Late Tsarist Russia*. Ithaca and London: Cornell University Press, 2001.

Golden, Peter. *An Introduction to the History of the Turkic Peoples: Ethnogenesis and State-Formation in Medieval and Early Modern Eurasia and the Middle East*. Wiesbaden: Otto Harrassowitz, 1992.

Goldman, Wendy Z. *Women, the State, and Revolution: Soviet Family Policy and Social Life, 1917–1936*. Cambridge: Cambridge University Press, 1993.

Grant, Bruce. *In the Soviet House of Culture: A Century of Perestroikas*. Princeton: Princeton University Press, 1995.

Hammoudi, A. "Segmentarity, Social Stratification, Political Power, and Sainthood: Reflections on Gellner's Theses." *Economy and Society* 9, no. 3 (August 1980): 279–303.

Hayden, Carol Eubanks. "Feminism and Bolshevism: The Zhenotdel and the Politics of Women's Emancipation in Russia, 1917–1930." Ph.D. dissertation, University of California, Berkeley, 1979.

Hayit, Baymirza. *Basmatschi: Nationaler Kampf Turkestans in den Jahren 1917 bis 1934*. Cologne: Dreisam Verlag, 1992.

Hellbeck, Jochen. "Laboratories of the Soviet Self: Diaries from the Stalin Era." Ph.D. dissertation, Columbia University, 1998.

Hirsch, Francine. "Empire of Nations: Colonial Technologies and the Making of the Soviet Union, 1917–1939." Ph.D. dissertation, Princeton University, 1998.

———. "Race without the Practice of Racial Politics." *Slavic Review* 61, no. 1 (Spring 2002): 30–43.

———. "The Soviet Union as a Work-in-Progress: Ethnographers and the Category *Nationality* in the 1926, 1937, and 1939 Censuses." *Slavic Review* 56 (Summer 1997): 251–78.

Hobsbawm, E. J. *Nations and Nationalism since 1780: Programme, Myth, Reality*. Cambridge: Cambridge University Press, 1990.

Hoffmann, David L., and Yanni Kotsonis, eds. *Russian Modernity: Politics, Knowledge, Practices.* New York: St. Martin's Press, 2000.

Holly, Ladislav. *Kinship, Honour, and Solidarity: Cousin Marriage in the Middle East.* Manchester and New York: Manchester University Press, 1989.

Holquist, Peter. "To Count, to Extract, to Exterminate: Population Statistics and Population Politics in Late-Imperial and Soviet Russia." In *State of Nations: Empire and Nation-Making in the Age of Lenin and Stalin,* edited by Ronald G. Suny and Terry Martin, pp. 111–44. Oxford: Oxford University Press, 2001.

Horowitz, Donald L. *Ethnic Groups in Conflict.* Berkeley and Los Angeles: University of California Press, 1985.

Humphrey, Caroline. *Marx Went Away, but Karl Stayed Behind.* Ann Arbor: University of Michigan Press, 1998.

Iazberdyev, A. *Izdatel'skoe delo v dorevoliutsionnom Turkmenistane.* Ashgabat: Ylym, 1993.

Iazlyev, Ch. *Turkmenskaia sel'skaia obshchina.* Ashgabat: Ylym, 1992.

Irons, William. *The Yomut Turkmen: A Study of Social Organization among a Central Asian Turkic-Speaking Population.* Ann Arbor: University of Michigan Press, 1975.

Istoriia sovetskogo turkmenistana, Chast' pervaia: 1917–1937 gg. Ashgabat: Ylym, 1970.

Ivanchenko, I. G. "Pravda i domysli ob odnoi neordinarnoi lichnosti (shtrikhi k politicheskomu portretu Khadjimurada Khodjamuradova)." *Izvestiia Akademii Nauk TSSR, seriia gumanitarnykh nauk,* no. 1 (1991): 36–46.

———. "Turkmen Azatlygy—Tragicheskii final mistifikatsii." *Izvestiia Akademii Nauk TSSR, seriia gumanitarnykh nauk,* no. 2 (1990): 29–36.

Iz istorii borby Kompartii Turkmenistana za kul'turnuiu revoliutstiiu (1925–1937 gg). Ashgabat,1968.

Kadyrov, Shokhrat. *Rossiisko-turkmenskii istoricheskii slovar',* vol. 1. Bergen, Norway: Biblioteka Almanakha "Turkmeny," 2001.

———. *Turkmenistan v XX veke: Probely i problemy.* Bergen, Norway: 1996.

Kaiser, Robert J. *The Geography of Nationalism in Russia and the USSR.* Princeton: Princeton University Press, 1994.

Kamp, Marianne. "Unveiling Uzbek Women: Liberation, Representation and Discourse, 1906–1929." Ph.D. dissertation, University of Chicago, 1998.

Kandiyoti, Deniz, ed. *Women, Islam, and the State.* London: Macmillan, 1991.

Kappeler, Andreas. *Russland als Vielvölkerriech: Entstehung, Geschichte, Zerfall.* Munich: C. H. Beck, 1992.

Keddie, Nikki R., and Beth Baron, eds. *Women in Middle Eastern History: Shifting Boundaries in Sex and Gender.* New Haven: Yale University Press, 1991.

Keller, Shoshana. "The Struggle against Islam in Uzbekistan, 1921–1941: Policy, Bureaucracy, and Reality." Ph.D. dissertation, Indiana University, 1995.

Khalid, Adeeb. "Nationalizing the Revolution in Central Asia: The Transformation of Jadidism." In *A State of Nations: Empire and Nation-Making in the Age of Lenin and Stalin,* edited by Ronald Grigor Suny and Terry Martin, 145–62. Oxford and New York: Oxford University Press, 2001.

———. *The Politics of Muslim Cultural Reform: Jadidism in Central Asia.* Berkeley and Los Angeles: University of California Press, 1999.

———. "The Politics of Muslim Cultural Reform: Jadidism in Tsarist Central Asia." Ph.D. dissertation, University of Wisconsin, 1993.

———. "Tashkent 1917: Muslim Politics in Revolutionary Turkestan." *Slavic Review* 55, no. 2 (Summer 1996): 270–96.

Khazanov, Anatoly. *After the USSR: Ethnicity, Nationalism, and Politics in the Commonwealth of Independent States*. Madison: University of Wisconsin Press, 1995.

———. *Nomads and the Outside World*. Cambridge: Cambridge University Press, 1984.

Khlevniuk, Oleg. "Les mècanismes de la 'grande terreur' des années 1937–1938 au Turkménistan." *Cahiers du monde russe* 39 (January–June 1998): 197–208.

Khodarkovsky, Michael. " 'Ignoble Savages and Unfaithful Subjects': Constructing Non-Christian Identities in Early Modern Russia." In *Russia's Orient: Imperial Borderlands and Peoples, 1700–1917*, edited by Daniel R. Brower and Edward J. Lazzerini, pp. 9–26. Bloomington: Indiana University Press, 1997.

Khodjakulieva, B. A. "Russko-tuzemnye shkoly v Zakaspiiskoi Oblasti (konets XIX–nachalo XX v.) *Izvestiia Akademii Nauk TSSR, seriia obshchestvennykh nauk*, no. 4 (1995): 13–18.

———. *Turkmenskaia natsional'naia intelligentsiia v kontse XIX–nachale XX v.* Ashgabat: Ylym, 1995.

Khoury, Philip S. *Syria and the French Mandate: The Politics of Arab Nationalism, 1920–1945*. Princeton: Princeton University Press, 1987.

Khoury, Philip S., and Joseph Kostiner, eds. *Tribes and State Formation in the Middle East*. Berkeley and Los Angeles: University of California Press, 1990.

Khudaiberdyev, Ia. *Obrazovanie Kommunisticheskoi Partii Turkmenistana*. Ashgabat: Turkmengosizdat, 1964.

Kirkwood, Michael, ed. *Language Planning in the Soviet Union*. London: Macmillan Press, 1989.

Kocaoglu, Timur. "The Existence of a Bukharan Nationality in the Recent Past." In *The Nationality Question in Soviet Central Asia*, edited by Edward A. Allworth, pp. 151–58. New York: Praeger, 1973.

Kolarz, Walter. *Russia and Her Colonies*. Hamden, CT: Archon Books, 1967.

Komatsu, Hisao. "The Evolution of Group Identity among Bukharan Intellectuals in 1911–1928: An Overview." *Memoirs of the Research Department of the Toyo Bunko*, no. 47 (1989): 115–44.

König, Wolfgang. *Die Achal-Teke: Zur Wirtschaft und Gesellschaft einer Turkmenengruppe im XIX Jahrhundert*. Berlin: Akademieverlag, 1962.

Kotkin, Stephen. *Magnetic Mountain: Stalinism as a Civilization*. Berkeley and Los Angeles: University of California Press, 1995.

Kreindler, Isabelle T. ed. *Sociolinguistic Perspectives on Soviet National Languages: Their Past, Present, and Future*. New York: Mouton, 1985.

Krylova, Anna. "Soviet Modernity in Life and Fiction: The Generation of the 'New Soviet Person' in the 1930s." Ph.D. dissertation, Johns Hopkins University, 2001.

Lapidus, Gail Warshovsky. *Women in Soviet Society: Equality, Development, and Social Change*. Berkeley and Los Angeles: University of California Press, 1978.

Lewin, Moshe. *Russian Peasants and Soviet Power: A Study of Collectivization.* New York: George Allen and Unwin, 1968.

———. *The Making of the Soviet System.* New York: Pantheon Books, 1985.

Lewis, Robert, ed. *Geographic Perspectives on Soviet Central Asia.* New York: Routledge, 1992.

Liber, George. "Korenizatsiia: Restructuring Soviet Nationality Policy in the 1920s." *Ethnic and Racial Studies* 14, no. 1 (January 1991): 15–23.

———. *Soviet Nationality Policy, Urban Growth and Identity Change in the Ukrainian SSR, 1923–1934.* Cambridge: Cambridge University Press, 1992.

Lorenz, Richard. "Economic Bases of the Basmachi Movement in the Farghana Valley." In *Muslim Communities Reemerge: Historical Perspectives on Nationality, Politics, and Opposition in the Former Soviet Union and Yugoslavia.* edited by Andreas Kappeler, Gerhard Simon, Georg Brunner, and Edward Allworth, pp. 277–303. Durham and London: Duke University Press, 1994.

Malia, Martin. *The Soviet Tragedy: A History of Socialism in Russia, 1917–1991.* New York: Free Press, 1994.

Manz, Beatrice, ed. *Central Asia in Historical Perspective.* Boulder, CO: Westview Press, 1994.

Martin, Terry. *The Affirmative Action Empire: Nations and Nationalism in the Soviet Union, 1923–1939.* Ithaca: Cornell University Press, 2001.

Massell, Gregory J. *The Surrogate Proletariat: Moslem Women and Revolutionary Strategies in Soviet Central Asia, 1919–1929.* Princeton: Princeton University Press, 1974.

Mel'kumov, V. G. *Ocherki istorii partorganizatsii Turkmenskoi oblasti Turkestanskoi ASSR.* Ashgabat: Turkmengosizdat, 1959.

Michaels, Paula A. "Medical Propaganda and Cultural Revolution in Soviet Kazakhstan, 1928–1941." *Russian Review* 59 (April 2000): 159–78.

Miles, William F. S. *Hausaland Divided: Colonialism and Independence in Nigeria and Niger.* Ithaca: Cornell University Press, 1994.

Nazarov, A. "Is istorii turkmenskogo literaturovedenii." *Izvestiia Akademii Nauk TSSR, seriia gumanitarnykh nauk,* no. 3 (1991): 46–51.

Northrop, Douglas. "Languages of Loyalty: Gender, Politics, and Party Supervision in Uzbekistan, 1927–1941," *Russian Review* 59, no. 2 (April 2000): 179–200.

———. "Nationalizing Backwardness: Gender, Empire, and Uzbek Identity." In *A State of Nations: Empire and Nation-Making in the Age of Lenin and Stalin,* edited by Ronald Gregor Suny and Terry Martin, pp. 191–220. Oxford and New York: Oxford University Press, 2001.

———. "Uzbek Women and the Veil: Gender and Power in Stalinist Central Asia." Ph.D. dissertation, Stanford University, 1999.

Ocherki istorii Kommunisticheskoi Partii Turkmenistana. 2d ed. Ashgabat: Izdatel'stvo Turkmenistan, 1965.

Ochs, Michael. "Turkmenistan: The Quest for Stability and Control." In *Conflict, Cleavage, and Change in Central Asia and the Caucasus,* edited by Karen Dawisha and Bruce Parrott, pp. 312–49. Cambridge: Cambridge University Press, 1997.

Palvanova, B. P. *Tragicheskie 30-e.* Ashgabat: Turkmenistan, 1991.

Park, Alexander. *Bolshevism in Turkestan, 1917–1927*. New York: Columbia University Press, 1957.

Pastner, Carroll McC. "The Status of Women and Property on a Baluchistan Oasis in Pakistan." In *Women in the Muslim World*, edited by Lois Beck and Nikki Keddie, pp. 434–52. Cambridge: Harvard University Press, 1978.

Pastoral Production and Society: Proceedings of the International Meeting on Nomadic Pastoralism, Paris 1976. Cambridge: Cambridge University Press, 1979.

Payne, Matthew J. *Stalin's Railroad: Turksib and the Building of Socialism*. Pittsburgh: University of Pittsburgh Press, 2001.

Penner, D'Ann. "Power, Pride, and Pitchforks: Farmer-Party Interaction on the Don, 1920–1928." Ph.D. dissertation, University of California at Berkeley, 1995.

Pierce, Richard. *Russian Central Asia, 1867–1917: A Study in Colonial Rule*. Berkeley and Los Angeles: University of California Press, 1960.

Roy, Olivier. *The New Central Asia: The Creation of Nations*. London: I. B. Tauris, 2000.

Rosliakov, A. A. "Politika Sredazbiuro TsK VKP v otnoshenii loyal'nykh elementov natsional'noi burzhuazii v 20-ykh godakh." *Izvestiia Akademii Nauk TSSR, seriia obshchestvennykh nauk*, no. 4 (1967): 10–16.

———. *Sredazburo TsK VKP: Voprosy strategii i taktiki*. Ashgabat, Turkmenistan, 1975.

Sabol, Stephen. "The Creation of Soviet Central Asia: The 1924 National Delimitation." *Central Asian Survey* 14, no. 2 (1995): 225–41.

Sahlins, Peter. *Boundaries: The Making of France and Spain in the Pyrenees*. Berkeley and Los Angeles: University of California Press, 1989.

Saray, Mehmet. *The Turkmens in the Age of Imperialism*. Ankara: Turkish Historical Society, 1989.

Sawyer, Jeren. "Turkmen Nationalism and Higher Education." *Central Asia-Caucasus Analyst* (on-line version), Field Reports, November 22, 2000.

Schoeberlein-Engel, John Samuel. "Identity in Central Asia: Construction and Contention in the Conceptions of 'Özbek,' 'Tajik,' 'Muslim,' 'Samarquandi,' and Other Groups." Ph.D. dissertation, Harvard University, 1994.

Scott, James C. *Weapons of the Weak: Everyday Forms of Peasant Resistance*. New Haven: Yale University Press, 1986.

———. *Seeing Like a State: How Certain Schemes to Improve the Human Condition Have Failed*. New Haven and London: Yale University Press, 1998.

Sengupta, Anita. *Frontiers into Borders: The Transformation of Identities in Central Asia*. London: Greenwich Millennium Press, 2002.

Shanin, Teodor. *The Awkward Class. Political Sociology of Peasantry in a Developing Society: Russia, 1910–1925*. Oxford: Clarendon Press, 1972.

Shikhmuradov, B. O., et al., eds. *Türkmen halkïnïng gelip chïkïshïnïng dünye yairaishïnïng we onung dövletining tarïkhïnïng problemalarï*. Ashgabat: Rukh, 1993.

Shryock, Andrew. *Nationalism and the Genealogical Imagination: Oral History and Textual Authority in Tribal Jordan*. Berkeley and Los Angeles: University of California Press, 1997.

Simon, Gerhard. *Nationalism and Policy toward the Nationalities in the Soviet Union*. Boulder, CO: Westview Press, 1991.

Slezkine, Yuri. *Arctic Mirrors: Russia and the Small Peoples of the North*. Ithaca and London: Cornell University Press, 1994.

——. "Imperialism as the Highest State of Socialism," *Russian Review* 59 (April 2000): 227–34.

——. "N. Ia. Marr and the National Origins of Soviet Ethnogenetics." *Slavic Review* 55 (Winter 1996): 826–62.

——. "The USSR as a Communal Apartment, or How a Socialist State Promoted Ethnic Particularism," *Slavic Review* 53 (Summer 1994): 414–52.

Slocum, John Willard. "The Boundaries of National Identity: Religion, Language, and Nationality Politics in Late-Imperial Russia." Ph.D. dissertation, University of Chicago, 1993.

Smith, Anthony. *The Ethnic Origins of Nations*. Oxford: Basil Blackwell, 1986.

Smith, Graham, Vivien Law, Andrew Wilson, Annette Bohr, and Edward Allworth. *Nation-Building in the Post-Soviet Borderlands: The Politics of National Identities*. Cambridge: Cambridge University Press, 1998.

Smith, Jeremy. *The Bolsheviks and the National Question, 1917–1923*. New York: St. Martin's Press, 1999.

——. "Delimiting National Space: The Ethnographical Principle in the Administrative Division of the RSFSR and USSR, 1918–1925." Paper presented at the conference "The Concept of Space in Russian History and Culture," Helsinki, Finland, June 1998.

——. "The Origins of Soviet National Autonomy," *Revolutionary Russia* 10, no. 2 (December 1997): 62–84.

Smith, Michael G. *Language and Power in the Creation of the USSR, 1917–1953*. Berlin and New York: Mouton de Gruyter, 1998.

Söyegov, M. "O iazykovoi politike v Turkmenistane v 20-e gody (po rabotam K. Sakhatova)." *Izvestiia Akademii Nauk TSSR, seriia obshchestvennykh nauk*, no. 2 (1987): 50–56.

——. *On Chïnar: Ilkinji Türkmen dilchileri ve edebiyatларï hakïnda ocherkler*. Ashgabat: Kuyash, 1993.

Stites, Richard. *The Women's Liberation Movement in Russia: Feminism, Nihilism, and Bolshevism, 1860–1930*. Princeton: Princeton University Press, 1978.

Suny, Ronald Grigor. "The Empire Strikes Out: Imperial Russia, 'National Identity,' and Theories of Empire." In *A State of Nations: Empire and Nation-Making in the Age of Lenin and Stalin*, edited by Ronald Grigor Suny and Terry Martin, pp. 23–66. Oxford and New York: Oxford University Press, 2001.

——. *The Revenge of the Past: Nationalism, Revolution, and the Collapse of the Soviet Union*. Stanford, CA: Stanford University Press, 1993.

——. *The Soviet Experiment: Russia, the USSR, and the Successor States*. Oxford: Oxford University Press, 1998.

Suny, Ronald Grigor, and Terry Martin, eds. *A State of Nations: Empire and Nation-Making in the Age of Lenin and Stalin*. Oxford and New York: Oxford University Press, 2001.

Tächmïradov, Tagangeldi. "Razvitie i normalizatsiia Turkmenskogo literaturnogo iazyka v Sovetskuiu epokhu." Avtoreferat dissertatsii. Ashgabat, 1974.

———. *Mukhammet Geldieving ömri we döredidzhiligi*. Ashgabat, 1989.

Tapper, Richard, ed. *The Conflict of Tribe and State in Iran and Afghanistan*. London: Croom Helm, 1983.

Tashliev, Sh. *Grazhdanskaia voina i angliiskaia voennaia interventsiia v Turkmenistane*. Ashgabat: Turkmenistan, 1974.

Thompson, Elizabeth. *Colonial Citizens: Republican Rights, Paternal Privilege, and Gender in French Syria and Lebanon*. New York: Columbia University Press, 2000.

Tibi, Bassam. "The Simultaneity of the Unsimultaneous: Old Tribes and Imposed Nation-States in the Modern Middle East." In *Tribes and State Formation in the Middle East*, edited by Philip S. Khoury and Joseph Kostiner. pp. 127–52. Berkeley and Los Angeles: University of California Press, 1990.

Tillett, Lowell. *The Great Friendship: Soviet Historians on the Non-Russian Nationalities*. Chapel Hill: University of North Carolina Press, 1969.

Timasheff, Lev. *The Great Retreat: The Growth and Decline of Communism in Russia*. New York, 1946.

Tohidi, Nayereh. "The Intersection of Gender, Ethnicity, and Islam in Soviet and Post-Soviet Azerbaijan." *Nationalities Papers* 25, no. 1 (1997): 147–67.

Vaidanyath, R. *The Formation of the Central Asian Republics: A Study in Soviet Nationalities Policy, 1917–1936*. New Delhi: People's Publishing House, 1967.

Viola, Lynn. *Peasant Rebels under Stalin: Collectivization and the Culture of Peasant Resistance*. Oxford: Oxford University Press, 1996.

Yuval-Davis, Nira, and Floya Anthias, eds. *Woman-Nation-State*. New York: St. Martin's Press, 1989.

Zenkovsky, Serge A. *Pan-Turkism and Islam in Russia*. Cambridge: Harvard University Press, 1967.

INDEX

adat. *See* customary law

affirmative action empire, USSR as, 71

Afghanistan, emigration to, 67, 193, 194

agriculture, 23, 31

Aitakov, Nadïrbai: background of, 68, 104–105, 184; and corruption, 111; on discrimination against Turkmen workers, 82; family of, 127–128; and indigenization commission, 77; and Popok, 123–124, 126; on location of capital, 66–68; and national delimitation, 55; and 1937–38 Terror, 127; on party factionalism, 119–120; rumor concerning, 211; and Turkmen alphabet committee, 142, 157

aksakgals (elders), 26, 30, 60, 107, 187

Aksentovich, Anna, 109, 236

All-Union Committee for the New Turkic Alphabet (VTsKNTA), 140, 153–154, 156–160, 163

Alparov, G., 133, 138

alphabet committees: all-union, 140, 153–154, 156–160, 163; Turkmen, 134, 142, 156, 159

alphabet reform, 133, 134, 138–143, 159, 164

ancestry, shared, 2, 6–7, 8, 17–21, 169. *See also* Oguz-Khan

Annamuhammedov (Turkmen official), 127

Arabic language, 48, 131; loan words from, 132, 136, 143–147, 161–162; and Muslim schools, 32; and saintly tribes, 62

Arabic script, 133, 138–143

aristocracy: and Russian colonial rule, 30–31; Turkmen lack of, 26, 171

Armenians, 65, 128n

Aronshtam, G.: and dual secretary system, 114, 118n, 119; and 1937–38 Terror, 128; and Popok, 123; on Russian language, 86–87

artel' collective farms, 212

Ashgabat, as location of capital, 9, 66–68

Atabaev, Gaigïsïz: background of, 68, 75, 104–105, 184; on Basmachi rebellion, 38, 121–122; on collectivization, 206; on divorce, 241–244; on European communists, 119; on female emancipation, 122, 245, 250, 252, 257; on land reform, 180; and national delimitation, 54–57, 62–63; and 1937–38 Terror, 127; and Popok, 123–124, 126; and Sähetmï-radov, 111–113; on Turkmen "figure-heads," 80–81; wife of, 94n

Atatürk, Kemal, 260

Austria, 45

Autonomous Soviet Socialist Republics, 50

autonomy, territorial: vs. internationalism, 57; and Leninist nationality policy, 14, 43–44; during Revolution and Civil War, 35–36, 39; Turkestani, 35. *See also* extra-territorial autonomy

Azerbaijani language, 135, 137–138; loan words from, 138n, 143, 145

Azerbaijanis, 136

Baluchis, 65, 181, 182

Bashkirs, 51

Basmachi rebellion, 38–39, 51, 60, 121–122, 208, 217

batraks (landless peasants), 175; and emigration, 218; and female emancipation, 222; and land reform, 180; preferential hiring of, 89; and village soviets, 187, 190, 192

Bayads, 61

bedniaks (poor peasants), 175, 183, 262; and collectivization, 210–211; and emigration, 218; and female emancipation, 222; and kulaks, 192–193; and land reform, 180–182; preferential hiring of, 89; and village soviets, 187–190, 193, 201

Beksler (Russian official), 90

Berdiev, Emir, 192

Bernshtam, A., 195

blood feuds, 10, 24, 25, 168, 170

Bogdanova, M. I., 157–158, 159

crimes of custom, 108, 245, 248–249, 252, 255, 257; and party members, 255–256. *See also* bride abduction; dakïlma; gaitarma; galïng; garshlïk; polygamy; underage marriage
customary law, 24, 262; and Islamic law, 26, 226; and land tenure, 177–178, 180; under Russian colonial rule, 30, 32; and Turkmen-ness, 49, 223, 265; and women, 234
Cyrillic script, 139, 141, 164, 264

Daihan (newspaper), 153
dakïlma (leviratic marriage), 252, 253
Dashhowuz: ceded to Turkmenistan, 65; and national delimitation, 63
daughters, 224, 240. *See also* bridewealth
disenfranchisement: and female emancipation, 231; and forced cotton production, 207; and kin rivalry, 190–191; of kulaks, 190–192; of Muslims, 35
divorce, 221, 239–245, 249; Islamic, 223–224, 239, 243
dual secretary system, 101, 110–120
Durdï (civil servant), 90
Durdïev (peasant), 243
Durdï Khan, Anna, 214
dynastic rulers, 18, 205. *See also* Bukharan emirate; Khivan khanate; Persian empire

education. *See* schools
Effendizade, Ferid, 135, 136
egalitarianism: among nomads, 170–74, 193–194, 225, 226; rhetoric of, 12–13, 72, 94
elders (aksakgals), 26, 30, 60, 107, 187
elites. *See* native Turkmen elite
emigration, 34, 193–194, 213–220, 262; and 1937–38 Terror, 128n; as resistance to land reform, 199, 203, 209
Ersarïs, 21, 61; "backwardness" of, 66–67; and Bukharan emirate, 27; and conflict with Tekes, 186; dialect of, 149, 151, 152; and Russian colonial rule, 184
ethnic categorization, 3, 19; difficulties with, 20, 41–43, 48–49, 60–62, 149–150, 262; Soviet rhetoric concerning, 47–48
ethnicity: "fictitious" claims of, 41, 61, 201; and identity, 3, 18, 31–32, 40; and statehood, 18

ethnic preferences, 44, 264; Russian resentment of, 13, 79, 84
ethnographic studies, 4, 5, 32, 49, 59–63, 172, 174, 193–194, 199–200, 225, 230, 262
Europeanization. *See* Russification
European languages, loan words from, 136, 143, 145, 146
Europeans: Central Asian definition of, 80n; hostility toward, 205; and Leninist nationality policy, 115; in OGPU, 95; in Turkmen Communist Party, 101, 108, 112–114, 117–120, 128; in zhenotdel, 227
Ewlad (saintly tribes), 62, 172, 187–188
extraterritorial autonomy, 45, 64

Faisulina (schoolteacher), 230
famine: and collectivization, 123, 202, 207, 209; and cotton cultivation, 208; during revolution and Civil War, 34, 36, 37, 199
female emancipation: vs. class priorities, 222, 241–247, 249, 255; coerced display of, 229–231; and colonialism, 224, 258–260; economic, 230; vs. national values, 222–223, 258; and Turkmen males, 202, 222, 228, 230, 239–240, 245; and veiling, 221, 235
feudalism, 4, 155, 157–158, 175, 195, 207n, 223
figurehead status of Turkmen officials, 80–81, 100–102, 111, 113–114, 117–119; official denials of, 114, 117–118, 120
Five-Year Plan, first, 11–12, 88, 190, 198, 202, 207, 215–216, 220
foreign words, 130, 132, 138, 143–150, 158–162

gaitarma (return of bride to parents), 245, 252, 253–254
galïng. *See* bridewealth
Garahanov, Allagulï, 150, 153, 158, 161
garshlïk (bride exchange), 246, 252–253
Geldiev, Muhammet: accusations against, 124, 126, 138, 155–156; death of, 124n; defense of Turkmen language by, 135–137; education of, 33–34, 76; and linguistic standardization, 145, 150–152, 162–163; posthumous denunciation of, 157–161; and script reform, 133, 142, 150; textbook by, 133, 138, 150

Karutskii (head of Turkmen OGPU), 192
Kary, Sultan, 65
Kazakhs: in civil service, 76–77; and collec-
   tivization, 209; discrimination against,
   47; educational preferences for, 70; as
   ethnic minority, 64; and jadidism, 33n;
   in Khivan communist party, 55; status of
   women among, 225; and term "Kirgiz,"
   47n; and territorial disputes, 60
Kazakhstan: republic of, 42, 50, 58; and
   Russian colonial rule, 28
Kerbabaev, Berdi, 76, 124, 126, 155, 156
Khalï, Sh., 144
Khalid, Adeeb, 33
Khïdïr-Alï, 41, 61
Khiva: and ethnographic studies, 60; and
   national delimitation, 42, 51–52, 55–57,
   59, 183; non-Russification of, 30, 40,
   75, 81, 184; during revolutionary period, 37–39; as Russian protectorate,
   28–32; Turkmen population of, 66; uprising in, 34
Khivan Communist Party, 55, 56, 58,
   104, 105
Khivan khanate, 27–28, 37–38
Khorezm. See Khivan khanate
kin groups: importance of, 21–25, 222,
   264; rivalry between, 189–192, 195–
   196, 265
kinship: and class, 11, 167–168, 181, 195–
   196, 262; and land tenure, 170; vs. state
   and individual loyalties, 8, 222, 223,
   265; terminology used for, 6n, 169n. See
   also blood feuds
Kirgiz, 47n
Kokand: autonomous government of, 35,
   38; Khanate of, 28
Kolkhozes, 204, 205, 209
Köneürgench, 197, 210
korenizatsiia. See indigenization
Koshchi Union, 180, 187, 201, 202
KPT. See Turkmen Communist Party
KUBT (Commission on the Improvement
   of Daily Life and Labor among Women),
   242–244, 251, 255
kulaks (rich peasants): blamed for unrest,
   208, 211, 215, 219; as class aliens, 11,
   175, 182, 188, 200, 201, 208, 215, 262;
   and descent groups, 183; and land reform, 181; liquidation of, 185, 189–193,
   203–204, 216–219; other groups redefined as, 193, 195–196, 200

Kulbesherov, Bäshim, 117
Kurama, 61
Kurds, 65, 172, 187
Kyrgyz: and jadidism, 33n; territory of,
   42, 50, 57–58

land reform, 4, 168, 175–182, 189, 202;
   active resistance to, 198–199, 203, 205–
   209, 217; passive resistance to, 180–
   181, 198, 200
land tenure: and social hierarchies, 172;
   systems of, 176–178, 179n
language: as ethnic criterion, 32, 48; and
   identity, 19, 20, 32, 33, 40, 129–130,
   134, 223; and nationhood, 3–5, 131
language difficulties: as barrier to Sovietiza-
   tion, 85–87, 108, 255; downplayed by
   OGPU, 95–96; and loan words, 144
language reform, 261; and Marxism-
   Leninism, 153–155, 158–160, 162–164;
   Moscow control of, 156–159; and
   supratribal dialect, 9, 130, 138, 148–
   153, 198
Latinization, 139–143, 146, 153, 159, 264
law. See customary law; Islamic law
Left Opposition, 116–118
left-right factionalism, 111–112, 120
Lenin, Vladimir Ilyich, 45, 211
Leninist nationality policy, 3, 5, 7, 13–14,
   143–48; Gosplan opposition to, 45–46;
   and Left Opposition, 116; and linguistic
   indigenization, 86; and nationalism, 95;
   and native elite, 72; and Turkmen communists, 53, 115
Leninsk. See Chärjew
leviratic marriage, 252, 253
linguistic conferences: of 1930, 146–148,
   152–162; of 1936, 159–164
linguistic indigenization, 84–88, 129; during first Five-Year Plan, 88; retreat from,
   97–98
literacy classes. See illiteracy
livestock: as bridewealth, 250, 257; communalization of, 195, 204–205, 209,
   211, 216, 219, 220; and emigration,
   214–217; raiding of, 22, 27, 60, 65; as
   variable source of wealth, 173, 194; veterinary care for, 189
loan words, 130, 132, 138, 143–150,
   158–162
local nationalism. See counterrevolutionary
   nationalism

Mägtïmgulï (poet), 95, 132, 151, 155
Mamedov (government official), 184
marital customs: and female emancipation, 11, 221–222; and national identity, 14, 258. *See also* bride abduction; bride-wealth; crimes of custom; dakïlma; gaitarma; garshlïk; polygamy; underage marriage
Marr, N. Ia., 153–154, 159
marriage, interethnic. *See* intermarriage
Martin, Terry, 5, 84
Marxism-Leninism, 10, 44, 262–265; and class theory, 108, 169, 174–175; and language reform, 153–155, 158–160, 162–164; and national question, 64
Massell, Gregory, 222, 244
medical care, 85, 109, 189, 198, 217, 230, 262
medreses. *See* Muslim schools
mekdeps. *See* Muslim schools
Mensheviks, 37
Mezhlauk, Ivan, 110, 128
Mezhnun (author of article), 147–148, 160
Mikhailov (Russian official), 89–90
Mikhailov, Fëdor, 173, 225
military service: and conscription, 189, 201, 202; and dynastic rulers, 27; during Revolution, 36–37; and Russian colonial rule, 34
minorities: non-Turkmen, 43, 64–65; Soviet policy concerning, 65
Mïrad, Klïch Övezmïrad, 192
Mïradali (rebel leader), 209, 212
Mountaineers, Republic of, 51
mülk (land tenure system), 177–179
Muslim dynastic rulers. *See* dynastic rulers
Muslims, disenfranchisement of, 35
Muslim schools: Atabaev on, 122; and civil service recruitment, 71, 78; communists educated in, 54, 105; and jadidism, 32–33; and old intelligentsia, 75–76

narratives, national. *See* identity narratives
national communists, 257
national delimitation of Central Asia: 6, 9, 51–59, 62–63, 70, 183–184, 200, 261; maps of, 52, 69
nationalism: and "anti-Russianism," 95; European concept of, 19, 31–32, 129n; hostility of OGPU toward, 95. *See also* counterrevolutionary nationalism

nationality policy. *See* Leninist nationality policy
national territories, 4, 19, 41–48; artificiality of, 2–3
nationhood, 42; and "backwardness," 46–47, 49; Central Asian concept of, 18; development of, 1–7, 261; as historical precondition for socialist internationalism, 44, 46, 183; Soviet rhetoric of, 223; Stalin's definition of, 48
native Turkmen elite, 5, 8, 261–263; ambivalence about Russification, 92–94; creation of, 4, 73, 78–79; use of democratic rhetoric by, 72. *See also* old intelligentsia
nativization. *See* indigenization
Naubatov, V., 66–68
Nazarov, Begjan: background of, 68, 81, 105; and indigenization commission, 77, 79, 81, 85; on location of capital, 66–68; and 1932–33 purge, 124–126; on script reform, 141–142
Nemchenko, M., 215–216
New Economic Policy (NEP), 182, 190, 206, 210
Nicholas II, 210
Nïyazov, O., 118
Niyazov, Saparmurat (Türkmenbashi), 1, 263, 265
Nodev, O. Ia., 127, 128
nomads, 7, 22–23, 264; and collectivization, 209, 210, 216, 220; egalitarianism of, 170–171, 193–194; ethnographic studies of, 60–61; and jadidism, 33; political ignorance of, 210; redefined as kulaks, 195; status of women among, 221, 225, 234; and territorial identity, 27–28, 42, 169
nonparty intellectuals, 75–76
Northrop, Douglas, 235
Nur, Ata, 210

oath, Turkmen national, 1
OGPU: and Basmachi rebellion, 122; and collectivization, 123n, 205, 209; and cotton production, 208; and emigration, 215–217; and female emancipation, 231; and land reform, 182; and liquidation of kulaks, 191–192; and tribal parity, 185; and Türkmen Azadlïgï, 124, 127, 156; and Turkmen-language press, 95–96; and village elections, 190–191

tribal policy, 167–169; and location of capital, 67; and parity, 183–186, 188
Trotsky, Leon, 116, 117
Trotskyism, 127; and Tumailov, 116. *See also* Left Opposition
TsKNA. *See* Turkmen alphabet committee
TsKNTA. *See* Turkmen alphabet committee
Tumailov, Mahmut, 115–118
Tumanovich, O., 226
Turkestan, 42; communist party of, 104, 105; and Islam, 30; and national delimitation, 51, 52, 57; Turkmen population of, 66
Turkey, 260
Turkic languages, 130, 132; administrative use of, 81; loan words from, 144, 145; non-standardization of, 48; phonetic system of, 139, 140
Turkish language, 33, 135
"Turkman" tribe, 61
Turkmen alphabet committee (TsKNTA, TsKNA), 134, 142, 146, 156, 159
Türkmen Azadlïgï, 124–127, 156
Türkmenbashi (Saparmurat Niyazov), 1, 263, 265
Turkmen Communist Party: career paths in, 80, 101, 114; and collectivization, 197, 212, 219–220; divided loyalties in, 210, 216, 220; factionalism in, 101, 110, 112–113, 117, 119–120; formation of, 100, 103–104, 110; and nonparty intellectuals, 75; recruitment into, 73; structure of, 4, 74, 102, 120; wives in, 109, 229–231, 255–256. *See also* dual secretary system; left-right factionalism
Turkmengosizdat (publishing house), 133, 155; and *Tokmak*, 87
Türkmen ili (journal), 133
Türkmenistan (newspaper), 73, 76, 85, 86, 124, 133, 135, 153; cited in *Tokmak*, 93; on intermarriage with Russians, 93–94
Turkmenkul't (Institute for Turkmen Culture), 124, 134, 150, 155, 159, 200
Turkmen language: administrative use of, 73, 84, 87, 89, 91, 264; dialects of, 9, 129, 132, 138, 149–151, 160–163, 262; phonetic system of, 147–48, 162, 163; promotion of, 133–138; psychological importance of, 85; scarcity of publications in, 86–87, 95–96; in schools, 73–74; standardization of, 39, 73, 130–132; and

Uzbek language, 60. *See also* language reform; linguistic conferences; linguistic indigenization; press, Turkmen-language
Türkmen medenieti (journal), 134, 156
Turkmen National Bureau, 84, 103; on location of capital, 66–68
Turkmen-ness: and ancestry, 6–9, 20, 21, 25–26; and customary law, 14, 26, 222–223; and Islam, 26; and nomadism, 23; vs. Russian-ness, 94–95; and territory, 43; vs. tribal identity, 94, 261
Turkmenovedenie (journal), 134, 156, 200
Turkmen republic: ethnic composition of, 64–65; founding of, 68–69; and independence from USSR, 1, 263–264; location of capital of, 66–67; provinces of, 68
Turkmenskaia iskra (newspaper): cited in *Tokmak*, 93; on slow pace of indigenization, 98; on Turkmen "figureheads," 81n; on Turkmen language, 87, 160n
Turkmen tribes: 7, 8, 21; conflict among, 17–18, 20, 24, 66; geographic distribution of, 19–21, 24, 66; map of, 22. *See also* Choudïrs; Ersarïs; Göklengs; Salïrs; Sarïks; Tekes; Yomuts

Uighur language, 145
Ukrainians, 47
underage marriage, 168, 245–251, 257
union republic status, 50–51
unveiling campaign, 221, 235–238; and yashmak, 236
uprisings: against Bolsheviks, 36, 38–39; against land reform, 12, 197, 209–212; against Russian colonial rule, 29, 34. *See also* Basmachi rebellion
Uzbekistan: and national delimitation, 50, 57, 63
Uzbek language, 33, 60, 72n, 136n, 145, 146; and Tajik language, 20, 48, 132
Uzbeks: in civil service, 76; and conflicts with Turkmen, 37–38, 51, 65; discrimination by, 47, 63; as ethnic minority, 64, 65; and Khïdïr-Alï, 41; in Khivan communist party, 55–56; preferences for, 70; and pan-Turkestanism, 47; status of women among, 221, 234, 236, 240n; and Tajiks, 19–20, 48. *See also* ethnic categorization, difficulties with

Vareikis, I., 49–50, 57
Vasiliev, P., 225, 226